Structural Reforms Without Prejudices

Structural Reforms Without Prejudices

Edited by

Tito Boeri, Micael Castanheira,
Riccardo Faini, and Vincenzo Galasso

With

Giorgio Barba Navaretti, Stéphane Carcillo,
Jonathan Haskel, Giuseppe Nicoletti, Enrico Perotti,
Carlo Scarpa, Lidia Tsyganok, and Christian Wey

OXFORD
UNIVERSITY PRESS

Great Clarendon Street, Oxford OX2 6DP

Oxford University Press is a department of the University of Oxford.
It furthers the University's objective of excellence in research, scholarship,
and education by publishing worldwide in

Oxford New York

Auckland Cape Town Dar es Salaam Hong Kong Karachi
Kuala Lumpur Madrid Melbourne Mexico City Nairobi
New Delhi Shanghai Taipei Toronto

With offices in

Argentina Austria Brazil Chile Czech Republic France Greece
Guatemala Hungary Italy Japan Poland Portugal Singapore
South Korea Switzerland Thailand Turkey Ukraine Vietnam

Oxford is a registered trade mark of Oxford University Press
in the UK and in certain other countries

Published in the United States
by Oxford University Press Inc., New York

© Fondazione Rodolfo Debenedetti, 2006

The moral rights of the author have been asserted
Database right Oxford University Press (maker)

First published 2006

All rights reserved. No part of this publication may be reproduced,
stored in a retrieval system, or transmitted, in any form or by any means,
without the prior permission in writing of Oxford University Press,
or as expressly permitted by law, or under terms agreed with the appropriate
reprographics rights organization. Enquiries concerning reproduction
outside the scope of the above should be sent to the Rights Department,
Oxford University Press, at the address above

You must not circulate this book in any other binding or cover
and you must impose the same condition on any acquirer

British Library Cataloguing in Publication Data
Data available

Library of Congress Cataloging in Publication Data
Data available

Typeset by Newgen Imaging Systems (P) Ltd., Chennai, India
Printed in Great Britain
on acid-free paper by
Biddles Ltd., King's Lynn, Norfolk

ISBN 0-19-920362-8   978-0-19-920362-8

10 9 8 7 6 5 4 3 2 1

Acknowledgements

The two studies that make up this volume were originally prepared for the sixth European conference of the Fondazione Rodolfo Debenedetti, which was held in Lecce in June 2004. This book draws a good deal on the discussion in Lecce, which involved a qualified audience of academicians, professional economists, representatives of unions and employers associations, industrialists, and policy-makers.

Needless to say, we are very much indebted to all those who attended that conference and contributed actively to the discussion. In particular, we wish to express our gratitude to Giuliano Amato, Vice President of the European Convention, for his insightful opening remarks on the single market and on European institutional integration.

We are most grateful to Carlo De Benedetti, who allowed this event to occur and opened the conference.

Financial support from the William Davidson Institute is also gratefully acknowledged.

Special thanks to Francesco Fasani, Roberta Marcaletti, and Domenico Tabasso, who assisted me in the organization of the conference and worked hard and skilfully to prepare the background material for this volume. I am also grateful to Simona Baldi and Paola Monti, who contributed to the final stages of preparation of the event. Micael Castanheira is grateful to the National Bank of Belgium for their financial support.

Tito Boeri

Contents

List of Figures	xi
List of Tables	xiii
List of Contributors	xv
Introduction	1

Part I. Contrasting Europe's Decline: Do Product Market Reforms Help? — 15
Riccardo Faini, Jonathan Haskel, Giorgio Barba Navaretti, Carlo Scarpa, and Christian Wey

1. Introduction	17
2. Competition and Economic Performance: A Brief Review of the Literature	21
3. The Maze of Services Regulation	24
3.1. A brief overview	24
3.2. Energy	25
Electricity	27
3.2.1. Pre-privatization structural issues	27
3.2.2. The EU reform agenda	28
3.2.3. Reform in the three countries	28
3.2.3.1. Privatization and structural change	28
3.2.3.2. Regulation and deregulation	31
3.2.3.3. Economic outcomes	31
3.2.4. Evaluation	34
Natural Gas	34
3.2.5. Pre-privatization structural issues	34
3.2.6. The EU reform agenda	35
3.2.7. Reform in the three countries	36
3.2.7.1. Privatization and structural change	36

Contents

3.2.7.2. Regulation and deregulation	38
3.2.7.3. Economic outcomes	38
3.2.8. Evaluation	40
3.3. Telecommunications	41
3.3.1. Pre-privatization structural issues	41
3.3.2. The EU reform agenda	41
3.3.3. Reform in the three countries	41
3.3.3.1. Privatization and structural change	41
3.3.3.2. Regulation and deregulation	43
3.3.3.3. Economic outcomes	44
3.3.4. Evaluation	46
3.4. Railways	47
3.4.1. Pre-privatization structural issues	47
3.4.2. The EU reform agenda	47
3.4.3. Reform in the three countries	48
3.4.3.1. Privatization and structural change	48
3.4.3.2. Regulation and deregulation	49
3.4.3.3. Economic outcomes	51
3.4.4. Evaluation	53
3.5. Professional services	54
3.5.1. Structural issues	54
3.5.2. The need for a reform agenda	55
3.5.3. The outcome of a slow reform	57
3.5.4. Evaluation	59
3.6. Retailing	60
3.6.1. Basic characteristics of the retail industry	60
3.6.2. The reform agenda	61
3.6.3. Implementation of the reform agenda in Germany, Italy, and the UK	63
3.6.4. Comparison of performance	66
3.7. Postal services	72
3.7.1. Postal service systems before liberalization	72
3.7.2. The reform agenda	74
3.7.3. Implementation of the reform agenda in Germany, Italy, and the UK	77
3.7.4. Comparison of performance	80
3.8. Water	82
3.8.1. Pre-privatization structure	82
3.8.2. The EU reform agenda	83

3.8.3. Reform in the three countries	83
3.8.3.1. Privatization and structural change	83
3.8.3.2. Regulation and de-regulation	85
3.8.3.3. Economic outcomes	86
3.8.4. Evaluation	88
4. The Changing Role of the Tertiary Sector	89
5. The Impact of Services Regulation	97
5.1. Productivity in manufacturing	97
5.2. Inward FDI	101
6. Looking Ahead: Will Liberalization Policies Succeed?	105
References	110
Appendix 1	116
Appendix 2	123
Comments	126
Olivier Blanchard	126
Jan Svejnar	135

Part II. How to Gain Political Support for Reforms — 141

Micael Castanheira, Vincenzo Galasso, Stéphane Carcillo, Giuseppe Nicoletti, Enrico Perotti, and Lidia Tsyganok

7. Introduction	143
8. Evidence and Theory of Reforms	151
8.1. Evidence about the reform momentum	151
8.2. Theories of reforms: a framework of analysis	157
9. Exploit a Parliamentary Majority	165
9.1. The 1986 Social Security Act in the UK	167
9.2. "Pushing reforms": the role of momentum	173
9.3. Strengths and caveats: a tale of three failures	180
10. Widen Your Political Base	187
10.1. *Flexicurity* in Denmark	189
10.2. Mass privatizations in Central and Eastern European transition countries	193
10.3. The season of reforms in Italy	199

Contents

11. Divide and Conquer	206
11.1. *Divide et Impera*	207
11.1.1. Privatize or corporatize: Telecom Italia versus France Telecom	210
11.1.2. Break vertical chain: intermediate goods	216
11.2. *Trickle-down effects*	219
11.2.1. Market power and gradual reforms	220
11.2.2. The 1994–1997 reforms of EPL in Spain	226
12. Exploit External Constraints	232
12.1. Škoda (Czech Republic) and AvtoZAZ (Ukraine)	233
12.2. The privatization of Škoda	235
12.3. The privatization of AvtoZAZ	239
12.4. Broader evidence	247
13. How to Reform: Pulling the Strings	249
References	255
Comments	263
Gérard Roland	263
Stefano Scarpetta	271
Final Remarks	280
Christopher Pissarides	280
André Sapir	283
Vito Tanzi	287
Index	297

List of Figures

3.1	Productivity in the electricity sector	32
3.2	Final net electricity prices for large industrial customers	32
3.3	Final net electricity prices for small industrial customers	33
3.4	Final net gas prices for small domestic customers	39
3.5	Final net gas prices for large industrial customers	40
3.6	Persons engaged in retail	69
3.7	Labour productivity per person employed	70
3.8	Hours worked per employee	70
3.9	Labour productivity per hour worked	71
4.1	The share of services in the value of final output: Italy versus the UK	92
4.2	The total share of services in the value of final output: Germany versus the UK	92
4.3	Italy: total indirect share of services in the value of manufacturing total output	93
4.4	Germany: total indirect share of services in the value of manufacturing total output	93
4.5.	United Kingdom: total indirect share of services in the value of manufacturing total output	94
4.6	The share of business activities in the value of final output: Italy versus the UK	95
4.7	The weight of network services in final output: Germany versus the UK	95
8.1	Regulatory reforms	152
8.2	Who reformed, and when?	153
8.3	The timing and scope of industry-level reforms	153
8.4	Employment protective legislation: number of reforms	154
8.5	Marginal pension reforms, 1985–1996	155
8.6	Changes in the degree of EPL, 1980s and 1990s	156
8.7	Gainers and losers from reform	163

List of Figures

9.1 Social spending over GDP in the UK, 1948–2002	171
9.2 Dynamics of payables, receivables, and wage arrears	176
9.3 Real GDP growth	177
9.4 Capital flight	180
9.5 Lega Nord votes in 1994 and expected seniority pensions in Italian regions	183
10.1 Developments in unemployment, structural unemployment, and rates of wage increases in Denmark, 1970–1998	190
10.2 Share of unemployed workers with seniority over 12 months, Denmark	192
10.3 Social security expenditure as a proportion of GDP in Italy	200
11.1 Workers' non-pecuniary rents and regulatory reform	211
11.2 Regulatory reform versus intermediate and final consumption	218
11.3 Product market rents and regulatory reform	221
11.4 Trade and FDI patterns in the OECD	222
11.5 Non-manufacturing regulation, services imports, and inward FDI, 1998	223
11.6 Regulatory reform and FDI openness	226
11.7 GDP and total employment changes (%) in Spain	228
11.8 Net employment variation by type of contract	229
11.9 Regular long-term employees as a proportion of the active population	230
12.1 Production of Škoda	238
12.2 Output in PPP	239
12.3 Production of AvtoZAZ	245
C2.1 Product and labour market reforms, 1982–1998	277
C2.2 Product market regulations and employment protection regulations, 1998	278

List of Tables

3.1	Labour productivity in telecommunications: real revenue per employee, 1991–2001	45
3.2	Employment in telecommunications, 1991–2001	45
3.3	Shares of railway traffic over total traffic, 1999	48
3.4	Shares of railway traffic over road traffic, 1991–2001	48
3.5	UK rail traffic: passengers, employees, and productivity, 1996–2002	51
3.6	Italian rail traffic: passenger, employees, and productivity, 1996–2002	52
3.7	Indices of regulation of professional services	58
3.8	Concentration ratios	67
3.9	Hypermarkets in Italy: numbers and employees	68
3.10	Implementation of Law 46/94: situation at June 2003	84
3.11	Average prices for water services in some cities, in Euro, 2001	87
4.1	Openness in manufacturing and services	90
4.2	The total share of services in the value of "manufacturing" final output	91
4.3	The total share of selected services in the value of "manufacturing" final output	94
5.1	Change in the rate of growth of labour productivity	100
5.2	Multinationals' employees rate	104
2A.1	OECD Input–Output tables (ISIC Rev. 3 Class.)	123
2A.2	OECD Input–Output tables (ISIC Rev. 2 Class.)	124
C1.1	Labour productivity levels in France, Italy, and the USA	127
C1.2	Labour productivity growth rates in Frances, Italy, and the USA	127
C1.3	Productivity levels and growth rates in retail in Europe and the United States	130
7.1	A simple typology of reforms	145

List of Tables

9.1 Vote shares and parliamentary seats in British elections, 1979–1992	169
9.2 Retireess' income by income group and composition	172
9.3 Votes and shares at the 1994 elections (lower house)	182
10.1 The effects of the reforms on net pension wealth by age	203
12.1 Private sector share in GDP	240
C2.1 The political economy of reforms	264

Contributors

Giorgio Barba Navaretti, University of Milan—Bicocca

Olivier Blanchard, Massachusetts Institute of Technology

Tito Boeri, Fondazione Rodolfo Debenedetti and Bocconi University

Stéphane Carcillo, Centre d'Economie de la Sorbonne (University Paris I and CNRS)

Micael Castanheira, Ecares, Brussels

Riccardo Faini, University of Rome "Tor Vergata"

Vincenzo Galasso, Bocconi University and IGIER

Jonathan Haskel, Queen Mary University of London, AIM—Advanced Institute of Management and CeRiBA—Centre for Research into Business Activity, UK

Giuseppe Nicoletti, OECD

Enrico Perotti, University of Amsterdam

Christopher Pissarides, London School of Economics

Gérard Roland, University of California at Berkeley

André Sapir, European Commission and Université Libre de Bruxelles

Carlo Scarpa, University of Brescia

Stefano Scarpetta, World Bank

Jan Svejnar, University of Michigan

Vito Tanzi, Inter-American Development Bank

Lidia Tsyganok, Ecares, Brussels

Christian Wey, DIW—Berlin

Introduction

This book offers unorthodox insights into an orthodox prescription. It dwells on the pros and cons of structural reforms in product and labour markets to try to find out why they are recommended by most economists and international organizations, but are rarely implemented or else are carried out at a very slow pace. There is no a priori about the net benefits of the reforms. The book is deliberately not reticent in highlighting the costs of these reforms since these costs may help to explain why reforms are so difficult to implement. We are in the domain of positive economics: reforms and their effects are described rather than recommended. Policy prescriptions are relegated to the final chapters of each part and to the comments.

The method which we adopt in the analysis of structural reforms is also rather unusual in this literature. Rather than drawing on cross-country comparisons—which often end up comparing apples with oranges, that is, countries with institutional configurations which are at the polar extremes—we carry out a case-studies analysis. We investigate the effects of reforms in different economic sectors and we assess the nature and strength of opposition to reforms in different policy areas. A word of caution is therefore needed: our findings are often related to a specific sector or policy domain and cannot be readily generalized. Yet they can shed some light on issues present to varying degrees in other sectors or policy areas.

What do we mean by structural reforms? We consider reforms that increase the size of product and labour markets. As previous volumes of this series have already addressed the effects of labour market reforms, our analysis of the *effects of reforms* is here confined to product markets, namely to the service sector, which is undersized and rather heavily protected from competition in Europe. The study of the *political obstacles*

Introduction

to reforms broadens somewhat the range of markets being considered. Not only is labour included, but also reforms modifying the governance structure of firms, hence the size of capital markets, are considered.

AN OUTLINE

A united Europe is still lacking a single market for services. A large number of unreformed, country-specific, regulations protect national service providers from domestic competition, and their services are not traded internationally. Often the state holds direct or indirect control over service providers, discouraging if not altogether preventing the entry of new firms. Monopolies in service provision are also protected in more subtle ways, for example, via licensing agreements, through the lack of recognition of curricula acquired elsewhere, by gaps in regulatory authorities, and by hidden subsidies. In this artificial and sheltered environment, services grow less and cost more to consumers and business units than elsewhere. While in the USA the tertiary sector generates roughly three-quarters of total value added, services hardly reach two-thirds of GDP (gross domestic product) in the European Union (EU). Differences in the costs of service provision between reformed and unreformed markets can be sizeable.

Lack of competition in some service sectors goes hand in hand with protection of other sectors and with labour market rigidities. There are clusters of institutional rigidities: a regulation in one area calls for regulations in another dimension. The strictness of the regulatory framework is indeed positively correlated across product and labour markets: the countries with the most restrictive provisions in labour markets also tend to protect service providers more heavily. Some European countries are "champions" in both respects.

Removing these "rigidities" is proving extremely difficult. Governments with short horizons are reluctant to cope with them as the costs of these reforms in terms of gross job and profit losses materialize immediately while the benefits in terms of growth and employment can be obtained only over longer time horizons. Even when governments genuinely wish to carry out reforms, they find fierce political opposition whenever they take the initiative. Available inventories of regulatory changes in product and labour markets in Europe point to an intensification of reform activity in recent years, especially in the labour market area. However, reforms are mostly marginal, rarely encompassing more than a single dimension at a time, and are sometimes undone in the following years (even by the same government!) through measures going in the opposite direction. This suggests that political obstacles are strong enough to induce policy reversals.

Citizens are often poorly informed about the costs of the status quo and the potential benefits of reforms. This is partly because those who have monopoly positions do not want their rents to be known by the public, and partly because it is the government itself that prefers to retain control, leaving citizens under the veil of ignorance. Only deliberate political choices can explain why those who contribute to public pension systems do not receive every year a statement informing them about what they are actually paying into the system and what they are likely to get out when they retire. A lack of information to consumers about the costs of services in other countries sharing the same currency is also likely to be a by-product of deliberate policy choices. What else could it be? Even governments that genuinely aim to carry out reforms fear that better informed citizens could become negative voters, since it is generally easier to document the costs of structural reforms rather than their benefits.

Still, cheating citizens is always a short-sighted policy. It can at best buy some extra time. It is not useful either at the commitment-building phase or when the task is to build up consensus for the reforms. Trust in governments is seriously hampered when the truth comes out. Moreover, although difficult, it is not altogether impossible to document the benefits of structural reforms. These benefits include also the potential synergies that can be achieved across reform trajectories; for example, the possibility that structural reforms in product markets foster reform in labour markets and vice versa. These spillovers can be quite sizeable.

This book is structured in two parts. The first part offers a balanced and sufficiently long-term analysis of the costs and benefits of structural reforms in selected service industries, namely electricity, natural gas, telecommunications, railways, professional services, retailing, postal services, and water. The second part focuses on the political–economic interactions that took place in a series of reforms that were implemented in the last twenty years. The range of reforms is wider than in the first part as it includes pension reforms and privatizations.

In this introduction, we confine ourselves to discussing some interactions between reforms carried out in different policy domains, as these "trickle-down" effects are relevant both in carrying out a cost-benefit analysis of reforms (the task set for Part I) and in devising ways to carry out politically difficult reforms, by choosing an appropriate sequencing of reforms (the task set out for Part II).

Introduction

SOME INTERACTIONS

As discussed above, there are relevant interactions among institutions operating in the various domains. For instance, the available indicators of the strictness of the regulatory framework in the product and labour market areas, which have been developed mainly by the OECD (1997, 1999, and 2004), point to a high degree of correlation between the two types of rigidities. The countries with the strictest regulations in product markets also feature stronger barriers to dismissals.

While cross-sectional clusters of "rigidities" have been documented by the literature, even going beyond these aggregate indicators (Bertola *et al.*, 2001; Nicoletti and Scarpetta, 2003), much less is known about their time-series properties. This is a serious shortcoming in the literature as labour market and product market institutions are not static at all. Rather, there is evidence of significant reform activity occurring in these areas. It is therefore important to analyse in some depth the nature and scope of these reform efforts as well as their interactions across policy domains.

There is some evidence that interactions between product and labour markets are also present in reform efforts. Regulatory changes in labour markets are more frequent at times of increased competitive pressures on product markets. (For example, they increased following the progress made in the completion of the EU Single Market Programme and after the introduction of the euro and associated price transparency and capital movements. There is less evidence on the opposite sequence: reforms of labour markets leading regulatory changes in the product market area.

In Europe, there has been an intensification of reform efforts in the labour market area in recent years. Importantly, this greater reform effort has not been paralleled by major variations in the values of the OECD aggregate indicators of labour market regulation. There are many reforms, but not much change in the aggregate indicators of the strictness of employment protection or in the generosity of unemployment benefit systems.

A possible interpretation of these developments is that there have been important changes in the environment in which these institutions operate, which have, on the one hand, increased the distortions associated with having these institutions in place and, on the other hand, induced stronger demand for protection. This would explain the greater reform efforts, but also the higher obstacles they face.

What type of environmental change has occurred in Europe in the 1990s? A key development has been the reduction of trade barriers and the progress made in the implementation of the Single Market Programme.

A more recent event is the introduction of the euro and its effects on capital flows and price transparency.

There are economic arguments, discussed in Bertola and Boeri (2004), suggesting that an increase in product market competition leads to pressures to reform the labour market and, more broadly, redistributive institutions. The issue is that any wedge between labour supply and demand has stronger costs in terms of foregone employment when labour demand is more elastic. Thus, unreformed labour markets have worse employment outcomes than before product liberalization. This creates pressure for a relaxation of employment protection, a lowering of the minimum wage, or a reduction in the scale of the tax and transfer scheme providing income support to people out of work. But, given that unreformed labour markets involve job losses, there are also pressures in the other direction: requests for more protection. Product market liberalization, on the one hand, increases the employment costs of the status quo and, at the same time, increases opposition to labour market reforms.

How about the reverse causal link, the one going from labour market liberalization to reforms of the product market?

Valuable insights in this respect come from a model developed by Blanchard and Giavazzi (2003), who consider labour market deregulation with given product market regulation. In particular, the effects of a decrease in the bargaining power of workers are considered. In the short run, workers give up rents; this leads immediately to a decline in the real wage and an increase in profits. This change in factor income distribution which results from the change in workers' bargaining power has no impact on unemployment. Thus, workers clearly lose out in the short run. In the long run, however, the larger rents to firms lead to the entry of new firms until the profit rate stabilizes again at the long-run equilibrium level. As more firms enter the market, competition increases, the mark-up decreases, leading to a decrease in the unemployment rate and an increase in the real wage. Indeed, in the long run, the unemployment rate is lower than before deregulation. In other words, labour market deregulation operates by altering the distribution of rents in favour of firms, leading to more competition in the long run, and lower unemployment. Thus, in the short run, a reduction in the bargaining power of workers does no more than simply redistributing rents between workers and firms. In the long run, however, the entry of firms induces changes in the level of unemployment. Labour market deregulation comes with a sharp intertemporal trade-off: lower real wages in the short run in exchange for lower unemployment in the long run.

Introduction

CAN THESE INTERACTIONS BE EXPLOITED TO WIN POLITICAL SUPPORT FOR REFORMS?

The literature reviewed above suggests that increased product market competition puts considerable pressure on institutions, which reduces the size of the labour market. At the same time, increased competition increases the demand for protection, providing powerful weapons to the opponents of reforms. How can resistance to labour market deregulation be reduced? And what can be done to speed up reforms in the product market area, which should also have an impact on the labour market?

Any politically feasible trajectory of reform of labour market institutions should recognize the rationale behind these regulations. Many of these provisions deal not only with distributional tensions, but also with market imperfections, especially as regards the possibility of obtaining insurance against adverse human capital shocks, idiosyncratic shocks to demand, and so on. Another important factor to be taken into account is that there are various ways and multiple instruments that can be used to deal with these risks. All this means that reforms need not take the form of simple deregulation; they can exploit the substitutability between different regulations.

A relevant example is provided by the so-called "UB/EPL trade-off": unemployment benefits (UBs) and firing costs or, more broadly, employment protection legislation (EPL) offer two alternative ways of protecting individuals against the risks of being unemployed . While EPL protects those who already have a job, and does not impose any explicit tax burden, UBs generally provide insurance to a larger portion of the labour force and are financed by a tax imposed on labour income. Economic theory provides a rationale for the substitutability between EPL and UB. Models assigning a welfare-enhancing role to these institutions (e.g. Pissarides, 2001) show that—when severance payments and notice periods in case of dismissals are chosen optimally—there is no role for unemployment insurance. The two institutions may also have important design features in common. For instance, when EPL involves only transfers from the employer to the employee (i.e. it is a severance cum notice period scheme), it may reduce to an experience-rated unemployment insurance scheme. However, job security provisions, in addition to payments from the employer to departing employees, typically involve judicial or administrative costs that are deadweight from the viewpoint of the individual employment relationship.

European countries use different combinations of the two institutions. Plotted against each other, measures of the generosity of the two institutions point to the presence of a trade-off between EPL and UBs: the

Introduction

countries adopting stronger dismissal restrictions tend to enjoy smaller unemployment insurance programmes, and vice versa. The trade-off has also been documented at the micro level: individuals who consider themselves to be protected by EPL are less willing to purchase state-provided unemployment insurance and their willingness to pay for UBs is lower than it is for individuals with a high subjective risk of job loss.

Why do countries resort to different combinations of employment protection and unemployment insurance to protect individuals against the risk of being unemployed? Ongoing theoretical work (e.g. Boeri *et al.*, 2003; Algan and Cahuc, 2006) suggests that such different configurations may correspond to cross-country differences in human capital endowments, age structure of the population, depth of capital markets and progressivity of tax and transfer systems. In particular, countries in which the median voter is a low-skilled insider, where capital markets are relatively underdeveloped, where there is a larger share of elderly workers, and where social policies are not properly targeted at the poor or where there are social santions against abuse state transfers may demand more EPL and less UB.

Under stronger competitive pressures and higher exposure to global demand shocks (Bertola and Boeri, 2004; Ljundqvist and Sargent, 2002), a case can be made for substituting employment protection regulations with temporary unemployment insurance, which can better reconcile worker protection and mobility, especially when job search effort is appropriately monitored. Similarly, search assistance, as well as a framework of subsidized training (or "lifelong learning"), can make it possible to cope with reallocation demands without burdening workers with an unfair share of the cost of transition. Overall, stronger competitive pressures tend to shift the balance of the two institutions in favour of mobility-friendly unemployment benefits, while employment protection is ill-suited to accommodate new demands for mobility. Unemployment benefits are also preferable to EPL on the grounds that they allow workers to seek for jobs which are hard to get because they require more specialized skills (Acemoglu and Shimer, 1999).

Thus, a first "political feasibility theorem" which is inspired by the above is that reforms of employment protection need to trade labour market flexibility off against state-provided unemployment insurance. The trade-off is likely to become more favourable when the educational attainments of the workforce are higher and when capital markets are deeper. Both developments tend to reduce the demand for EPL at any given level of unemployment insurance.

Many European countries would seem to have followed this trajectory, according to the Fondazione Rodolfo Debenedetti (fRDB) database: focusing on those countries which had the strictest EPL provisions to start with, in Portugal a combination of reforms reducing the strictness of employment protection and increasing the generosity of unemployment benefits in the following two years has occurred seven times, and in Italy five times.

UNBUNDLING

Many institutional reforms are asymmetric in that they change regulations only for a subset of the population. Reforms of EPL, in particular, have often been parametric, involving only specific segments of the workforce. Unbundling reforms is therefore a viable strategy to implement politically difficult reforms. The task is first to identify those groups which are more prone to accept the reforms and then differentiate changes in regulations according to these asymmetries in political preferences. As it is undesirable for equity and also efficiency reasons (Blanchard and Phillippon, 2003; Bentolila and Dolado, 1992) to create long-lasting differences in the way different socio-economic groups are treated, it is also important to devise ways to gradually extend the reform to everybody.

Two fields where this approach has been successfully implemented are employment protection legislation and pension reforms, where preferences over reform options are deeply shaped by individuals' characteristics.

Political support for reforms of EPL by different socio-economic groups can be clearly illustrated by a survey carried out by Fondazione Rodolfo Debenedetti in April 2002 using a representative sample of Italians (1,000 individuals aged 16 to 80). All respondents were asked whether they preferred a flexible "labour market regime in which it is relatively easy to find a job, but it is likewise easy to lose a job" or a "rigid labour market in which jobs are difficult to find but last longer". In particular, being aged more than 55 yields a 20 per cent higher probability (than the baseline) of voting in favour of employment protection. Low educational attainments also work in favour of stronger employment protection ($+12\%$) and even more so in combination with the fact of having lost a job ($+40\%$). Finally, residence in depressed labour markets (e.g. in the Mezzogiorno) also increases support for employment protection. Thus, reforms of EPL are more likely to win support if concentrated on certain socio-economic groups, such as high-skill types, the young, and those living in relatively dynamic labour markets.

Political support for pension reforms likewise interacts meaningfully with personal characteristics. Once more, this can be better appreciated with the help of survey data. Such surveys suggest that individual features, such as age, income, and education, play an important role in shaping the evaluation of these reform options. In particular, younger, more educated, richer, males tend to approve more of reforms shrinking the size of pay-as-you-go systems, while the fact of being member of a trade union, living in a poor region, or having a left-wing ideology works in the opposite direction.

Clearly not all of these heterogeneities in preferences can be exploited in devising feasible reform trajectories. For instance, there are constitutional rules or simply just ethical considerations preventing the enforcing of reforms which create long-lasting asymmetries across workers with different educational attainments, let alone ideology. Other asymmetries can instead be exploited: many pension reforms in Europe (e.g. the Italian 1995 reform, the Swedish 1998 reform) involved only the youngest workers, leaving the rules for older workers unaltered. The reason for creating these two-tier systems is essentially political: younger workers are more favourable to pension reforms reducing the state monopoly in retirement provision and expanding the scope of complementary, private pensions.

A similar approach underlines the introduction of flexible contractual arrangements limited to new hires or to school-leavers (as in the case of contracts combining fixed-term durations and a training component). In principle, these reforms eventually change the rules for everybody. As young workers age, all pensions will be paid according to the new rules; as labour turnover changes the stock of jobs, only the new contracts are enforced. The crucial issue is the length of the transition from one system to another: too long a transition exposes a country to the risk of getting caught in an equilibrium with a two-tier regime in place (Saint-Paul, 2000). In this respect, the Swedish pension reform was much better than the Italian one. The former spared only 10 per cent of workers from the new (less generous) rules, while in Italy the new defined contribution (DC) rules were introduced on a flow, pro-rata, basis for no more than 60 per cent of the eligible population. Only in 2065 will the transition to the new system be complete.

To summarize, reforms done "at the margin" or the unbundling of reforms offer a very powerful way to enforce politically difficult reforms. The trick is to devise them in such a way as to gradually extend the new rules to everybody. There are indeed potential distortions associated with maintaining a two-tier system in place for a long time: the speed of the transition from the old to the new rules is therefore crucial in this reform strategy.

AN "IMPOSSIBILITY THEOREM": REFORM AT THE MARGIN AND THE PRODUCT MARKET

As discussed above, governments can exploit the asymmetric impact of labour market reforms across individuals within the working age population and across the heterogeneity in preferences over public policies resulting from these asymmetries.

Unfortunately, this reform strategy does not seem to be viable in the case of product markets. A marginal reform (similar to those applied in the labour market) in a specific sector (e.g. in the provision of a public utility) would result in a market applying with different sets of rules to different firms. On the one hand, incumbent firms would operate under the traditional set of protection and rents (i.e. government subsidies). On the other hand, new entrants would be forced to operate without these rents. This cannot work if the incumbent firm (the former monopolist) can easily drive the new competitive fringe away from the market.

There is indeed a fundamental difference between product market and labour market reforms. In the latter case, marginal reforms are politically feasible and widespread. In the former case, reforms need necessarily to be more fundamental, and need to completely change the set of rules which govern the competitive structure. Marginal reforms in the product market are just not sustainable.

In the absence of the possibility of engineering marginal reforms, radical reforms in a specific industry turn out to be politically very difficult, for at least two reasons. First, the lobbying power of existing incumbents is strong. Aware of the risk of radical reforms, existing monopolists are likely to oppose by all means any radical reform proposal. Some form or rent splitting is likely to take place in this dimension. The second reason is more subtle, and has to do with the marginal propensity to push and resist reform by the active population. Arguably, the mass of voters within the population would certainly have the *aggregate* political power to enforce a radical reform in a specific good sector. The issue is whether such political power is exploited in equilibrium. As noted by several observers in the past, each individual tends to see her/his position in the economic system more as a worker rather than as a consumer. This asymmetry has an obvious impact on the reform process. While individuals are willing to demonstrate and oppose structural reforms in the labour market, the same political energy seems to be absent when lobbying for radical reforms in the product market. Within the European history of the last ten years, there are plenty of examples of protracted strikes aimed at opposing structural reforms of the European welfare states (e.g. Italy, 1994 and 2002; France 1995 and 2006). By contrast, the same people have never engaged in long strikes aimed at implementing market reform for specific industries.

The above may also help to explain why there seems to be a stronger status quo bias in product markets than in labour markets. In product markets, reforms unavoidably hit the incumbents, while in labour markets it is possible to concentrate regulatory changes on new entrants. Marginal reforms are a powerful factor leading to convergence of institutions as they are more successful in countries which need more deregulation of labour markets: temporary contracts increased in those countries where the rules for incumbents were most restrictive.

DELEGATING POWER TO SUPRANATIONAL AUTHORITIES

If marginal reforms are feasible in labour markets, while they are not in product markets, there is another reform strategy which is more feasible in product than in labour markets. This is the possibility of delegating power to supranational authorities in order to achieve reforms while being able to shift the blame onto someone else. It is the "Ulysses and the Sirens" approach which, after all, was used in the case of monetary policy in the European Monetary Union (EMU) in the idea that a central bank located sufficiently far from political pressures would be better placed to fight inflation.

This strategy is ultimately what lies behind the success of European countries in liberalizing their product markets in the early 1990s. EU competition policy, in the form of elimination of anti-competitive agreements, liberalization of monopolistic sectors, control of mergers between firms, and monitoring of state aid, has been very important in liberalizing product markets and in preventing the undoing of earlier reforms.

This involvement of supranational authorities is not a viable reform strategy in the case of labour market reforms. The issue is that there should be sound economic arguments for having supranational authorities in charge of policies in this area. In the case of product markets, the externalities associated with greater competition are self-evident. In the case of labour market and social policies, there is a strong case for keeping decentralized, country-level, decision-making in place. Public insurance schemes, for instance, can be better run at a decentralized level. There is also evidence of diseconomies of scale in social security provisions as the most effective social security systems (those achieving more redistribution relative to the resources allocated to them) in Europe are those of the smallest EU members. Finally, there are country-specific clusters of institutions and imposing the same approach on all may result in the worst of the various systems. It is much better to rely on competition among systems, forcing reforms which imitate best practice.

Unsurprisingly, attempts to shift responsibility onto someone else, sufficiently far from domestic pressures, in the case of labour market or pension reforms (e.g. the so-called Maastricht for pensions proposed under the Italian Presidency of the EU) have so far been unsuccessful.

Overall, shifting responsibilities to supranational authorities is a viable strategy if there is a strong case for delegating power to higher levels of decision-making. Arguments based on the theory of fiscal federalism (Oates, 1999) suggest that this case is strong in product markets, but not in labour markets.

References

Acemoglu, D. and Shimer, R. (1999), "Productivity Gains from Unemployment Insurance", NBER Working Paper no. 7352, National Bureau of Economic Research.

Algan, Y. and Cahuc, P. (2006), "Civic Attitudes and the Design of Labour Market Institutions: which Countries can Implement the Danish Flexicurity Model", CEPR D.P. no. 1928.

Bentolila, S. and Dolado, J. (1993), "Who are the Insiders?", Centre for Economic Policy Research (CEPR) Discussion Paper no. 754.

Bertola, G. and Boeri, T. (2004), "Product Market Integrations, Institutions and the Labour Markets", mimeo.

—— and Nicoletti, G. (eds.) (2001), *Welfare and Employment in a United Europe*, Cambridge, Mass.: MIT Press.

Blanchard, O. and Giavazzi, F. (2003), "Macroeconomic Effects of Regulation and Deregulation in Goods and Labor Markets", *Quarterly Journal of Economics*, 118(3), 879–908.

—— and Philippon, T. (2003), "The Decline of Rents, and the Rise and Fall of European Unemployment", mimeo.

Boeri, T., Conde-Ruiz, J. I., and Galasso, V. (2003), "Protecting Against Labour Market Risk: Employment Protection or Unemployment Benefits?" CEPR Discussion Paper no. 3990.

Ljungqvist, L. and Sargent, T. J. (2002), "The European Employment Experience", CEPR Discussion Paper no. 3543–2002.

Nicoletti, G. and Scarpetta, S. (2003), "Regulation, Productivity, and Growth: OECD Evidence", *Economic Policy*, no. 36.

Oates, W. (1999), "An Essay on Fiscal Federalism", *Journal of Economic Literature*, 37, 1120–49.

OECD (1997), *The OECD Report on Regulatory Reform*, Paris.

—— (1999), *EMU: Facts, Challenges and Policies*, Paris.

—— (2004), *Employment Outlook*, Paris.

Pissarides, C. (2001), "Employment Protection", *Labour Economics*, 8, 131–59.

Saint-Paul, G. (2000), *The Political Economy of Labour Market Institutions*, Oxford: Oxford University Press.

Part I

CONTRASTING EUROPE'S DECLINE: DO PRODUCT MARKET REFORMS HELP?

Riccardo Faini, Jonathan Haskel, Giorgio Barba Navaretti, Carlo Scarpa, and Christian Wey*

---

* We are grateful to an anonymous referee for insightful comments and to Laura Anselmi, Laura Brigoni, Chiara Criscuolo, and Alessandra Tucci for their invaluable help in preparing this report.

1
Introduction

In 2001, faced with the US economic slowdown, European policy-makers were quite confident that Europe could become the leading engine of growth for the international economy. Strong macroeconomic fundamentals, including low inflation, the lack of current account imbalances, and an increasingly healthy public finance situation, all boded well for the future prospects of the continent's economy. Most of these expectations were much too optimistic. The economic slowdown since 2001 has been substantially more pronounced in Europe than in the USA. By and large, Europe has yet to find the recipe for endogenous self-sustained growth.

The mediocre growth performance has prompted new concerns about Europe's long-term economic prospects. Particularly worrying is the fact that, in contrast to the USA, productivity growth has been stagnant. In the absence of sustained growth in total productivity, many of the objectives of the Lisbon Agenda will be difficult, if not impossible, to attain. Inadequate productivity growth may also be at the heart of Europe's competitiveness problem, as epitomized in particular by the steady erosion of world exports market shares and the increasingly limited ability to attract foreign direct investment.

Do product market reforms have some bearing on Europe's poor growth and productivity record? This is the central question addressed by this report. There is considerable agreement that widespread rigidities in European markets are among the main factors responsible for Europe's growth record. So far, much of policy-makers' and public attention has been devoted to reform of labour markets and the pension system. Yet, pervasive inefficiencies and distortions are not limited to labour markets but are significant features of product markets as well.

In what follows, we focus on the tertiary sector. We do so for three main reasons. First, services account for most of the unfinished reform agenda.

Second, they are relatively less exposed to international competition. Third, the sector plays a key role as a supplier of inputs to manufacturing. The combination of these three factors—weak international competition, an uncompetitive domestic environment, and strong downstream intersectoral linkages—make us conjecture that services have become a crucial determinant of international competitiveness.

Under these circumstances, the call for further liberalization in services should be overwhelming. It is not, as shown by the stalling of the reform process. There are indeed concerns that this process might encourage job losses, lower investments in infrastructure and that the benefits of increased competition do not trickle down to final users through price reductions and better quality. Liberalization is a difficult process that many European countries have been able to implement only as a consequence of Directives of the European Commission. Sectoral specificities also matter in determining the effects of liberalization policies, with sectors often reacting quite differently to reforms as a function of their initial technological and demand conditions. These concerns are often raised by interests groups, but may also find support in the theoretical literature, which shows that increased competition does not necessarily result in greater dynamic efficiency, particularly as far as innovation is concerned (Aghion *et al.*, 2002; Etro, 2004). More generally, in a second-best situation, there is no guarantee that sectoral reforms will improve efficiency. Broad-based reforms may be more effective (Blanchard and Giavazzi, 2003), but their implementation may none the less face the opposition of well-entrenched and politically powerful specific factors.

Notwithstanding these concerns, the broad consensus in the academic community and among policy-makers is that the benefits of competition outweigh any eventual costs. The consensus rests on three key arguments. The first is that well-designed product market reforms can play a key role in boosting productivity growth, as shown by recent OECD research (Nicoletti and Scarpetta, 2003). The second is that many labour market rigidities are intrinsically linked to product market distortions (Blanchard and Giavazzi, 2003; Jean and Nicoletti, 2002; Bertola and Boeri, 2002). In particular, inefficient regulations typically generate economic rents that in turn foster additional labour market rigidities. Hence, reforming product markets may facilitate structural changes in labour markets as well. Finally, there is now also some evidence that inadequate regulation stifles investments (Alesina *et al.*, 2003).

One key shortcoming about the emerging consensus is that too often it skirts over the sectoral details of reforms. Yet, this is a key step in assessing

Introduction

the success of the reform effort. Looking beyond the averages is essential to understanding why some reforms have not fully delivered or, in some cases, may even have failed. The features of the reform experiences and their effects are often industry specific, depending on sectoral factors such as market conduct and technological conditions. Hence, reduced form models, such as those used in the literature, will often fail to account for some of the key factors that may affect the relationship between competition and performance. Equally crucially, efficiency is just one, albeit crucial, indicator of the impact of regulatory reforms. Other aspects, such as price and employment, also have a bearing on the evaluation of such reforms. In this report, therefore, we take a close look at the sectoral details of reforms and at their outcomes. At the same time, we also take a relatively broad view compared with the literature of the impact of regulatory reforms and consider their impact on other sectors in the economy. Indeed, services—the main focus of our report—are increasingly linked, through input–output linkages, to the rest of the economy, in particular to manufacturing. Changes in the efficiency of providing services inputs may therefore have a marked impact on the cost conditions and the competitiveness of the economy as a whole.

We therefore proceed in two main directions. The first is to take stock of reform efforts in key services in a number of European countries, by focusing on three case studies: Germany, Italy, and the UK. The choice of the sample is dictated by the need to consider a set of representative countries in the European arena as well as by the desire to focus on a sufficiently wide range of country experiences. The features and the effects of reforms will be examined for individual sectors, as regulatory issues and their effects are industry specific: the problems faced by network industries like energy or communications are substantively different from those concerning business services like accountants or lawyers. So far, most of the attention at the European level has focused on reform of the regulatory framework in the network industries. Other sectors, including the wholesale and the retail sectors as well as professional services, while quite crucial in terms of competitiveness and efficiency, have not been equally emphasized.

A second feature of this report is that it examines also the indirect effects of the tertiary sector as a supplier of key inputs for manufacturing. Generally, the debate on services focuses on their effects on final consumption, whereas input–output linkages are seldom considered (see, however, Allegra *et al.*, 2004, and Nicoletti and Scarpetta, 2003, for two noticeable exceptions). However, services account for an important share of the total output value of other economic activities like manufacturing. In this respect, the efficiency of the tertiary sector has important implications for the efficiency of other economic activities.

Our key finding is that, although reforms are difficult to implement and do not always deliver the expected gains, particularly in the short term, deregulation of services in all three countries analysed is found to be associated with faster productivity growth and competitiveness both in the service sector and in the rest of the economy. This latter result is largely due to the fact that services play a much more pervasive role in the overall economy than generally acknowledged, as they are fundamental inputs to most non-service activities like manufacturing and agriculture. Consequently, changes in efficiency, quality, and costs of services delivered trickle down in large competitive gains in the overall economy. The bottom line is that liberalization in services has the potential to bring large welfare gains and governments need to persevere in their effort to reform the service sector.

The structure of this part is as follows. First, it briefly reviews the literature on the relationship between deregulation and productivity and growth. Second, it examines at considerable length reform efforts in key services in Germany, Italy, and the UK. The reader uninterested in the details of individual regulatory reforms may skip the relevant sections without any loss of continuity. In Chapter 4, the report turns to economy-wide issues and relies on input-output analysis to document how the tertiary sector plays a large and growing role as a supplier of inputs for manufacturing. In the following chapter, the report examines the impact of deregulation of services on the manufacturing sector by focusing on two key indicators, productivity growth and the ability to attract foreign direct investment. Chapter 6 offers some conclusions and discusses the prospects for further liberalization in the market for services. The part also has two appendices, one summarizing the literature on competitiveness, privatization, and efficiency and the other summarizing the sectoral classification of input-output tables.

2

Competition and Economic Performance: A Brief Review of the Literature

Theory does not provide an unambiguous answer as to the impact of competition on economic performance.[1] Empirical evidence, however, while not fully unanimous, suggests that more competition raises productivity. Both policy-makers and the academic community agree that the benefits of competition outweigh any eventual costs.

First, imperfectly competitive markets are typically inefficient. By equating marginal costs to marginal revenues rather than to prices, they produce at inefficiently low levels. However, such static costs are not very significant. Empirical evidence shows that they amount to just a few decimal points of a percentage point of GDP.

A stronger case in favour of a competitive environment comes from considering the incentives for cost efficiency. It is often argued that competition may strengthen such incentives and prompt firms' owners to better monitor their managers. While the owner of a monopolistic firm should be keen to monitor his managers, his task may be greatly complicated by the lack of an obvious benchmark.

An even stronger case in favour of competition is that it boosts the incentives for innovation. The standard argument is that a reduction in production costs brought about by a technological advance would be fully captured by a competitive firm rather than being eroded by a decreasing marginal revenue schedule. However, if barriers to entry are not too high, a monopolistic firm may have a strong incentive to keep innovating simply to keep its potential competitors at bay and preserve its hefty

---

[1] See Appendix 1 for a more thorough discussion of the link between competition and economic performance.

monopolistic rents (Etro, 2004). Aghion *et al.* (2002) argue that the relationship between market structure and innovation is hump shaped with either a highly competitive or a highly concentrated environment fostering innovation. Again, empirical evidence is somewhat inconclusive. The typical finding is that large firms innovate more. Yet, this may simply be due to the fact that such firms are better innovators and, as such, have comparatively larger market shares.

Finally, in addition to raising the productivity of existing firms, competition can also raise productivity growth via the process of entry and exit. Empirical evidence shows that entry and exit of firms account for a large and increasing share of aggregate productivity growth.

A different but related issue is whether privatized firms are more efficient than public enterprises. There are a number of reasons to believe that this may the case, namely the closer alignment of shareholders' and managers' objectives and the more limited scope for rent-seeking behaviour.[2]

The typical way to examine the link between competition and performance is to relate some indicators of market structure (say price cost margins, concentration indices) to performance indicators such as productivity and innovative activity. Nicoletti and Scarpetta (2003) take a different route and assess the link between productivity growth and the OECD indicator of regulatory restrictions. They focus therefore on the policy determinants of product market competition. One key advantage of their indicator is its exogeneity, provided political economy factors are neglected. Their main finding is that privatization has a systematically strong effect on productivity growth. The effect of restrictive regulations is more mixed, but works mainly by slowing down convergence towards the best productivity performers.

Most existing empirical research, however, is based on reduced form models which may fail to capture the comprehensive set of factors affecting the relationship between competition and performance, such as market conduct and technological conditions. The features of reform experiences and their effects vary considerably and are often industry specific. Any attempt to assess such effects only through cross-country and cross-industry regressions is bound to run into great difficulties. For this reason, in the following chapter we present a set of industry-specific case studies that examine the reform experiences of three sample countries,

---

[2] See Appendix 2 for a detailed analysis.

Germany, Italy, and the United Kingdom and take stock of their main effects in terms of productivity, employment, and prices.

Moreover, available works are generally focused on the direct link between a competitive environment and economic performance. In doing so, they largely overlook the possibility that costs and productivity inefficiencies in a given sector may spill over to other sectors through input-output linkages. As noticed earlier, this type of pecuniary externalities is likely to be particularly relevant for the tertiary sector. First, this is a highly regulated and imperfectly competitive sector. Second, it is relatively less exposed to international competition. Third, its role as a supplier of inputs to manufacturing is very significant and has been growing quite markedly over recent decades. In Chapters 4 and 5 we rely on input-output analysis to document these trends and their effects on competitiveness.

3
The Maze of Services Regulation

3.1. A brief overview

Dismantling the dominant position of an incumbent firm is a daunting task. Even in Britain, the initial reforms in sectors such as gas, electricity, and telecommunications were characterized by little restructuring of incumbents and substantial limitations to competition. Liberalization is a difficult process that many European countries implemented only as a consequence of Directives of the European Commission. This seems to suggest that institutions which are further away from local specific interests tend to be more market oriented than national governments.

Political commitment to reform is key to its implementation. However, sectoral specificities also matter in determining the effects of liberalization policies. Indeed, the post-liberalization path of employment and prices is found to vary considerably among sectors, sometimes unfavourably.

Liberalization has definite positive effects on *productivity*. However, most of the boost to productivity seems to come from a reduction in employment relative to its initial possibly excessive levels. In some cases, productivity may increase even well before privatization and liberalization; as shown for instance by Italy's electricity sector, incumbent firms may boost their efficiency-enhancing efforts in anticipation of a more competitive environment.

As for *prices* and *employment*, the picture is mixed. In some cases (retailing, professional services, telecommunications), liberalization has been associated with greater competition, either because the sector was naturally competitive (and regulation was simply a way to protect producers), or because rapid technological progress has allowed entrants to bypass the incumbent's network and to offer innovative products. Product differentiation (in particular, product improvements) seems to have been a key factor in developing competition in telecommunications. In these cases, prices have decreased and employment has increased, thanks to rapid output growth.

For other network industries, the picture is less satisfactory. Faced with limited product and process innovations and a strong natural monopoly element, competitors have found it harder to bypass a strong incumbent, sometimes also because of regulatory shortcomings. In sectors such as energy, water, railways, and postal services, the most visible effect of reforms has been a reduction in the initial overmanning. Productivity has typically risen, mostly reflecting the decrease in employment, rather than a post-liberalization boom in output.

Quite crucially, most often efficiency gains did not fully translate into lower prices. Several explanations are possible. In energy sectors, expectations about the impact of reforms were probably too optimistic, and did not fully take account of the large role of fuel costs in determining user prices of electricity or in the cost of long-term wholesale supply of gas. More to the point, prices did not decrease as much as expected partly because of the limited competition that countries were able and willing to introduce. Equally crucially, the reform process involved a number of sectors where prices were initially below average costs, thereby requiring heavy public subsidies. In sectors such as railways or water, market-oriented reforms that brought prices in line with costs were bound to result in substantial increases in prices. Finally, the alleged need to fund large infrastructural investments has also resulted in relatively high prices, particularly when regulation has maintained a price-setting role.

Given the extreme relevance of differences across countries and across sectors, because of both starting conditions and technological features, an analysis of the impact of market reforms is needed that allows for the heterogeneity of sectoral reform experience. In what follows, we illustrate the different cases separately.

3.2. Energy

The common European framework has been designed through two Directives approved in the second half of the 1990s, and on this basis national plans have been further developed in the member countries. At the beginning of 2003, two new Directives were approved, with relatively minor innovations. The first steps in the liberalization process have so far concentrated on the removal of public restrictions on upstream activities, on the definition of non-discriminatory access conditions to introduced network infrastructures, but minor requirements on vertical separation have been introduced, where nothing more than a legal separation between the subjects operating different stages of the activity is required, and the development of competition where possible.

The effects of restructuring are quite clear—despite some difficulty in interpreting the data for a sector in transition—as for employment and productivity. The excessive levels of employment which prevailed before the reform appear to have been trimmed considerably, and this has not prevented quality increases. Productivity, as a result, has increased substantially. However, the behaviour of prices has been less satisfactory, reflecting also the difficulty in establishing effective competition, which even in UK experience has required several years of trials and error.

Asymmetries among countries are quite substantial. Countries which have operated a more aggressive separation have allowed the regulator to operate in a clearer situation, reducing cross-subsidies and granting new entrants a relatively level playing field, with positive effects on competition. In countries (Germany being a prominent example) where vertical integration remains widespread and where unclear rules are in place, competition is extremely slow to develop and consumers do not benefit from the opening up of the market, which remains mostly formal. Public ownership is also very important, but plays an ambiguous role; in France it appears to slow down the development of a market, while in Italy state-owned firms appear to maximize profit in a market where regulation is getting more and more relaxed.

Several important asymmetries also exist between the two sectors under observation (gas and electricity), which generally point to gas as the more problematic situation:

- Wholesale competition in electricity is relatively easy, although often very imperfect, while take-or-pay contracts drastically limit access to gas wholesale. Although the Directives only protect take-or-pay contracts signed before 1999, the duration (20–30 years) of these contracts makes the distinction between old and new contracts significant only beyond a reasonable time horizon.

- Vertical integration remains particularly strong in the gas sector, where coordination problems are less cogent than in electricity. The political decision to protect vertical integration in gas markets seems to have little economic basis.

- Access to international gas infrastructures is limited, as they seem to be outside the scope of both regulatory and antitrust norms in the EU. Given the relevance of imports in most EU countries, this means that the owners of international networks—which are often integrated with firms selling gas—may effectively foreclose a market.

The liberalization process is under way in all European countries, but much remains to be done. The apparent opening of markets, where most customers are formally free to choose their supplier, does not always translate into lower prices. Competition remains limited because countries have been lenient towards incumbents (even the UK story in the early years confirms that) and greater effort must be exerted in this direction.

Electricity

3.2.1. *Pre-privatization structural issues*

The electricity industry has for a long time been dominated by vertically integrated industries, owning and controlling generation, transmission, local distribution, and final sales of the sector. Although different countries had different structures, vertical and horizontal integration usually went hand in hand.

In England and Wales, generation and transmission came under together in the monopolistic Central Electricity Generating Board (CEGB), while twelve Area Boards (ABs) were responsible for the distribution and selling of electricity to consumers. In Scotland, there were two vertically integrated Boards, while in Northern Ireland, the NIE was responsible for the small vertically integrated system. In Italy, Enel was vertically integrated from generation to transmission, distribution, and final sales, while some private firms in generation and some local public utilities in distribution prevented a total monopoly.

In Germany, there were nine vertically integrated supra-regional companies (*Verbund*) operating on a supra-regional scale, which in 1995 covered about 79 per cent of generating capacity, plus a large number of regional and municipal firms. While generation was dominated by supra-regional companies, the final market was split quite evenly among *Verbund* companies (33%), regional (36%), and municipal firms (31%).

As for ownership, the state owned most assets in the UK and in Italy, while Germany was a complex case where cross-ownership and (partial) ownership by financial groups were very common.

As in most European countries, prices were set by a public body in the UK and Italy. Germany sticks out as an exception, as access tariffs and wholesale prices were based on private agreements among market participants, while only final prices for domestic customers were determined by a public body (the Länder governments).

In the UK and in Italy, some restructuring took place before the European initiative. In 1992, Enel, which was part of the public administration, became a limited company (S.p.A.) with a plan to eventually privatize it. Privatization however started only in November 1999, when one-third of Enel was put on the market. The government still holds a controlling share of Enel. In the UK, a much more radical reform took place in 1990, and it inspired the subsequent European liberalization process.

3.2.2. The EU reform agenda

The main EU Directives were approved in 1996 and 2003. The main principles are the following:

- vertically integrated firms must separate the accounts of different segments ('unbundling');
- access to the network is regulated by the notion of free third party access (TPA), under tariffs that may be either regulated or negotiated with the owner of the network;
- large clients are 'eligible' to choose the supplier they prefer;
- since the 2003 Directive, all countries are supposed to have an independent regulator, and unbundling must entail the creation of different companies (legal separation).

These principles are stated in a very weak way, in that they leave member countries substantial margins of freedom. A country such as France implemented the necessary minimum, while the UK largely anticipated the Directive with a radical liberalization plan. Germany and Italy took an intermediate position, with more radical vertical separation and more transparent pricing in Italy and quicker market opening but difficult network access in Germany.

3.2.3. Reform in the three countries

3.2.3.1. PRIVATIZATION AND STRUCTURAL CHANGE

The UK, well before European Directives, paved the way for reforms and has since represented a benchmark. The Central Electricity Generating

Board was split into a transmission company and three generating companies: National Power and PowerGen (privatized in 1991) and Nuclear Power (which remained state owned until 1996). The generators competed to sell power to electricity suppliers and eligible customers in a wholesale market called the Electricity Pool, which took daily price bids from every power station and selected the cheapest ones.

At the outset, the wholesale market was extremely concentrated, as the main private producers were almost always price setters. Subsequent entry by new generators and the change in the rules of the game have altered the picture (the pool system ended in 2001 and the New Electricity Trading Agreements—NETA—have started operating, ending the system based on one price for all in favour of a pay-as-bid system). Now the market is considerably fragmented, and the initial joint dominance of National Power and PowerGen has come to an end.

The transmission network was given to the National Grid Company (NGC), an independent firm which was privatized in 1991, with limitations on the participation of generators and other electricity firms in its shareholding. Since then, it has operated as a neutral transmission system operator (TSO) under a price cap. As for distribution, the ABs were replaced by 12 Regional Electricity Companies (RECs), which were sold to the public in December 1990.

Vertical integration still remains present, however. Several RECs have supply businesses and Eastern is one of the largest generators in England and Wales. Most RECs are now active in the supply of gas as well as electricity. Further sales of the other RECs' supply businesses are expected, following restrictions to ensure that each regional electricity distribution business—which is a local monopoly—is held in a separate corporate entity, ringfenced from all other activities carried on within the licensee's group. Mergers and acquisitions were allowed to take place after 1995. Of the 12 RECs in England and Wales, eight were taken over by US electricity companies; two by UK-based water companies; and one by Scottish Power; Southern Electric merged with Scottish Hydro.

Distribution and transmission remain regional and national monopolies and are price controlled by the independent electricity authority, now called OFGEM, which also tried to introduce competition in ancillary services such as metering and installation of connections to the distribution network.

Other countries looked to the British experience as a model of radical reform, entailing privatization, and a division between regulated sectors and segments in competition. The EU Directives owe a lot to the British experience, and so does their implementation at national level.

In Italy, the government aimed at copying the British experiment, but the lobby defending Enel proved to be too strong, so that Italy stopped halfway. Later governments tried to develop competition wholesale, but the lobby defending the privileges of large customers buying cheap energy from France has so far managed to protect that source of energy (about 16 per cent of total consumption) from open competition.

Enel's position has been restrained in all segments, but never with the energy that would probably have been necessary. In the upstream market, no firm can have more than 50 per cent of capacity, and Enel was forced to sell some plants (but still remains close to dominance in generation). The wholesale market is organized as a pool market, along the lines of the initial British example. Bilateral physical contracts have become the normal way of exchanging electricity in Italy, so that the electricity exchange will remain totally marginal (not more than 10% of transactions are expected to take place through this market).

The transmission network has been operated by a state-owned operator (Grtn), although the privatization is under way (and the role of Enel as well as other electricity companies is still undecided). In distribution, the share of former municipal companies has increased, following the decision that Enel should sell part of its local network; local public firms proved to be the only lobby in the sector which proved stronger than Enel.

The thresholds for customer eligibility were established in order to accelerate the process of market opening relative to the dates set in the Directive. Since July 2004, all non-domestic clients are eligible. Eligible clients represent at present more than 60 per cent of total energy sold in the country. Distributors selling energy to franchise (non-eligible) customers must buy the energy for these customers, through a single buyer which is also part of the state-owned Grtn group.

In Germany, the 1996 Directive was implemented with substantial scepticism. Not much has changed compared with the previous institutional set-up. Only with the implementation of the new 2003 Directive will an independent regulatory authority be introduced—eliminating what has been an absolute exception in the European situation. Self-regulation (bordering on collusion) is the common way of tackling the issues of network access. Disputes are settled through national and regional antitrust authorities.

Vertical integration of transmission and other segments remains widespread. After implementation, a general restructuring of the network has taken place, halving the number of large network operators. Only four national network operators remain (RWE, EnBW, E.On, Vattenfall Europe), with 35 regional distributors and about 800 municipal distributors; most of these firms are vertically integrated.

The distribution network is owned and operated by regional and municipal firms. Only a separation of accounts is envisaged for these firms.

3.2.3.2. REGULATION AND DEREGULATION

The UK and Italy have chosen to have an independent energy regulator. In both countries, access to the transmission network is open to third parties on the basis of conditions set by the regulatory authority on the basis of an RPI − x system.[1]

While for the UK this was a choice that fitted their legal tradition, in Italy the introduction of an independent authority has generated substantial debate over its power and its autonomy. In particular, the idea that price determination is left to an administrative body with limited political interference proved hard to digest. Not surprisingly, the weight of government 'guidelines' in the decision process of the authority has increased substantially over time.

Germany is the only European country to choose negotiated TPA, a feature that will have to change soon as the 2003 Directive is implemented. Under the Associations' Agreements, since 1998 grid access can only be denied if the use of lignite coal is endangered; this provision particularly protects the East German lignite (brown coal) industry, which is considered a stranded asset—akin to nuclear power in the UK. However, numerous allegations of abuse of dominant position have been raised against German network operators; absent regulatory interventions, the self-regulatory model has proved unsuitable to define the rules of the game when new entrants try to penetrate the market.

3.2.3.3. ECONOMIC OUTCOMES

Data on productivity are not easy to obtain in any country, especially given that the industry is in transition, and that the borders of the firms and of the industry in general are continuously changing; this makes data extremely hard to interpret. However, both Italian data in the period of leading up to actual restructuring and UK data immediately after

---

[1] Where the regulatory authorities set the regulated price as a function of the overall retail price index (RPI) minus an efficiency (x) factor.

Contrasting Europe's Decline

privatization show that very substantial overmanning existed and that productivity gains have been undeniable (see Fig. 3.1).

In assessing the impact on prices, one must control for the behaviour of input prices, in particular of oil, gas, and coal, whose fluctuations may be considered largely responsible for observed price changes. By and large, however, with the exception of the UK, post-liberalization price performance has been less than fully successful (see Figs. 3.2 and 3.3).

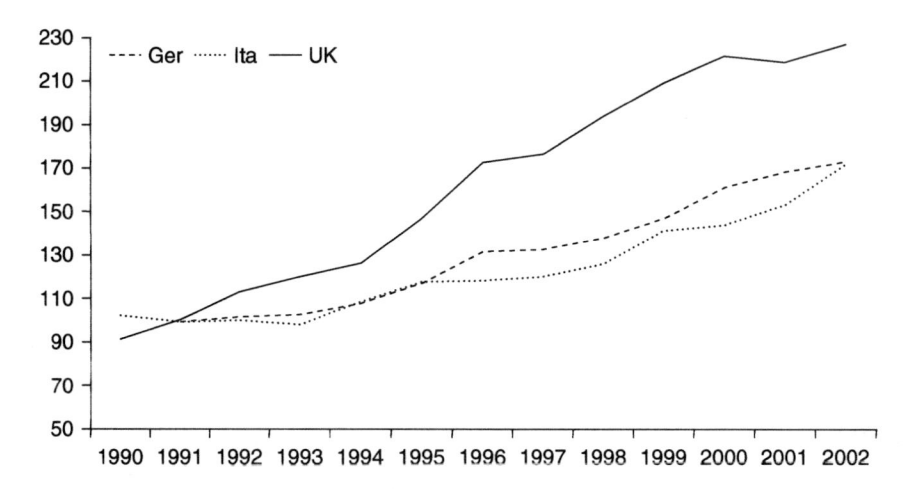

Fig. 3.1 Productivity in the electricity sector
Source: Own elaboration from OECD STAN database for industrial analysis.

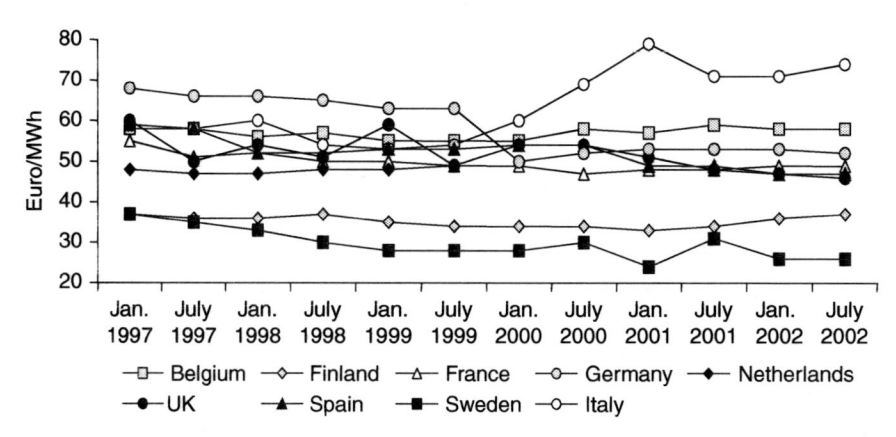

Fig. 3.2 Final net electricity prices for large industrial customers (category Industrial 1G, 24 GWh/year)
Source: Eurostat.

The Maze of Services Regulation

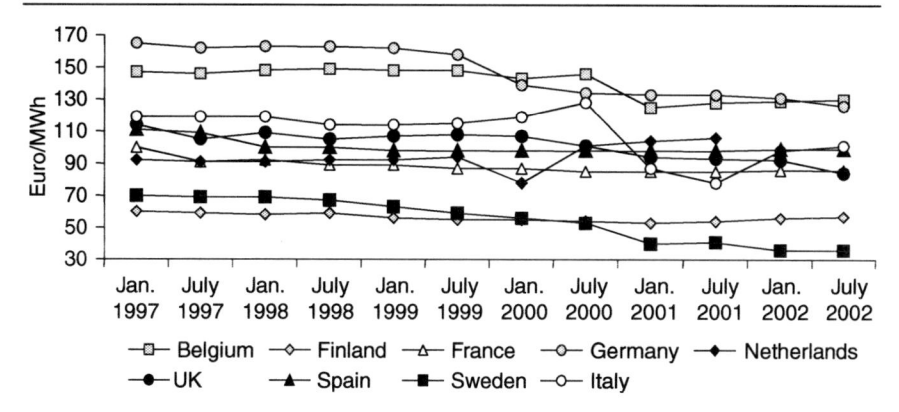

Fig. 3.3 Final net electricity prices for small industrial customers (category Industrial Ib, 50 Mwh/year)
Source: Eurostat.

In the first years of the UK experience, the limited wholesale competition left substantial margins for strategic behaviour in the pool. Only subsequent interventions (price caps, forced divestments by the main firms, new entries, and eventually the introduction of the New Electricity Trading Agreements (NETA)) managed to prove that competition may be effective.

Italy—a latecomer relative to the UK—is still in the initial phase of market opening, where rules are uncertain, the market power of the main generator very high, and the possibility of strategic manipulation of wholesale prices very high. A different story should be told about Germany, where market fragmentation was much higher even before the European Directives, and where prices are kept high by a tradition of self-regulation as the normal way of organizing markets; German prices still remain among the highest in Europe.

Coming to final prices dynamics, in all three countries liberalization proceeds quite quickly from a formal viewpoint, albeit large customers seem much better equipped to exploit the potential of open markets. Small customers are usually still protected by regulation, whose performance is in general considered with favour, especially if one compares final prices with fuel prices.

In no country in our sample is the quality of service considered a problem, and available data indicate a clear positive trend in this respect. Clearly, entrusting the regulator with the task of monitoring quality has proved to be a better model than leaving it to the incumbent (typically State owned) firms.

3.2.4. Evaluation

The development of competition in the electricity markets can be considered partially satisfactory. The UK example proves that there are no insurmountable obstacles in the path towards liberalization, although in the early years competition was very limited.

Productivity indices show clear improvements, and firms within the sector have benefited, often changing from initial situations where they were inefficient State owned monopolies to the current situation where they are (very) profitable firms. The results for final consumers are still uncertain, but the UK experience, where competition and regulation had more time to unfold, is encouraging, and even in Italy regulated prices for final consumers seem to have somehow protected them from the increase in fuel prices.

Natural gas

3.2.5. Pre-privatization structural issues

In most European countries, national or local monopolies were the normal way of organizing the gas industry until the 1990s. In the UK, British Gas controlled distribution and supply under a monopolistic regime. Similarly, in Italy, the state-controlled Eni group controlled national production, imports (under long-term take-or-pay contracts), storage, the high pressure transmission network, sales to large customers, and one-third of distribution to domestic customers. Some fragmentation was present only in the latter segment of the market, where several municipal firms are historically active.

Germany was (and still is) somehow different, with a few large firms and massive cross-participation among these firms and between gas firms and other energy firms (in particular, oil). The main market operator was Ruhrgas, owned by a consortium of coal and steel industries, utilities, and national and foreign oil companies. Private ownership is widespread upstream, while local governments are very active in distribution and final sales.

As in electricity, little regulation was present in Germany before 1998. Agreements among firms would often define exclusive territories which ruled out competition. Final prices were checked *ex post* to control possible abuses of dominant positions.

Overall, there seems to be little or no correlation between the organization of the industry and the degree of dependence on imports: while UK demand can be wholly met by national production, Italy traditionally imports about two-thirds of final consumption.

3.2.6. *The EU reform agenda*

In natural gas, the key document is the Directive 98/30/CE, setting August 2000 as the deadline for the definition of national policies. In 2003, we have had a second Directive, which has added little to the previous situation, in that most countries were already compliant with its new provisions (again, as for electricity, with the notable exception of Germany).

These Directives are very similar in nature to those approved in the electricity sector, with emphasis on unbundling of activities, open third party access to essential facilities (pipelines as well as storage facilities). Issues such as the promotion of competition or privatization are, however, absent from these Directives.

The structural features of the gas market are such that probably a much deeper intervention was called for. For instance, while the TPA principle is easy to establish, it is known that many types of transport tariffs exist (entry–exit; distance related; stamplike) and that the effects of each type of tariff on competition may substantially differ. For instance, an entry-exit tariff entails a payment which only depends on the cost associated with pumping the gas in and out of the network, a cost which may vary from point to point in the network, also depending on the local balance between demand and supply. A distance-related tariff requires instead a payment proportional to the distance between the supplier and the consumer, and it thus penalizes suppliers who do not have a well-established local network of storage sites, especially foreign competitors or new entrants. A stamplike tariff contemplates a fixed charge which only reflects average costs. Unfortunately, the Directives do not specify much, and the Commission's preference for entry-exit tariffs—as a way to balance the need to have cost-reflective tariffs and to favour competition—is expressed only in documents with no binding effect.

A key feature of the gas industry is the presence of long-term (20–30 year) contracts which bind international producers to national resellers. These contracts are generally characterized by take-or-pay clauses, which commit the national buyer to pay a set annual amount to the international producer for the right to buy a pre-specified amount of gas, whether or not that gas is actually withdrawn. These contracts impose a substantial risk on the national reseller, in that the annual amount has to be paid even if the reseller does not manage to sell the contracted quantity.

The Directive therefore decided to protect firms endowed with such contracts—at least those contracts signed before the Directive itself—granting the gas purchased under take-or-pay clauses privileged access to transport pipelines provided the sale of such gas is considered essential for the financial security of the firm. This had a triple anti-competitive effect.

First of all, an exception to the TPA principle introduces an undesirable asymmetry among players, typically favouring large firms, which hold most take-or-pay contracts. Second, as we will see, the same firms are often vertically integrated with network owners, and therefore may find in this clause an easy way to justify other forms of discrimination against competitors. Third, firms who have such contracts have a large quantity of gas at zero marginal cost, and this makes them potentially very aggressive against entrants; if potential entrants anticipate this effect, take-or-pay contracts have a remarkable anti-competitive effect.

A final feature of these long-term contracts is the presence of 'destination clauses', namely provisions which prohibit a national firm from reselling the gas purchased outside its national boundaries. Needless to say, this strengthens market segmentation and reduces the possibility of competition within the continent. However, it is only recently, well after the Directives, that the Commission has tried to convince non-EU producers to eliminate such clauses. Although the issue is objectively complex, having to do with clauses in private contracts with non-EU firms, this delay has raised some doubts about the effectiveness of the reforms.

3.2.7. Reform in the three countries

3.2.7.1. PRIVATIZATION AND STRUCTURAL CHANGE

As in electricity, the UK has represented a benchmark for other EU countries, in that the privatization of British Gas (BG, previously a monopoly) took place in 1986. However, here liberalization has been much slower than in electricity; indeed, BG was privatized with the same management, maintaining the same structure, and introducing very light price controls. The continuous presence of this element has characterized the British gas industry since the beginning of the restructuring phase.

Some liberalization upstream was introduced, in that rival gas suppliers were given permission to enter the market. However, they had to buy gas from North Sea operators who sold most of their output to British Gas (and were presumably reluctant to upset their major customer), and then ship it through British Gas pipes, at charges set by British Gas, to gas consumers with individual, confidential, contracts. Not surprisingly, practically no entry occurred, until numerous complaints by competitors and external observers induced further changes. In February 1997, the company voluntarily demerged into Centrica (the supply business) and BG Transco (the transportation business). This vertical separation of the transportation network is now recognized as a key aspect of the development of competition in this sector. Now supply to final customers is a fully liberalized activity.

In Italy, the dominant position of Eni has been tackled since 2000, but the separation of the network and the supply businesses of Eni is purely legal. As for the upstream market, some 'antitrust ceilings' to its market shares have been introduced: no operator can enter more than 75 per cent of gas into the national transport network; this threshold will be reduced by 2 per cent each year until 2010, with a final market share of 61 per cent. Moreover, from January 2003 to December 2010 no firm will be permitted to sell more than 50 per cent of gas to final customers. Notice that Eni is still allowed to choose to whom it wishes to sell its gas wholesale, so that the effectiveness of such provisions is very dubious. Gas distribution has traditionally been extremely fragmented. Here we see an opposite trend compared to upstream activities. While in the latter we have a slow trend towards fragmentation of supply, in distribution we have an increased consolidation, carried out through acquisitions of small distributors and the shrinking role of local authorities as direct providers of the service. While in 1997, Italy was served by 732 different distributors, in 2003, 'only' 453 distributors are operating.

Germany implemented the Directive very quickly (1998), but took particular care to leave the situation as it was. As with electricity, no regulator for the natural gas market in Germany was envisaged, and antitrust authorities (until the implementation of the 2003 Directive) oversaw market operations. Vertical integration between the different segments of the activity still remains the most common way of organizing the sector. Only the unbundling of accounts (the weakest form) was envisaged. Wholesale, no specific intervention in the largest firms was envisaged by the Energy Bill. This was justified given a relatively fragmented market structure.

The definition of access conditions is left to an agreement among the firms in the gas sector. Access tariffs are not regulated, but negotiated (as in electricity, and here again we have a unique case in Europe). The existence of supra-regional, regional, and local networks provokes a "pancaking" effect, whereby fragmentation leads to very high final access charges. The structure of tariffs (which are distance related, penalizing imported gas) and other conditions for balancing are considered as relevant obstacles to competition and new entry.

3.2.7.2. REGULATION AND DEREGULATION

When market structure is characterized by substantial vertical integration and the presence of dominant firms, behavioural regulation has a more difficult task. As all countries opted for integrated structures involving local or national monopolies, regulation becomes particularly important also to guarantee that competition is left sufficient room. In this respect, the situation appears particularly critical in Germany.

Both in the UK and in Italy, a price regulation scheme in the form of RPI − x was imposed in monopoly segments, namely final prices for small users and for transport and storage of gas. Prices are set by an independent regulator. In contrast, Germany kept relying on a mixture of self-regulation, which borders on collusion, and on the (naturally imbalanced) negotiation between network owners and users.

Tariffs for gas transport have been set on the basis of different criteria in different countries. While in the UK and in Italy their structure is such that competition is favoured even by those entrants which are distant from final demand, in the German situation tariffs are distance related and this especially penalizes foreign competitors.

In Britain, supply to larger users was left unregulated after privatization, anticipating the distinction which the Directive introduced later between eligible and franchise customers. Now all customers large or small, in all three countries, are free to choose their supplier. However, as we will see, the development of competition appears slow.

3.2.7.3. ECONOMIC OUTCOMES

As in electricity, reliable productivity data are difficult to produce, but different indices point towards substantial declines in employment and increases in output. The effects on prices are equally difficult to measure with precision, as world prices oscillate, and it is hard to build a sensible counterfactual.

The limited scope of competition has generated controversies in all countries. In the UK, the post-privatization period was characterized by regulatory battles between BG—accused of discriminating between its industrial customers—and the regulator. Also for this reason, restraints on BG were introduced, in order to allow its rivals access to wholesale gas. Even these measures, however, only allowed a very gradual development of competition. It was not until the early 1990s, when British Gas negotiated specific (and rapidly declining) targets for its market share, and took several steps to help rival suppliers, that competition really took off. Only total market opening has been able to bring about a change. Roughly a quarter of domestic gas consumers now buy from a company different from the local distributor (very often their local electricity company), in part because the regulator allowed British Gas to set prices which recover most of the costs of past gas purchases at what had become above-market prices, while new suppliers based their prices on the lower current prices.

While, in Britain, full supply competition has resulted in significant price reductions for residential customers who do switch but relatively little switching of suppliers, in other countries, total market opening has not proved as effective (see e.g. Fig. 3.4). In Italy, not one case of a domestic customer switching to a new supplier has so far been reported since January 2003. Therefore, the authority still maintains control over prices for small customers.

In Germany, limited network access and the absence of clear regulations seem to favour total market segmentation, whereby suppliers, whether upstream or downstream, share the market with little or no effective competition. The Third EU Benchmarking Report indicates that gas prices in Germany are stable for all categories of final customers, while they are falling in almost all other EU countries. Switching rates in Germany are

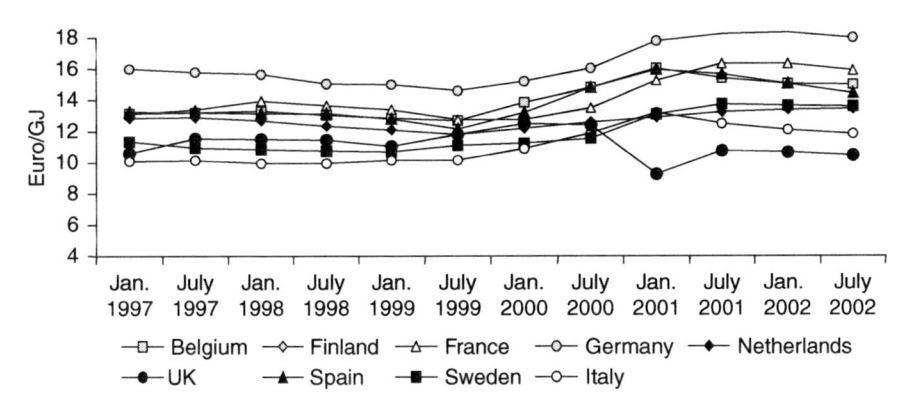

Fig. 3.4 Final net gas prices for small domestic customers (8.37 GJ/year)
Source: Eurostat.

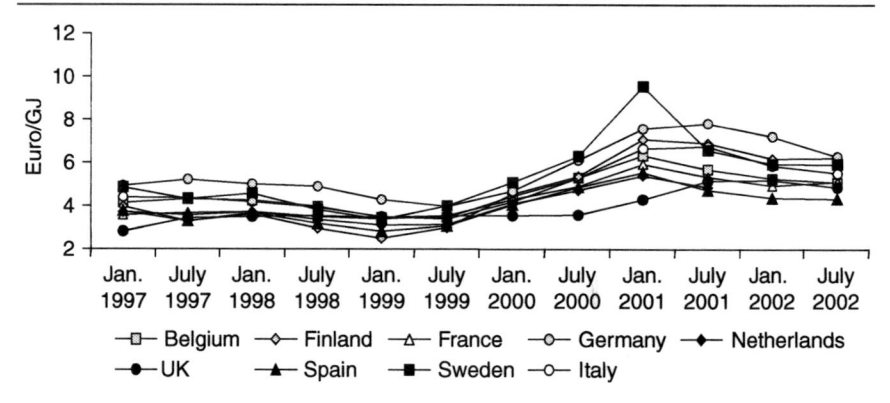

Fig. 3.5 Final net gas prices for large industrial customers (41,860 GJ/year)
Source: Eurostat.

also extremely low (5% for industrial customers, less than 2% for domestic customers), confirming the impression that competition is extremely weak throughout the country. As a result, German gas prices for large customers are the highest in Europe (see e.g. Fig. 3.5).

The data on quality for the three countries are fairly sparse, and they show no clear trend in either direction.

3.2.8. Evaluation

Even the UK, the leader in these reform processes, has had a hard time introducing competition in natural gas. The protection of incumbents is a common feature of the industry in the EU, and despite important formal steps, such as the introduction of competition downstream, the reforms have not proved effective, absent an easy access to gas wholesale. Given the difficulty in obtaining gas (which can be produced only in limited quantities) and given the dominant position of the incumbents upstream, market opening may be a mere formality when the market structure is heavily distorted. In European gas markets, vertical integration seems to remain the rule, and either concentration is extremely high (as in the UK or in Italy), or market segmentation is such that the country is divided into local monopolies (in Germany, we are not far from this limit case).

The performance of gas markets is positive as regards productivity, but these productivity gains have only limited positive effects on consumers (especially small ones); while the aggregate outcome of the reform process is positive, the distribution of the benefits does not seem to be well balanced.

3.3. Telecommunications

3.3.1. Pre-privatization structural issues

In the UK, the Post Office became a near-national monopoly in telephone services from 1912 onwards. At that time, the Post Office was a government department headed by a Minister, but it eventually became a conventional nationalized industry, a "public corporation", in 1969. Similarly, in Italy, at the beginning of the 1990s, the Italian telephone service consisted of one state-owned operator (Telecom Italia). In Germany, Deutsche Telekom AG had the monopoly on voice telephony up until 1 January 1998.

3.3.2. The EU reform agenda

Until the mid-1980s, most European countries were characterized by legally protected monopolies. The Green Paper of 1987 was the first document on liberalization, followed by Directives in 1988 and 1990, but the formal start of the current European liberalization process is the Full Competition Directive of 1996 (1996/19/EC).

While the initial approach was favourable to entrants, the approach of the latest Directives of 2002 is to create a level playing field. Five Directives were issued, the most relevant being the Framework Directive 2002/21/EC. The general approach is to eliminate whenever possible restrictions to entry, to allow TPA on the basis of regulated tariffs linked to long-run incremental costs and to favour local loop unbundling. It is also advised that regulation should be replaced as soon as possible by antitrust control, and the traditional discretionary power of regulatory authorities should be limited (and subject to veto by the European Commission).

3.3.3. Reform in the three countries

3.3.3.1. PRIVATIZATION AND STRUCTURAL CHANGE

In the UK, British Telecom was privatized in 1984. However, in 1982, before privatization, the government licensed another network competitor, Mercury, and began a 'duopoly policy' to develop an alternative national network. Initially, competition from Mercury was ineffective as the interconnection agreement between BT and Mercury was unfavourable to Mercury. After 1987, Mercury did begin to emerge as a serious competitor to BT in some areas but BT's market share was eroded only slowly. 1990–1 saw a review of the duopoly policy and the end of the policy, with alternative licences being offered. There has been substantial entry of companies reselling bulk fixed line minutes. Progress in unbundling the local loop has been slow however. In addition, since the early 1990s, mobile telephony has grown very substantially, with estimates suggesting that 85 per cent of the eligible population possess mobiles. There are five licence holders and there has also been entry by mobile virtual network operators.

In Italy, the implementation of the European Directive in Italy (starting in 1997) led to the end of the legal monopoly of Telecom Italia in January 1998. During the 1990s Telecom Italia was sold to private investors. Telecom Italia remains a vertically integrated operator in fixed telephony, owning most of the fixed line network and being extremely strong in the final segment. There is TPA in the network of Telecom Italia, and tariffs are regulated. The local loop was unbundled only very recently. Other companies are free to develop their own network, and some network competition is actually taking place. More than 200 firms have a licence to operate various services (vocal services, installing networks, running private networks) at both national and local level, and about one-half of them already operate in the sector. Most operators are resellers, that is, use the existing network to offer services at competitive prices, but an increasing number of operators—very often linked to public utilities active in other regulated sectors, such as energy or water—are now working in the cable business. In terms of revenues from final customers, therefore, Telecom Italia's share of fixed revenues has fallen from practically 100 per cent in 1996 to around 85 per cent in 2000 (Bonaccorsi *et al.*, 2001).

One of the most significant aspects of the Italian market is the tremendous development of mobile telephony: mobile telephony now represents about 50 per cent of the market. There are three main operators, but entry in 3G telephony has only just begun and is expected to provide new opportunities for competition. Telecom Italia also controls the main mobile operator (TIM), whose market position is, however, not as strong as in fixed telephony.

The German market was deregulated on 1 January 1998 with licence holders for new fixed services reliant on DTAG for access to local loops. The price of access is set equal for all entrants. Since 1 January 1998, it has been possible for consumers to use a five-digit carrier identification number to select a cheaper provider than the incumbent for long-distance calls. As a result, there has been a wave of entry (OECD, 2002): in 2003,

180 companies were providing voice telephony services in Germany. More than 40 per cent of the minutes of national long-distance calls and foreign calls are now carried by competitors of the incumbent. In total, therefore, the competitors have a market share of 22 per cent.

3.3.3.2. REGULATION AND DEREGULATION

Since BT was the first major UK privatization, and therefore one of the first major privatizations in Europe, it is worth setting out the regulatory pattern in some detail since it set the style for other regulation types. The government established in 1984 an independent regulator, the Director General of Telecommunications, with statutory duties that required the regulator to ensure that the company could finance its activities. The details of the company's regulation were enshrined in its licence, a contract that could only be revoked with 25 years' notice. The regulator would be allowed to impose a change against the wishes of the company, however, if the matter was referred to the then Monopolies and Mergers Commission (the UK's competition authority, now the Competition Commission), and the MMC supported the change. The regulator was also subject to judicial review of his decision-making. If the company felt that the regulator had not followed the proper procedures, or that the decision taken was manifestly unreasonable, it could ask a court to review the matter. This system of checks and balances was designed to protect the company's interests, while ensuring that the regulator could still control its behaviour.

The regulation method chosen was RPI $-$ x of a particular tariff basket, with price caps also on line rental and the bill for the median user. Supply, value added network supply (VANS), and mobile services were unregulated initially, with mobile termination rates regulated since 1998. Since cable and mobile phone companies can now offer fixed link telecommunications services in direct competition to BT, effectively only BT's inland phone charges are now regulated.

Tariffs for final customers in Italy used to be decided by a governmental body, and are now free, subject to the supervision of Agcom (the national authority for communications, an independent administrative body, created in 1997). Competition is, however, subject to the scrutiny of the antitrust authority.

German regulation consists of two elements, price caps for final customers for basket of goods and interconnection fees. Price caps are set by

RPI − x and the interconnection charges in force so far have been based on an international market comparison.

3.3.3.3. ECONOMIC OUTCOMES
Productivity and Employment

Haskel (1991) presents data on total factor productivity in BT. Data are taken from company accounts, where labour inputs are the headcount total from the accounts, and gross capital inputs are derived using a perpetual inventory method. Year-by-year Tornqvist indices of the changes in total factor productivity (TFP) were calculated and geometric averages then taken over several years. Whereas between 1972 and 1978, BT TFP grew by 0.6 per cent p.a., growth rates rose to 3.2 per cent p.a. between 1978 and 1984 and were then at 3.0 per cent p.a. between 1984 and 1994 (recall that BT was privatized in 1984). Whereas in other industries firms improve their productivity significantly in the run-up to privatization, but fail to maintain the same level of efficiency growth afterwards, in the case of BT, improvements of performance appear to have been sustained even after 1984.

That liberalization leads to improvements in efficiency is quite evident in the case of Germany. According to OECD (2002), Deutsche Telekom's productivity rose by more than 13 per cent a year on average in the last three years, with a peak of 26 per cent in 1998, immediately after liberalization. In the two years preceding liberalization, gains averaged 6 per cent p.a.

Unfortunately, data on TFP are not available for our three sample countries. For the sake of comparison, we rely on labour productivity data. Consistently with the evidence on TFP, Table 3.1 shows that labour productivity rose quite markedly in the three sample countries. The good news is that improvements in performance were not achieved because of labour shedding: employment was indeed stable throughout, as shown in Table 3.2.

Prices

In the most recent UK price review (from 2000), prices for some services wgill fall by more than 13 per cent and services in prospectively competitive markets cannot rise by more than RPI + 0 per cent. The OECD reports very positive developments in Germany. Since market liberalization, the price of long-distance calls has dropped by up to 95 per cent,

Table 3.1 Labour productivity in telecommunications: real revenue per employee, 1991–2001

	1991	1993	1995	1997	1999	2001	Annual Growth 1991–2001 (%)
Germany	126,005	155,659	212,133	202,659	229,027	236,044	6.05
Italy	173,375	182,763	201,359	254,629	266,888	296,325	5.05
United Kingdom	116,107	129,824	186,411	212,054	246,036	241,156	7.06

Source: OECD (2002).

Table 3.2 Employment in telecommunications, 1991–2001

	1991	1993	1995	1997	1999	2000	2001	Annual Growth 1991–2001 (%)
Germany	225,628	234,000	217,900	215,624	221,400	240,700	241,800	0.07
Italy	104,714	93,172	91,802	93,782	100,026	95,809	90,880	1.04
United Kingdom	224,197	185,505	153,166	168,740	206,500	230,300	231,500	0.03

Source: OECD (2002).

along with substantial reductions in the cost of mobile phone calls and Internet access. The prices for long-distance calls, Internet use charged by the minute, and mobile telephony are, according to the OECD, amongst the lowest in Europe. In Italy, the plethora of offers that each customer faces, all characterized by two-part tariffs and numerous complex clauses, makes it difficult to construct an average price index. This problem is made even more complex as Istat, the official Italian Statistical Office, provides data that do not distinguish between fixed and mobile telephony.

Quality of service

We have scant evidence on this point and it is limited to the UK, probably because quality is not easy to access and measure. In general terms, quality was initially seen as a problem in the UK, particularly as to what constitutes serviceable public phone boxes. Regulatory targets were set to deal with quality matters. At present, problems have apparently been sorted out in fixed line telecoms, with BT and OFTEL agreeing measures and OFTEL monitoring performance, which is generally acknowledged to be good. Measures such as the percentage of successfully connected calls show good performances, for example 97.5 per cent in 2000 Q4.

3.3.4. Evaluation

Telecommunications are probably the most dynamic sector among those considered, especially for technological reasons. Competition seems to develop quite quickly in all sectors (fixed line, mobile, Internet), with a substantial and positive impact on the sector's economic performance. This happens despite the fact that in all countries examined the incumbent firm has been granted a position of advantage for a substantial period. Unlike other sectors, here the quick development of the technology, the continuous expansion in the range of possible services and possible quality increases give entrants a much better chance of effectively competing.

The range of services in this sector is expanding continuously, so that employment has increased substantially. Productivity—which is not easy to measure, given the changes in the range of services—also seems to increase quite rapidly. This sector thus provides an example where liberalization boosts output and does not conflict with job creation.

Entry is substantial, although it varies significantly from segment to segment. In newer markets such as mobile telephony and Internet services, entry has produced relatively balanced situations, where the existence of a large firm does not prevent competitors from getting important market shares. In fixed telephony, the incumbent still maintains a substantial advantage. However, in the three countries considered, for both local and long-distance calls consumers have substantial freedom of choice. Although the market shares of the incumbent are still well above the level which traditionally indicates likely market dominance (50%), prices have fallen substantially, especially in the long-distance segment, where competition is more intense. The quality of service, measured by availability and reliability of services and by availability of the latest technologies for network connection, is on the rise; in particular, investments in new technology seem to be directly due to competition from entrants.

Therefore, in this sector, despite the persistence in certain segments of dominant positions, consumers seem to benefit from substantial price cuts and investments in new technologies. Productivity and employment also increase. It is, however, difficult to determine to what extent this is due to liberalization, restructuring, and competition, rather than to the considerable technical progress we observe in this sector.

3.4. Railways

3.4.1. Pre-privatization structural issues

The railway network in Britain was built by the private sector in the nineteenth century. It was gradually nationalized in the twentieth century. The railways started to lose money in the mid-1950s and according to the Beeching Reports (1963, 1965) total route mileage was reduced by a third. Finances got worse in the 1970s and early 1980s and subsidies rose (at 1999/2000 prices) from £600 m. in 1968 to £1.6 bn. by 1985–6. The Italian railways were run by a state-owned monopolist (Ferrovie dello Stato), which was part of the public administration until 1999 when it was turned into an (unlisted) limited company. The service was characterized by considerable public subsidies. German railways were nationalized in 1920. As in the UK, public subsidies mushroomed, and in 1993, state railroads were in a deficit of DM 16 m. and DM 67 bn. in debt.[2]

3.4.2. The EU reform agenda

The railway industry in Europe has been liberalized over the last 13–15 years. The EU Directive 91/440 was a landmark in the process of liberalization of the sector. As with other network industries, the Directive envisaged a separation between the infrastructure and those activities that could be opened up to competition. The European Commission wanted to increase competition and reverse the average EU downward trend in rail market share relative to other transport modes, which is shown in Tables 3.3 and 3.4.

The main European Directive dictating the guidelines for liberalization, EU Directive 91/440 EEC, stipulates:

- separation of infrastructure from operation, with compulsory separation of accounting and recommended separation of institutions;
- non-discriminatory rules and prices for track access;
- competition in transit and international combined freight.

EU countries responded differently to EU reforms. The UK liberalized the industry even beyond the requirements of the EU directive, Italy just implemented the minimum number of requirements, and Germany was in-between.

---

[2] Peter Häfner, "Feature: Restructuring Railways Part 2, The Effects of Railroad Reform in Germany", www.jrtr.net/jrtr08/f27_haf.html, 2 June 2004.

Table 3.3 Shares of railway traffic over total traffic, 1999 (in % based on tonne/km performed)

	Passengers	Goods
UK	7	10
Italy	6.2	8
Germany	—	14.5
European Union	6.1	13.4

Source: DG Energy and Transport.

Table 3.4 Shares of railway traffic over road traffic, 1991–2001 (in % based on tonne/km performed)

	1991	2001
Great Britain	4.93	5.51
Germany	8.05	8.72
Italy	6.75	5.77
European Union	7.13	6.83

Source: Transport Statistics Great Britain, international comparisons.

3.4.3. Reform in the three countries

3.4.3.1. PRIVATIZATION AND STRUCTURAL CHANGE

In 1992 in the UK, a White Paper proposed privatization and rail was privatized between 1995 and 1997. The industry was separated (vertically and horizontally) into more than 100 companies in order to foster competition in the contestable elements of the business. Restructuring initially took place within the public sector and the companies thus created were later sold. The key change was the separation of track infrastructure (considered to be a natural monopoly) from train operation (considered to be contestable). Regarding infrastructure, in 1994, most of the fixed railway infrastructure was transferred to Railtrack, which was a separate company from BR, but still government owned. The company was then privatized in 1996. At the same time, BR's infrastructure services were reorganized into seven infrastructure maintenance and six track renewal companies, which were also privatized between February and July 1996. As for operation, BR's rolling stock was divided into three companies that leased rolling stock (rolling stock companies, or ROSCOs). The ROSCOs (also privatized in January/February 1996) lease locomotives and carriages to the passenger train operating companies. Six heavy maintenance depots provide services to ROSCOs (these were privatized in April and June 1995). The right to run passenger train services was franchised to 25 private sector train operating companies (TOCs). TOCs lease almost all of their rolling stock from the

ROSCOs, and pay Railtrack for access to track and stations. Freight operations were separated into six companies (later consolidated into two) and privatized between December 1995 and November 1997. In addition, many other BR central services operations were sold to private sector companies or management teams. In 2002, following a series of fatal accidents, Railtrack was taken into government control and the regulatory bodies rationalized. This restructuring process is still under way.

In Italy, rail is still wholly owned by the Ministry of Economics and Finance. In 2000, the activities of the national monopolist Ferrovie dello Stato (FFSS) were divided between several newly created limited companies (yet not listed and wholly owned by the FFSS). In particular, RFI (Rete Ferroviaria Italiana) owns and manages the railway tracks, while Trenitalia owns and manages all carriages and trains (and has non-exclusive authorization to run the railway service). Within Trenitalia, there has been an unbundling of accounts and management among three divisions, namely "Passengers" (for long-distance passenger trains), "Local transport" (for regional and local passenger services), and "Cargo" (for the transport of merchandise).

As for Germany, Deutsche Bahn AG (DBAG) was formed in 1994, following unification, out of the merger between Bundesbahn and Deutsche Reichsbahn, the Eastern and the Western monopolists. DBAG is owned by the federal government and in turns owns about 36,000 km of track and over 90 per cent of the market share in rail transport. It operates passenger transport (long distance and regional), freight transport, rail track, and railway stations. In 1998, these activities were divided between separate companies, still owned by the DBAG holding. There are plans to float DBAG on the stock market.

One of the EU's conditions regarding railways is that there should be independence between infrastructure and transport divisions. In Germany, there is an independent company that owns the infrastructure DB netz, but this is still owned by DBAG. Private companies that want to run rail services must apply to DB netz.[3] As a result of this, third party participants in the market are appealing for an independent regulator and/or for a transfer of track into federal property.

3.4.3.2. REGULATION AND DEREGULATION

As part of the UK reorganization, two regulatory bodies were also created. The Office of Rail Regulator (ORR) was created principally to regulate

---

[3] Please refer to www.x-rail.net/render.asp?0 = 2801&c = 4, 2 June 2004.

Railtrack. The Office of Passenger Rail Franchising (OPRAF) is mainly responsible for awarding franchises, paying subsidies, and regulating the TOCs. Rail Users' Consultative Committees (RUCCs) were established to work with OPRAF in protecting the interests of rail users. Safety regulation was placed with the Health & Safety Executive.

As for Italy, the main European Directive dictating the guidelines for liberalization, Directive 440/91, was implemented in Italy only in July 1998, with the Decree no. 277/98. Up till then, the regulatory framework was almost non-existent, in that everything revolved around an arm's length relationship between the Ferrovie dello Stato (FFSS) and the Ministry. Prices were determined directly by a governmental body (CIPE). In 1992, the licence given by the state to FFSS had implemented EC Regulations 1191/69, 1107/70, and 1893/91. This licence includes two contracts. The first is the Service Contract, which defines the "public services" the FFSS is obliged to provide to passengers. This excludes "commercial services" such as long-distance passenger services and freights. The Contract also sets prices and public subsidies. The second licence is the Programme Contract, which defines the transfers the state makes to FFSS to cover infrastructure costs and the reciprocal commitments of the state and the FFSS as regards the development of the network and the carriages.

Since 1997, competence over regional and local passengers has been granted to the regions, so that the Service Contract has lost part of its relevance. Economic regulation is still in the hands of a governmental body (CIPE) which determines the prices and conditions for accessing the network. Also, quality control is done by CIPE on the basis of data provided by regulated firms. This implies that there is no distinction between the regulator and the only shareholder of the quasi monopolist, FFSS.

Regarding competition, RFI, which owns the track—despite being a limited company, part of a holding that also owns Trenitalia, the largest player in the competition for the right to use the network—acts as a body with a public mission and has to certify the technical suitability of potential competitors to operate the service. Competition is allowed only for merchandise transport and long-distance international trains; to date there is some competition for goods transport, but very few examples in the passengers' segment. Competition for the right to operate passenger services may start, but it is seriously limited by two factors: (*a*) Trenitalia is the owner of all trains and carriages previously owned by FFSS and (*b*) Law 146/1999 states that potential competitors must prove that they already have the necessary carriages and personnel to run the service when they apply for the right to do so.

Italian price regulation works as follows. Until 1999, the prices of final services were determined by CIPE (a governmental body), taking into account the firm's costs, and were revised without a fixed schedule. Given vertical integration, no distinction was ever made between the price for the use of the network and the price of the train service. In 1999, EC Directives 18/95 and 19/95 on access to the railways network were implemented. Thus, the government instructed CIPE to design the rules for third party access (including the methodology to determine access prices), which were approved in the same year (CIPE decision 180/1999).

In Germany, the DBAG introduced a price system for using rail infrastructure. It is based on prices per train kilometre on the different line sectors. There are ten line types and twelve train categories, resulting in a considerable number of fee combinations, but there are still strong elements of discrimination in favour of DBAG.

3.4.3.3. ECONOMIC OUTCOMES

Productivity

Table 3.5 shows data on UK rail traffic. Passenger kilometres provided have risen and employment has fallen sharply, with an apparent rise in productivity. One has to be careful about these data, however, since employees working for external contractors providing services previously carried out by BR are no longer counted as rail workers.

A similar outcome emerges for the Italian case. In Italy, comparative analyses carried out up until the mid-1990s indicate that Italian railways were characterized by low labour productivity, high labour costs (at purchasing power parity (PPP)), considerable overmanning, low quality of services (measured by the percentage of trains arriving on time). Prices

Table 3.5 UK rail traffic: passengers, employees, and productivity, 1996–2002

	1996	1997	1998	1999	2000	2001	2002
Passenger km	38,748	41,698	43,597	46,287	46,505	47,394	47,974
Relative to 1996	100	107.61	112.51	119.46	120.02	122.31	123.81
Employees	75	43	50	49	49	50	51
Relative to 1996	100	57.33	66.67	65.33	65.33	66.67	68.00
Passenger km/employee	516.64	969.72	871.94	944.63	949.08	947.88	940.67
Relative to 1996	100	187.70	168.77	182.84	183.70	183.47	182.07

Source: Transport Statistics of Great Britain, 2004.

Table 3.6 Italian rail traffic: passengers, employees, and productivity, 1996–2002

	1996	1997	1998	1999	2000	2001	2002
Passenger km (million)	44,782	43,591	41,392	40,971	47,133	46,675	45,956
• long range	25,442	24,642	23,398	22,843	27,537	27,307	25,973
• regional transport	19,340	18,949	17,994	18,129	19,596	19,368	19,983
Passenger km	100.0	97.3	92.4	91.5	105.2	104.2	102.6
Employment (large firms)	100.0	97.7	95.5	92.9	89.8	85.8	81.6
Productivity (passenger km/employees)	100.0	99.7	96.8	98.5	117.2	121.5	125.8

Source: Istat, Annuario Statistico.

were considerably lower than the European average, and the service was made financially viable thanks to large public subsidies. As shown by Table 3.6, productivity in Italian rails has risen in recent years, particularly because of labour shedding.

Cost reductions of about 20 per cent have also been observed in the German rail market.[4]

Prices

From December 1979 to 1999, UK prices rose by 45.7 per cent. Regarding Italian prices, for passenger' fares, in 1999 CIPE decided to introduce a price-cap rule on a basket of Trenitalia fares on medium and long-distance travel. The formula is the typical $RPI - x + k$, where k should take into account qualitative improvements over the period. For the first regulatory period, x was set equal to zero while k was set at 3.5 per cent, conditional on the effect of the targets set by the Ministry of Transport on cost savings and quality standards. In the first two years, the standards were actually met by Trenitalia, and the first two price increases (January 2001 and 2003) were allowed. However, in December 2001, the Ministry of Economics and Finance blocked the price increases for fear of inflation, and prices of medium and long-distance trains have not changed since.[5]

[4] Please refer to www.x-rail.net/render.asp?0 = 2801&c = 4, 02 June 2004.

[5] In the same period, energy prices have also been frozen, but only for three months (automatic adjustments following wholesale price increases now take place only every 6 months). The reasons for this difference are probably two fold. In energy sectors, price changes are directly linked to changes in input prices. Most important, energy firms are partially private and are listed on the stock-market. The importance of privatization appears clear.

Quality of service

Regarding quality in the UK rail industry, the rapid expansion in demand since privatization, without a corresponding increase in network capacity, has caused considerable delays and cancellations after privatization. Public confidence has been further eroded by three major accidents in four years (killing a total of 42 people). Italian quality is hard to obtain, given the absence of an external regulator. However, the speed of trains and their reliability is considered better than it used to be.

3.4.4. Evaluation

Assessing the impact of liberalization is a complex task. First, the post-liberalization period is in most cases very short. Second, countries have liberalized at a very different pace. Third, adequate statistics on the sector are scarce. Nonetheless, it would seem that productivity increased substantially in the post-liberalization period, sometimes as reflecting lower employment and higher output (the UK) and in other cases simply because of a fall in employment (Italy). However, as we have seen, these data must be treated with caution. The evolution of prices is even more difficult to assess. First, train prices were initially unprofitably low (Italy) and will have to be raised in the aftermath of liberalization. Second, continuing high prices were justified by the need to pay for major infrastructural investments (Germany). Third, with the exception of the UK, train prices are still regulated by the executive who also owns the rail companies (Italy). Finally, quality has been controversial, particularly in the UK. The verdict on safety and quality is at worst "not proven". What can be said, however, is that the rapid expansion of demand in the UK was not met by a corresponding increase in network capacity. The lack of a substantive impact on investment, particularly in infrastructure, has by and large been the weak spot of the liberalization process.

Summing up, the review of the three case studies has highlighted the following problem areas:

- A proactive approach to competition is required. As with other network industries, third party access is insufficient to generate effective competition. The incumbent should be asked to divest part of its fixed assets, that is, locomotives and carriages, to be leased by potential competitors willing to enter the market.

- The employment impact of liberalization is largely negative, explaining the widespread resistance to liberalization. More data, however, are needed to assess whether the loss of railway jobs was offset by employment growth in subcontracting firms.

- Last, but not least, the liberalization schemes do not seem to provide adequate incentives for investment, particularly in infrastructure. It is not clear that privatized infrastructure fares better on this score than when publicly owned. However, even if infrastructure stays in public hands, a clear regulatory framework will be required to guide investment decisions. Excessive discretion by public officials, in setting prices or in modifying existing price-setting rules, would increase regulatory risk and discourage investment.

3.5. Professional services

3.5.1. *Structural issues*

"Liberal" professional workers such as lawyers, architects, or notaries operate in a market where there is no concern for natural monopolies, where supply is typically very fragmented, but where regulatory interventions are very common. The traditional justification is that informational asymmetries between professionals and consumers are so strong that competition may be unable to provide consumers with sufficient protection. On top of this, professionals' representatives often argue that competition among professionals may even be harmful for consumers, in that it may undermine any incentive to give a high quality service. In some countries (e.g. Italy), a third argument is put forward, and sometimes accepted by the law, according to which a professional's activity is different from a firm's activity, and has a particular dignity and status to preserve. For these and other reasons, a sector where the fragmentation of supply would suggest that free competition should be the natural way of organizing transactions is instead subject to a multitude of restrictions, sometimes enforced through professional bodies (self-regulation), and often administered directly by some public agency.

Self-regulation seems to be the most common form of intervention for professions across Europe, but the extent and content of regulation may vary substantially from country to country. The general argument in favour of self-regulation is that the verifiability of quality is particularly limited in the service sector and calls for regulation carried out by peers, that is, those who have a concrete possibility of understanding what limitations can be sensibly introduced to a professional's activity and of properly monitoring what their colleagues have done. In this direction, one could conceive that some restrictions on competition may be called for, if one could prove that such restrictions effectively help the production of high quality and ultimately are in the consumers' interest.

However, self-regulation entails the risk of collusion between the regulator and the professionals, in that the (self) regulating authority may choose not to operate in the interest of the community, but in order to maximize the profession's profits. This is reflected in some of the restrictions that were traditionally present in these sectors:

- (minimum) professional fees are determined by the professional association;
- the entry process is managed by the same association as organizes an entry test, which may be more or less restrictive depending on the country and the profession, but which in practice means that the professionals have control over the number of their future competitors;
- advertising is severely restricted, and certainly prohibited in the way it is carried out either in other sectors (industrial goods, but also financial services) or in other countries (e.g. the USA);
- in some countries, the profession could be exercised only by individuals, and not by companies, so that, for instance, engineering firms used to face restrictions on their operations;
- the lack of mutual recognition of university degrees, necessary to exercise a profession, has represented a traditional barrier to entry by foreigners.

3.5.2. *The need for a reform agenda*

Professional services do not fall squarely into the mandate of European institutions. A key issue is whether they are relevant to the creation of a single market or to the development of competition in the whole Union—in which case, the Commission would recover a role in the economic regulation of such activities. By and large, however, professional services are non-tradables, thereby allowing member states to object to any interference by European bodies.

This weakens any intervention by the European Commission, whose attempts to intervene on the subject clash both with the defence of national prerogatives and with the claim that professions should be excluded from general competition principles. Indeed, no Directive has ever been proposed, and only one (less binding) "Communication" has been issued, in February 2004. However, Commissioner Monti in particular has begun several projects on professions, stressing the economic cost of the regulation of professional services and how this may represent a burden in the attempt to improve the Union's competitiveness; restrictive regulation of professional services is alleged to hamper the implementation of the Lisbon Agenda, and this by itself should allow EU institutions to have a say.

In particular, the European Commission has on numerous occasions tried to bring professions back into the area where competition law should at least normally apply, claiming that one should distinguish between the very few restrictions on open competition which may be useful to preserve the incentive to high quality and those—probably the vast majority—which are totally unnecessary to this end.

Despite the Commission's repeated outcries, the obvious fact that competition may be in danger when the regulator has an interest in colluding with the regulated agents, seems to be of no concern at all to many European governments, and particularly so in Germany and Italy, where professional organizations not only have been given responsibility for quality control and the protection of consumers, but are also still in charge of determining professional fees and entry conditions to the market, and impose other limitations on the competition among members of the profession.

The optimal extent of this protection and its compatibility with a reasonable development of competition are at the core of the debate on professional services in the whole European Union, but economic theory does not suggest that in general minimum prices have a positive effect on quality. Several instruments could be used to increase quality.

One could be certification, which simply implies a public declaration that certain training has been carried out by the professional; in this case, everybody would be allowed to enter the business and the consumers, made aware of the "productive process" that remains behind the provision of the service, should be free to choose which level of training they consider adequate for their needs. A further step may be to require a licence, that is, not allowing those who do not have a given background to exert a profession.

In Europe, licensing—which entails public control on entry—has been preferred to simple certification, and the list of pre-requisites to enter a certain profession may vary from country to country, but typically represents a sizeable entry barrier. However, it is hard to see why price controls, which in general do not positively affect incentives—at the margin—to provide quality, should be introduced. Admittedly, economic theory is fairly inconclusive as to the impact of regulations on quality. Yet, it fails to provide any general argument that restrictions on competition boosts quality. More crucially, advocating far-reaching restrictions on competition, including those that "*per se*" clearly harm consumers, on the ground that this "might" help to protect quality is hardly acceptable. There is no evidence whatsoever to support the claim that where price competition and advertising are allowed the quality of professional services has decreased (and that this decrease is not compensated by sufficiently lower prices).

Another common aspect of the regulation of professions is that severe restrictions on advertising by professionals are often introduced. These restrictions on competition are typically considered by these professional organizations as necessary to avoid the risk that "excessive" competition may negatively affect quality and to preserve the "dignity" of the professional's status. The recurring concern for the quality of the service is to some extent understandable, but whether these restrictions to competition are necessary (or even useful) to protect consumers from services of insufficient quality is still to be proven.

Restrictions on advertising also have dubious effects. They can hardly be justified on economic grounds, and in fact they are often defended on the basis of the idea that advertising conflicts with the "dignity" of the professional status. This, however, entails greater difficulties for new entrants to get established, and therefore adds yet another entry barrier. Access to the profession is already full of obstacles (entry tests and sometimes long periods of compulsory—often unpaid—training are typical in these fields). When looking at the differences in these restrictions across professions, their rationale is too often obscure: for instance, why does the Italian system require three years of compulsory training for qualified accountants and not for doctors?

3.5.3. *The outcome of a slow reform*

The recurring calls by the EC for the modernization of the professions are certainly well founded, and relevant given the significance of professional services in firms' costs. Although in many countries we observe a trend towards liberalization, the resistance to the removal of anti-competitive restrictions is still strong.

The current situation is still characterized by many traditional features, but some aspects are changing. The idea that a profession may be exercised not only by an individual, but also by a more entrepreneurial entity (a large law firm, or engineering firm) is more and more accepted even in Italy. In the same way, in many countries officially set professional fees increasingly tend to be considered as merely indicative.

Yet, the pace of liberalization is exceedingly slow. We have little information on prices, but the fact is that restrictions on advertising remain quite widespread, sometimes because of legal requirements, sometimes as a result of self-regulation. While the entry of large multinational organizations in traditional professions (such as engineers or lawyers) is an encouraging development, the removal of a number of entry barriers as regards young professionals is very slow and not univocal; it is quite clear that stronger moves in that direction would help employment in this sector.

Differences in the pace of liberalization among member states are still very relevant, as shown in Table 3.7.

Quite clearly, the UK stands out as a much more open market. It was not always so. A tradition of protection of professions has long been in place in the UK as well. The key regulatory change was to bring the professions within the ambit of UK competition law. Professions were previously excluded from the main provisions of competition law; a price-fixing agreement between the members of the professions was not illegal, for example, unless it was contrary to wider European competition law. All this changed with the Competition Act, 1998, when anti-competitive agreements between enterprises providing professional services were prohibited unless specifically exempted on the grounds of sufficient consumer benefit. However, limits on advertising and marketing by accountants, solicitors, and barristers still exist, and recommended fees still exist for architectural work and legal probate work.

Table 3.7 Indices of regulation of professional services

Professional service	Germany	Italy	UK
Lawyers	6.5	6.4	3.5
Notaries	11.0	10.7	—
Accountants	6.1	5.1	3.0
Architects	4.5	6.2	0.0
Engineers	7.4	6.4	0.0
Pharmacists	5.7	8.4	4.1
Mean	6.9	7.2	2.1

Note: The index increases with the extent of regulation.
Source: IHS Questionnaire 2002 and other sources in Paterson et al. (2003).

The Italian situation is more complex, in that a number of "protected" professions exist, where exercising the profession requires an admission by the professional body. This body also has the right to set professional fees, which in some cases are compulsory, at least for certain work (e.g. for public administration). In other cases, dubbed as "recognized" professions, the licence to exercise the profession is granted by the public administration and not by a professional body; this second category includes professions such as journalists, alpine guides, and ski instructors. It is very unclear why there should be a need to have passed a public exam before exercising such professions; a simple certification seems to be more than sufficient to guarantee the public interest. For most sectors, the German case is extremely similar to the Italian one, as can be seen from Table 3.7.

The case of notaries in Italy is particularly interesting, in that the law specifies the maximum possible number of notaries in each area of the country, considering parameters such as the size of the population, the extent of business, the size of the territory, and making sure that for each position there is a population of at least 8,000 people and that each position is associated (in expectation) with a given minimum income. The number of positions is revised every ten years, and the evolution of the number of positions over time is extremely slow (+7% since 1976).

Where self-regulation is in place, the national professional councils dictate norms of conduct and monitors whether members of the profession act accordingly. These norms, collected in a "deontological code", range from purely ethical recommendations to clear restrictions on competition among members (which seems to imply that most aspects of competition are "unethical"). For these professions, self-regulation has the force of law, in that the power of professional bodies stems from the ordinary law. The actual functioning of professional markets is fortunately more flexible, in that it is more and more accepted that "official" professional fees apply only to certain cases, and that normally fees can be negotiated with each client (within the "cap" of official fees). The notion of market prices is creeping into the professional world, but this is happening very slowly. The size of the lobby affected by these regulations and their proximity to the world of policy-makers seem to be key elements which make it likely that the future will provide no revolution.

3.5.4. Evaluation

The call for further liberalization by the European Commission is certainly warranted. However, national and local resistance is extremely strong.

The claims that current restrictions on competition are justified and necessary to protect consumers appear misleading; in most cases, they simply represent ways to protect professionals from competition.

The crucial question is what needs to be done to liberalize the sector. Price liberalization, namely the elimination of regulated professional fees, would certainly be a step in the right direction. Yet, its impact may be limited given that, increasingly, professional fees are only indicative. Banning restrictions on advertising is also likely to improve matters, even though the impact of such a measure on competition is a priori ambiguous. Where matters would most likely improve is if (only) *informational advertising* (e.g. on professional fees) became legitimate, so that younger professionals could attract more clients. Finally, the elimination of the current strict controls on entry is probably an area where improvements are more likely. Substituting the current system of licences (where entry requires obtaining a public licence) with a system of simple *certification* (where entry is free, but where the public authority certifies that the entrant has certain qualifications) would eliminate an important barrier.

The key measure, however, would be to subject professional services to competition law. This is the main lesson of the UK experience. We have seen how professional services increasingly cater to firms and play a substantive role in determining their international competitiveness. In this context, the traditional argument in favour of continuing restrictions on competition in the professional services sector, namely the need to protect uninformed consumers, is even weaker than it used to be.

3.6. Retailing

3.6.1. *Basic characteristics of the retail industry*

Historically, retailers were regarded as mere ciphers in the distribution channel. Accordingly, their main function was to work as pure intermediaries just to enable the flow of goods and services between suppliers and consumers. Very little value added was contributed. This perception has changed dramatically when it became clearer that retailers were able to become much more active and powerful agents in their own right.

The main business of retailing can be split into two parts (see Oxford Institute of Retail Management, 2004). First, retailers provide locations where final consumers make transactions to acquire goods and services.

Second, retailers facilitate and encourage transactions by providing variable support services, including displays, stocks, cash, and credit facilities. These marketing activities allow retailers to gather information on consumer behaviour that producers typically do not have access to. With the concentration of retail ownership, powerful retail chains have emerged which act as gatekeepers for producers and play a major role in the price formation process. While this has raised anti-competitive concerns (see e.g. OECD, 1999), it has also created efficiencies by allowing for growth of new product categories—including own label products—and the development of new retail outlet formats in new locations.

With the emergence of new retail formats and new technologies (such as Electronic Point of Sale), the retail sector has witnessed considerable changes in most developed countries. Supermarkets and hypermarkets have moved retail activities from downtown areas to out-of-town and edge-of-town retail centres and shopping malls. Giant corporations such as Wal-Mart Stores that operate internationally and rank among the largest companies in the world have entered the scene.

3.6.2. The reform agenda

Europe's retailing sectors have been liberalized in the last decades. While deregulation efforts in the UK can be traced back to the 1980s, liberalization of Germany's and Italy's retail markets began in 1996 and 1998, respectively. We can identify three types of regulations which have traditionally restricted competition in the retail business by protecting small retailing units, both against market entry in general and the establishment of new large forms of retailing. In this regard, liberalization targets opening hours and concession restrictions as well as planning and construction restrictions. Quite surprisingly, another source of restricting retailing has come from competition policy rules and fair trade laws, which condemn several pricing and trading practices as anti-competitive and unfair. In the following, we briefly describe the nature of these restrictions.

Opening hours

Perhaps the most prominent retail regulation has been the restriction of opening hours. Regulations on shopping hours have traditionally been put in place for religious reasons. However, protection of employees by unions also often plays a role. As a result, opening hours have been restricted not only on Sundays and religious holidays but also during the week and on Saturdays. Those laws—also called "Blue Laws"—restrict personal action in order to promote "morality" (see Grünhagen and Mittelstaedt, 2001). For example, in the UK blue laws can be traced back to the Fairs and Market Act of 1448, which was extended in the first half of the twentieth century as a result of political pressure. In Germany, store opening hours were, until June 1996, based on the store-closing law (*Ladenschlussgesetz*) of 1956 that had been originally established to protect employees and to regulate the booming demand in post-war Germany. The law kept stores closed after 6 p.m. on weekdays and restricted even Saturday shopping to no later than 2 p.m. Only once a month (and during the Christmas season) were stores allowed to stay open two hours later on "long Saturdays". Similar restrictions were imposed in Italy.

Planning and construction restrictions

Regulations concerning commercial real estate, zoning, and construction are among the greatest barriers to the development of retail services (OECD, 2000). In most countries, special urban planning regulations apply to retail premises and restrict planning and construction of new retail outlets with respect to choice of location and outlet size. Such regulations potentially lead to rigidities and uncertainties that may hamper modernization of the industry. Often, these regulations are delegated to local authorities. Local lobbies may then influence the decision processes and may make entry more difficult for outsiders.

In Italy, entry into retail markets became regulated with the introduction of a public licence system during the fascist regime in 1926 and a city planning law (Legge urbanistica) which dates back to 1942. In 1971, a new trade law came into force which accommodated new retail formats such as supermarkets. With that law, the licensing policy remained extremely restrictive until 1998, when the liberalization process took off with a general reform of the Italian retail trade sector (see Potz, 2002, for an overview). In the UK, the Town and Country Planning Act of 1947 has been the cornerstone of the planning system of the UK retail sector after the Second World War (see Potz, 2003). In Germany, regional and urban planning laws have been restricting entry into retailing (for a survey, see Bahn, 2002).

Competition and fair trade policy

Competition policy and fair trade regulations may restrict retailers' pricing strategies *vis-à-vis* consumers (as e.g. marginal cost and loss leader pricing below) and retailers' contracting terms with suppliers (as e.g. slotting allowances or rebate schemes). For example, in Germany, the Rebate Law of 1933 restricted sales and discounts. Similar restrictions were effective under the retailing regime created during the fascist period in Italy.

Competition policy can also restrict concentration through merger control and its policy towards buyers' associations. With the emergence of large retail chains and significant concentration of retail markets in some countries, competition authorities have started to watch this sector more closely (see e.g. Dobson Consulting, 1999, or OECD, 1999).[6]

This list of regulations, while highlighting the most important aspect of Europe's liberalization agenda for the retail sector, is, of course, not exhaustive. In particular, waste recovery systems are problematic as they are often organized by industry organizations that may serve anti-competitive purposes or deter the entry of foreign firms by raising rivals' costs.

3.6.3. Implementation of the reform agenda in Germany, Italy, and the UK

As there is no EU-wide approach that governs liberalization in this sector, the overall picture remains mixed and a comparison of national regulatory regimes is a complex task. While many regulations have been relaxed, many remain in force, and some regulations have even become more restrictive. Moreover, the decision process whether or not to impose restrictions is often delegated to local authorities, thereby making any cross-country comparison more complex.[7] Nevertheless, inspection of the three countries' moves towards deregulating the retail sector reveal clear differences with respect to the above-mentioned restrictions traditionally imposed on the retailing sector.

United Kingdom

It is fair to say that the United Kingdom has taken the lead within Europe in terms of both time and scope. The liberalization process started in the UK with the Thatcher government, when planning requirements for out-of-town developments were eased. This induced growth of large-scale retailing which has not been matched by any other country in the EU so far.

Most prominently, the United Kingdom enjoys the most liberal approach towards opening hours, such that there are virtually no

---

[6] For a survey of the economic theories of buyer power and an analysis of its sources, see Inderst and Wey (2003).
[7] See also Boylaud and Nicoletti (2001) for an attempt to construct indices measuring regulatory reforms.

restrictions during weekdays. The Sunday Trading Act, which was enacted on 26 August 1994, forms the legal basis for shopping hours on Sundays, and provides for at most six hours of trading by all retailers. However, as described by Grünhagen and Mittelstaedt (2001), even these restrictions are not fully effective as fines on violations were rather negligible.

Planning and construction restrictions had already been deregulated in the 1980s. After a long period of *laissez-faire* policy regarding planning permission in the United Kingdom, recent policies, however, show a more restrictive pattern, which remains largely unresolved today. The McKinsey Global Institute (MGI, 1998) has reported that, between 1993 and 1996, the UK government voted for a series of planning restrictions establishing that local planning authorities should promote the development of small retail stores in town centres. At the same time, the ruling prescribed restrictions on concessions of planning permissions for extensions of existing stores outside town centres.

Competition policy does not restrict pricing and sales policies much in the UK. However, merger control has become stricter, which is documented by the recent acquisition of Safeway, one of the leading retailers in the UK. In its recommendation to the Office of Fair Trading, the Competition Commission concluded that the proposed acquisition by the three largest retailers, Asda, Sainsbury, and Tesco, of the whole or part of Safeway should be prohibited. Regarding the proposed acquisition by Wm Morrison Supermarkets, which was the smallest among the potential acquirers, the Competition Commission recommended that the takeover be allowed.[8] However, the acquisition was made subject to strong remedies, which required divestment of many grocery stores.

Germany

In Germany, the liberalization process started on 1 November 1996 when the new trading time legislation went into effect, expanding the country's rigid store hours during weekday evening hours and on Saturdays (Bundesministerium für Wirtschaft, 1996). With the new legal regime, stores were allowed to remain open between the hours of 6 a.m. and 8 p.m. on weekdays and until 4 p.m. on Saturdays. Sundays are still a day of rest, but for the first time bakeries were allowed to make and sell

---

[8] The report of the UK Competition Commission, entitled "Safeway plc and Asda Group Limited (owned by Wal-Mart Stores Inc); Wm Morrison Supermarkets plc; J Sainsbury plc; and Tesco plc: A report on the mergers in contemplation" is available on the Internet: http://www.competition-commission.org.uk/rep_pub/reports/.

fresh bread and rolls on Sunday and open as early as 5.30 a.m. every day. Since then, opening hours have been gradually liberalized. In 2003, the lower parliament sanctioned that stores could stay open till 8 p.m. on Saturday. In September 2004, the legislative chamber that represents the German states (*Bundesländer*) unanimously urged the federal parliament to give them authority to set store hours at the states' level. With this initiative, shopping may become a 24/6 (i.e. 24 hours a day and six days a week) business in Germany in the foreseeable future. While these developments show that there is an overall tendency to push the liberalization of opening hours further, Germany remains behind the UK or the USA, where shopping is virtually a 24/7 activity.

Another important step towards deregulation was the annulment of the rebate law (*Rabattgesetz*) in 2001 which restricted discounts and several promotional activities since 1933. In 2004, the biennial sales regulation, which had coordinated retail pricing behaviour since the 1950s, came to a final close. Large-scale retailing, however, still faces pricing restrictions in Germany. Despite the strong position of discounters, large-scale supermarkets are confronted not only with planning and construction restrictions but also with restrictions on promotional activities (like loss leader pricing). An instructive case is Wal-Mart's experience with the German Cartel Office (*Bundeskartellamt*). Wal-Mart entered the German retail market in 1998 by buying the 21-unit Wertkauf chain. In 1999, Wal-Mart started an aggressive "Always Low Prices" programme, which was declared illegal by the Cartel Office. Quite interestingly, the pricing behaviour was forbidden on the grounds that it constituted an abuse of a dominant position (see Arndt and Knorr, 2004). While Wal-Mart's market share is extremely low, its financial resources were taken as proof of market dominance.[9] This case illustrates that competition policy is still protecting small businesses and with this tends to unfold entry-deterring effects, which are somehow evidenced by Wal-Mart's failure to enter German markets with a business model which is extremely successful in more liberalized countries as the USA or the UK.

Regulations concerning construction and planning permission have not so far been affected by Germany's move towards liberalization (the last amendment of the respective law, the *Baunutzungverordnung*, dates back to 1993).

---

[9] More information on the case can be found on the website of the German Cartel Office: http://bundeskartellamt.de.

Italy

Law 114 of 1998 (DLgs. 144/98, Legge Bersani) provided the impulse for a reform of the general rules for this sector. The new approach limits considerably the needed authorizations to start a new business. However, many authorizations are still required for outlets of middle or large size.

The principles on liberalization have not been taken to an extreme so far. In the case of opening hours, shops may not be open for more than 13 hours a day, between 7 a.m. and 10 p.m. Sunday is the usual closing day, and local authorities may decide to have an additional half-day of closing for all retailers. However, exceptions are envisaged for tourist areas and in particular periods of the year.

Moreover, the Legge Bersani leaves considerable autonomy to local authorities, in particular regions and municipalities. This entails that there is no unified national framework dictating all relevant rules for the sector, as many aspects of considerable importance are delegated to a local level. Most regions still envisage quantitative planning regarding the number of large retail compounds in each sub-area of the territory (see Potz, 2002, for an early account of these developments). Overall, the procedure for obtaining a licence is still in a state of flux and not easy to assess at this point. However, although territorial policy is still in the hands of local authorities, which are free to authorize (or deny the authorization for) the opening of large commercial centres, large distribution is developing.

Overall, we may conclude that the UK has taken the lead in deregulating domestic retailing. With respect to planning and construction restrictions, recent developments are less clear, and there appears to be a tendency to impose hurdles on the expansion of out-of-town hypermarket retailing. The fear of "high-street flight" is also present in Italy and Germany, and tends to impede structural change. While Italy used to have the most restrictive procedures for obtaining a concession, it has recently made considerable progress. In Germany, a move towards liberalization of planning and construction restrictions is hardly detectable. However, in terms of opening hour restrictions and fair trading provisions, Germany has implemented significant changes.

3.6.4. *Comparison of performance*

Attention to the retail sector has increased recently as economists have started to search for the sources of productivity growth at industry level (see e.g. MGI, 1991). The retail sector has been identified as a main source

Table 3.8 Concentration ratios (%)

	1993*	1996*	2000**
Germany	45	45	62.4
Italy	11	12	28.8
UK	50	56	63.7

Sources: *Dobson Consulting, 1999; **M + M EUROdata (www.mm-eurodata.de).

of the much better performance of the USA when compared with the EU. van Ark et al. (2003) report that from 1995 to 2000 total factor productivity in retail trade increased in the USA by 6.9 per cent while the EU only experienced an increase of 1.4 per cent. Moreover, the contribution of value added by the retail trade industry to the total economy is significantly larger in the USA with 6.3 per cent when compared to the EU, where the retail trade industry only contributes 4.8 per cent to the total economy in terms of value added. It may well be the case that these differences can be explained by the significant regulations imposed on retail businesses in Europe which are absent in the USA. Neither opening hour regulations nor land regulations impose significant restrictions on retailers' business strategies. Although there have been investigations of buyer power and slotting allowances, antitrust policy has not so far restricted large retail chains' pricing, contracting, and takeover strategies much.[10]

The structural changes are best documented by the changing market structure of the retail sector. Table 3.8 provides the concentration ratio CR5 for the three countries, which measures the market share of the five largest firms within the retail grocery business.

Concentration has increased markedly from 1996 to 2000. As retail regulations have traditionally favoured small-scale retailing, it is not surprising that deregulation has led to more concentrated retail markets.

A higher concentration ratio may reflect a larger role for supermarkets and hypermarkets. As these retail formats are characterized by large outlets, one should expect overall a lower outlet density per inhabitant in more concentrated countries. Dobson Consulting (1999) confirms this conjecture and reports the highest outlet density among the three countries for Italy, with 500 inhabitants per outlet. The UK has the lowest outlet density with 1,667 inhabitants per outlet and Germany lies in between with 1,111 inhabitants per outlet. As a larger inhabitant per outlet ratio should lead to higher turnover per outlet, the abilities of retail

---

[10] See FTC (2001) for an investigation of slotting allowances and Balto (1999) for a study on retail mergers in the USA.

Table 3.9 Hypermarkets in Italy: numbers and employees

	1999	2000	2001	2002
Hypermarkets				
• Number	251	304	349	359
• Employees	40,431	52,178	62,923	63,399

Source: ISTAT (2003).

firms to exploit economies of scale are markedly different. From this perspective, one may expect the largest productive efficiencies to be realized in the UK, with the lowest being found in Italy.

Dobson Consulting (1999) has also collected instructive data on the role of large retail formats; namely, hypermarkets with 2,500 sq. m. and supermarkets with 400–2,499 sq. m. per outlet. In 1996, hypermarkets in the UK accounted for 45 per cent of national aggregate turnover in the food industry, which is a 29 per cent change since 1980. In contrast, in Germany, hypermarkets only achieve a market share of 24 per cent, while Italy reports a share of 13 per cent. More recent data for Italy provided by ISTAT (2003) show, however, that Italy has made significant progress in the last few years. Table 3.9 shows that the number of hypermarkets has increased from 251 in 1999 to 359 in 2002. During that period, the number of employees in that segment has increased by more than 50 per cent.

Of course, a higher concentration ratio and a high share of hypermarkets, which allow for convenient one-stop-shopping by consumers, go hand in hand with the monopolization of retail markets. While the associated buyer power can lead to better input prices, it is not entirely clear whether these gains are passed on to the consumers. Consumer prices may rise if competition is hurt too much. Discounters are an important disciplining force in retail markets. In this regard, Germany is rather unique. The four largest discounters in Europe are all of German origin, namely, Aldi, Lidl, Tengelmann, and Rewe. Dobson Consulting (1999) reports that discounters account for roughly 30 per cent of total food industry turnover in Germany, while their role is much smaller in the UK and Italy, where their markets shares are 11 per cent and 10 per cent, respectively.

This overview of the retail market structures in the three countries can be summarized as follows. The UK has the most concentrated retail industry where hypermarkets play a major role, while Italy has the most fragmented market where both hypermarkets and discounters have yet to gain significant importance. In Germany, the picture is somewhat

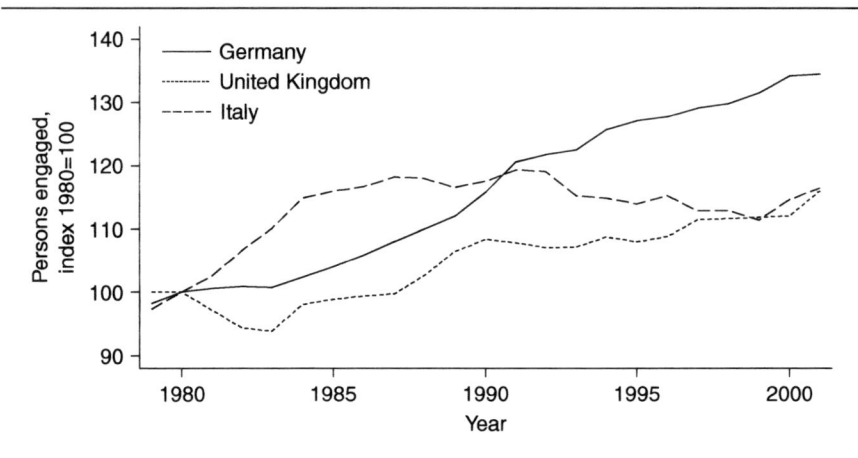

Fig. 3.6 Persons engaged in retail, index 1980 = 100
Source: O'Mahaony and van Ark (2003).

mixed. Concentration has almost reached the UK level, but hypermarkets are only of minor importance, while discounters are a major part of the German retail industry. Overall, there is a trade-off between the exploitation of productive efficiencies associated with large-outlet retailing and intense competition. The UK seems to lead in terms of the former but may suffer from less competition at the outlet level.[11] Competitive forces appear to be highest in Germany, with its large share of discounters and balanced oligopolistic supply structure. In Italy, a fragmented market structure prevails which has not experienced dramatic changes so far.

Using the data provided in O'Mahony and van Ark (2003), we now describe the evolution of employment and labor productivity in the three countries.[12] The number of people employed in the retail industry has increased in all three countries over the last decades. From 1979 to 2001, the number of people employed increased in Germany from 2.5 to 3.5 million, from 2.8 to 3.4 million in the UK, and from 2.0 to 2.4 in Italy. These trends are depicted in Figure 3.6, where we set 1980 as the base year. The evolution though is quite different in these countries. Notably, Germany has experienced a steady increase in employment, while for the others employment growth has been much slower.

O'Mahony and van Ark (2003) also provide data for the value added contributed by the retail industry. This allows us to calculate labour

---

[11] Interestingly, *Fortune* consistently ranks British retail companies, such as, for example, Asda as the most profitable major food retailers in the world.
[12] The data is available online at http://www.eco.rug.nl/medewerk/Ark/ark.htm.

Contrasting Europe's Decline

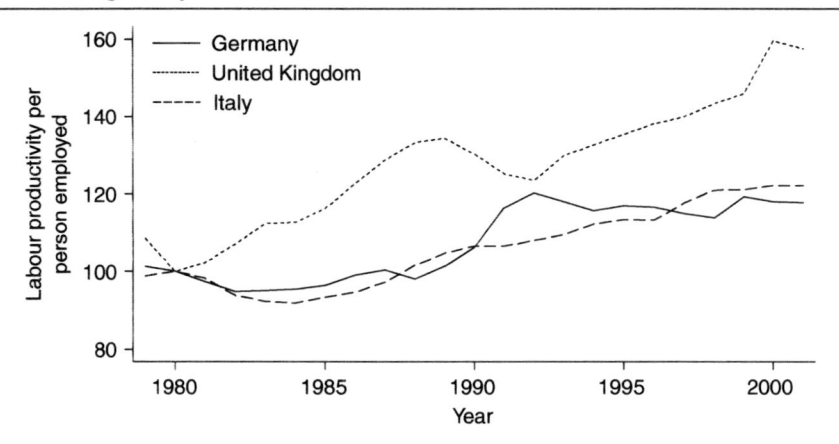

Fig. 3.7 Labour productivity per person employed, index 1980 = 100
Source: O'Mahony and van Ark (2003); own calculations.

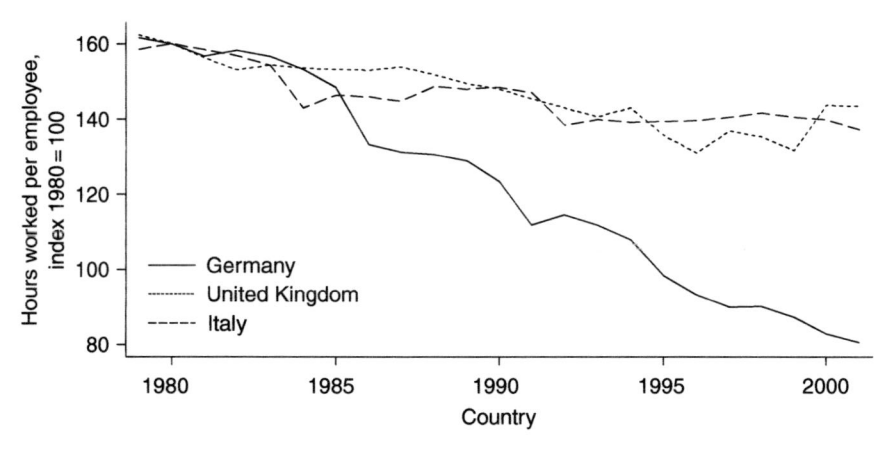

Fig. 3.8 Hours worked per employee, index 1980 = 100
Source: O'Mahony and van Ark (2003); own calculations.

productivity. Figure 3.7 shows that labour productivity per person has increased in all three countries over the last 20 years. However, the patterns are markedly different. While Italy and Germany exhibit similar patterns of labour productivity growth, the UK experienced a tremendous growth period from the early 1990s onward, resulting in a large productivity gap between the UK and the other two countries.

However, for a meaningful productivity comparison, allowance must be made for the fact that Germany experienced a substantial reduction in the number of hours worked per employee (see Fig. 3.8). This may be explained by collective bargaining agreements concerning the reduction

The Maze of Services Regulation

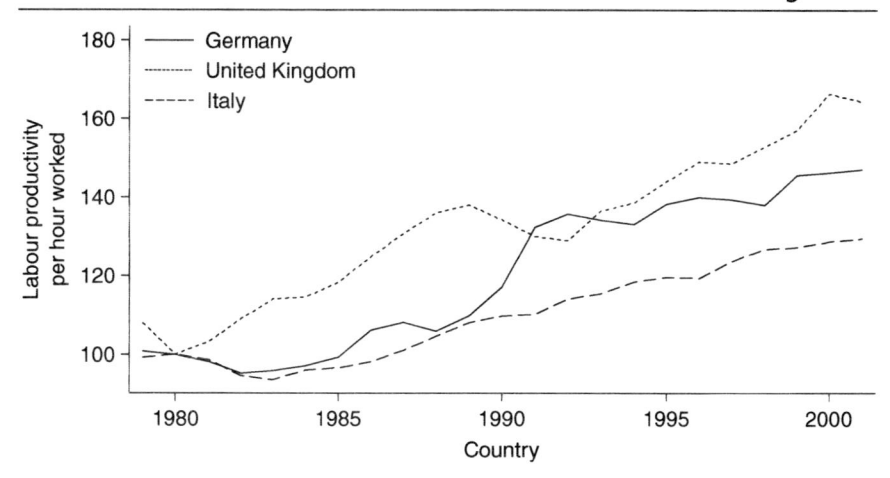

Fig. 3.9 Labour productivity per hour worked, index 1980 = 100
Source: O'Mahony and van Ark (2003); own calculations.

of working hours and the increase in the number of part-time workers. From 1996, the deregulation of shop closing hours may have further contributed to the increase of part-time workers such that the overall number of hours worked per employee decreased.

Figure 3.9 examines labour productivity per hour worked and therefore controls for changes in working time per employee. Taking this factor into account, we see that Germany's labour productivity increased more substantially, particularly in the 1990s, a fact which was absent in Figure 3.7. Still, the fact remains that the UK has achieved the highest productivity growth over the last decades, followed by Germany, with Italy lagging.

Overall, one can argue that the UK presents the most liberalized model, while Germany's and Italy's retailing structures appear to be more regulated. Moreover, labour markets are generally more rigid in Germany and Italy compared to the UK, lending further support to the view that the UK has created the most liberalized retailing environment among the three countries. These differences may be responsible for the rankings of productivity growth in the three countries, with the UK experiencing the highest growth followed by Germany and Italy, in that order. However, the liberalization process has just started in Germany and Italy, and it remains to be seen how the markets evolve when compared with the UK, where deregulation began with the Thatcher government.

3.7. Postal services

3.7.1. *Postal service systems before liberalization*

Mail service has traditionally been a governmental activity. National postal service systems were first developed by monarchs in France and in the UK. For instance, the post delivery system in the UK goes back to 1516 when Henry VIII appointed Sir Brian Tuke as his Master of the Posts, to ensure the King's mail was carried safely. At that time, the mail services were almost exclusively for the King and the use of the post service by the public was not encouraged. In 1660, the British postal monopoly law was enacted upon the restoration of Charles II, which lasted until the last decade when the liberalization process we are exploring in this section began.

In the mid-nineteenth century, universal national post systems were introduced all over Europe. The UK was a leader in this regard. In 1840, key reforms were introduced by Rowland Hill in England that lowered postage rates to affordable levels and introduced uniform national postage rates. With these reforms, the "Penny Post" of prepaid postage was set up.[13] Within the next 15 years, roadside post boxes and residential postal slots were opened and in 1870 the first postcards were introduced as a cheap alternative to letters. In 1883, parcel post and in 1919 the first regular international airmail service had been opened between London and Paris. Postal service delivery became a mass market phenomenon.

Until the 1980s, postal services were typically administered by governmental departments or as a national industry together with national telecoms. This changed, for example, in 1981 in the UK when the two services were split.[14] Until then, competition played no role in Europe's postal industries. Even though the quality of national postal services varied across states and was often administered by loss-making and possibly overstaffed and inefficient monopolies, most business experts regarded the integrated mail service network as a natural monopoly which had to be controlled by governmental action. In the 1980s, however, this assessment changed, when high-end competitors and cross-border competition entered the scene, and was later reinforced by better transportation and communications technologies. So-called "air couriers" had

---

[13] With the Penny Post, the first postage stamp, the Penny Black, was also created.
[14] In 1990, Royal Mail Parcels became Royal Mail Parcelforce, an independent division of Royal Mail and in 1992 Royal Mail was again restructured.

started to expand their businesses to a considerable scale in the 1970s. They provided extra fast and reliable transmission of business documents.

Moreover, both couriers and some post offices began to offer "remail" services on a scale that threatened the foundations of the international postal system and was a precipitating event of the European liberalization reforms. It is, therefore, instructive to examine the case of remail more closely (see Campbell, 2002, and Stumpf, 1997). Remail refers to the practice of posting mail in a country other than the country where the sender resides. For instance, a company with an office in country A might prepare a large mailing at home and transport the mail in bulk by private express to country B for posting to addressees in that country or another country (including country A). Using telecommunication technologies, the sender might even send the data to the foreign country and have its mail produced there. Misalignment between international and domestic postage rates as the main reason for the evolution of remail. As early as 1924, the Universal Postal Convention had agreed on a provision to discourage mailers from remailing mail into the original sender's country (so-called ABA-mail). In the 1970s and 1980s, the Universal Postal Convention repeatedly authorized interception and surcharging of remail. However, the breakthrough for letter remail occurred in 1986 when the US Postal Service modified its postal monopoly regulations and explicitly permitted export of US-origin letters for remailing abroad. As has been described by Campbell (2002), this led European post offices to compete for large quantities of international remail from the USA. In several initiatives and agreements, European post operators tried to discourage competition for international remail, which led to a formal complaint by the International Express Carriers Conference to the European Commission about the anti-competitive activities of European post offices. The subsequent legal struggle strongly influenced the 1992 Postal Green Paper (COM(91) 476 final; adopted 11 June 1992). That paper found that national post offices tended to impede progress to a single market, and that the quality and performance of postal services in the EU member states, which were typically administered by possibly inefficient monopolies, were rather mixed. The Postal Green Paper initiated the liberalization process of the postal service markets in the EU.

Overall, the national post office has been among the oldest governmental services. The integrated national network of mail service was long regarded as a natural monopoly, so that duplication of national postal service networks, and hence, competition appeared not to be desirable. As a consequence, competitive played no role in national postal industries.

As competition increased, pressures for regulatory changes towards less interventionist regulation began to develop. While market forces were predominantly confined to international mail transmission, they also triggered the internal liberalization of domestic postal service markets in the EU.

3.7.2. The reform agenda

The road map to liberalization of the postal service market is prescribed by the Directive on Postal Services (Directive 97/67/EC), which was adopted in December 1997, and the amendment Directive 2002/39, which was adopted in June 2002 by the Council and the Parliament.[15] The amendment is also part of the "Lisbon strategy" of the European Council for transforming the EU into the most competitive and dynamic knowledge-based economy.

The EU Directives have the potential to present the biggest overall shift in the national postal service regulations of the EU member states since the monarchies granted monopoly rights in the seventh century and the introduction of the universal national post systems in the mid-nineteenth century, which set up the basic regulatory structure that prevailed until the end of the twentieth century. At the most general level, the Directives' intention is a gradual and controlled market opening and further limiting of the service sector that can be protected from competition. At the same time, the new regulatory framework aims at increasing the quality of universal service. In line with the subsidiarity principle, the Postal Directive left EU member states considerable discretion in terms of liberalizing their national postal systems. The reforms agenda requires member states

- to build national regulatory authorities,
- to develop universal service policies,
- to determine reservable areas for the incumbent operator, and
- to implement an authorization procedure for new post operators.

National Regulatory Authority

The Directive requires member states to set up a National Regulatory Authority (NRA) for the postal sector that is independent of the incumbent

---

[15] Directive 2002/39/EC of the European Parliament and of the Council of June 2002 amending Directive 97/67/EC with regard to the further opening to competition of Community postal services (OJ L176, 5.7.2002, p. 21).

postal operator. The NRA should ensure compliance with the obligations arising from the Directive.

Universal service policy

The universal service policy consists of quality provisions and tariff principles governing the pricing of universal services and access prices to dominant operators. Quality standards for universal services seek to harmonize and improve the quality of universal postal service of the incumbent operator and market entrants. Precisely, Article 3 of the Postal Directive states: "All Member States shall ensure that users enjoy the right to a universal service involving the permanent provision of a postal service of specific quality at all points in their territory at affordable prices for all users".

The Directive defines minimum criteria for (i) the scope of universal service, (ii) delivery requirements, (iii) access conditions, (iv) quality of service, and (v) complaints and redress procedures. The universal service provision shall cover national and cross-border postal service of domestic postal items weighing up to 10 kilograms (but not more than 20 kilograms) and delivery of incoming cross-border postal packages weighing up to 20 kilograms. Moreover, the Directive states delivery requirements, access requirements for the public, and quality of service provisions.

Assessing tariff policies for universal services is a complicated and still pretty much unsettled issue. In general, the Directive states that the provision of universal service prices must be "affordable", "geared to costs", and "transparent and non-discriminatory". Although access prices for private mailers can be bargained over freely, they too have to adhere to these principles. Mandatory access to the incumbent's delivery network is derived from the observation that mail delivery exhibits substantial economies of scale (Rogerson and Takis, 1993, and Panzar, 2002).

Maximum reservable area

An important feature of the Postal Directive is the segmentation of the postal service market into a reservable area and a competitive area. The reserved area grants a statutory monopoly to the universal service provider. The reserved area applies only to letters and addressed direct mail. The remaining postal markets for newspaper delivery, unaddressed direct mail, parcels, and express mail are not reservable in EU member states, so that competition should prevail in these segments.

The underlying rationale for the reservable area is to ensure a smooth transition process towards a fully competitive postal market. This would allow the restructuring of the incumbent universal service provider so as to improve its quality and to become more competitive *vis-à-vis* foreign competitors. As has been forcefully argued by Hellwig and Paulus (2002), this kind of monopoly licence creates the risk of interrupting the entire liberalization process. Governments may be tempted to engage in industry policies such as national champion building. Moreover, reserved areas may very well impose negative externalities on competitors in the non-reserved area by depriving them of the benefits of larger-scale operations.

The maximum reservable area is defined in terms of letter weight and a multiplier applied to the basic public tariff. The higher the letter weight and the higher the value of the multiplier, the larger is the exclusive monopoly granted to the universal service provider. Currently, the reserved area is set at letters of 100 grams and for which the transportation charge is less than three times the public tariff. Prior to 2003, the weight and price limits were 350 grams and five times the basic tariff, respectively. By 2008, these limits should be reduced to 50 grams and 2.5 times the basic tariff.

Authorization policy

A critical part of the Postal Directive is the authorization provision for postal services, which applies to both public and private operators. Clearly, competitors cannot apply for authorization for the reserved area. The Directive prescribes two types of authorization for the non-reserved area: individual licences and general authorization. As has been detected in Wik-Consult (2004), there is a great deal of confusion among the NRAs about the scope of authorization and the general authorization process. As a rule, individual licences are typically required for all universal services. The much less demanding general authorization is usually granted for all remaining postal services.

The Directive also sets transparency and accounting standards for the universal service provider and a complaints procedure. Finally, it is worth mentioning that universal service providers are typically exempted from value-added taxes, while competitors are not.[16]

Overall, this short summary of the reform agenda shows that the liberalization strategy taken in the EU appears to be quite modest. The reservable area is an outright protection of the incumbent's monopoly position. The authorization process imposes further restrictions on the

---

[16] This issue is not mentioned in the Directives.

emergence of a competitive market structure. Finally, universal service provisions and tariff policies can potentially impose a deterrent effect on competitors. While these considerations lead one to expect not too much from the liberalization of postal services in Germany, Italy, and the UK, we will also see in the next section that within those limits different degrees of liberalization have been pursued with potentially measurable effects on the country's performance in postal services.

3.7.3. Implementation of the reform agenda in Germany, Italy, and the UK

In all three countries, postal reform started in 1997, when new postal laws came into force. Quite interestingly, in principle, those laws provide for the full liberalization of postal markets. However, none of the three countries opened postal markets completely to private suppliers, as the laws also provided for a transitional period where the incumbent could retain its monopoly power in large parts of the national postal markets.

Since the 1997 Postal Directive and its amendment became valid on 1 January 2003, national postal laws evolved, however.[17] Germany and the UK changed their laws in 2002 while Italy followed one year later in 2003.

National Regulatory Authority

Comparison of the NRAs and the implementation procedures of the Directives chosen by the three countries reveal some interesting differences. Among the large member states, only the UK has established a dedicated and truly independent postal regulator, Postcomm. In contrast, in Italy, the independent postal regulator is closely tied to the ministry in charge of postal affairs. The independence from the ministry of the public postal operator is, therefore, likely to be unclear. In Germany, postal regulation has been moved to the telecommunication regulator (Regulierungsbehörde für Telekommunikation und Post; abbreviated as RegTP), which is not necessarily committed to devoting sufficient resources to proper supervision of the postal sector.

The resources devoted to the NRAs differ in the three countries. Wik-Consult (2004, table 4.7.1, p. 87) reports that the budget of Postcomm in the UK was 1,208,000 euro while the Italian NRA's budget in the same year was only about 847,000 euro.[18] In terms of professional staff (i.e. lawyers,

---

[17] The following sections draw heavily on the latest report by Wik-Consult (2004), commissioned by the European Commission.
[18] Germany did not report that number in the Wik-Consult report.

economists, or other persons with advanced degrees of expertise), Germany announced that all its 25 employees were professionals, while Italy announced that only six out of 20 employees belonged to that category.

The procedures for implementing the Postal Directive also reveal some striking differences between the three countries. The UK delegated most of the policy decisions required by the Directive (such as the scope of the reserved area, the authorization procedures for non-reserved sectors, or the quality of service) and all of the administrative decisions to the NRA.[19] Only issues related to the quality of the universal service, such as frequency, maximum weight of parcels, and so on, which are required to meet the needs of consumers, remain with the parliament. In sharp contrast, in Italy, the entire implementation process is undertaken by the ministry of postal services. In Germany, the policy decisions are left to the parliament, while the NRA decides on administrative issues.

These observations suggest that in the UK relatively more independence with regard to political pressures and the incumbent operator's interests has been achieved than in Germany or Italy. As described in detail by Hellwig and Paulus (2002), the independence of the regulatory authority appears to be of particular importance in the postal service sector. Referring to the extension of the expiration date of the statutory monopoly to the end of 2007 in Germany, they note that this served the union's interests, the government's interests, and the Deutsche Post AG's management interests.[20] The union feared lay-offs at the technologically lagging Deutsche Post AG and the government enjoyed the prospect of increased revenues from the privatization of its public company. Finally, the Deutsche Post AG's management should have been happy to secure their monopoly profits. In order to counter political pressure that tries to delay or even stop the liberalization process, independence of the NRA is likely to lead to outcomes more in line with the original goals of the reform agenda laid down in EU Directives.

Universal service policy

In Germany, Italy, and the UK, the universal service providers are public limited companies. While all countries provide universal service requirements for domestic postal letters weighing up to 10 kilograms, the Postcomm in the UK has recently adopted a universal service definition based

---

[19] See Wik-Consult (2004: 30 ff.) for more information on the implementation procedures in EU member states.

[20] The Deutsche Post AG is the universal service provider in Germany.

on an assessment of the needs of postal users. This has led Postcomm to exempt most of the bulk mail service and parcels from the universal provision.

Universal service prices are subject to *ex ante* regulation in all three countries. Wik-Consult (2004: 72–3) has detected an interesting difference between the UK and the German downstream access price policy of Postcomm and the RegTP, respectively. Both laws require the universal service provider to provide access to competitors. However, the German postal law does not allow for downstream access within the reserved area. Moreover, Postcomm sets access prices based on the costs of providing the service, while the RegTP has adopted the avoided costs methodology which includes overhead contributions and hence leads to a much higher access prices.

Reserved areas

The reserved area defines the extent to which the postal market remains completely monopolized. While Italy and Germany have limited their reserved areas to the boundaries for the maximum reservable area set by the Directive, the UK has taken the most market-oriented approach in this regard. The 2002 UK postal law no longer provides for a reserved area. In contrast, in Italy and Germany, domestic and incoming cross-border mail is reserved for the universal service provider. Moreover, in Germany, direct mail, which is essentially printed matter mail, remains a statutory monopoly for the incumbent operator. While this segment is not part of the reserved area in Italy, outgoing cross-border mail remains a reserved area.

Based on these considerations, it may very well be the case that entrants in the UK face the most attractive regulatory environment. They have the opportunity to obtain licences for bulk mail, direct mail, and outgoing mail. As the UK has tried to commit credibly to the termination of the reserved area entirely by 2007, entrants may enter with the prospect of stepping into the remaining letter segment in the near future.

As the scope of monopoly protection is larger in Germany and Italy when compared with the UK, it is likely that the adverse effects a protected monopoly licence should have on competition are also more pronounced in those countries. The monopoly licence prevents competitors from realizing the economies of scale associated with postal service delivery. The monopoly prices obtained in the reserved area can be used for cross-subsidization purposes. Another consequence of these concerns is that the reserved area also impacts negatively on competitors in the unreserved areas.

Authorization policy

The authorization policy determines the conditions under which new firms can enter into the universal service markets and the postal markets outside the universal service area. In terms of the number of authorizations for competitors inside the universal service area, in effect, at the end of the year 2003, Germany is performing much better than the UK and Italy. In Germany 1,020 licences were in effect, while the UK and Italy reported 18 and 331, respectively (see Wik-Consult, 2004: 58). This indicator, however, hardly reflects the presence of barriers to entry. For example, bulk mail has been exempted from universal service provisions in the UK. Accordingly, this segment can be entered in the UK without a licence. Turning to authorizations for competitors in the domain outside the universal service area, we find a similar picture. As Germany and the UK do not require any authorizations in that area, they also reported no issued licences, while Italy reported 1,356 authorizations in effect in 2003 (see Wik-Consult, 2004: 64).

Overall, comparison of the liberalization reforms shows that the countries have implemented the reforms required by the Directives at a relatively low level (the exception being the UK). Differences in liberalization strategies have become more visible with the implementation of the amended Directive into national postal laws in 2002–3, with a more pro-competitive approach being followed in the UK.

3.7.4. *Comparison of performance*

A comparison of letter items per inhabitants between the USA and the three EU countries, Germany, Italy, and the UK, reveals large growth potential in the EU. While in the USA 706 letter items per inhabitant and year are delivered, the UK figure stands at 325, followed by Germany with 250, with Italy lagging behind at 115. Abstracting from many particularities of the US postal market—as, for example, the fact that many cheques are sent by post—we may nevertheless infer from these significant differences that there is unexploited growth potential in the three EU countries.

There are basically two criteria to assess the relative performance of the reforms undertaken: the evolution of the market structure in the liberalized segments of postal service markets which accounts for the bulk of incumbent operators' revenues and the overall performance of the universal service provider.

The WIK-Consult (2004) study reports extremely high market shares of the incumbents in liberalized universal service segments all over Europe (see also Postal Services Commission, 2005, and RegTP, 2003). In Germany, the incumbent operator's market share was about 96 per cent (RegTP, 2004) by the end of 2003 and in the UK, Royal Mail's market share in the licensed letter market reached 99.7 per cent in 2003. Contrasting this with the fact that 32 per cent of the licensed letter post market in Germany was open to competition by the end of 2003 and some 30 per cent in the UK, one is left with the conjecture that severe barriers to entry remain in force.

One obvious entry barrier follows from the fact that the reserved area is significantly larger than the licensed part in terms of total revenues. The share of liberalized post volumes as a function of the weight threshold has been estimated by Wik-Consult (2004: 98). They calculate that a reserved area for letters weighing less than 100 grams would on average open 18 per cent of the overall letter market to competition. A reduction of the reserved area to letters weighing less than 50 grams (which is envisioned by 2008) would open not more than 25 per cent of the letter post market to competition. Consequently, sales volumes of the incumbent operator remain much larger than rivals' market shares for the foreseeable future. This allows the incumbent operator to realize economies of scale while competitors find it hard to cover the fixed costs associated with setting up a delivery network. Hellwig and Paulus (2002) also point to one-stop-shopping advantages which reinforce the incumbent operator's dominance.

With the transformation of universal service providers from governmental departments or quasi state enterprises into ordinary corporations, many have expanded their business activities considerably. The German universal service provider—the Deutsche Post AG—has engaged in a number of takeovers at home and abroad, and is now quoted on the stock exchange. This appears to be particularly problematic, as the German state holds 62.6 per cent of shares directly or indirectly according to the Deutsche Post AG's annual report (see Wik-Consult, 2004: 102). There is also a trend towards brand proliferation that deepens the degree of vertical integration of the universal service providers, which, again, raises concerns regarding foreclosure activities of less integrated competitors.

In terms of prices for 20 gram letters, the UK has the lowest tariff with 50 eurocents, followed by Germany with 55 eurocents, and Italy with 62 eurocents (Wik-Consult, 2004). A similar pattern is obtained for other letter categories. With these prices, the Deutsche Post AG achieved most of its profits from the mail segment according to its own annual reports, although most of its fixed and common costs were attributed to the letter segment. Profitability in the licensed area is typically much lower, also in light of falling prices. It is, therefore, not surprising that private operators make almost no profits while the incumbent operator expands its business into adjacent markets, which they can cross-subsidize by their letter post margins (see also Hellwig and Paulus, 2002: 197).

While it is generally not easy to make productivity comparisons because of data limitations, Wik-Consult (2004: 159) reports the highest labor productivity index increase from 2000 to 2002 for Germany, with Italy and Britain following in that order. Investigation of the sources of these developments, however, reveals that the UK achieved its productivity growth by increases in mail volumes, with employment only mildly increasing. In contrast, Germany and Italy faced decreasing letter volumes and avoided declining productivity only by substantial employment reductions. The UK development, therefore, appears to be more favourable than Germany's and Italy's developments.

Overall, we can conclude that the liberalization process of postal services has only just started and that no dramatic changes have occurred so far. Competitors have entered licensed areas but remain small when compared with incumbent operators. In all three countries, the reserved area of letter services remains too large to induce substantial competition in letter markets. Recently, the UK has followed a more forceful liberalization route than Germany and Italy. While this may pay off in the future, it remains to future research to explore the consequences of different and more ambitious liberalization strategies.

3.8. Water

3.8.1. *Pre-privatization structure*

Water is one the last public sectors to be brought under the realm of reform and further enhancement for consumers. In the UK, water was nationalized in 1973, having previously been owned by municipal authorities. Prices were determined by national price setting. In Italy, the water service has always been considered a local service, and only since 1990 (Law 142/90) may the service be provided by limited companies. It is reckoned that in 1996 about 8,100 independent subjects were managing at least one part of the water service in the country; 42.5 per cent of the population were provided for by local public firms, 49.5 per cent by municipalities, and 8 per cent by private firms (Comitato per la vigilanza sulle risorse idriche, 2000). Prices were determined locally, with little national coordination or compelling national guidelines.

In Germany, the Act on the Regulation of Matters relating to Water came about in 1957 and was most recently amended in 2001. The German system of water and sewerage consists of thousands of fragmented utilities. There are about 6,500 water suppliers and 8,000 wastewater treatment companies.[21] Municipalities are largely responsible for these utilities, along with medium-sized enterprises. In 1996, more than 80 per cent of the German population received their water supply from publicly owned enterprises and 1.6 per cent of total water service is provided by private companies. In contrast to French, English, and Welsh policy, German water policy is in public hands.

3.8.2. The EU reform agenda

The main goals of the EU regarding water policy are protection and improvement of the water environment and contribution to sustainable, balanced, and equitable water use.[22]

3.8.3. Reform in the three countries

3.8.3.1. PRIVATIZATION AND STRUCTURAL CHANGE

In the UK, the ten Water and Sewerage Companies (WASCs) were privatized in 1989 as natural monopolies. Each company has a licence to operate a monopoly in either water or sewerage or water supply only within their licensed area. It was envisaged that product market competition might develop but this did not happen. The regulator has therefore concentrated on introducing yardstick regulation of water companies in the absence of competitive pressure. In addition, there were 29 privately owned water companies which existed before 1989.

After privatization, the number of companies has fallen from 39 to 23 due to mergers. OFWAT helped introduce competition for some users via inset appointments for large users and greenfield sites (the threshold was reduced in 2000 to 100 megalitres per year). This has reduced tariffs for large users. Most smaller customers, who are the majority of customers, do not have a choice of supplier and water companies are a monopoly. Thus, there are price controls for licensed water and sewerage services.

In Italy, the restructuring of the water industry started in January 1994 with Law 36/94. The 1994 law starts from the following principles: (i) the

---

[21] Stefan Gramel, Results of a Case Study on the Water Supply in the region Frankfurt/Germany.
[22] EEB: A Review of Water Services in the EU under Liberalisation and Privatisation Pressures, www.eeb.org/activities/water/special-report-water-services.pdf, June 1 2004, p. 5.

water service should be considered as an integrated service, including water treatment and disposal; (ii) the integrated service should be provided on the basis of larger areas, to be defined locally according to hydrologic and administrative criteria (optimal territorial areas, ATO); (iii) within these ATO, the service will be coordinated and investment will be centrally determined by a plan; (iv) the tariff should be regulated and should be such as to guarantee coverage of all costs, and in particular investment should be encouraged; and (v) the creation of a national body to supervise the service (not an actual Authority). The 1994 law envisages four different important stages of change: (i) forming the ATO; (ii) investigating the current situation and investment needs; (iii) approving the investment plan; and (iv) awarding the licence for the management of the plan and of the service.

In June 2003, the situation regarding the implementation of the law is as shown in Table 3.10.
This has led to a substantial rationalization of the providers of different water services operating in the country, with the water service now (or shortly to be) organized by 91 bodies (although within each ATO there could be more than one provider of the water service and—for few years—more than one price for the service).

Turning to structural issues, in Italy, while prior to the 1994 reform the provision of the service was extremely fragmented, one of the key elements of the reform is the notion of an integrated water service and the provision that in all areas coordination among different phases should be encouraged and promoted. Planning is concentrated in each ATO, and refers to all phases of the service. However, the law does not explicitly envisage that the whole service should be provided by the same entity. Therefore, in each ATO—at least in principle—different firms might run different phases of the service; however, as already stated, the drive towards a total horizontal and vertical integration of the service within

Table 3.10 Implementation of Law 46/94: situation at June 2003

	ATO envisaged	ATO formed	Investigations completed	Plans approved	Management licences awarded
Italy	91	84	66	40	25
North	44	38	22	6	7
Centre	19	19	16	13	13
South	28	27	28	21	5

Source: Bardelli and Muraro (2003).

each ATO is quite substantial. Thus competition is "for" the market, with the key to efficiency being vertical integration.

German privatization has been slow. In 1999, the part privatization of the Berliner Wasserbetriebe took place, 50.1 per cent of the shares remaining in the possession of the Land Berlin, 49.9 per cent was held by a consortium consisting of the French corporation Vivendi, the multi-utility company RWE, and the Allianz insurance company.[23] Competition is likely to rise with an increasing number of suppliers and with an increased likelihood of consumers changing to another supplier. The municipalities who essentially control water services can decide up to what degree private participation can be allowed. A number of public–private partnerships have therefore arisen. Between 1971 and 1990, around 14 per cent of Germany's water was delivered by public–private companies and by 1998, this share rose to 22 per cent.[24]

3.8.3.2. REGULATION AND DEREGULATION

UK regulation is done by RPI − x using yardstick regulation to help estimate x. OFWAT uses such analysis whereby less efficient firms are required to reduce prices (and hence costs) by more than more efficient firms. To this end, the MMC has been reluctant to allow water mergers, reporting that the value of the loss of one water company by merger with another would have a present value of £50–250 m.

Italian prices are likewise now regulated, and this regulation will be enforced in each ATO once the ATO is actually operating as envisaged by the law. This regulation is based on a national formula (the "normalized method"), which is a complex mixture of cost-of-service and price-cap elements. Its primary explicit goal is the coverage of all costs, so that subsidies are ruled out. The price-cap element proceeds by each ATO determining a reference price, to which the prices in different parts of the area will have to converge. This reference price is a standard cost plus an allowance for different regional costs, with the standard costs determined by country averages.

Turning to Germany, wastewater disposal costs are passed on to the consumer and may or may not include a profit. Price mechanisms for water supply systems are not under the municipalities, being instead

---

[23] Bundesministerium für Wirtschaft und Technologie, Optionen, Chancen, und Rahmenbedingungen einer Marktöffnung für eine nachhaltige Wasserversorgung. Endbericht, July 2001, p.15.
[24] Stefan Gramel, Results of a Case Study on the Water Supply in the region Frankfurt/Germany.

under the antitrust agency. Water supply utilities must demonstrate that their prices are not higher than those of comparable companies and suppliers. There are no uniform rules or formulas to be administered, cases are considered on an individual basis.

3.8.3.3. ECONOMIC OUTCOMES
Productivity

UK evidence suggests the cost efficiency of water companies has improved significantly since privatization under the pressure of yardstick regulation and takeover pressure. The NAO report the following. OFWAT have made extensive use of yardstick competition and made efficiency savings since 1990 as follows: base operating expenditures (costs of delivering a fixed service), 3–37 per cent for individual companies, quality enhancement, up to 30 per cent, and capital maintenance expenditure up to 15 per cent.

Prices

UK prices have actually risen since privatization (until April 2000), but this was to fund the very large investment programme. In the 1999/2000 review, OFWAT cut average prices by 13 per cent in 2000/1, with price caps expected to cut prices by £25 in real terms between 2000 and 2004/5. Between 1995 and 2000, however, companies did pass on rebates to consumers owing to efficiency savings being passed on by regulatory action.

Italian water prices are seen as extremely low by international standards, as Table 3.11 shows.

Also in the light of this, water firms have substantially increased prices throughout the decade. The Istat national price index for drinking water indicates that between 1990 and 2003 these prices have more than doubled. This has happened, however, without clear coordination among the providers of the water service and without a clear national directive. In the near future, water prices are expected to increase by about 50 per cent over the next 15 years.

Quality of service

The UK government has given the water regulator a role on quality. At first, the regulators were limited to publishing quality statistics, but the Competition and Service (Utilities) Act of 1992 gave customers the right to compensation for specific instances of bad service, or the failure to reply to correspondence. Following huge investment, there has been an improvement in quality; reductions in the number of properties

Table 3.11 Average prices for water services in some cities, in Euro, 2001

	No. of clients	Average price per m^3
Amsterdam	1,258,756	1.81
Antwerp	557,052	1.85
Athens	3,860,000	0.91
Barcelona	2,693,000	1.45
Berlin	3,450,000	5.10
Brisbane	879,000	1.53
Bristol	1,100,000	0.88
Brussels	995,184	1.94
Budapest	1,974,341	0.52
Copenhagen	499,840	4.20
East-West Midlands (UK)	7,446,000	2.46
Gelsenkirchen	2,479,000	2.16
Hamburg	1,992,000	4.31
Helsinki	556,900	2.36
Los Angeles	3,833,400	1.51
Maastricht	1,142,000	1.67
Marseille	1,254,751	2.65
New York City	9,000,000	1.40
Oslo	535,000	1.20
Perth	1,376,000	1.26
Stockholm	1,135,000	1.96
Sydney	4,029,000	1.63
Tokyo	11,676,650	1.76
Zurich	783,700	3.83
Average	2,687,774	1.98
Rome	3,000,000	0.70
Turin	1,367,813	0.74

Source: Peruzzi (2003).

subject to unplanned supply interruptions, a fall in properties at risk of low pressure from 1.8 per cent in 1990/1 to 0.11 per cent in 2000/1, and a fall in properties subject to sewer flooding (0.05 per cent in 1992/3 to 0.03 per cent in 2000/1).

Italy is lagging behind, in particular as regards purification, where in 2002 the EC issued a fine for late implementation of Directive 91/271/CEE, implemented in 1999. Aqueducts serve about 96 per cent of the population, sewage serves about 84 per cent of the population, while the coverage ratio for purification is on average 73 per cent, but falls to 60 per cent in certain areas of the country. Distribution pipelines and sewage are about 30 years old, while sewage networks are more recent (16 years). Some very substantial losses in drinking water are documented. Although it is hard to distinguish actual physical losses from unaccounted sales, on average 42 per cent of water flowing through pipelines is not "officially" delivered and accounted for, with peaks close to 60 per cent in whole regions.

Finally, German standards for water are being steadily adapted to the European Committee for Standardization (CEN) and are converging upon EU standards.

3.8.4. Evaluation

Assessing the impact of the reform process is a difficult task. First, the post-liberalization period is very short, with the exception of the UK. Second, countries' efforts to liberalize differ markedly. Rationalization rather than liberalization seems to have been the driving motive of reform in Italy and Germany. Third, adequate statistics on the sector are relatively scarce. None the less, it would seem that productivity increased substantially in the post-liberalization period. The evolution of prices is even more difficult to assess. First, water prices were initially unsustainably low (Italy) and will have to be raised on both economic and environmental grounds. Second, price increases were justified by the need to pay for major infrastructural investments (UK). Third, there is no indication that quality has been deteriorating following reform. A more worrying note comes from the behaviour of investment, which has collapsed in Italy and was sustained in the UK only thanks to high prices.

Summing up, the review of the three case studies highlights the following problem areas:

- First, competition, when it was introduced, was mostly competition for the market rather than in the market. Attempts to foster competition in the UK did not succeed.
- Second, the impact on prices has not been favourable either because prices were initially too low and needed to be raised or because high prices were used to pay for a large infrastructural investment programme. Whether there are better ways to fund such programmes is an open issue.
- Third, there is no indication that restructuring and liberalization have had a negative impact on quality.

4
The Changing Role of the Tertiary Sector

The tertiary sector is increasingly playing a larger role, particularly in advanced countries. Its GDP share has increased from 62 per cent in 1970 to around 74 per cent in 2000 in the USA and from 52.2 per cent to 70 per cent in the EU-15 during the same period. Hence, reform in services, as described in the previous section, is bound to have a substantial impact on the overall economy. In this section, we document the growing linkages of the service sector with the rest of the economy and how liberalization has contributed to increasing such linkages. In the next section, we pull the threads together and assess the impact of service liberalization on downstream sectors.

Typically, the trend towards the tertiary sector's greater GDP weight is supposed to reflect the shifting pattern of consumers' demand, away from goods and towards services. This is only part of the story, however. The growth in the tertiary sector is also a function of its increasing role as a supplier of inputs. The sector is therefore likely to be a key determinant of competitiveness, however defined. This is even more so given that, as we shall see later in this section, the sector has been highly regulated—and still is, despite the best efforts of the European Commission—and, even more crucially, is much less exposed to international competition. The combination of uncompetitive domestic regulations and protection against imports is bound to strengthen the monopoly power of service firms and weaken the competitive position of those domestic firms that rely more intensively on service inputs.

In what follows, we rely mainly on input–output analysis to uncover the links between the tertiary sector and the rest of the economy. We define the tertiary sector in a fairly broad manner by excluding only manufacturing, mining, agriculture, and construction. Defined this way, the tertiary sector includes a number of "industrial" activities such as energy production and distribution. Our choice is motivated by the desire to consider those activities that are highly regulated—and energy still is—and relatively less open to international competition.

We begin by asking three main questions. First, is it true that the service sector, as previously defined, is less open to trade? Second, is it relatively more regulated and more protected against competitive pressures? Third, how large is its role as a supplier of inputs?

Concerning the first question, the answer is unquestionably positive. While services are increasingly tradable, they remain substantially less open than manufacturing. We look at import penetration coefficients defined as the ratio of imports to domestic gross output. We also consider a broader measure of trade openness, defined as the sum of exports and imports over gross output. We focus on our three country samples, Germany, Italy, and the UK. For manufacturing in Germany, the average value of import penetration is 31 per cent, that of trade openness 63 per cent. The contrast with services is sharp. Import penetration ratios stand at 2 per cent, total trade openness at 5.4 per cent. Turning to the UK, which is substantially more open than Germany, the contrast between manufacturing and services is none the less equally sharp. For manufacturing, import penetration stands at 43 per cent, total trade openness at 77 per cent; for services, the figures are 3.8 and 10.9 per cent respectively. At the other side of the openness spectrum we find Italy. Once again, however, we find that both import penetration and openness ratios are substantially larger in manufacturing. We conclude that services are much less open to international competition (Table 4.1).

Turning to the second question, the available evidence indicates that while manufacturing has increasingly been exposed to the forces of competition, such a trend is much less pronounced for services. Indeed, in the past, the main source of protection for manufacturing were impediments to international trade. However, the Uruguay Round of trade

Table 4.1 Openness in manufacturing and services

	Germany		Italy		UK	
	Import penetration	Trade openness	Import penetration	Trade openness	Import penetration	Trade openness
Manufacturing	0.3082	0.6337	0.2303	0.4224	0.4332	0.7715
services	0.0221	0.0543	0.0227	0.0592	0.0383	0.1090

Source: OECD Input–Output Tables: Germany 1995, Italy 1992, and United Kingdom 1998.

The Changing Role of the Tertiary Sector

negotiations has led to a major dismantling of non-tariff barriers to trade and a further reduction in customs duties. Merchandise trade is therefore increasingly unrestricted and manufacturing firms must compete globally. Manufacturing protection has therefore declined and so has its cross-country variance. For services, the picture is much less reassuring. First, the General Agreement on Trade in Services (GATS)—that is, the attempt to open services to international trade—has had a difficult life since its inception. Moreover, the drive towards domestic de-regulation of services has been quite uneven, with some countries decisively forging ahead towards a more liberal regulatory regime with others instead lagging behind (Nicoletti and Scarpetta, 2003; OECD, 2004). The cross-country variance in services regulation has, if anything, increased.

The third question concerns the role of the service sector as a supplier of inputs to manufacturing. We look at both direct and total input coefficients. The former measure the direct weight of a given service in the cost structure of manufacturing. The latter allow also for the fact that such a service was also an input to other sectors that supply inputs to manufacturing. The total coefficients are clearly preferable as they more fully capture general equilibrium effects.

The first and most remarkable finding is that services as a whole are indeed key suppliers of inputs to other sectors of the economy. Excluding mining and petroleum products, their share in the value of final sales are between 37 and 56 per cent in the UK, between 35 and 51 per cent in Germany, and between 32 and 46 per cent in Italy. These are extremely large values. Moreover, they have been growing over time (Table 4.2). While much caution is needed in comparing input-output matrices at different points of time, we see from Table 4.2 that for all three countries the average, either weighted or unweighted, share of services in the total value of final sales has been steadily increasing.

Figures 4.1 and 4.2 focus on the latest available input–output matrices and show the sectoral weights of the service sectors for our three sample

Table 4.2 The total share of services in the value of "manufacturing" final output

	Germany			UK			Italy	
	1986	1990	1995	1984	1990	1998	1985	1992
Unweighted average	0.3024	0.3089	0.3408	0.2376	0.3865	0.4501	0.2905	0.3633
Weighted average 1	0.3528	0.3590	0.4102	0.2585	0.4072	0.4454	0.3091	0.3761

Note: 1 With sectoral value-added weights.
Source: OECD Input–Output Tables.

Contrasting Europe's Decline

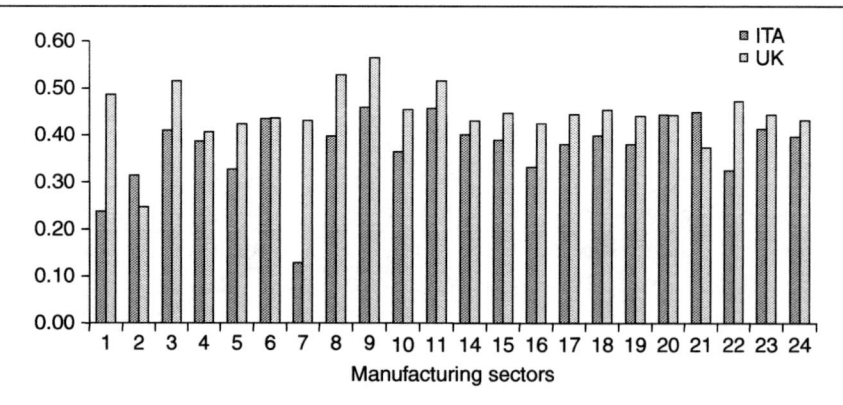

Fig. 4.1 The share of services in the value of final output: Italy versus the UK
Source: OECD Input–Output Tables: Italy 1992 and UK 1998.

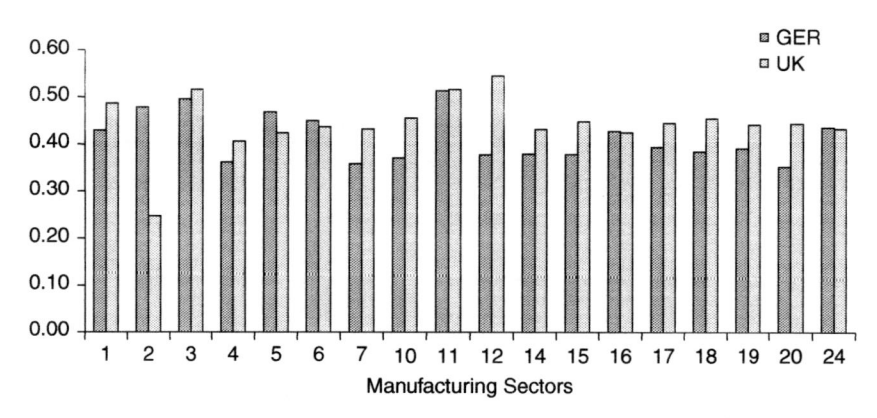

Fig. 4.2 The total share of services in the value of final output: Germany versus the UK
Source: OECD Input–Output Tables: Germany 1995 and UK 1998.

countries. Visual inspection seems to suggest that, by and large, services account for a larger share of manufacturing output in the UK compared to either Italy or Germany. Less casual tests confirm this impression. A pairwise sectoral comparison (Fig. 4.1) between Italy and the UK indicates that the weight of services is significantly larger (i.e. the gap is greater than 5%) in the UK for 18 sectors out of 24. The hypothesis that on average UK manufacturing sectors make a larger use of services inputs is also confirmed by a simple one-sided test of equality of means. The hypothesis of equal means is strongly rejected at 99.9 per cent significance levels. Similar findings apply to Germany, where the hypothesis of equal means is rejected at a 99.5 per cent level.

We should also note that the importance of the tertiary sector as factor of production to other industries is often underestimated because only direct effects are generally taken into account. The difference between direct and indirect effects is large, as documented by Figures 4.3 to 4.5. The total weight of services in the value of manufacturing sales is substantially larger than its direct weight. Hence, a large share of services inputs bought by manufacturers is embedded in other inputs and will not be immediately visible to buyers.

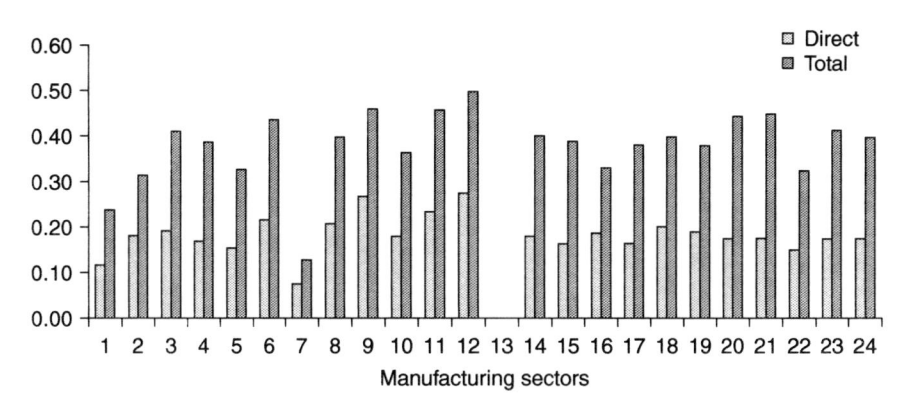

Fig. 4.3 Italy: total indirect share of services in the value of manufacturing total output
Source: OECD Input–Output Tables: Italy 1992.

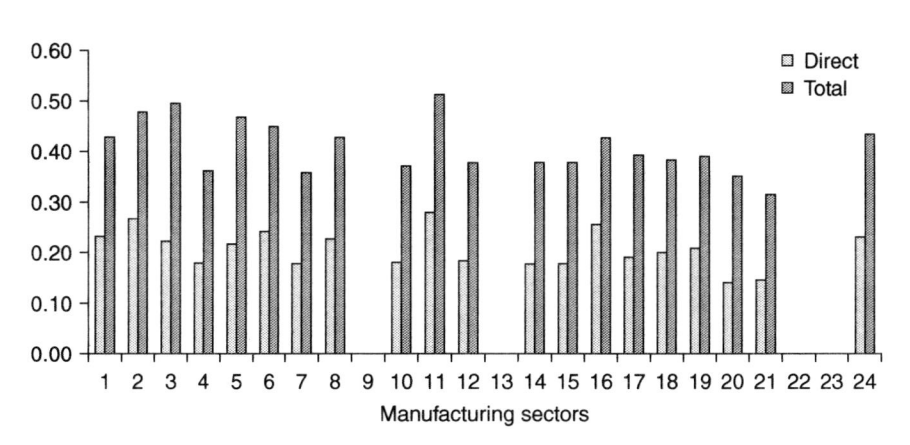

Fig. 4.4 Germany: total indirect share of services in the value of manufacturing total output
Source: OECD Input–Output Tables: Germany 1995.

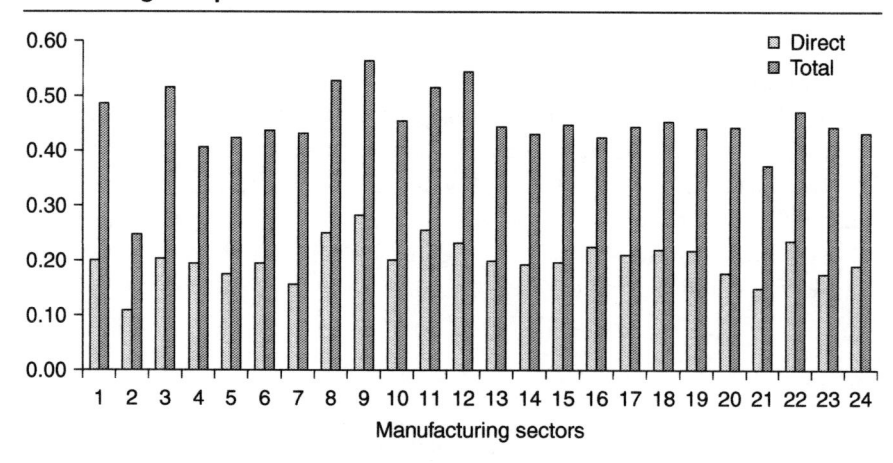

Fig. 4.5 United Kingdom: total indirect share of services in the value of manufacturing total output

Source: OECD Input–Output Tables: United Kingdom 1998.

Table 4.3 The total share of selected services in the value of "manufacturing" final output

Services	Germany	UK	Italy
Network services	0.0797	0.1167	0.1089
Financial services	0.0866	0.0910	0.0915
Wholesale and retail trade	0.0697	0.0667	0.0735
Other business activities	0.1057	0.1055	0.0679
Total	0.3417	0.3799	0.3418

Note: Weighted average of total input–output coefficients, with sectoral value-added weights.
Sources: OECD Input–Output Tables: Germany 1995, Italy 1992, and UK 1998.

We can probe somewhat deeper into the contribution of services by disaggregating them. We distinguish four sectors: network industries, trade, finance, and other business services. We find that the contribution of each subsector is broadly balanced (Table 4.3).

The weight of services therefore does not simply reflect the growing role of finance. Interestingly enough, business services—professional and other services—account for a substantial share (around 10 per cent on average) of gross sales in all three countries. Accordingly, weak competition in this sector is likely to have a substantial impact on the competitiveness of manufacturing. Again, there are major differences among countries. For instance, business activities account on average for a much larger share of final output in the UK than in Italy (Fig. 4.6). Similarly,

The Changing Role of the Tertiary Sector

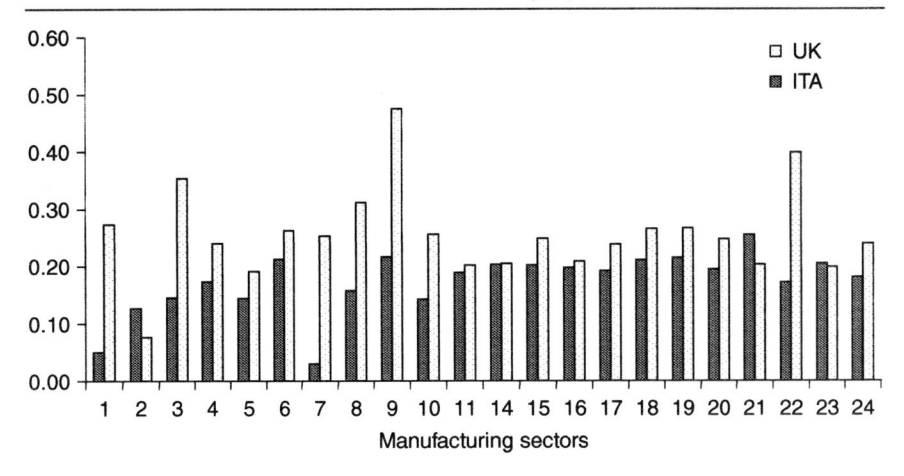

Fig. 4.6 The share of business activities in the value of final output: Italy versus the UK
Source: OECD Input–Output Tables: Italy 1992 and UK 1998.

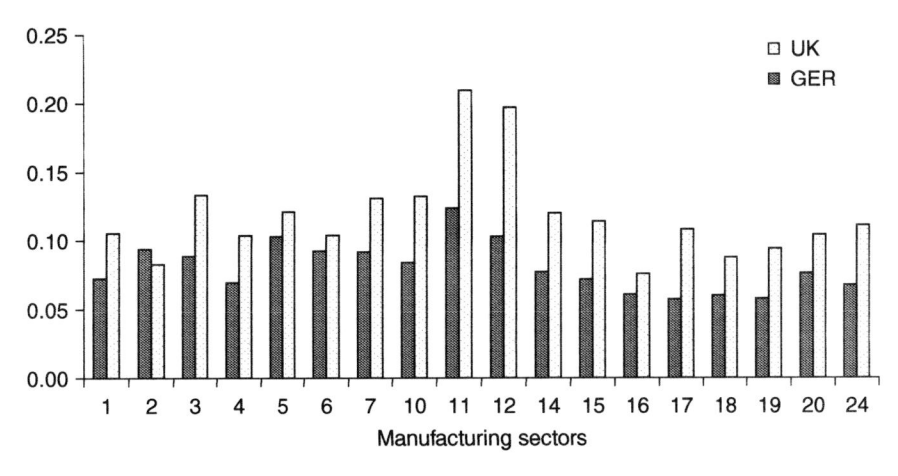

Fig. 4.7 The weight of network services in final output: Germany versus the UK
Source: OECD Input–Output Tables: Germany 1995 and UK 1998.

network industries play a much more significant role in the UK compared to Germany (Fig. 4.7).

One final word of caution is in order. The evidence so far only documents the substantial role of service inputs. It does not allow any inference as to the costs at which those services are provided. Suppose, for instance, that uncompetitive regulations lead to higher service prices. Recall that input–output matrices are generally computed at current prices. Hence, the impact of a change in prices on the input–output coefficients cannot be signed unambiguously but will depend on the price elasticity of the demand for such input. What can be safely said, however, is that services play a crucial role as a supplier of inputs for other sectors in the economy. The costs and the quality of service inputs are bound therefore to be a key determinant of the performance of the whole economy.

5
The Impact of Services Regulation

5.1. Productivity in manufacturing

In this chapter, we illustrate how regulation in services affected the performance of other sectors in the economy through input–output linkages.

We have seen how final consumers have generally benefited from the process of deregulation and liberalization in the service sectors. In the aftermath of liberalization, quality and productivity in the service industries appear to have improved for our sample countries. Similarly, prices have often declined, albeit by a very limited amount. In what follows, we assess whether intermediate users of services have also gained from liberalization. As shown in Chapter 3, services account for a large and growing share of total output for other sectors in the economy. Better quality and lower costs of key inputs should help boost the performance of intermediate users. Accordingly, we check whether gains in competitiveness and efficiency in services have trickled down to intermediate users.

Our analysis compares the performance of 24 non-service (mostly manufacturing) industries in Germany, Italy, and the UK. For lack of a better term, we shall refer to these sectors as manufacturing, even though they also include mining and agriculture. Labour productivity (real value added per employee) is our first performance indicator. We take labour productivity rather than total factor productivity as our measure of performance since it is most easily computed and is less amenable to measurement errors. Differences between labour and total factor productivity are a function of the changes in the capital intensity of production, which in our regression will be mostly picked up by sectoral dummies.

The impact of regulation on sectoral manufacturing performance is a function of both the intensity of service regulation and the intensity of service usage. The latter, however, is itself a function of prices, and hence of regulatory conditions. Given that input–output matrices are generally computed at current prices, the impact of a change in prices on the input–output coefficient cannot be signed unambiguously but will depend on the price elasticity of the demand for such input. To cope, at least partly, with the endogeneity of service usage, we rely on the average value of such indicators across our sample countries.

We focus on the impact of the regulation of two key services: network industries (transport, telecommunications, and energy) and business-related activities (mostly professional services). Either sector accounts for a substantial share of the value of manufacturing output. We do not include in our analysis financial services, as they raise a set of altogether different issues, or the trade sector, on the ground that wholesale trade—a major supplier of inputs to manufacturing—has been fully liberalized and at any rate cannot be distinguished from retail trade in input-output tables.

Despite the best efforts of the OECD, data on regulation are still sparse. The main exceptions are network industries for which fairly reliable and broadly comparable cross-country data on the regulatory framework exist for a relatively long period. We seek to measure how each manufacturing sector (k) is affected by existing regulations in the markets for its inputs from network industries (j). As noticed earlier, this will depend both on the extent of regulation in sector j and the weight of sector j as an input to k. Accordingly, to measure the exposure of manufacturing industry k in country c to regulation in network services, we define the following indicator:

$$R^{NET}{}_{kc} = \sum_j^n \frac{(R_{jc} \bar{d}_{jk})}{\sum_j \bar{d}_{jk}} \quad (5.1)$$

where, R_{jc} is the OECD index of restrictive regulations for individual network services j (e.g. telecommunications) in country c and $\bar{d}_{jk}$ is the country average of the direct and indirect contribution of service j to manufacturing industry k. $R^{NET}{}_{kc}$ is therefore a weighted average of the individual network services regulations, with the weight equal to the (relative) input coefficient of such services in the manufacturing sector k.

As for business activities, we follow two alternative strategies. Our earlier discussion indicates that regulation of professional services varies considerably across countries and that, by and large, the UK is the least regulated country. Therefore, we proxy differences in regulation by country dummies. Our measure of exposure to regulation of business services in country c is simply:

$$R^{BA1}{}_{kc} = D_c \sum_i^a \bar{d}_{bik} \qquad (5.2)$$

where D_c is a country dummy equal to one when the country is c and zero otherwise and $\bar{d}_{bik}$ is the average across the three sample countries of the direct and indirect contribution of business service i (e.g. accountants) to manufacturing industry k. Accordingly, except for the country dummies, R^{BA1} is country invariant. Alternatively, we rely on the recently developed indicators of the restrictiveness of business services regulations developed by Paterson et al. (2003). We then define a new indicator (R^{BA2}) along the lines of eqn. (5.1). Notice that R^{BA2} varies both across sectors and among countries.

We investigate the link between manufacturing performance and regulation in services by relating the average growth in labour productivity in 24 manufacturing sectors to a set of country dummies, sectoral dummies, and at least one of our indicators of regulation in services inputs, $R^{NET}{}_{kc}$ and $R^{BAi}{}_{kc}$. We also test and impose the restrictions that $R^{NET}{}_{kc}$ and $R^{BA2}{}_{kc}$ have the same coefficient. Finally, we allow for a lagged adjustment of labour productivity growth. Our base equation is:

$$\Delta glp_{kc} = \alpha_0 glp_{kc} + \alpha_1 R^J{}_{kc} + \alpha_2 D_c + \alpha_3 D_k + \varepsilon_{kc} \qquad (5.3)$$

The change in labour productivity growth (Δglp_{kc}) is measured as the difference between average productivity growth in 1997–9 and 1994–7. D_c and D_k are country and sectoral dummies respectively.

Econometric estimates are reported in Table 5.1. Country dummies were never jointly significant and have been excluded from all the reported equations. In column 1 we present the results with $R^J = R^{BA2}$ in column 2, with the country dummies properly defined to capture the impact of business services regulations (see eqn. 5.2); in column 3 with $R^J = R^{NET}$; and, in column 4, after imposing the restriction that the coefficient of $R^{NET}{}_{kc}$ is equal to the coefficient of $R^{BA2}{}_{kc}$.

Our results suggest that a market-friendly regulatory environment has a definite impact on productivity growth. The impact of our regulatory indicator, however defined, is consistently negative and statistically significant.

Our dynamics are too simple and our sample too short to say much about the adjustment path. What can be said, however, is that our estimates capture a number of stylized facts. We know that the UK is by far the least regulated country. However, at the beginning of the period, productivity growth in most manufacturing sectors was lower there than in either Germany or Italy. In the following few years, the UK productivity gap fell markedly (reversing sign in several cases), a fact that our estimates attribute to a favourable regulatory environment rather than more trivially to a simple country effect. In the end, therefore, it was a better regulatory framework that allowed UK firms to more fully capture new technological opportunities or, more modestly, to escape the fate of declining productivity growth that has characterized many industries in Germany and in Italy.

By and large, these results are only illustrative as they rely on a small sample and fairly imperfect indicators of regulation. They suggest none the less that the regulatory framework may have a role in boosting the productivity performance of UK manufacturing and bringing it into line with, and often above, that of Germany and Italy. Our results also indicate that a better regulatory environment in any given sector may trickle down to other downstream sectors in the economy. These

Table 5.1 Change in the rate of growth of labour productivity (OLS estimation)

	(1)	(2)	(3)	(4)
Glp	−0.3390	−0.3572	−0.3418	−0.3390
	(0.2395)	(0.2369)	(0.2268)	(0.2295)
R^{BA1}_{ITA}		−0.5968 *		
		(0.1787)		
R^{BA1}_{GER}		−0.3513 **		
		(0.1958)		
R^{BA1}_{UK}				
R^{BA2}	−0.1904 *			
	(0.0624)			
R^{NET}			−0.0957 *	
			(0.0345)	
$R^{NET+BA2}$				−0.0665 *
				(0.0224)
Constant	0.0517 **	0.0322	0.0394	0.0454 **
	(0.0255)	(0.0215)	(0.0265)	(0.0255)
Observations	56	56	56	56
R–squared	0.6548	0.6927	0.6564	0.6581

Notes:
Single asterisk (*) stands for significance at 5% level.
Double asterisk (**) stands for significance at 10% level.
Robust standard errors in brackets.

input–output linkages are seldom considered (see, however, Allegra *et al.*, 2004, and Nicoletti and Scarpetta, 2003, for two noticeable exceptions). Aggregate productivity analyses exclude them by definition, while sectoral or firm-level analysis typically focus exclusively on variables that are related to the sector of interest.

5.2. Inward FDI

One important channel through which regulation in services may negatively affect the efficiency of manufacturing is by discouraging the inflows of foreign direct investment (FDI). We assess, in this section, how regulation in services affects FDI inflows in manufacturing in the three sample countries.

Why is it important to look at FDI? FDI has important effects on productivity and growth, the main reason being that FDI contributed to gross capital formation, often in a way that is at least partly additional to domestic investments. Moreover, the activities of multinational enterprises (MNEs) in a host country are generally more efficient than those of national firms. Consequently, average productivity would be higher the higher the inflows of FDI, even if they were to fully crowd out domestic investments (see Barba Navaretti *et al.*, 2004, ch. 7, for a review).

The evidence on this point is overwhelming and not controversial. Several studies have compared the performance of national firms and multinationals in the UK (Griffith, 1999; Griffith and Simpson, 2001; Conyon *et al.*, 2002; Girma *et al.*, 2001; Görg and Strobl, 2002; Criscuolo and Martin, 2003; Harris, 2002; Harris and Robinson, 2002), Italy (Benfratello and Sembenelli, 2002), and the USA (Howenstine and Zeile, 1994; Doms and Jensen, 1998). They all find that MNEs have higher productivity, whether measured as labour productivity or total factor productivity. For example, Griffith and Simpson (2001) find for the UK that labour productivity is higher in MNEs than in national firms by 42 to 77 per cent. When they use total factor productivity (thereby allowing for the greater use of other inputs by foreign firms) the MNE premium is still around 5 per cent.

This gap in productivity is partly explained by the fact that MNEs are inherently different from national firms: they are larger, they invest more, they are more capital intensive, they spend more on R&D, they have more skilled personnel. When all these factors are controlled for, the gap in productivity becomes much smaller, although it rarely disappears. However, from the point of view of the host country, this is irrelevant. What matters is that MNEs are more productive, if not more efficient, than national firms. Why this is the case (because they are large or because their headquarters are in a foreign country) is not important. Namely, MNEs are unique bundles of inputs and activities which are not provided by domestic firms.

MNEs also have effects on the efficiency of national firms in the host country. First, they raise competition in the host market. The consequences here are double-edged. National firms either become more efficient or they go bust. Second, MNEs, by enlarging the size of overall economic activities in a given country, generate pecuniary externalities (e.g. cheaper supply of inputs). Third, their activities may give rise to technological spillovers, especially when they use better technologies; they train local employees; they work with local suppliers and customers. The evidence on this point is controversial, in that it is not always possible to identify positive effects on national firms. Görg and Greenaway (2001) survey all the available econometric studies on this issue. They find that results depend heavily on the methodology used. However, the effects are either positive or not significant and there is virtually no evidence supporting the view that MNEs have negative effects on the efficiency of national firms. Moreover, recent studies on the UK, based on large panels of data, find that MNEs have large and positive effects on national firms (Haskel *et al.*, 2002 and Griffith *et al.*, 2003).

Consequently, regulation of services by hindering FDI flows may negatively affect productivity. Now, why should we expect regulation of services to hinder FDI? Other things equal, multinationals (MNEs) decide where to locate their plants by taking into account costs of production in alternative locations. As non-tradable services, like energy or lawyers, account for a large share of these costs, their price, their efficiency, and their quality are important factors affecting a country's attractiveness to FDI. This effect is important, independently of the basic underlying motives for a firm investing in a given country. Whether MNEs are looking for promising markets (these are conventionally dubbed as horizontal FDI) or cheap factors of production (vertical FDI), they have anyway to rely partly on products and especially services which cannot be imported. We have shown earlier (Table 4.1) that import penetration in services is very limited in the three sample countries.

Consistently with this prediction, we find that FDI plays a much larger role in the UK, where services are least regulated, than in Germany and in Italy. The average share of inward FDI in gross capital formation between 1997 and 2002 was 28.2 per cent in the UK, 15.5 per cent in Germany, and 4.2 per cent in Italy (UNCTAD, 2003).

The Impact of Services Regulation

Although individual countries compete fiercely to attract FDI, policy-makers rarely consider that the lack of liberalization of services can have detrimental effects on FDI flows. UNCTAD compiles a ranking of countries as *potential* attractors of inward FDI. It then compares it to a *real* ranking based on the amount of FDI inflows that actually took place. Regulation of services is not used to compile the *potential* index. Therefore it can be tentatively considered as one of the determinants of the gap between effective and potential rankings. Italy's effective position is 108th, but its potential rank is 26th. These indices, while highly imperfect, suggest that the gains in FDI inflows for countries like Italy could be very large, if hindering factors like regulation of services were to be lifted.

Up to this point we have looked at the link between regulation and FDI in fairly general terms. If our conjecture that a misguided regulatory framework discourages FDI holds true, then such an effect should be particularly pronounced in those sectors that are heavy users of services inputs. To capture both the weight of services input and the degree of regulatory intervention, we rely again on our set of indicators, R^{NET}_{kc}, R^{BA1}_{kc}, and R^{BA2}_{kc}. We also need to compute a measure of the relative size of FDI in a given manufacturing industry. Data on FDI flows are not available at a sufficient level of disaggregation. Therefore, we rely on data on the activities of MNEs, and specifically employment data, which are compiled by the OECD (OECD, 2004). Our measure is $mner_{jc}$, the share of employment in foreign affiliates of multinationals in country c and sector j.

We can now investigate the link between manufacturing performance and regulation in services by relating our measure of FDI to a set of country dummies, sectoral dummies, and our indicators of regulation in service inputs, R^{NET}_{kc}, R^{BA1}_{kc}, and R^{BA2}_{kc}. Specifically, we estimate the following regressions:

$$mner_{kc} = \alpha_0 + \alpha_1 R^J_{kc} + \alpha_2 D_c + \alpha_3 D_k + \varepsilon_{kc} \qquad (5.4)$$

Econometric results are reported in Table 5.2.

The main finding is that regulation, however measured, has a negative impact on FDI. As for productivity, country dummies are not jointly significant and are dropped from the reported equation.

Note that these estimations are carried out for a cross-section of a limited number of industries. This evidence, while suggestive, should not be taken as conclusive. However, it supports the presumption that the lack of

Table 5.2 Multinationals' employees rate (OLS estimation)

	(1)	(2)	(3)	(4)
R^{BA}_{ITA}		−0.6878		
		(0.4266)		
R^{BA}_{GER}		−1.5989 *		
		(0.4364)		
R^{BA}_{UK}				
R^{BA}	−0.4798 *			
	(0.1509)			
R^{NET}			−0.1754 *	
			(0.0774)	
R^{NET+BA}				−0.1386 *
				(0.0526)
Constant	0.1628 *	0.1103 *	0.1056 *	0.1276 *
	(0.0522)	(0.0457)	(0.0350)	(0.0414)
Number of observations	48	48	48	48
R–squared	0.7155	0.8556	0.6710	0.6870

Notes:
Single asterisk (*) stands for significance at 5% level.
Double asterisk (**) stands for significance at 10% level.
Robust standard errors in brackets.

liberalization of the service industries affects productivity and growth through a variety of channels. Its effect on FDI flows is certainly important in this respect.

6
Looking Ahead: Will Liberalization Policies Succeed?

According to the case studies of Germany, Italy, and the UK, liberalization has positive direct effects on productivity in services, but does not always result in declining prices and employment gains. Liberalization seems to have positive effects on productivity, which—almost invariably because of a reduction in employment relative to excessively high levels—increases in all cases where its measurement is possible and reliable. Productivity may even increase well before privatization and liberalization, in anticipation of an increasingly competitive environment.

As for prices and employment, the evidence is more mixed. Prices decline and employment increases when liberalization is actually successful in fostering competition. This happens either in naturally competitive industries, where regulation is simply a way to protect producers, or when technological progress allows entrants to offer new products or forces the incumbent to be more innovative himself. Telecommunications are the best example of this virtuous pattern.

Effects are less positive in industries characterized by limited product and process innovations, where natural monopoly elements do not allow competitors to easily bypass a strong incumbent. More to the point, prices did not decrease as much as expected, partly because of the limited competition that countries were able or willing to introduce. Moreover, liberalization has taken place in sectors where prices were initially well below average cost. Notwithstanding the continuation of subsidies, in sectors such as railways or water, market-oriented reforms are bound to raise prices so as to cut operating losses and fund investments. Finally, in energy sectors, expectations on the effectiveness of reforms were probably excessive. Users' prices are still largely determined by fuel costs and taxation and large investments are required to raise efficiency.

The tertiary sector was found to play a large and increasing role as provider of inputs in manufacturing and agriculture. The benefits of product market reforms therefore go well beyond their direct sectoral impact. In particular, the tertiary sector provides a substantial share of intermediate inputs to manufacturing and therefore plays a key role in affecting industrial and more broadly economic competitiveness. Input-output analysis was used to show that the increasing weight of services in employment and GDP reflects not only the shift in consumer demand towards services but also the greater weight of services as providers of inputs to other sectors of the economy. Services, indeed, increasingly cater to business. This is true for trade, energy, finance, and professional services.

Accordingly, we find that service inputs account on average for more than 40 per cent of the value of production in other sectors. Moreover, this share has been steadily increasing since the mid-1980s for the three sample countries. For example, in the UK it rose from 25 per cent in 1984 to 45 per cent by the end of the 1990s. This rise was faster and larger than the increase in the overall GDP weight of services. This increased from 62 per cent in 1970 to around 74 per cent in 2000 in the USA and from 52.2 to 70 per cent in the EU-15 during the same period.

When we decompose the total share of the tertiary sector into the contributions of individual industries—network industries (transport, energy, and telecommunications), trade (retail and wholesale), finance and other business activities (e.g. lawyers, accountants, and so on)—we find that the contribution of each industry is broadly balanced. Interestingly, professional services, which are often considered less important than network industries or finance, account for a substantial share (around 10% on average) in all three countries.

A key finding is that, while business-oriented services are increasingly tradables, they remain substantially less open than manufacturing. Whereas import penetration, defined as the ratio of imports to domestic gross output, ranges between 23 per cent and 43 per cent in manufacturing, it varies between 2 and 3 per cent in services. The finding that services are not exposed to international competition has two main implications: first, that national regulations are the only effective channel to raise competition and, second, that activities using them as inputs cannot resort to cheaper imported alternatives. Seen in this light, the finding that restrictive regulations significantly hamper productivity growth in downstream sectors is not that surprising.

Widespread rigidities in the supply of key largely non-tradable inputs from the service sector also discourage foreign direct investment—and therefore deprive the host country of a number of beneficial externalities, like further gains in wages and productivity. The effectiveness of business services is a key factor in the location of multinational enterprises. FDI, whatever the reason for carrying it out (to enter new markets or to save on costs), needs an efficient network of suppliers and producers' services. While traded inputs can be imported, non-tradable inputs—and we have seen that services are much less tradable compared to goods—must be purchased locally. Their availability and their costs are therefore instrumental in affecting the investment decision of multinational corporations. Inefficient regulations that hamper the quality and the variety of business services have been found to discourages foreign direct investment in all the sample countries.

Services, therefore, are a key determinant of economic competitiveness. High quality, efficient, and competitively priced services carry strong cost savings for other sectors. Even when the gains of reforms in the tertiary sector itself are small, they get magnified when the indirect effects on the rest of the economy are also taken into account. Pervasive rigidities in much of the tertiary sector are likely to penalize manufacturing production, particularly in those sectors that are more exposed to international competition, and to discourage foreign direct investment.

Overall, our results help to explain a number of stylized facts. We know that the UK is by far the least regulated country. However, at the beginning of the period, productivity growth in most manufacturing sectors was lower there than in either Germany or Italy. In the following few years, the UK productivity gap fell markedly, a fact that our estimates attribute to a favourable regulatory environment rather than more trivially to a simple country effect. In the end, therefore, it was most likely a better regulatory framework that allowed UK firms to better capture new technological opportunities or, more modestly, to escape the fate of declining productivity growth that has characterized many industries in Germany and in Italy.

Service liberalization has, however, met with strong resistance. There have been repeated calls to treat services differently. The need to provide universal service, in energy and telecoms, is often mentioned as a reason for such special and differential treatment. Other sectors—professional services in particular—have claimed that they should be granted an exception given the pervasiveness of informational asymmetries and the need to ensure quality for unprotected users. We are unconvinced by these arguments. First, there is no evidence whatsoever that universal service obligation has been undermined by liberalization. Second, there is no reason why restrictions on competition will necessarily ensure higher quality. Actually, the opposite is likely to be true as suggested by both theory and empirical analysis. Similarly, informational asymmetries are not a unique feature of professional services. We therefore see no reason why services, including professional services, should not be fully subject to competition laws.

In light of the many benefits associated with the liberalization of producer services, it is somewhat puzzling why national governments have not pushed the reform agenda in this sector more decisively. This political economy puzzle is addressed in the companion paper by Castanheira *et al.* (2004). We none the less offer some simple speculations.

The evidence collected in Castanheira *et al.* (2004) suggests that the short-run employment impact of liberalization may be unfavourable. For many sectors, the combination of pervasive overmanning, large productivity gains, and inelastic demand meant that employment had to fall in the aftermath of liberalization. Moreover, sectoral employment losses are not always easily absorbed. If labour is at least to some extent sector specific, then some aggregate employment losses are virtually unavoidable. It is not too surprising therefore to find that liberalization is typically opposed by labour. Moreover, the support for liberalization may be further undermined by the fact that prices fell only moderately in the post-liberalization period.

It is also surprising that support for liberalization has not been boosted by sectors using services as inputs. A standard result in the political economy of trade literature is that sectors that cater mainly to other producers find it harder to get protection. This argument may not fully apply to the case of services because users of services are more dispersed, and therefore less keen to mobilize in favour of liberalization, than users of intermediate goods. Also, our evidence shows how the total weight of services in the value of manufacturing production is substantially larger than its direct weight. Hence, a large share of services inputs bought by manufacturers is embedded in other inputs and will not be immediately visible to buyers. To the extent that buyers are not fully aware of these general equilibrium effects they will lobby less vigorously for liberalization.

Political economy considerations only partly account for the limited success of liberalization policies. The design of such policies needs also to be improved. Half-hearted liberalization that fails to deliver lower prices may be self-defeating to the extent that it will not be able to garner the public support necessary to proceed further. Regulatory authorities need to be truly independent from the executive and be given a clear mandate. Equally crucially, the regulatory framework must be stable and predictable. Otherwise, investment will suffer most, creating widespread bottlenecks and further undermining support for liberalization.

Yet, the fact remains that liberalization in services has the potential to bring large welfare gains in terms of higher productivity and higher FDI throughout the economy. So far, liberalization of services has proceeded mainly at the urging of the European Commission. It is to be hoped that national governments throughout Europe will recognize the large economic dividends that a better regulatory framework for services can elicit. Far-reaching reforms in this area should represent a top priority for economic policy. Unfortunately, the waning commitment towards the Lisbon agenda does not leave much room for optimism in this respect.

References

Aghion, P., Bloom, N., Blundell, R., Griffith, R., and Howitt, P. (2002), "Competition and Innovation: An Inverted U Relationship", NBER Working Paper no. 9269.

Alesina, A., Ardagna, S., Nicoletti, G., and Schiantarelli, F. (2003), "Regulation and Investment", NBER Working Paper no. 9560.

Allegra, E., Forni, M., Grillo, M., and Magnani, L. (2004), "Anti Trust Policy and National Growth: Some Evidence from Italy", *Giornale degli Economisti*, 63(1), 69–86.

Arndt, A. and Knorr, A. (2004), "Wal-Mart in Deutschland: Eine verfehlte Internationalisierungsstrategie", *Orientierungen zur Wirtschafts- und Gesellschaftspolitik*, 99(1/2004), 44–50.

Bahn, C. (2002), "Die Bedeutung der lokalen Regulierungssysteme in Berlin für den Strukturwandel im Einzelhandel", WZB Discussion Paper FS I 02–103, Wissenschaftszentrum, Berlin.

Baily, M. N., Hulten, C., and Campbell, D. (1992), "Productivity Dynamics in Manufacturing Plants", *Brookings Papers on Economic Activity, Microeconomics*, 187–249.

Baldwin, R., Lipsey, R., and Richardson, J. (eds.) (1998), *Geography and Ownership as Bases for Economic Accounting: Studies in Income and Wealth*, Chicago: University of Chicago Press.

Balto, D. A. (1999), "Supermarket Merger Enforcement", Antitrust Report (Aug.).

Barba Navaretti, G., Venables, A. J., Barry, F., Ekholm, K., Falzoni, A. M., Haaland, J., Midelfart, K.-H., and Turrini, A. (2004), *Multinational Firms in the World Economy*, Princeton: Princeton University Press.

Bardelli, L. and Muraro, G. (2003), "L'offerta e la regolamentazione dei servizi idrici: l'esperienza italiana", in G. Muraro and T. Valbonesi (eds.), *I Servizi idrici tra mercado e regole*, Rome: Carocci Editore, 347–83.

Bartelsman, E. J. and Dhrymes, P. J. (1998), "Productivity Dynamics: U.S. Manufacturing Plants 1972–1986", *Journal of Productivity Analysis*, 1(9), 5–33.

—— and Doms, M. (2000), "Understanding Productivity: Lessons from Longitudinal Microdata", *Journal of Economic Literature*, 38 (Sept.), 569–94.

Benfratello, L. and Sembenelli A. (2002), "Foreign Ownership and Productivity: Is the Direction of Causality so Obvious?", Centro Studi d'Agliano Working Paper no. 166.

Bertola, G. and Boeri, T. (2002), "EMU Labour Markets Two Years on: Microeconomics Tensions and Institutional Evolution", in M. Buti and A. Sapir (eds.), *EMU and Economic Policy in Europe*, Cheltenham: Edward Elgar.

Bishop, M. and Green, M. (1995), "Privatization and Recession—The Miracle Tested", Centre for the Study of Regulated Industries, Discussion Paper no. 10, London.

—— and Kay, J. (1988), *Does Privatization Work?* London: Centre for Business Strategy, London Business School.

References

——and Thompson. D. (1992), "Regulatory Reform and Productivity Growth in the UK's Public Utilities", *Applied Economics*, 24(11), 1181–90.

——— (1994), "Privatisation, Internal Organization and Productive Efficiency", in M. Bishop, J. Kay, and C. Mayer (eds.), *Privatisation and Economic Performance*, Oxford: Oxford University Press.

Blanchard, O. and Giavazzi, F. (2003), "Macroeconomic Effects of Regulation and Deregulation in Goods and Labor Markets", *Quarterly Journal of Economics*, 118(3), 879–908.

Bonaccorsi, A., Cambini, R., Giuri, P., and Riccardi R. (2001), "Non Ergodic Properties of the Dynamics of Industry Concentration", LEM Working Paper 2001/12, presented to European Meeting on Applied Evolutionary Economics, Vienna, 13–15 Sept. 2001.

Boylaud, O. and Nicoletti, G. (2001), "Regulatory Reform in Retail Distribution", *OECD Economic Studies*, 32, 253–74.

Bundesministerium für Wirtschaft (1996), "Bericht über den Stand der Umsetzung des Aktionsprogrammes für Investitionen und Arbeitsplätze", 20 Mar.

Button, K. J. and Weyman-Jones, T. G. (1992), "Ownership Structure, Institutional Organization and Measured X-Inefficiency", *AEA Papers and Proceedings*, 82(2), 439–45.

——— (1994), "X-Efficiency and Technical Efficiency", *Public Choice*, 80, 83–104.

Campbell, James I., Jr. (2002), "Remailing—Catalyst for Liberalizing the European Postal Markets?" In G. Kulenkampff and H. Smit (eds.), *Liberalization of Postal Markets*, Bad Honnef: WIK Wissenschaftliches Institut für Kommunikationsdienste.

Carter, C. and Williams, B. (1959), *Investment in Innovation*, Oxford: Oxford University Press.

Castanheira, M., Galasso, V., Carcillo, S., Perotti, E., Nicoletti, G., and Tsyganock, L. (2004), "How to Gain Popular Support for Reforms?" Report prepared for Structural Reforms without Prejudices, Sixth European Meeting of the Fondazione DeBenedetti.

Caves, R., Bailey, S. D., et al. (1992), *Industrial Efficiency in Six Nations*, Cambridge, Mass.: MIT Press.

——and Barton, D. (1990), *Efficiency in US Manufacturing Industries*, Cambridge, Mass.: MIT Press.

Comitato per la vigilanza sulle risorse idriche (2000), Relazione annuale al Parlamento sullo stato dei servizi idrici.

Commission of the European Communities (1992), Green Paper on the Development of the Single Market in Postal Services, COM(91) 476 final (adopted 11 June 1992).

Conyon, M., Girma, S., Thompson, S. and Wright, P. W. (2002), "The Productivity and Wage Effects of Foreign Acquisition in the United Kingdom", *Journal of Industrial Economics*, 50(1), 83–102.

Criscuolo, C., Haskel, J., and Martin, R. (2004), "Productivity, Restructuring and Globalisation", draft paper.

Criscuolo, C., Haskel, J., and R. Martin (2002), "Multinationals, Foreign Ownership and Productivity in UK businesses", mimeo.

Davies, S. and Caves, R. (1987), *Britain's Productivity Gap*, Cambridge: Cambridge University Press for NIESR.

Directive 97/67/EC of the European Parliament and of the Council of 15 December 1997 on common rules for the development of the internal market of Community postal services and the improvement of quality of service (OJ L15, 21/02/1998, p. 14) amended by Directive 2002/39/EC of the European Parliament and of the Council of 10 June 2002 amending Directive 97/67/EC with regard to further opening to competition of Community postal services (OJ L176, 05.07.2002, p. 21).

Dobson Consulting (1999), "Buyer Power and its Impact on Competition in the Food Retail Distribution Sector of the European Union", Report produced for the European Commission, DG IV, Brussels.

Doms, M. E. and Jensen, J. B. (1998), "Comparing Wages, Skills, and Productivity between Domestically and Foreign-Owned Manufacturing Establishments in the United States", in Baldwin *et al.* (1998), 235–55.

Etro, F. (2004), "Innovation by Leaders", *Economic Journal*, 114, 281–303.

Foster, L., Haltiwanger, J., and Krizan, C. J. (2001), "Aggregate Productivity Growth: Lessons from Microeconomic Evidence", in Edward Dean, Michael Harper, and Charles Hulten (eds.), *New Development in Productivity Analysis*, Chicago: University of Chicago Press.

FTC (2001), Report on the Federal Trade Commission Workshop on Slotting Allowances and Other Marketing Practices in the Grocery Industry, Report by the Federal Trade Commission Staff, Washington, DC.

Geroski, P. (1990), "Innovation, Technical Opportunity and Market Structure", *Oxford Economic Papers*, 42, 586–602.

Geroski, P. (1990), "Innovation and The Sectoral Impact on Productivity", *Economic Journal*, Royal Economic Society, 101(409), 1438–51.

Girma, S., Greenaway, D., and Wakelin, K. (2001), "Who Benefits from Foreign Direct Investment in the UK?", *Scottish Journal of Political Economy*, 48(2), 119–33.

Görg, H. and Greenaway, D. (2001), "Foreign Direct Investment and Intra-Industry Spillovers: A Review of the Literature", GEP Research Paper no. 2001/37, Globalisation and Labour Markets Programme, Nottingham, Leverhulme Centre for Research on Globalisation and Economic Policy.

—— and Strobl, E. (2001), "Multinational Companies and Productivity Spillovers: A Meta-Analysis", *Economic Journal*, 111(475), F723–F739.

Green, A. and Mayes, D. (1991), "Technical Efficiency in Manufacturing Industries", *Economic Journal*, 101, 523–38.

Griffith, R. (1999), "Using the ARD Establishment Level Data to Look at Foreign Ownership and Productivity in the United Kingdom", *Economic Journal*, 109, 416–42.

—— Redding, S. J. and Simpson, H. (2003), "Productivity Convergence and Foreign Ownership at the Establishment Level", CEPR Discussion Paper no. 3765.

References

—— and Simpson, H. (2001), "Characteristics of Foreign-Owned Firms in British Manufacturing", The Institute for Fiscal Studies Working Paper no. 01/10.

Griliches, Z. and Regev, H. (1992), "Productivity and Firm Turnover in Israeli Industry 1979–88", NBER Working Paper no. 4059.

Grillo, M. (2004), "Alle radici di una 'Economia che non gira'", *Il Mulino*, 53(3).

Grünhagen, M. and Mittelstaedt, R. A. (2001), "The Impact of Store Hours and Redistributive Income Effects on the Retail Industry: Some Projections for Germany", *International Review of Retail, Distribution and Consumer Research*, 11, 49–62.

Harris, R. (2002), "Foreign Ownership and Productivity in the United Kingdom—Some Issues When Using the ARD Establishment Level Data", *Scottish Journal of Political Economy*, 47, 318–55.

—— and Robinson, C. (2002), "The Effect of Foreign Acquisitions on Total Factor Productivity: Plant-Level Evidence from U.K. Manufacturing, 1987–1992", *Review of Economics and Statistics*, 84(3), 562–8.

Hart, O. D. (1983), "The Market Mechanism as an Incentive Scheme", *Bell Journal of Economics*, 14, 366–82.

Hart, P. and Clarke, R. (1980), *Concentration in British Industry 1935–75*, Cambridge: Cambridge University Press.

Haskel, J. (1991), "Imperfect Competition, Work Practices and Productivity Growth", *Oxford Bulletin of Economics and Statistics*, 53(3), 265–80.

—— Pereira, S. and Slaughter, M. (2002), "Does Inward Foreign Direct Investment Boost the Productivity of Domestic Firms?", NBER Working Paper no. 8724.

—— and Sanchis, A. (1995), "Privatisation and X-Inefficiency: A Bargaining Approach", *Journal of Industrial Economics*, 43(3), 301–21.

—— and Szymanski, S. (1992), "The Effects of Privatisation, Competition and Restructuring on Productivity Growth in UK Manufacturing", Queen Mary and Westfield College, Department of Economics, Discussion Paper no. 286 (Jan.).

Hellwig, M. and Paulus, M. (2002), "Liberalization of German Postal Markets?" In G. Kulenkampff and H. Smit (eds.), *"Liberalization of Postal Markets"*, Bad Honnef: WIK Wissenschaftliches Institut für Kommunikationsdienste.

Hermalin, B. E. (1992), "The Effects of Competition on Executive Behaviour", *Rand Journal of Economics*, 32, 350–65.

Howenstine, N. and Zeile W. (1994), "Characteristics of Foreign-Owned U.S. Manufacturing Establishments", *Survey of Current Business*, 74, 34–59.

Inderst, R. and Wey, C. (2003), "Buyer Power and Supplier Incentives", WZB Discussion Paper SP II 2003-05, Wissenschaftszentrum, Berlin.

ISTAT (2003), *Annuario Statistico*.

Jean, S. and Nicoletti, G. (2002), "Product Market Regulation and Sectoral Wage Premia in Europe and North America: An Empirical Investigation", OECD Economics Department Working Paper no. 318.

Johnson, G. (1990), "Work Rules, Featherbedding and Pareto-Optimal Union-Management Bargaining", *Journal of Labour Economics*, 8, S237–S259.

Mankiw, N. G. and Whinston, M. D. (1998), "Free Entry and Social Efficiency", *Rand Journal of Economics*, 17, 48–58.

Martin, S. and Parker, D. (1997), *Privatisation*, Cheltenham: Edward Elgar.

MGI (1998), "Deriving Productivity and Growth in the UK Economy", MGI Reports (Oct.), McKinsey Global Institute, available at http://www.mckinsey.com/knowledge/mgi/.

—— (2001), "U.S. Productivity Growth", 1995–2000, MGI Reports (Oct.), McKinsey Global Institute, available at http://www.mckinsey.com/mgi/publications/us/.

Nickell, S. (1996), "Competition and Corporate Performance", *Journal of Political Economy*, 104, 724–46.

—— Vainomaki, J., and Wadhwani, S. (1992), "Wager, Unions, Insiders and Product Market Power", CEP Discussion Paper 077, Centre for Economic Performance, LSE.

Nicoletti, G. and Scarpetta, S. (2003), "Regulation, Productivity and Growth: OECD Evidence", OECD Economics Department Working Paper no. 347.

OECD (1999), "Buying Power of Multiproduct Retailers, Series Roudtables on Competition Policy DAFFE/CLP(99)21", Paris: OECD.

—— (2000), "Assessing Barriers to Trade in Services: Retail Trade Services", OECD Working Paper, Paris.

—— (2002), "Competition and Regulation Issues in Telecommunications", DAFFE/COMP (2002)6, Paris.

—— (2004), *Economic Outlook*, Paris.

Olley, S. and Pakes, A. (1992), "The Dynamics of Productivity in the Telecommunications Industry", NBER Working Paper no. 3977, Cambridge, Mass.

O'Mahony, M. (1999), *"Britain's Productivity Performance 1950-1996: An International Perspective"*, London: National Institute for Economic and Social Research.

—— and van Ark, B. (eds.) (2003), *EU Productivity and Competitiveness: An Industry Perspective: Can Europe Resume the Catching-up Process?*, Luxembourg: Office for Official Publications of the European Communities.

Oxford Institute of Retail Management (2004), "Assessing the Productivity of the UK Retail Sector", Templeton College, University of Oxford, Apr.

Panzar, J. (2002), "Reconciling Competition, Downstream Access and Universal Service in Postal Markets", in M. A. Crew and P. R. Kleindorfer (eds.), *Regulation and the Nature of Postal and Delivery Services*, Boston: Kluwer Academic Publishers, 93–115.

Parker, D. and Martin, S. (1995), "The Impact of UK Privatization on Labour and Total Factor Productivity", *Scottish Journal of Political Economy*, 42(2) (May), 201–20.

Paterson, I., Fink, M., and Ogus, A. (2003), "Economic Impact of Regulations in the Field of Liberal Profession in Different Member States", Institute for Advanced Studies, Vienna.

Peruzzi, P. (2003), "Le tariffe dei servizi idrici dopo la riforma della legge 36/94", mimeo.

Pollitt, M. (1999), "A Survey of the Liberalization of Public Enterprises in the UK since 1979", in M. Kagami and M. Tsuji (eds.), *Privatization, Deregulation and*

References

Institutional Framework, Tokyo: Institute of Developing Economies, Japan External Trade Organization.

Postal Services Commission (2005), *Annual Report 2004–5*, London: Postcomm.

Potz, P. (2002), "Die Regulierung des Einzelhandels in Italien: Grundlagen und Einfluss auf die Handelsstruktur", WZB Discussion Paper FS I 02–104, Wissenschaftszentrum, Berlin.

—— (2003), "Die Regulierung des Einzelhandels im Grossraum London", WZB Discussion Paper SP III 2003–203, Wissenschaftszentrum, Berlin.

Regulierungsbehörde für Telekommunikation und Post (RegTP) (2003a), Sechste Marktuntersuchung für den Bereich der lizenzierten Postsendungen, Bad Honnef.

—— (2003b), Sixth Market Study in the Field of Licensed Postal Items, Bad Honnef.

—— (2004), Siebte Marktuntersuchung für den Bereich der lizenzpflichtigen Postdienstleistungen, Bad Honnef.

Rogerson, C. and Takis, W. (1993), "Economies of Scale and Scope and Competition in Postal Services", in M. A. Crew and P. R. Kleindorfer (eds.), *Regulation and the Nature of Postal and Delivery Services*, Boston: Kluwer Academic Publishers.

Rosen, A. (1989), "Bargaining over Effort", Centre for Labour Economics, London School of Economics, Discussion Paper no. 351, rev. July 1990.

Scharfstein, D. (1988), "Product Market Competition and Managerial Slack", *Rand Journal of Economics*, 19(1), 147–55.

Schumpeter, J. A. (1943), *Capitalism, Socialism and Democracy*, New York: Harper and Row.

Stumpf, U. (1997), "Remailing in the European Community: Economic Analysis of Alternative Regulatory Environments", in M. Crew and P. Kleindorfer (eds.), *Regulation and the Nature of Postal and Delivery Services*, Boston: Kluwer Academic Publishers.

UNCTAD (2003), *World Investment Report 2003*, Geneva: UNCTAD.

van Ark, B., Inklaar, R., and McGuckin, R. H. (2003), "The Contribution of ICT-Producing and ICT-Using Industries to Productivity Growth: A Comparison of Canada, Europe, and the United States", *International Productivity Monitor*, Centre for the Study of Living Standards, no. 6 (spring), 56–63.

Varian, H. R. (1995), "Entry and Cost Reduction", mimeo, University of Michigan.

Vickers, J. S. (1995), "Concepts of Competition", *Oxford Economic Papers*, 47, 1–23.

Waddams Price, C. (1999), *"Efficiency and Productivity Studies in Incentive Regulation of UK Utilities"*, address to the Sixth European Workshop on Efficiency and Productivity Analysis, mimeo, Warwick Business School.

Wik-Consult (2004), *Main Developments in the European Postal Sector*, Study for the European Commission, Bad Honnef.

Wragg, R. and Robertson, J. (1978), "Post War Trends in Employment, Productivity, Output, Labour Costs and Prices by Industry in the UK", Department of Employment Research Paper no. 3, London: HMSO.

APPENDIX 1

COMPETITION, PRIVATIZATION, AND PERFORMANCE

A1. Introduction

Competition can raise productivity growth in two ways. First, competition can raise the productivity of existing enterprises. Studies that emphasize this contribution are, for example, Nickell (1996), on the impact of competition on existing firms. Second, competition can raise productivity growth via the process of market selection. In turn, this is potentially composed of two effects. First, low productivity establishments may exit and be replaced by higher productivity entrants and second, higher productivity incumbents may gain market share. There are a number of theoretical papers on the issue, and recently there has been growing evidence of its importance (see e.g. Bartelsman and Doms, 2000, for references).

A2. Competition and productivity within firms

Let us think of the firm as consisting of owners, managers, and workers. Within the firm, there is a set of contracts between these groups. Outside the firm, competitive pressure comes from competition in the product market and/or the capital market. Competitive pressure presumably alters the behaviour of one or more of these groups. We might then think of two distinct effects:

(a) with a given contractual/bargaining relation within the firm, competition may affect effort incentives;
(b) competition may affect the type of contracts that can be written between agents in the firm.

A2.1 Competition and within-firm contracts

Consider first competition and within-firm contracts. Much recent work on X-inefficiency has modelled X-inefficiency as caused by inefficient effort levels exerted by managers (see e.g. Vickers, 1995). Why might such effort be inefficient? Consider an owner trying to devise a suitable wage contract for a manager.

If owners link managerial compensation to output, this would reward high effort and so induce efficiency. A potential problem arises if owners cannot observe managerial effort and managers are risk averse. Hence owners cannot observe whether high output is due to high managerial effort or good fortune (e.g. good weather on a farm). Tying rewards to output exposes managers to a lot of risk.

What are the effects of competition in this setting? Suppose there was another similar firm in the market. The basic idea is that such competition increases the information available to the principal when they write the contract with their agent. Suppose, for example, that the only source of random shocks to measured output is the weather, and suppose that the two firms are in the same weather area. Then the manager would be happy to accept a contract that rewards her based not only on her output but on the relative output of the other firm. If the weather shocks are correlated, the output of the other firm will fall in response to a bad shock, thus showing the principal that the agent did indeed work hard, but suffered an adverse shock. So basing reward on relative output introduces an insurance element into the contract which improves welfare.

Unfortunately, the picture is a little more complicated when one considers the correlation of measured output between the firms in a little more detail. Suppose the unobservable component of measured output has two components: the unobservable ability of managers and random weather. Then the output correlation between the firms depends on the between-firm correlation of managerial effort, managerial ability, and weather. Suppose, first, that there is very high correlation of managerial ability levels and low correlation of weather effects. Then, conditioning an agent's contract on rival managers' output might have a poor incentive effect. For if the agent knows that her rival's output is mostly due to ability, rather than bad luck, she might reduce her effort in the expectation of receiving part of her reward based on her rival's ability. Since both managers behave in this way, there is a free-rider effect, and so conditioning rewards on rivals may lead to poor effort outcomes.

These complications also affect the desirability of competition in dynamic models, in particular the ratchet effect (a manager perceived as having high ability in period 1 might get a tighter contract in period 2). Suppose information from the market improves the estimate of underlying managerial ability. Although this might be good for insurance, it worsens the ratchet effect.

A2.2 Competition and outside firm forces

The above section dealt with how competition affects the structure of contracts within a firm and therefore X-inefficiency. How does competition influence effort for a given set of contracts or bargaining relation?

The most obvious form of competition is from the product market. Models here have looked at the influence of competition on the X-inefficiency of managers and of workers.

A2.2.1 *Agency models* An influential early paper was Hart (1983). Here firms are either managerial or entrepreneurial. Managerial firms are run by managers who wish to minimize effort. Owners observe the firm's performance, but cannot observe the firm's costs, which are a mix of managerial effort and random shocks. Such firms are therefore X-inefficient due to this agency problem and the manager's assumed utility functions mean that owners set managers a fixed profit target. Entrepreneurial firms, by contrast, are profit maximizers and have no X-inefficiency.

Hart was concerned, to show how the presence of entrepreneurial firms (this is the sense in which he examines competition) affected X-inefficiency in managerial firms. With no entrepreneurial firms in the market, consider a shock that lowers all costs. Such a shock provides the opportunity for managers to shirk whilst still fulfilling their profit targets and so X-inefficiency will increase. Suppose now that there are also entrepreneurial firms in the market and assume cost shocks are correlated between both sets of firms. With low costs, the entrepreneurial firms will expand. Product prices will fall. Managers in managerial firms will find it more difficult to fulfil profit targets and so will have to raise effort. So competition reduces X-inefficiency in the sense that managers find it harder to "take" favourable shocks in the form of reduced effort.

Scharfstein (1988), however, showed the result depends critically on his assumed managerial utility function In Hart's model, managerial utility functions were such that owners simply issued managers with a fixed profit target.[1] With more general utility functions, contracts can be more complicated and competition might not necessarily raise productivity. See Hermalin (1992), who sets out the various effects and shows there are no clear conditions under which any one effect dominates.

A2.2.2 *Bargaining models* A number of models have examined effort (typically worker effort) as the outcome of a bargain between firms and workers, rather than an agency relation (Rosen, 1989; Johnson, 1990; Haskel, 1991; Nickell *et al.*, 1992). The bargaining approach is appealing for many economies since detailed survey data suggest that bargaining over effort (crew sizes, manning levels, and so on) is widespread. Note that there is no need for unions in this model; Johnson (1990) reports widespread bargaining over crew sizes in the USA, which is predominantly non-unionized.

These models generally proceed as follows. Output depends on employment, capital, and "effort". So increased effort raises productivity. Firms and workers bargain over the level of effort (and perhaps other variables such as wages) and the firm then sets employment. In the bargain, firms desire high effort and low wages

---

[1] Hart assumed that managers were infinitely risk averse with respect to incomes above some particular level. So contracts were limited to those specifying a single profit target, since managers did not care about incomes above this level and would not accept contracts below this level. Hence managers are X-efficient when cost shocks mean that costs are high, but X-inefficient when costs are low.

to raise profits. By contrast, workers desire low effort and high wages to raise utility. The effect of bargaining is to transfer some of the profits of the firm to the workers, depending on bargaining power. In the simplest models, workers simply take reduced effort as part of profits (and perhaps increased wages). Competition lowers the surplus available to bargain over and raises the marginal employment loss for workers in raising their wages. Workers are therefore forced to take at least part of the reduced surplus in the form of reduced slack or X-inefficiency.

One problem with these models is that, like the agency models, they too depend quite a lot on preferences. Consider a union with a much stronger preference for low effort relative to high wages. Increased competition shrinks the cake and the union knows that it must give something away to the firm in the bargain. It is perfectly possible that such a union might agree to work for a much lower wage but only in return for lower effort. The firm is happy to accede to this demand if the effect on profits of lowered effort is outweighed by the effect of lowered wages.

A3. Competition and the selection of organizations

In the above models, competition affects the efficiency of an organization. In the context of these models, welfare implications relate to a given organization. However, competition might very well affect the mix of organizations. It is worth noting first that there is a classic result concerning the *welfare* effects of competition and entry, namely that in free market equilibrium there is *too much* entry (Mankiw and Whinston, 1988). In this model, competition does not alter the cost structure of firms, as in the models above, but simply increases the number of firms in the market. Consider a Cournot market of *ex ante* identical firms, where entry requires a fixed cost F, after which firms produce at exogenous costs MC. Suppose a regulator allows free entry into the market. This improves allocative efficiency as prices fall towards MC. But since each firm's output falls, productivity is *worsened* as firms produce further up the AC curve (the business stealing effect, since it occurs as new firms enter the market). This negative externality turns out to outweigh the positive externality that extra production confers on consumers.

As Vickers (1995) and Varian (1995) have pointed out, all firms are identical in this model. What if an entrant were more productive? Then welfare might be increased, even with reduced economies of scale, if the output were shifted to the more efficient new entrant (a positive externality that Vickers (1995) christens the "business shifting" effect; (see also Varian, 1995). This again turns out to depend on the set-up of the model.[2]

---

[2] All these effects are of competition on the level of productivity. Competition might affect productivity growth if it affected innovation. Theoretical results are mainly divided as to whether more competition encourages innovation. Schumpeter (1943) argued that monopolies were more likely to innovate since they had the profits out of which to finance innovations. Subsequent theoretical work has looked instead at situations where firms have equal access to capital markets so that these "deep pockets" considerations do not arise. Results here are typically ambiguous.

A4. Empirical evidence

Since theory is ambiguous, what of empirical work? There are a number of currents in the work.

A4.1 *Frontier studies*

First, frontier production studies. As Button and Weymarn-Jones (1994) remark, although many studies estimate inefficiency, few explore its relation to competition. Among these are the findings of the multi-industry study for the UK reported in Green and Mayes (1991) and for the USA, reported in Caves and Barton (1990) (see Caves *et al.*, 1992, for further information and other countries). These studies use a similar methodology across countries and so have the advantage of being comparable, and are specifically designed to look at the issue of competition and efficiency. Their findings are rather inconclusive. For example, Caves and Barton (1990) and Green and Mayes (1991) calculated a range of frontier-based inefficiency indices for industries in 1977 and regressed them on a number of industry-level variables of interest. As for concentration, neither study found any significant linear relation between industry concentration and any of the inefficiency measures. Both studies found a significant non-linear, U-shaped relation between concentration and inefficiency, such that both unconcentrated and concentrated industries were associated with inefficiency. In the UK, the minimum inefficiency occurred at a five-firm concentration ratio of 40 per cent, whilst in the USA maximum efficiency was at a four-firm concentration ratio of 34.8 per cent (sample mean 39.7%), after which efficiency fell with concentration. Results were similarly mixed for other variables such as import penetration.

Turning to data envelopment analysis (DEA), Button and Weyman-Jones (1994) survey 23 DEA studies of X-inefficiency, and for nine of them, construct a 1/0 dummy variable which decreases with the degree to which competition, private ownership, or a lack of regulation characterize the industry in question. They find a negative rank correlation between this measure and efficiency. So this is consistent with the idea that more competitive industries are more efficient, although, as the authors stress, the results can be regarded as suggestive at best.

A4.2 *Non-frontier studies*

As for non-frontier methods, a number of recent studies have taken industry or plant-level panel data and regressed productivity levels on competition levels and growth, using the panel structure to control for unobservable industry or firm fixed effects. As for industry work, Carter and Williams (1959) found a positive correlation between productivity and concentration for 12 British industries, 1907–48, whilst Wragg and Robinson (1978) found a negative correlation for 82 industries, 1963–73 (although they included output as a regressor, making interpretation difficult). Hart and Clarke (1980) report no significant effects of concentration on labour productivity (measured relative to the USA) for a number of industries and

Appendices

countries, although they do not include controls such as capital beyond concentration, plant size, and country and industry dummies. Davies and Caves (1987) also examine productivity and productivity growth for 100 UK industries relative to the USA but find no effects of concentration in explaining the inter-country difference. Haskel (1991) finds that falls in concentration are associated with increases in productivity, suggesting that more competition raises productivity.

Finally, Geroski (1990) has studied the impact of competition on innovation (and in turn innovation on productivity growth, see Geroski, 1991). The key correlation established is that increased concentration lowers innovations. The data is for 73 MLH industries where two cross-sections have been created using averaged data for 1970–4 and 1975–9. To the extent that innovation feeds into productivity growth, then this supports the notion that the level of competition raises productivity growth.

Turning to firm-level work, Nickell (1996) uses data on 148 firms, 1975–86, to explore the influence of competition on both the *level* and *growth* of productivity. Competition is measured by the market share of firms in the relevant three-digit industry (a measure that varies over time and firms) and by a questionnaire response to the enquiry "have you more than five competitors in the market for your products" (a 1/0 variable, that varies over firms). The two most significant effects are that the (two-period lagged) level of market share lowers the level of productivity and that the competitors' effect raises productivity growth. Thus, these effects suggest that competition both raises productivity (as found in the industry studies) and raises productivity growth.

The final current of empirical work is the work that looks at the role of reallocation in explaining productivity growth. Many of these recent studies are surveyed in Bartelsman and Doms (2000). A significant early contribution was that of Bartelsman and Dhrymes (1998). They used US data to document that aggregate US TFP 1970–80 rose very substantially, but unweighted average plant-level TFP declined or was flat. Since aggregate TFP is a weighted average of the individual, this suggests that much of productivity growth is due to changes in the weights. Changes in the weights are themselves due to reallocation, suggesting that reallocation is important in explaining productivity growth. For US telecommunications, Olley and Pakes (1996) found a similar importance of reallocation, particularly after the deregulation of the industry.

Baily *et al.* (1992), Foster *et al.* (2001), and Griliches and Regev (1992) presented explicit accounting decompositions of productivity growth into the contributions of continuers, entrants, and exitors. Foster *et al.* (2001) found, for example, that entry and exit accounted for 26 per cent of US manufacturing productivity growth in 1977–87. Criscuolo *et al.* (2004) find entry and exit accounted for 25 per cent of productivity growth over a five-year period in the UK in the 1980s and 50 per cent in the 1990s.

A5. Privatizations and performance

Precise evidence on productivity, privatization, and competition requires the study of particular firms. A number of studies exist for the UK (see e.g. Bishop and Kay, 1988; Bishop and Thompson, 1992; Bishop and Green, 1995; Haskel and Szymanski, 1992; Parker and Martin, 1995; and Pollitt, 1999). Many of these results are summarized in Haskel and Green (2001) who set out a number of findings. First, public sector firms were typically very inefficient before privatization. Second, privatization itself is not strongly associated with rises in TFP, while pre-privatization restructuring and increased market competition were associated with a rise in TFP. Third, most of the rise in labour productivity was due to fast labour shedding. The finding that privatization itself does not seem to be correlated with productivity growth is intriguing, but whether the commitment to privatize, which can only be obtained by privatizing, is essential to getting the gains from pre-privatization restructuring remains an open question that is unlikely to be econometrically testable.

Turning to international evidence, O'Mahony (1999) calculates labour productivity in the gas, electricity, and water sectors in the G5 countries. These data are of interest since they provide an international productivity comparison. The UK had the lowest level of productivity throughout the 1970s and 1980s, and it is hard to identify any change in trend between 1973 and 1990. From 1990 onwards, however, labour productivity growth more than doubles, to 9 per cent a year, so that the UK overtakes France, and closes the gap with the other countries in the sample. Productivity growth in the other countries only rose slightly, on average, from 2.4 per cent in the 1980s to 3.1 per cent between 1990 and 1996, and so an exogenous technical change is unlikely to be responsible for the acceleration in the UK. This would appear to provide evidence of an effect from privatization and tightened regulation but since the dates of privatization of gas, electricity, and water vary one cannot conclude for sure whether it is the result of privatization, pre-privatization restructuring, or regulation.

APPENDIX 2

OECD INPUT–OUTPUT TABLES CLASSIFICATION BY SECTORS

Table 2A.1 OECD Input–Output tables (ISIC Rev. 3 Class.) (classification by sector)

Sector	OECD IO Industry	ISIC Rev. 3 Class.
Agriculture, Hunting, Forestry and Fishing	1	01–05
Mining and Quarrying	2	10–14
Food Products, Beverages and Tobacco	3	15–16
Textiles, Textile Products, Leather and Footwear	4	17–19
Wood and Products of Wood and Cork	5	20
Pulp, Paper, Paper Products, Printing and Publishing	6	21–22
Coke, Refined Petroleum Products and Nuclear Fuel	7	23
Chemicals Excluding Pharmaceuticals	8	24 ex. 2423
Pharmaceuticals	9	2423
Rubber and Plastics Products	10	25
Other Non-Metallic Mineral Products	11	26
Iron & Steel	12	271, 2731
Non-Ferrous Metals	13	272, 2732
Fabricated Metal Products, Except Machinery and Equipment	14	28
Machinery and Equipment, N.E.C.	15	29
Office, Accounting and Computing Machinery	16	30
Electrical Machinery and Apparatus, N.E.C.	17	31
Radio, Television and Communication Equipment	18	32
Medical, Precision and Optical Instruments	19	33
Motor Vehicles, Trailers and Semi-Trailers	20	34
Building and Repairing of Ships and Boats	21	351
Aircraft and Spacecraft	22	353
Railroad Equipment and Transport Equipment N.E.C.	23	352, 359
Manufacturing N.E.C.; Recycling	24	36–37
Electricity, Gas and Water	25	40–41
Construction	26	45
Wholesale and Retail Trade; Repairs	27	50–52
Hotels and Restaurants	28	55
Transport and Storage	29	60–63
Post and Telecommunications	30	64
Finance, Insurance	31	65–67
Real Estate Activities	32	70
Renting of Machinery and Equipment	33	71

Table 2A.1 (*Contd.*)

Sector	OECD IO Industry	ISIC Rev. 3 Class.
Computer and Related Activities	34	72
Research and Development	35	73
Other Business Activities	36	74
Public Admin. and Defence; Compulsory Social Security	37	75
Education	38	80
Health and Social Work	39	85
Other Community, Social and Personal Services	40	90–93
Private Households with Employed Persons and Extra Territorial Organization and Bodies SBFD+j	41	95–99

Notes:

Germany 1995, Italy 1992, and United Kingdom 1998. OECD Input–Output Tables follow the classification.

Sectors 8 and 9, 20, 21 and 22 are not separately available for Germany and they are included respectively in sectors 8 and 20. Sector 13 is not available.

Sectors 12 and 13 are not separately available for Italy and they are included in sector 12.

Table 2A.2 OECD Input–Output tables (ISIC Rev. 2 Class.)

Sector	OECD IO Industry	ISIC Rev. 2 Class.
Agriculture, Forestry and Fishing	1	1
Mining and Quarrying	2	2
Food, Beverages and Tobacco	3	31
Textiles, Apparel and Leather	4	32
Wood Products and Furniture	5	33
Paper, Paper Products and Printing	6	34
Industrial Chemicals	7	351, 352 ex. 3522
Drugs and Medicines	8	3522
Petroleum and Coal Products	9	353, 354
Rubber and Plastic Products	10	355, 356
Non-Metallic Mineral Products	11	36
Iron & Steel	12	371
Non-Ferrous Metals	13	372
Metal Products	14	381
Non-Electrical Machinery	15	382 ex. 3852
Office and Computing Machinery	16	3852
Electrical Apparatus, N.E.C.	17	383 ex. 3832
Radio, TV and Communication Equipment	18	3832
Shipbuilding and Repairing	19	3841
Other Transport	20	3842, 3844, 3849
Motor Vehicles	21	3843
Aircraft	22	3845
Professional Goods	23	385
Other Manufacturing	24	39
Electricity, Gas and Water	25	4
Construction	26	5

Table 2A.2 (*Contd.*)

Sector	OECD IO Industry	ISIC Rev. 2 Class.
Wholesale and Retail Trade	27	61, 62
Restaurants and Hotels	28	63
Transport and Storage	29	71
Communications	30	72
Finance and Insurance	31	81, 82
Real Estate and Business Services	32	83
Community, Social and Personal Services	33	9
Producers of Government Services	34	
Other Producers	35	
SBFD + j	36	

Notes:

Germany 1986 and 1990, Italy 1985, and United Kingdom 1984 and 1990. OECD Input–Output Tables follow the classification.

Sectors 8 and 18 are not separately available for Germany; they are included in sectors 7 and 17 respectively.

Sector 20 is not separately available for Germany. Railway engines and wagons are included in sector 14; tractors, excavators, etc. are included in sector 15; bicycles are included in sector 21.

Comments

Olivier Blanchard

This report builds on the collective knowledge of the many authors, it contains an enormous amount of factual information about many sectors and many countries, and it is likely to serve as a standard reference in the future.

I learned a lot from it. My comparative advantage is surely not to argue with the specific findings. It may instead be to put the results of the study in the larger context of the effects of deregulation on productivity and employment, and the now traditional comparison between the USA and Europe. I shall expand briefly on six points.

1. ARE THINGS REALLY SO BAD (ON THE PRODUCTIVITY FRONT)?

Quoting from the introduction of the paper: "There is considerable agreement that widespread rigidities in European markets are among the main factors responsible for Europe's growth record".

Sure, there are many rigidities in Europe. Sure, output growth could be higher. But is the reality so bad? I believe that some of the European self-flagellation is excessive, and the diagnosis should be nuanced.

Table C1.1, using data from the OECD, gives numbers for labour productivity levels for France, Italy, and the USA. I choose France because I know it well, Italy because of where we are, and the USA as the standard benchmark. Labour productivity is constructed as the ratio of GDP, measured in 1995 PPP prices, to total hours worked. The conclusions are clear: France and Italy were far behind the USA in 1970. They are roughly at the same level as the USA today.

Table C1.1 Labour productivity levels in France, Italy, and the USA

Year	France	Italy	USA
1970	16.0	16.5	23.2
1990	30.4	30.7	30.1
2002	38.2	37.4	37.2

Table C1.2 Labour productivity growth rates in France, Italy, and the USA

Period	France	Italy	USA
1970–80	3.5	3.8	1.3
1980–90	2.8	2.3	1.3
1990–2000	1.6	1.2	1.4
(1995–2000)	1.6	1.0	2.2

Can these numbers be taken at face value? Don't these numbers reflect the fact that European countries boost labour productivity by replacing workers by machines and by setting a high minimum wage, therefore eliminating low productivity workers from the employment pool? I have looked at these two issues in a recent paper (Blanchaid and Landier, 2002). My conclusion is that, while both factors are relevant, they do not radically change the conclusions. Looking at total factor rather than labour productivity, it looks like a close race, and while the USA is probably ahead, it is not ahead by very much.

Table C1.2 gives labour productivity growth (with labour productivity defined in the same way as in Table C1.1) by decade since 1970, again for France, Italy, and the USA.

Two facts are striking. First, labour productivity growth has been substantially higher in France and Italy than in the USA since 1970. This is the good news (although it is old news, as it was already implicit in Table C1.1). Second, the gap between French or Italian productivity growth on the one hand, and US productivity growth on the other, has steadily decreased. Indeed, for the most recent period (1995–2000), it has reversed, and, while the table stops in 2000, the reversal appears to have continued so far in the 2000s. This is the bad news.

There are, however, two ways of interpreting this bad news: One is as a steady deterioration of the European performance, starting in the 1970s. The other is at the natural end of catch-up as productivity levels have converged, plus additional danger signs since the mid-1990s.

The two interpretations point to potentially different factors. Under the first, one naturally thinks of rigidities as progressively asphyxiating Europe, steadily reducing its growth since 1970. Under the second, which has my preference, the problem is more recent, dating perhaps from the mid-1990s. The slowdown in productivity growth is due to catch-up and does not reflect badly on Europe. What is worrisome is that the USA appears to have recently found a second youth, while Europe is still looking. The questions then are why, and what in particular, is the role of differences in product market regulation. This brings me to the second point.

2. THE POST-1995 POOR PERFORMANCE AND THE ROLE OF REGULATION

Much work has gone into trying to understand the divergence of productivity growth rates across the two sides of the ocean since the mid-1990s. I am a consumer, not a producer of this research. I have a lot of admiration for what has been done already, in particular that of van Ark and co-authors (2002a, 2002b). I am not sure, however, that we, as a profession, have the story tied down. The time series are short, the measurement problems gigantic. (There are also complex macro factors at work. Take the example of Spain which has had roughly zero measured total factor productivity growth since 1990. There is little question that low measured total factor productivity growth and the large unemployment decline during the same period must be related. The question is how. Is it due to the re-employment of low productivity workers—so, to measurement problems, which would disappear if we weighted workers properly? Or is it for real, with firms facing a trade-off between TFP and employment? The questions are obviously central to thinking about the future of Spain. But they are relevant for other European countries as well.)

What do we know with reasonable confidence?

We know that the GDP share of the IT producing sector, the sector with very high productivity growth, is smaller on average in Europe than in the USA (the European average hiding, however, substantial heterogeneity across countries). Does this smaller share point to problems with goods market regulation? I am not sure. To me, it points more to problems with the education system, with credit and financial markets, with the financing of R&D.

We are less sure about the role of differences in the use of IT by firms. US firms spent more on IT than their European counterparts in the 1990s, but, in retrospect, one is not sure that all that money was well spent. Case study evidence, for example from the McKinsey studies on the use of IT in specific sectors in France, Germany, and the USA (1997, 2001, 2002), does not point to major differences. In most cases, European firms appear to be just as eager, and just as able, to introduce IT as are their US counterparts.

One sector stands out as accounting for much of the difference between the US and European productivity growth since 1995: the trade sector, especially retail trade. (The other sector singled out by van Ark et al. is "securities". The problems of measurement of productivity in the financial sector seem so large in that case that I am not sure how much weight we can put on the finding.) This indeed points to a potential role of goods market rigidities: retail trade is organized very differently across the two sides of the Atlantic. Retail trade does not fall under Brussels' mandate to make goods markets more competitive, and thus has largely escaped deregulation. Many European countries still have tight national and local regulations, from restrictions on opening hours, to zoning restrictions on what can be built where. This brings me to my third point.

3. A CLOSER LOOK AT THE RETAIL TRADE SECTOR

What do the data say about differences in productivity in retail trade across countries, and do they indeed point to regulation as the culprit?

Here again, except for my participation in the McKinsey studies, I am a consumer, rather than a producer, of research. And I must admit to being a fairly confused consumer.

First, this is a case where visiting the kitchen makes you less enthusiastic about the meal. Measuring productivity in the retail trade sector is an accounting nightmare. For example: value added data are rarely available. What is typically available is gross margins, so that the cost of intermediate inputs other than the goods purchased for resale is not taken into account. The price deflator typically measures the price of goods sold (the PCE deflator), rather than the price of services provided. (As Martin Baily has reminded us, in the USA, the retail sector with the highest measured productivity growth is electronics....) When one attempts to measure total factor productivity rather than labour productivity, measuring capital is nearly impossible. Values of capital, including land at market value make capital much larger in European countries, where stores tend to be in the centre of town, and land prices are much higher. Approximating, as is often done, capital by square footage leads instead to a smaller value of capital in Europe relative to the USA (stores are smaller in Europe, largely because they are on more

Table C1.3 Productivity levels and growth rates in retail in Europe and the United States

	FRA	DEU	UK	USA	EU
Labour productivity growth					
van Ark 1990–95 (%)	1.3	0.2	2.6	2.3	1.1
van Ark 1995–2000	0.9	−0.2	3.5	6.9	1.4
Labour productivity					
O'Mahony 1999	98	78	61	100*	
McKinsey 2000	98	90		100*	
Food retail (McKinsey)					
Modern segment	107	86		100*	
Traditional segment	77	70		48	
Share of modern	60%	81%		92%	
Δ share trad 80–95	−23%	−17%		−9%	

Note: * 100 by normalization.

expensive real estate). And using square footage does not seem promising if one of the goals of a study is to find the effects of IT capital on productivity in the sector.

With these caveats duly registered, Table C1.3 gives the numbers I have been able to collect for labour productivity levels and growth rates in the retail trade sector for a number of European countries (in this case, I could not get numbers for Italy), and for the USA.

I draw three conclusions from the table.

The first two lines, coming from the work of van Ark *et al.*, give the numbers for labour productivity growth since 1990. They show much higher labour productivity growth in retail trade in the USA than in Europe since the mid-1900s—6.9 per cent versus 1.4 per cent. The American "Wal-Mart" miracle, documented by McKinsey (2001), does not appear to have had a European counterpart.

It is this pair of numbers which has led many to blame goods market rigidities in Europe: what Wal-Mart could do, European retailers would not or could not do.

The next two lines do not quite fit this simple theme however. They give labour productivity levels, from studies by O'Mahony et de Boer (2002) and McKinsey (2002). Both studies suggest roughly similar levels of productivity for France and the United States—surely not what the simple rigidities story would suggest. The laggard appears to be the UK, a country relatively unregulated relative to its continental European counterparts! This again is not good news for the rigidities thesis. (A side, but relevant, remark. I have a hard time getting a sense of the UK productivity level or growth rate in retail trade. The numbers on UK productivity growth in the

Comments

retail trade sector from van Ark in line 2 of Table C1.3—which are the numbers cited in Part I by Faini *et al.*—are high. But the numbers constructed by Basu *et al.* (2003) are extremely low, indeed negative for the second half of the 1990s. I could not trace the difference in findings.)

The last two lines of the table try to get at what lies behind the surprisingly similar levels of productivity in France and the USA. They are taken from the McKinsey study of *food retail* in France, Germany, and the USA (2002). The study measures productivity levels separately for the modern and the traditional segment, and this leads to an interesting conclusion. For *both* the modern and the traditional segment, productivity is higher in France than in the USA! The last two lines of the table show why this does not translate into a higher average productivity level in France: the share of the modern sector is much smaller in France than in the USA.

Let me again insist on the fact that all these numbers must be taken with more than a grain of salt. But, such as it is, the picture which emerges is interesting: format by format, retailers are as efficient or even more efficient in France than in the USA. But the various policies put in place in France to protect small businesses in the centre of towns lead to a larger share of small retailers, and thus a productivity level which is lower than it could be. Are these policies justified? Their design is often mediocre, and sometimes counterproductive. But their goal, keeping the centre of cities alive, can surely not be rejected a priori.

4. DEREGULATION AND PRODUCTIVITY GROWTH

Whether Europe is or is not behind the USA, it is still the case that deregulation—or, for most of the sectors this study is looking at, better regulation—would allow for substantial improvements in productivity.

This is indeed the credo of most economists. It is also the conclusion of the sectoral studies summarized in the report by Faini *et al.* One may wonder whether the correlations prove causality. My impression from the McKinsey studies—which go into the entrails of particular sectors, and often allow the tracing of the specific effects of deregulation more convincingly—is that they do. I shall add three examples to the discussion given in part I, all from services, and all taken from McKinsey (2002):

The first is mobile telephony. Labour productivity today is about twice as high in France as it is in the USA. The main reason appears to be simple, but perhaps surprising: good regulation, which has limited the numbers of mobile operators in France relative to the USA, and allowed for economies of scale while maintaining a high degree of competition.

The second is road freight. One of the characteristics of road freight is that the technology is simple, and inputs and outputs relatively easy to measure. This makes it easy to link productivity growth to specific actions (load rate for trucks, truck size), and in turn specific actions to regulation. There, the story is one of large increases in productivity in road freight in France in the 1990s. And most of the increases can be directly traced back to deregulation—the development of the European internal market, the elimination of restrictions on foreign carriers, and other national reforms.

The third is an example *a contrario*. France often boasts of the efficiency of its electricity generation and distribution system. Indeed, labour productivity was slightly higher in France than in the USA in the early 1990s. Since then, however, productivity growth has been lower in France than in the USA, and France now appears to be slightly behind. Why? One factor—admittedly only one—is the considerable pressure from the French government on EDF to hire approximately 10,000 employees over the period. *Stricto sensu*, this example points more to the dangers of state ownership than of regulation; but the two are closely linked.

5. DEREGULATION AND EMPLOYMENT

Another big issue studied in Part I is the effect of deregulation on employment. It is useful here to take a short theoretical detour.

At the aggregate level, deregulation is likely to be good for employment. Deregulation increases productivity. The macro evidence is that such increases in productivity decrease unemployment for a while, if not for ever. Deregulation decreases monopoly power and thus decreases prices given wages. Put another way, deregulation increases real wages effectively paid by firms. This is also likely to decrease unemployment, at least for some time.

These are, however, aggregate effects. At the level of the sector being deregulated, the effect of deregulation on employment is definitely ambiguous. Higher productivity leads to a decrease in employment for a given level of output. Lower prices, induced either by higher productivity or/and by reduced monopoly power, lead to an increase in demand and thus an increase in output. Which effect dominates is ambiguous.

The conclusion of Part I is that, in most of the cases studied, sectoral employment decreases. This again fits with the sectoral evidence from the McKinsey studies. One of the main effects of deregulation is a decrease in X-inefficiency. In the short run, this almost always means lay-offs. In the longer run, higher productivity could lead to higher output and higher employment; in fact, I have not yet seen a sectoral study in which employment recovers or more than recovers. (Employment has obviously increased in telecommunications in the 1990s. But how much is due to deregulation, how much is due to the introduction of new products, indeed how many of the new products introduced have been introduced because deregulation made it possible, is hard to establish.)

The conclusion that deregulation, even if it increases employment at the aggregate level, is more likely to decrease than increase employment in the sector being deregulated, is an important one, one that politicians are unlikely to ignore. This takes me to my last point.

6. DEREGULATION AND LABOUR MARKET REFORMS

Europe needs reforms not only in the goods market, but also, and perhaps more so, in the labour market. This raises the issue of the interactions between the two. This is something I have explored in a paper with Francesco Giavazzi (2003). Let me just state what I see as the relevant conclusions in the present context.

Deregulation lowers monopoly rents for firms; it also leads to higher entry and exit, to higher reallocation. Both changes put pressure on a number of labour market institutions. If workers try to extract the same level of rents, or keep the same level of employment protection for example, some firms are likely to go bankrupt.

However, deregulation is likely to weaken unions. To the extent that unions are about transferring some of the monopoly rents to workers, smaller rents means a smaller scope for transfer of rents to the workers, weaker unions. Why join a union if there are no rents to appropriate in the first place? Faced with this problem, unions may either retreat to the sectors protected from deregulation (e.g. the public sector) and continue to fight for rents there. Or they can modify their strategy, for example by actively participating in and influencing the reform process. Some unions choose the first route, some the second.

The optimistic scenario is then one in which the pressure from deregulation on labour market institutions, together with either weaker or reformed unions, leads to reforms in the labour market. The pessimistic scenario is one in which labour market institutions are adjusted too slowly in response to changes in the goods market, squeezing firms' profits, and potentially leading to bankruptcies. (The two scenarios are played out in the airline industry.) We are likely to see a mix of both scenarios played out in Europe over the coming decade.

References

Basu, S., Fernald, J., Oulton, N., and Srinivasan, S. (2003), "The Case of the Missing Productivity Growth: Or, does Information Technology Explain Why Productivity Accelerated in the United States but Not in the United Kingdom?" *NBER Macroeconomics Annual 2003*, Cambridge, Mass.: MIT Press, 9–63.

Blanchard, O. (2004), "The Economic Future of Europe", *Journal of Economic Perspectives*, 18(4) Fall 3–26.

—— and Giavazzi, F. (2003), "Macroeconomic Effects of Regulation and Deregulation in Goods and Labor Markets", *Quarterly Journal of Economics*, 118(3) Aug. 879–909.

—— and Landier, A. (2002), "The Perverse Effects of Partial Labor Market Reform: Fixed Duration Contracts in France", *Economic Journal*, 112 (June), pp. F214–44.

McKinsey Global Institute (1997), *France and Germany*.

—— (2001), *U.S. Productivity Growth, 1995–2000*, Washington, DC., Oct.

—— (2002), *Reaching High Productivity Growth in France and Germany*, Oct.

O'Mahony, M., and de Boer, W. (2002), "Britain's Relative Productivity Performance: Updates to 1999", London: National Institute of Economic and Social Research, Mar.

van Ark, B., Melka, J., Mulder, N., Timmer, M., and Ypma, G. (2002*a*), "ICT Investment and Growth Accounts for the European Union, 1980–2000", Report to the European Commission, Sept.

—— Inklaar, Robert, and McGuckin, Robert (2002*b*), "Changing Gear: Productivity, ICT Investment and Service Industries: Europe and the United States", Groningen Growth and Development Centre, Research Memorandum GD-60, Dec.

Jan Svejnar

The authors have produced a very informative and interesting study. They tackle important issues and carry out innovative analysis combining case studies with econometric analysis. They use data that have particular strengths but also some limitations, and their results are credible but with some unusual twists.

The starting point of the analysis is the idea that Europe started the twenty-first century with good macroeconomic conditions and high expectations for growth, but that these expectations were unfortunately too optimistic. According to the data cited by the authors, Europe has recently been characterized by stagnant productivity growth, erosion of its exports market share, and increasingly limited ability to attract FDI. In this context, the authors explore the question of whether product market reforms boost productivity and other structural changes (e.g. in labour markets). In particular, they ask whether product market reforms are related to Europe's poor growth and productivity record. They focus on product markets since labour markets have already received attention, and within the product markets they emphasize the importance of reforms in the tertiary sector, as they see this as being the unfinished agenda.

In the analytical section, the study first takes stock of reforms in key services. It provides in-depth case studies of Germany, Italy, and the UK, and examines network industries as well as the trade sector and professional services. It assesses the direct and indirect effects of the tertiary sector on the whole economy.

The first key finding is that deregulation of services leads to productivity growth in the service sector and the economy as a whole. The important caveat is that these improvements are not evident in the data in the short run and that the strength of these results varies across sectors (e.g. telecoms v. railways or water). The second major finding is that services constitute a key input for the economy as a whole and are a major determinant of the economy's competitiveness. Yet, services are not very tradable and rigidities in their supply discourage FDI.

The results are based on two types of data. First, as mentioned above, the authors provide substantive case-study information from Germany, Italy, and the UK. This case-study analysis is based on in-depth information gathering and is quite all-encompassing.

Second, the authors carry out an econometric analysis of the determinants of performance, using the change in the growth of labour productivity (Δglp) and the change in the share of workers working in foreign affiliates of multinationals ($\Delta mner$) in 24 non-service industries as their dependent variables. The *glp* data cover the period 1994–9, while the *mner* data are for *1997–9*. The principal explanatory variables are three quantitative indicators of service sector regulations: R^{NET}—an index based on the OECD index of regulation of individual network services and the input–output (I–O) linkage of a given service sector to a given industry, R^{BA}—country dummies (for regulation of business activities) combined with the average I–O linkage of a given service sector to a given industry across the three countries, and R^{NET+BA}—the strictest level of regulation for network industries taken as the level of regulation of business services (similar to R^{NET}).

I have two points with respect to the use of R^{NET}. First, for policy purposes it would be informative if one separated the index of regulation from the weight of a given service in a given industry and entered them as separate regressors. This would enable the reader to assess the extent to which it is the regulation or the value of the input–output linkage that matters. Second, it would be useful to discuss in more detail the composition of the OECD index and report estimates from regressions using the individual components of the index, rather than the index itself, as explanatory variables. The regression coefficients from this specification would provide the implicit weights and knowing the effects (weights) of individual components of the index would allow one to use the results more readily for formulating appropriate policy recommendations. As to R^{BA}, these weighted country dummies are equivalent to including weighted country-specific effects in the regression. This is a clever approach but note that R^{BA} but could also be capturing other effects than regulation of business.

The econometric strategy consists of running a simple partial adjustment model with *R*s and sectoral fixed effects as the explanatory variables and using the change in *glp* and in *mner* as the dependent variables. The authors use one long-difference observation per industry (i.e. a cross-section of differences) and estimate the equations by ordinary least squares (OLS).

The issues that arise with respect to this methodology are the following: the model is very parsimonious, raising the issue that there may be other important explanatory variables that are absent, thus potentially giving rise to an omitted variable bias. Sectoral dummies (if finely defined) could capture other effects and control for time-invariant endogeneity (selection) issues. The long-differencing approach reduces severely the number of observations. One could alleviate this problem (and increase the number of observations) by using data from the early 1990s and early 2000s. Finally, while the authors examine the effects of R on the change in *mner*, it would be also of interest to look at the effects of R on the level of *mner*.

The results of the econometric analysis suggest that in the 1990s R^{NET} and R^{NET+BA} had negative effects on the growth of *glp* and *mner* and that *glp* and *mner* increased in the UK (the less regulated economy as opposed to the more regulated economies of Germany and Italy). These findings provide support for the hypotheses advanced in the study and they are consistent with the case-study information. Given the methodology, the major outstanding question is whether there are other (omitted) factors that could be bringing about these results.

Overall, this is an important study that yields interesting, albeit somewhat tentative, empirical evidence and identifies a key area for policy work. I see two fruitful extensions in future research. One is to re-estimate a fuller model with more data. The other is to use the I–O analysis to identify other sectors of the economy that have strong forward linkages and where policies could improve the efficiency of the whole economy.

It is also of interest to consider what other factors may be keeping Europe back. My assessment is that they relate to limited entrepreneurship and venture capital, investment in and organization of research and development (R&D), deployment of human capital, and leadership as well as perception of leadership (see also Svejnar, 2004; Basu *et al.*, 2005). Let me briefly consider each of these factors.

The relatively limited emphasis on entrepreneurship and venture capital dates from the technology-driven financial bubble of the mid-to-late 1990s. In the USA, the bubble translated into abundance of venture capital, which in turn resulted in more risk-taking, invention, and innovation. In Europe, the system generated less venture capital and resulted in less entrepreneurship. The stronger tradition in Europe of becoming an employee rather than an entrepreneur probably also played a part.

The R&D issue is complicated because in some areas, such as GSM (global system for mobile communication) technology, Europe has been the leader. However, on average, firms in Europe have been doing less research than those in the USA and Japan. Some innovations (e.g. in biotech) have been restricted by Europe's own policies. In other areas (e.g. information technology) Europe is widely viewed as being behind in both production and use of the sector's products. Finally, Europe is known to be slower in transferring scientific results into applications.

The human capital challenge is in part related to R&D and it has several components. First, there is the brain drain from Europe to the USA. While there are flows in both directions, the net flow is from Europe to America and on many measures it is the best people who move. The second aspect is arguably an insufficient allocation of the best human capital to producing new knowledge. This is sometimes captured by the phrase, "the best minds prefer to be bankers rather than scientists". While this is true, it is to be noted that the same problem arises in America. Where the two regions differ is that the USA has developed a system whereby there is a sizeable group of first-generation Americans (immigrants) who enter and stay in the US scientific establishment. Finally, Europe has a much more acute medium-term problem of an aging population, which means that an increasingly small share of the population has and deploys productively their human capital. Naturally, the impact of all these factors is magnified by the existence of human capital externalities (spillovers).

Finally, on a more speculative level, there is the issue of Europe's leadership and perception of leadership. It stems from the observation that in many areas the timing of US economic activities leads the rest of the world, including Europe. This is observed with respect to economic growth, business cycles, and even the daily price movements on the stock markets. Given that Europe and the USA are similar sized economies, the question naturally arises as to why the European economy does not take more of a lead—why, for instance, it does not become the engine of world growth in periods when the US economy slows down. Part of the answer lies in real US leadership, stemming from the fact that it has historically represented the concentration and diffusion of major innovations and has a greater homogeneity of policies and economic activity across regions. However, part of the problem is that Europe does not project the image of leadership and influence to the same extent as the USA. This in turn forms global perceptions and expectations of Europe as being a follower rather than a leader relative to the USA.

The factors identified in the present and past volumes provide valuable guidance for European policy-makers. Having eliminated most of the obvious inefficiencies, the US economy is operating near its potential, thus being forced to advance through innovations rather than a combination of innovations and elimination of gross inefficiencies. Europe, in contrast, still has tremendous unexploited possibilities. It is the largest free-trade zone in the world, has a single currency, and is increasingly able to act as a unified economic power. Properly designed policies could indeed help the European economy to advance substantially towards or ahead of the USA. The question is whether Europe is ready to realize this potential.

References

Basu, S., Estrin, S., and Svejnar, J. (2005), "Employment Determination in Enterprises under Communism and in Transition: Evidence from Central Europe", *Industrial and Labor Relations Review*, 58(3), 353–69.

Svejnar, J. (2004), "Can We Turn Europe's Differences to Business Advantage? Europe Poised to Move Up a Geas", *European Business Forum*, 17, 7–10.

Part II
HOW TO GAIN POLITICAL SUPPORT FOR REFORMS

Micael Castanheira, Vincenzo Galasso, Stéphane Carcillo, Giuseppe Nicoletti, Enrico Perotti, and Lidia Tsyganok

7
Introduction

Since the 1980s, when the Thatcher government initiated a programme of massive privatizations and liberalizations, many OECD countries have gone through a large number of structural reforms in crucial sectors of the economy, such as labour and product markets, and the welfare state. This flurry of reforms demonstrates the rise of a new paradigm among economists, often referred to as the "Washington consensus".[1] Most of these reforms aim at liberalizing the financial and product markets; reducing rigidity in the labour market; retrenching the welfare state; and decreasing the government's involvement in production, through privatizations. Yet, while some attempts were highly successful and led to structural changes in the economy, other reform plans failed to receive the necessary political support.

Indeed, some deep reform measures leading to the liberalization of relevant markets were initially implemented, but later overturned—casting some doubt on their economic efficiency or rather on the stability of their political support. Here, we refrain from addressing the economic efficiency of the reforms, which has instead been analysed in the Part I for the case of product markets, although we do acknowledge that in a second-best world, some of these reforms may actually fail to be beneficial.

We concentrate on the political feasibility of these reforms, in an attempt to provide some policy advice on how to push forward with structural reforms. Reforms may occur in a variety of economic environments; may have different impacts on economic agents; may take place

---

[1] A notable example of this consensus is represented by the effort made by the World Bank to set the stage for the reform of pension systems in Latin America (see World Bank, 1994); interestingly, a recent World Bank publication (see World Bank, 1994); interestingly, a recent World Bank Publication (see Holzmann and Hinz, 2005) integrated the previous suggestions with new considerations aimed at emphasizing also the role of public provision in retirement income.

under several political institutions; and may be implemented by policy-makers with different political strength. This variety of situations does not allow for a unique, one-fits-all reform strategy. Our analysis is hence based on a case-study approach, which emphasizes the crucial role of economic and political framework conditions. In particular, we consider different reform scenarios. Each scenario identifies some relevant economic aspects, such as the structure of the markets or welfare systems to be reformed, and political elements, such as the relative political strength of the policy-makers. These economic aspects characterize the nature of the opposition to a reform plan. Far-reaching reforms may trigger wide opposition within the population;[2] but narrower reforms that affect less extended yet entrenched interests may also prove equally unpopular, and thus difficult to pass. Some political and institutional (as well as cultural and social) features of the countries instead characterize the relative political strength of the policy-makers—and hence their ability to push forward with reforms—but also how the opposition to reform may materialize—for instance, whether through the threat of electoral back-lashes or though lobbying and strikes.

Our case studies include a broad array of economic areas—such as labour and product markets, the welfare state, and privatizations—and of political institutions, ranging from majority systems, such as the UK, to proportional systems and consensus democracies, such as Denmark, to hybrid systems (Italy), and to new democracies (Russia and the Czech Republic). Although this methodological approach may fail to identify universal "laws", we are confident that the wide range of economic and political framework conditions analysed in our case study will allow us to draw some common lessons on how to design politically feasible reforms. The recipes for reform emerging from this report will hence depend on the overall economic and political scenario, as characterized in particular by the relevant economic and political players and their—often opposing—interests; by the initial structure of the markets to be reformed; by the political institutions in place; by the (electoral) incentives of the policy-makers; and by the existence of external constraints. Table 7.1 provides a classification of our case studies according to a simple economic and political dichotomy: as the relevant economic feature we identify the extent of the interests affected by a reform—whether broad or narrow—while the crucial political feature is represented by the relative political strength of the policy-makers.

---

[2] Economic efficiency clearly plays a role in this discussion by helping to define the size of the opposition.

Introduction

Table 7.1 A simple typology of reforms

		Political features	
		Strong policy-maker	Weak policy-maker
Economic impact of the reform	Broad	Pensions (UK, Italy, France)	Pension (Italy)
		Privatization (Russia)	Labour market (Denmark) Privatization (Eastern Europe)
	Narrow	Privatization (UK)	Telecom (Italy, France) Labour Market (Spain) FDI (various countries)

Our theoretical framework of analysis is deeply rooted in the recent political economy literature of reform (see Chapter 8). Through the analysis of different scenarios, we examine the preferences and interests of economic *actors*—such as consumers, workers, firms, unions, and retirees—and their key role in shaping the economic response to a reform; the economic *rents*, which capture the gains from reforming, as well as the intensity of the opposition to these measures; and the *political institutions*, that is, the rules regulating the economic and political interactions among these different agents.

A common denominator to *all* the reform processes analysed here is that the policy-makers have to undergo two important stages which determine the success or failure of the reform: a *commitment building* stage, and a *coalition building* stage. Interestingly, our case studies show that governments adopted different strategies during these two stages, depending on a set of economic and political framework conditions. For each reform experience, we identify the crucial components that explain why commitment and coalition building were a success or a failure. Our hope is that, by describing a relatively large set of reforms, and by categorizing them along these "strategies", we can provide some guidance to the "reformers" in different scenarios. The case studies we provide may help them understand how they could use their political strength, the benefits associated with the reform plan (or the information they have about these benefits) to carry out the reform successfully.

Why do policy-makers decide to undertake a reform process and hence to commit their political capital to its implementation? The seminal reasons behind a reform vary widely across reforms, countries, and sectors and, therefore, so do the policy-makers' initial motivations. Beside the ideological push for reform—coinciding with the Washington consensus—demands to implement structural reforms in a given market often originate from technical progress and globalization. Substantial reductions in scale economies, the introduction of new technologies, and increased international competition (e.g. in transport and energy industries) create new opportunities to provide services. They reduce barriers to entry, and make users realize that there are costs to keeping some markets highly regulated. Supranational legal constraints—for instance related to trade agreements, to IMF conditionality loans, or to the Maastricht Treaty—have also constituted powerful triggers for structural reforms (see Chapter 8).

Yet, policy-makers often need to build a large political and social consensus around their reform plan. How could they achieve this crucial support, which eventually determines the political success or failure of a reform attempt? Again, the successful strategy depends largely on the economic sector expected to experience the changes, and on the political institutions of the country where the reform is debated. In our case studies, we identify both the common and specific elements of successful reform processes, and we compare these successes to situations that led to failure. For instance, we observe cases in which the choice of an appropriate "strategy" was the essential driver of success. Yet, simply mimicking a strategy that proved successful under a given scenario may easily feed failure under a different set of framework conditions. It is thus important to provide broad-ranging evidence of the different "recipes for reform" that were used under different scenarios. In fact, one of the important lessons of our exercise is that no "one-size-fits-all" policy recommendation can be drawn.

Despite significant diversity in the reform experiences we cover, some lessons can be drawn about the reform strategy to use, given the market to be reformed and the country's political institutions. For instance, our analysis of the reforms that affect the population at large, such as the labour market and the welfare state, illustrates that clearly defined groups with vested interests—namely, insiders for the labour market, and retirees for the welfare state—emerged in opposing the reform measures. In consensus democracies—such as Denmark, Italy, and, to a lesser extent, Spain—the packaging and the pace of reforms had to be targeted so as to circumvent opposition; to buy approval by the lobbies and unions that represent the interests of these groups. Long transition periods, which effectively sheltered middle-aged workers and retirees from the effects of pension reforms, were engineered in the Italian pension reforms. Gradual, piecemeal, labour market reforms were implemented in Spain, to reduce

Introduction

their impact on tenured workers. On these occasions, the reform process was rather gradual (and thus slow) but, having built a large public consensus, these governments had secured wide political support for their reforms, and hence reduced the risk of reversal. The experience proved different in the UK, partly due to the existence of a different system of political representation. Under the majoritarian representation rule, governments typically face less resistance—or they can circumvent it more easily. Therefore, reforms can be more sudden and radical, as shown by the Thatcher experience in the UK, which included the 1986 pension reform and the privatization of several major state-owned enterprises. These reform measures clearly hurt some on the fringes of the population but were ultimately used by the Conservative government of Mrs Thatcher to build additional support for the Tories among the upper and upper-middle classes of the population. Yet, the lack of popular consensus, together with genuine questions about the efficiency of these reforms, led to subsequent reversals, as with the case of Blair's 1999 pension reform.

In the *product market*, the approach of the government has to be somehow different. In this market, interest groups are less clearly divided along ideological party lines. Vested interests cross the left–right, worker–employer division lines, and develop converging incentives. Workers and employers, blue and white collar, bureaucrats and consumers, tend to join forces in many non-manufacturing industries. In these markets, almost independently of the political strength of the policy-maker, successful reformers appear to have generally followed a "divide and conquer" strategy: targeted changes to existing regulations led to the division of vested interests. However, to achieve these ends, the pace of reform ought to be slow; it must create the conditions for a smooth and continuous reform process rather than appeal to a big-bang reform. Sometimes, this process also calls for reforms in other markets. Our analysis suggests that reforms in one market—for instance, the product market—may well spill over to other markets—such as the labour market—both by creating political momentum and by modifying background economic conditions.

We also cover some reform experiences in transition economies. The contrast between the conditions faced by their governments can be more starkly contrasted, and additional lessons can also be drawn for OECD countries. External constraints played a more prominent role in these countries, since most reforms were inescapable. Moreover, transition countries had to establish simultaneously the role of economic and political governance. We review some of the mass privatization programmes that took place there, and show that many were precisely designed to target *political* motives. The role of political governance and external constraints was crucial in the privatization of the main Czech and Ukrainian car makers. Our case studies clearly illustrate that, while the prospect of future EU membership allowed the Czech government to commit to an efficient privatization plan, the excessive freedom of action of the Ukrainian government led to the protection of particular lobby groups and politicians, at the expense of economic efficiency and, ultimately, of the population at large.

The typology of reform experiences analysed here is thus extremely large and varied. Policy-makers must be aware of the wealth of strategies used by their fellow reformers, and take stock of what made some reform attempts successful while others failed. This report highlights the most salient features of several reform processes according to their different economic and political scenarios and discusses some useful "recipes" for reform. Chapter 8 provides broad-brush evidence of the pace of reform over time, across countries and sectors, and reviews some major theoretical elements of the political economics literature of reforms. Then, each of the following chapters investigates a specific scenario and an associated strategy.

In Chapter 9, we concentrate on the reform opportunities that emerge when a government *exploits its parliamentary majority*. Classical examples of this situation are the privatizations and pension reforms carried out in the UK by the Thatcher government. When backed by a large parliamentary majority, the policy-makers' only constraint is typically the need to win a future election, which provides ample freedom of action in most cases. Yet, this strategy is not always valuable. The desire to rely exclusively on a parliamentary majority was probably the cause of failure in many other reform attempts—such as Berlusconi's 1994 pension reform plan in Italy, Juppé's 1995 labour market reform in France, and Rasmussen's 2001 labour market reform in Denmark. This mix of successes and failures suggests that other institutional elements are crucial, such as the (lack of) internal cohesion in coalition governments or the existence of strong opposition. A strong parliamentary majority can thus be boldly insufficient to generate sufficient coalition building.

Chapter 10 discusses an alternate strategy that policy-makers tend to use when they do not enjoy sufficiently strong political power, and when they address reforms in broad-reaching sectors that affect a large fraction of the population. In the absence of a large parliamentary majority or in the presence of strong opposition in the economic or social arena, policy-makers *widen the political base* for their reform, by

Introduction

resorting to social dialogue and to a more consensual style. The need to gather wider social and political support induces policy-makers to increase the share of winners from the reform, while raising expenses for the losers. Examples of this strategy are the postponed implementation of the *measures to future generations* in the 1992 and 1995 Italian pension reforms, and the adoption of consensual measures in the Danish labour market.

In Chapter 11, we consider instances in which widening the political base for reform may still be desirable, but is practically unfeasible. This economic scenario typically emerges when the benefits from reform are dispersed among many economic agents, postponed to future generations and perhaps highly uncertain—as, for example, with the liberalization of a "strategic", traditionally highly regulated market—whereas costs are highly visible and relatively concentrated. Since buying out the opposition of vested interests is too costly or would largely limit the scope for reform, policy-makers must resort to a different strategy. The recipe adopted by successful policy-makers—particularly when liberalizing non-manufacturing industries—is to *"divide and conquer"*. This strategy aims at disentangling entrenched vested interests by concentrating the costs of the reform on particular groups. Successful adoption of this recipe includes the privatization of Telecom Italia, which had already been corporatized and had offered private contracts to its employees; and can be contrasted with the experience of France Telecom. Often this *"divide and conquer"* strategy calls for a reform to be initiated gradually, that is, in one particular market or sector to start with. Then, the effects of this first step can trickle-down to other markets over time, as the rents appropriated on these markets are reduced. Examples of such trickle-down effects include the Spanish labour market reform of the 1980s that—by liberalizing temporary contracts—induced a reduction in the relevance of permanent contracts and eventually made the reforms of the 1990s possible.

Chapter 12 takes a different angle on policy-making by recognizing that several successful reforms were actually implemented under the tight pressure of *external constraints*. Although strong governments may prefer to be free to select their reform options (see Chapter 9), governments facing strong opposition may need to rely on external constraints to increase their bargaining power in the coalition building phase and to limit the opposition of lobby groups. The recipe provided in this chapter is hence to *exploit* external constraints, such as those imposed by World Trade Organization (WTO) rules, the Stability Pact, or International Monetary Fund (IMF) conditionality rules. Recent economic history

How to Gain Political Support for Reforms

provides several successful examples of how external constraints imposed by EU laws or treaties increased the pace of structural reforms in Europe. Yet, Chapter 12 essentially concentrates on the reform experience of two transition countries—the Czech Republic and Ukraine—and of their major national car producers—Škoda and AvtoZAZ—to highlight the role of commitment to reform provided by a truly external constraint; in this case, the external anchor of the European Union.

8
Evidence and Theory of Reforms

8.1. Evidence about the reform momentum

During the last 30 years, OECD countries have experienced a large number of structural reforms in several crucial sectors of the economy. To gain some perspective over the magnitude of this process, we can look at the reforms implemented in non-manufacturing industries over the past decades. We use a data set that concerns reforms in seven non-manufacturing industries for 21 OECD countries over the period 1975–98: air transport, road freight, rail transport, telecommunications, postal services, electricity and gas supply. The main reforms include privatization, liberalization of access to potentially competitive markets, restructuring of vertically integrated industries, and the elimination of price controls in competitively supplied services. Regulatory tightness has conventionally been measured using a decreasing scale, such that a "6" denotes the most restrictive competition and private governance, and a "0" denotes the least restrictive conditions. Structural reforms thus induce a move along this 6–0 scale. Summarizing reforms in this way is convenient for providing a broad-brush historical view of developments in different (OECD) countries and industries as well as for analyzing reform patterns quantitatively.

Product market reform has a long history in OECD countries, beginning with trade liberalization (an unfinished business) and continuing with the liberalization of international financial flows. Besides these *external* changes, the past 30 years have also witnessed a concerted movement of *domestic* structural policies towards increased reliance on markets. However, in many cases, moving from abstract statements in favour of competition to the actual implementation of liberalization and competition policies proved difficult, especially in non-manufacturing industries.

How to Gain Political Support for Reforms

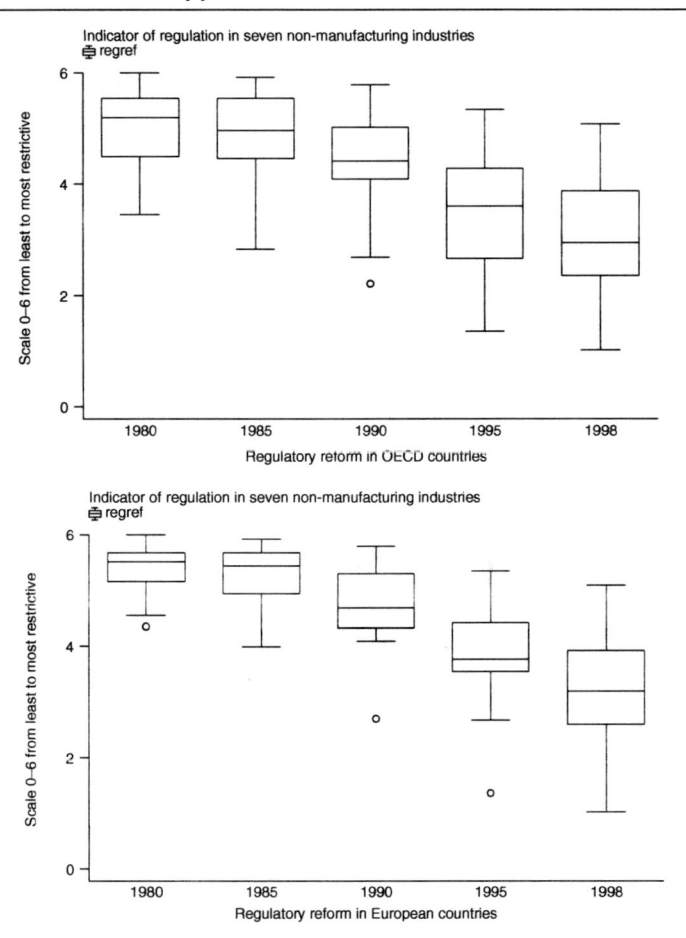

Fig. 8.1 Regulatory reforms
Source: Nicoletti (2006).

Figure 8.1 suggests that, on average, reform policies have succeeded in lowering regulations that restrict competition and private governance in the OECD area. However, the regulatory environment still displays significant cross-country variance. Compare, for instance, Greece, Switzerland, and Italy, where regulation has barely changed, and the UK, New Zealand, United States, or Australia, where extensive reforms have been implemented in all industries (Fig. 8.2). Strikingly, at least over this period, dispersion is more accentuated among European countries, despite efforts at harmonization through the so-called Single Market Programme.

Looking at the extent of reforms across industries, Figure 8.3 shows that in some sectors—such as road freight, air transport, and

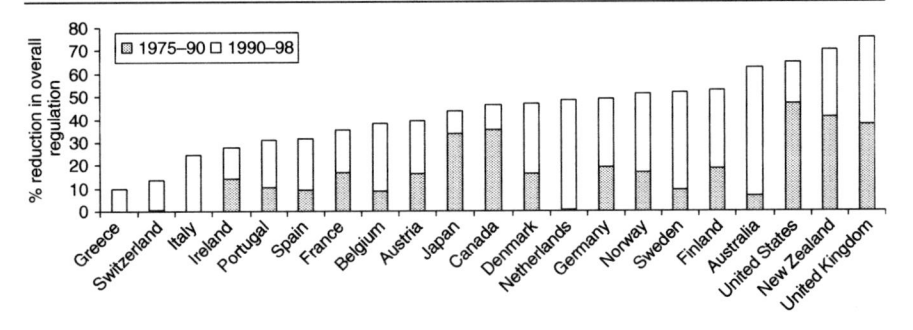

Fig. 8.2 Who reformed, and when?
Source: Nicoletti (2006).

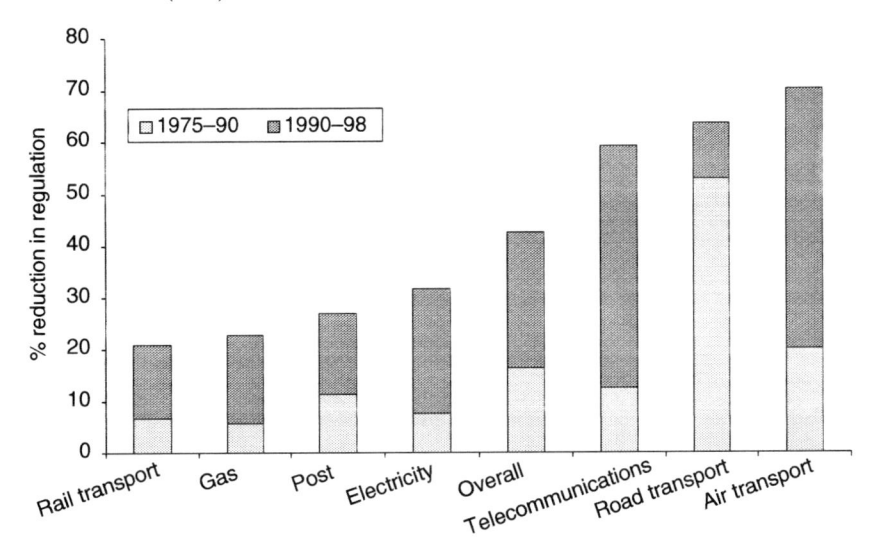

Fig. 8.3 The timing and scope of industry-level reforms
Source: Nicoletti (2006).

telecommunications—regulation was completely overhauled. In others—such as gas, postal services, and rail transport—reforms were minor.

The timing of reforms differs widely across countries, with the USA, UK, New Zealand, Canada, and Japan beginning their reforms in the early 1980s, while the Netherlands, Australia, and Sweden only began reforming in the second half of the 1990s (Fig. 8.2). The timing of reforms also differs significantly across industries. Industries where reforms were implemented early include road freight and, to a different degree, air transport. In the other industries, reforms were implemented much later, if at all (Fig. 8.3). Industries least affected by natural monopoly elements were liberalized first and more extensively. This is indeed where the fewest complexities are likely to arise after liberalization, the need of re-regulation appears to be minor, and the benefits seem most clear-cut.

Alongside these deregulation and liberalization trends, other reform measures went in the opposite direction. For instance, while the welfare state was (at least partially) retrenched in several countries (e.g. Italy and the UK), its generosity increased in Spain. Similarly, while some markets are liberalized, others become increasingly regulated. For instance, the labour market witnessed increased waves of regulation for some categories of workers, and the level of unemployment benefits was increased on several occasions.

Although this ambivalent approach may appear contradictory, many of these measures may actually have been introduced as compensating measures; to obtain public support for the former reforms, through a *quid pro quo* exchange. This has been the case particularly in the labour market where, to gain popular support for their reforms, governments have had to implement countervailing measures targeted at possible veto players, such as the unions. Figure 8.4 provides a striking illustration of this attempt at compensating specific groups: governments that increased flexibility in the labour market also implemented measures that partially undid their main reforms (note that disaggregating the data country by country would provide the same evidence).

A similar pattern can be observed for pensions. Before 1997, euro-area countries were also intensifying the process of pension reform. However,

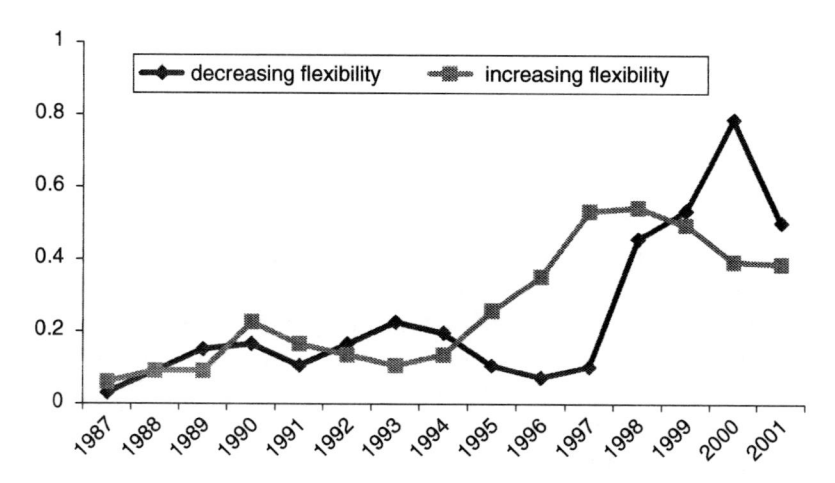

Fig. 8.4 Employment protective legislation: number of reforms
Source: Bertola and Boeri (2004).

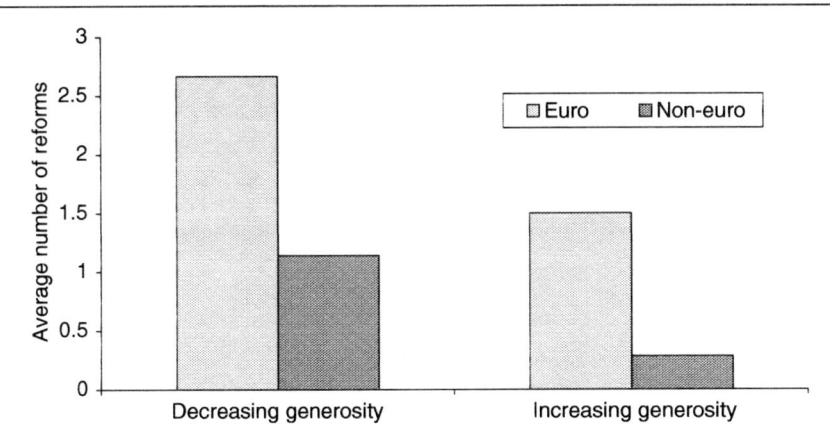

Fig. 8.5 Marginal pension reforms, 1985–1996
Source: Bertola and Boeri (2004).

despite this intensity, reforms were never unidirectional. As shown in Figure 8.5, over the 1985–96 sub-period, there were as many attempts to curtail the benefits of state pensions, as there were presents being made through increases in generosity.

Interestingly, after 1997, euro-area countries sharply accelerated the pace of their reforms, in the direction of decreasing the generosity of their systems. This evidence is in line with the argument of Bertola and Boeri (2004): the increased degree of competition among euro countries may lie at the core of the accelerated pace of reforms in these countries. Their argument is simple and powerful: the higher is international mobility, the more salient the weaknesses of a given country become. Therefore, to avoid a massive outflow of firms, these countries are forced into an accelerated pace of reforms (see also Chapter 12 for more detail about the effects of external constraints on the government's capacity to reform).

Summing up, governments who want to implement reforms in one direction may have to take countervailing steps, to gain support from specific groups. Next, international competition may help accelerate the pace of reforms. Taken together, these two arguments suggest that, although the reform process accelerated noticeably throughout the 1990s, the political constraints faced by some countries may have prevented them from deeply affecting the way in which their markets operate. Some "protected" markets were left virtually untouched; and some reform efforts turned out to be simply unsuccessful, as some reform attempts were blocked due to the strong opposition of some crucial economic, social,

How to Gain Political Support for Reforms

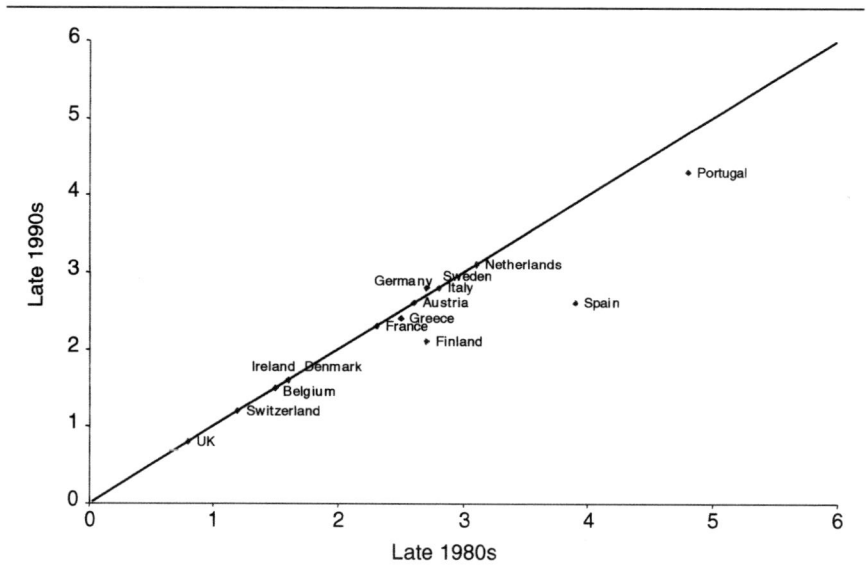

Fig. 8.6 Changes in the degree of EPL, 1980s and 1990s
Source: OECD, Employment Outlook.

and/or political forces. Exceptions, if any are found in countries that faced more strenuous external constraints.

Figure 8.6 confirms this intuition. This figure uses another indicator, also developed by the OECD, that describes the degree of regulation of labour markets. Similar to the index developed for product market regulation, low values of the index indicate highly liberalized markets, whereas a value closer to 6 indicates a highly regulated market. Along the horizontal (vertical) axis, one can read the value of this index for the late 1980s (late 1990s). Next to the country points, we also drew a line that indicates a situation in which no change would have occurred over a period of ten years. Strikingly, most countries remain close to this diagonal line, despite the high number of reforms that occurred.

Which are the main exceptions? A first exception, not visible on this figure, is Great Britain, which undertook its package of forceful liberalization reforms during the 1980s (see also Chapter 9). A second exception is Spain, which suffered from the highest level of unemployment in Europe (this peaked at about 20% in 1994). Such a high level of unemployment played the role of a major external constraint, by increasing the cost of the status quo (see also Chapter 11). The next two exceptions are Finland and Portugal, which had to take steps to adjust their economies to face the single market and avoid lagging behind.

8.2. Theories of reforms: a framework of analysis

Political incentives, economic incentives, and skills are all necessary to initiate and implement reforms. To disentangle the various *motivations* behind the reform initiatives described in the following chapters, one should distinguish the *economic rewards* of reform, from the various actors' *political will* to support or oppose a reform. While the first report focused on assessing the realized benefits from various reform experiences, this report concentrates on the latter aspect. We compare sets of reforms across countries and industries and try to identify which distinctive element of the political strategy made an attempted reform successful or unsuccessful. To this end, we identify four broad categories of political "recipes" that were used by governments, and analyse why a given reform was tailored one or another to make it politically sustainable.

Abstracting from realized benefits is not meant to imply that economic needs do not play an important role. The above evidence instead suggests that changing economic conditions are key to providing proper incentives to adjust the functioning of markets through such reforms. Increased competition increases the value of improving the economic competitiveness of domestic markets. We would thus expect that reforms start to take place when existing legislation is no longer consistent with the current economic environment, for example, because of technological developments or because of trade liberalization.

Yet, the evidence provided in the previous section emphasizes substantial differences in the cross-country timing of reforms, despite the likely synchronized materialization of economic benefits—especially when linked to technological shocks. These differences in reform experiences may be due to different *political determinants* of the reform process: the *ideology* of the policy-maker, the *system of political representation*, and the relative power of different *groups of actors* (parties, lobbies, and voters).

Besides economic incentives, the reform process can only start if a crucial player—the policy-maker—or of a group of players—for example, certain pressure groups—decide that they have to intervene to tip the scales in favour of the reform. Depending on their identity and position, they tend to assess the potential benefits and costs of passing a reform differently. Potential benefits are for instance:

- *Economic*, as political actors close to the policy-maker may derive economic benefits from implementation of the reform. For example, lowering severance payments will benefit employers.

- *Ideological*, as the policy-maker may find a personal benefit in bringing the functioning of the country closer to his or her personal ideal views.
- *Political*, since ensuring the success of the reform may make the party of the policy-maker more popular, thereby increasing the chances of re-election.

Of course, the potential costs are the exact mirror of these benefits: for instance, if the reform fails, the opposition party may get elected (political loss), and implement a reform that goes in the opposite direction (ideological and economic losses).

The political economics literature addresses these issues by studying the role of collective action processes (such as voting procedures, interest group activity, constitutions) in resource allocation and rent distribution, while the theory of institutions, pioneered by Douglass North, helps us understand institutional reforms. This literature can be divided into different subcategories focusing on specific problems and types of interaction. In particular, Castanheira and Esfahani (2003) identify *three groups of actors* that influence policy-making in a specific manner; *three types of interaction games* among these actors; as well as the objective of these actors: to gain control over (economic or other types of) *rents*.

Actors

We identify three different classes of actor that intervene in collective action processes: *the public*, who acts as *voters* when there are elections; *special interest groups* (or: *lobbies*), who can influence policy decisions by other means than elections (mass media campaigns, demonstrations, and so on);[1] and, finally, *political elites* (or, for short, *politicians*) who are identified as the actors who set the agenda, make choices, and can impose their decisions.

The interactions among these different groups are of course complex. The *voters* will have a comparatively stronger influence on reforms that affect the population at large (e.g. for labour market or pension reforms). By contrast, lobby groups will have more power in reforms that hit specific groups of the population, in which case voters' motivation to interfere with the process is lower (e.g. over the deregulation of intermediate goods markets, privatizations, and so on). Of course, which special interest

---

[1] Grossman and Helpman (2001) provide an in-depth and enlightening analysis of the role of special interest groups.

groups oppose or support most intensely a reform depends on the target of the latter. Lastly, politicians have more or less leeway depending on the institutional set-up.

Rules

Institutions provide a specific framework of interactions among these agents. Again, the literature tends to analyze these different processes separately. It is only recently that theoretical developments have allowed us to begin to understand how these different processes interact with one another. We can distinguish at least three different types of interactions: *democratic voting procedures*; *lobbying*; and *constitutional arrangements* that regulate the power and the freedom of action of political elites.

VOTING

One approach to the political economy of public policy is to focus on the interactions among *voters*. Voters differ in their preferences over policy outcomes, and democratic elections allow the selection of the proposal that is supported by a majority of the electorate. Anticipating the likely outcome of such elections, which type of proposals do politicians endorse? The literature showed that office-motivated politicians have an incentive to propose the platform that is most preferred either by the *median voter* (Hotelling, 1929; Downs, 1957; Black, 1958) or by the *average voter* (Hinich et al., 1972; Hinich, 1977; Lindbeck and Weibull, 1987 and 1993). The politician's focus on one or the other depends on certain characteristics of the elections (see Persson and Tabellini, 2000 and Mueller, 2003 for a survey).

LOBBYING

A different (and complementary) approach is to focus on the role of *special interest groups* (SIGs). The contribution of this approach is to show how SIGs influence policy-making beyond their role as voters. Coordinated actions by SIG members allows actors with common interests to interfere with policy-making, by eliciting specific information that favours them, by offering block political support, and/or financial contributions to politicians' causes. The politicians' decision is then biased towards these interest groups (see e.g. Olson, 1965, 1982; Becker, 1983; Baron, 1994; and Grossman and Helpman, 2001). The weight of these groups can also be explained by their relative cohesiveness at the election stage (Lindbeck and Weibull, 1987), or their level of organization (Olson, 1982). This may induce inefficient policy choices when lobbies have unbalanced access to policy-makers (Grossman and Helpman 2001). By contrast, efficiency is restored when all lobbies have equal access to the politician's ear and lobbying is socially costless (Bernheim and Whinston, 1986; Krueger, 1974).

CONSTITUTIONAL ARRANGEMENTS

The third approach to political economy modelling is to concentrate on the institutional arrangements that allow the public to constrain ruling politicians. For instance, since lobbies can influence policy-making beyond their voting power, allowing or forbidding campaign contributions will influence the lobbies' ability to manipulate policy-making. Some institutions are clearly suboptimal in that regard. For instance, Acemoglu *et al.* (2003) show how weak institutions may allow dictators to expropriate citizens by using divide-and-rule tactics. Stronger institutions impose constitutional checks and balances that limit the rulers' ability to exploit such societal divisions. In short: "When institutions are strong, citizens demand rights; when institutions are weak, citizens beg for favors" (Acemoglu *et al.*, 2003: 1).

THE ROLE OF POLITICAL REPRESENTATION

The system of representation is also important. Proportional systems reduce the power of ruling politicians to implement policy or reforms but also lower the party's accountability (Lijphart, 1999); whereas majoritarian representation provides more leeway to the politicians in designing their most desired reform. As a counterpart, this system makes the incumbent fully accountable to his electorate (see Chapter 9 and Crepaz, 1998). Moreover, politicians may divert rents even in strong democracies. Persson *et al.* (1997, 1998, 2000, and 2003) and Diermeier and Feddersen (1998) demonstrate that existing constitutions face a systematic trade-off between efficiency and rent extraction. For instance, Persson *et al.* (2000) show that stronger separation of powers puts tighter limits on the amount of rents diverted by politicians, but also generates suboptimally low provisions of public goods. Conversely, institutional arrangements that generate a better equilibrium provision of public goods tend to have weaker separation of powers, and therefore larger amounts of rent diverted by the politicians.

Rents

The motivations of the different actors in their political interactions are certainly many. Still, given the focus on *economic* reforms, it is quite natural for us to emphasize *economic rents*. Reaping these rents might be the immediate goal of only some, but it definitely is a necessary instrument for anyone who wants resources to attain his/her political objectives. This is to stress that even though we focus on economic rents, the logic of our argument does not preclude ideological motivations. Whether economic rents are a final goal or an intermediate tool, each group of actors will have an incentive to gain access to these rents. Focusing on economic rents is also a way to assess whether introducing other motivations is needed to understand the success of reforms. Perhaps surprisingly, it appears that, while ideology and national traditions are crucial to understanding why a reform process gets started in a particular way, they are much less relevant to understanding the reaction of voters, lobbies, and other potential veto players. In most cases, buying out additional support or taming oppositions does not take much more than appropriately allocating economic rents.

The standard prediction is that, when the amount of rents that can be appropriated is large and concentrated, groups will better organize themselves to gain access to these rents. Oppositions between organized groups will become fiercer, and more resources will be dissipated in the process (Olson, 1982).[2] This is the reason why farmers are politically more active in countries that receive larger subsidies from the Common Agricultural Policy; this is also the reason why bigger and more cohesive industries manage to effectively lobby for stricter regulatory frameworks, and why it proves more difficult to reform existing pension systems, the more generous and inefficient they initially are.[3] Clearly, other framework conditions largely affect the reform process, and need not be directly linked to these political aspects. The purpose of the case studies is also to provide more detail regarding these contingencies in specific cases.

---

[2] Evidence demonstrates that the presence of abundant resources can turn out to be a curse for economic growth. This curse tends to be even more pronounced when institutions are weaker, i.e. implicitly when lobbying becomes more effective. There are thus strong reasons to believe that abundant resources essentially generate a *political economy curse* (see Acemoglu et al., 2003; Castanheira and Esfahani, 2003; and Robinson et al., 2002).

[3] See also Blanchard and Giavazzi (2003) for an analysis of the links between product market and labour market reforms.

How to Gain Political Support for Reforms

The status quo bias

The establishment of welfare systems or the existence of dominant positions in crucial markets tends to generate a *status quo bias*. Despite the potential gains to be reaped from reforming, actors opposing the changes have a higher propensity to dominate decisions: "Why do governments so often fail to adopt policies that economists consider to be efficiency-enhancing?... The answer usually relies on [the fact that] the gainers from the status quo are taken to be politically 'strong' and the losers to be politically 'weak,' thereby preventing the adoption of reform", is how Fernandez and Rodrik (1991: 1146) introduce their theory of status quo bias.

This theory is based on the uncertainty that reforms generate: while those who stand to lose from the reform are easily identified, those who stand to gain may face substantial individual uncertainty. This uncertainty generates a double hurdle for reforms: to attract majoritarian support, a reform must attract both *ex ante* and *ex post* support. An example will illustrate this point (see Fig. 8.7). Consider a population divided in two sectors: *L* is the sector that will *lose* from the reform, and *G* is the sector that *gains*. *Ex ante*, 54 per cent of the population works in sector *L*. *Ex post*, 64 per cent will be working in sector *G*. Therefore, a majority of the population (64%) gains from the reform process: those who are already present in sector *G* (46% of the population) and the additional 18 per cent who will move from one sector to the other.

Yet, a majority of 54 per cent may block the reform *ex ante*. Assume that the reform increases the pay-offs of anyone in sector *G* by 10, while decreasing the pay-offs of anyone in sector *L* by 9. Those initially in sector *L* hence face a two-third is probability of staying in their sector and lose 9, and a one-third probability of moving and gain 10. The uncertainty as to *who* would be able to change sector implies that anyone initially in sector *L* faces an expected pay-off of $-8/3$. They will thus oppose the reform. Since this sector initially represents a majority, the reform can be blocked democratically. This simple example characterizes a typical status quo bias: if the government ever managed to impose its reform, a majority would oppose its reversal as well. This is a fundamental feature of the status quo bias: whether the status quo is the pre-reform or the post-reform state, a reform put to the vote would be rejected by a majority.

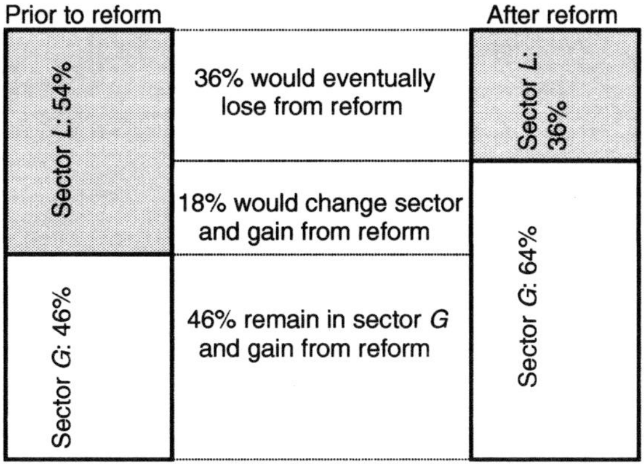

Evidence and Theory of Reforms

Prior to reform		After reform
Sector L: 54%	36% would eventually lose from reform	Sector L: 36%
	18% would change sector and gain from reform	Sector G: 64%
Sector G: 46%	46% remain in sector G and gain from reform	

Fig. 8.7 Gainers and losers from reform
Source: Authors' calculations.

Gradual versus one-off reforms

This shows that the uncertainty faced by individuals (*individual uncertainty*) is sometimes sufficient to maintain the status quo, whether efficient or not. In addition, there may also be *aggregate* uncertainty concerning the eventual effects of a reform. In the example above, the reform was known to generate a gain of 10 in sector G. Assume instead it is equally likely to generate a pay-off of 1 or a pay-off of 19. On average, the *expected* payoff is still 10. However, if the reform yields 19, the expected pay-off for a person in sector L would become positive! Gradual reforms may in that case help the government gain popular support for its reform. Assume the reform can be divided into two steps. If the first step generates almost no loss for those in sector L but, at the same time, elicits information regarding the actual pay-offs of the full reform, even those in sector L may support the first step and, eventually, the second. Next, if there are more than two groups in the population, the government can exploit divide-and-rule tactics to buy support from a different majority in favour of each component of the reform. The gradual implementation or an appropriate sequencing of reforms can thus prove an appropriate way of circumventing political oppositions[4] (Dewatripont and Roland, 1992 and 1995).

---

[4] Interestingly, many of these issues of *gradualism versus big bang* reforms were raised primarily to address the situation faced by Eastern European countries during their transition to a market economy. However, the lessons learned from their experience are now proving valuable for the reform processes faced by other countries in the world (Roland, 2000).

How to Gain Political Support for Reforms

According to this broad theoretical framework, we identify four relevant scenarios for reforms. These are, of course, not an exhaustive list of possible situations, neither are they mutually exclusive. With each scenario, we associate a strategy or "recipe" for reform based on the case-study experience outlines in the following chapters.

- In a scenario characterized by strong concentration of power in the hands of the policy-makers—and hence also by large political accountability—a reform attempt in markets that do not feature overly strong entrenched interests may be carried out by *exploiting this political power or parliamentary majority*. Policy-makers may not even need to justify their course of action upfront, nor to spread the economic benefits of the reform onto the widest possible group of actors. Yet, their electoral concerns, combined with a high degree of political accountability, will eventually require these reform policies to improve—or at the very least not to reduce—the well-being of the voters in their constituency. Power is thus key in this strategy; it explains most successes *and* failures.
- Policy-makers lacking a substantial concentration of power—perhaps because of coalition government—can instead adopt a consensus building strategy to reform by *tailoring the reform package to widen the political base*. Instead of confronting oppositions, these governments indulge in spreading the benefits of their reform, to attract wider political support.
- Another relevant scenario may be defined according to the characteristics of the institutions or markets to be reformed, rather than by the political strength of the policy-makers. In the presence of strong entrenched interests, when some specific groups are both too strong to be confronted at once and too expensive to buy out, policy-makers may adopt a strategy of *divide and conquer*. Under this strategy, governments target the benefits of their reforms at specific subgroups, so as to undermine intra-group cohesion.
- In several circumstances, the reform efforts of policy-makers are largely induced by the existence of external constraints (e.g. international laws or regulations) that make reforms inescapable. Almost regardless of their intrinsic political power and of the market or institution to be modified, the policy-maker may hence *exploit these external constraints* to carry out the reform.

9
Exploit a Parliamentary Majority

Structural reforms—by changing the economic environment and affecting the political arena—typically create winners and losers in both fields. When policy-makers implement reform measures, they alter the status quo. Often, these changes produce "sure losers" from the reforms—and hence strong opposition—whereas the size of the gains, their timing, and their distribution across the population may be uncertain. In light of the theoretical literature presented in the previous chapter, this requires that the government bypass *ex ante* political constraints: it must first be able to *impose* its reform on the population. Popular support for the post-reform situation may then materialize in a second phase, when individual uncertainty has been resolved.

This chapter analyses a scenario in which reforms featuring definite current costs but only uncertain future benefits are carried out by strong governments—backed by large parliamentary majority. The strength of the policy-makers, as measured by their political support, clearly enhances the possibility of reforming; yet, it typically increases their political accountability to the population at large. Since also strong governments have electoral concerns, and since unpopular reforms may undermine their chances of re-election, this increased accountability may thus act as a deterrent to reform. Under this political and economic scenario, governments may choose to impose a reform on an unwilling population, with the expectation that—once given the necessary momentum—political support may be obtained among the winners from the reforms. Examples of this strategy covered in this chapter are, primarily, the pension reforms enacted by the Thatcher government in the 1980s, but also the rather less successful reform attempts in Italy and Denmark.

This ability to impose a reform on voters, with the objective of overcoming the status quo bias, requires that a government be sufficiently "strong". In light of the main dimensions highlighted before, strength may result from different sources: either *institutional rules* make an incumbent naturally strong, or the *actors* facing the reformer are sufficiently weak. Majoritarian representation systems tend to make the incumbent comparatively stronger, thanks to the winner-takes-all feature of the election. Presidential systems also feature this comparative power, since a single representative is offered more leeway to impose his or her agenda on the parliament. Next, the *actors* facing the reformer can make a difference. The opposition may be in a weak bargaining position if is not represented by well-organized groups. Consider a purely electoral politics framework, in which only the voters have the power to block a reform. Since voters can only intervene at the time of elections, they have to wait for the subsequent poll. Yet, if economic actors adapt sufficiently fast to the new system, their opposition will have waned by the time of the election. Finally, if a seminal reform disrupts opposition when passed successfully, it may create *momentum* and new reforms may become feasible.

This confrontational style to reform typically arises in reforms that are not targeting specific sectors, but rather affect—at least potentially—every voter, and are prominent in the political debate at the time of elections. This is why most reform attempts covered here relate to pensions and to the labour market. Indeed, unions can interfere with both reform processes, but their role is comparatively less prominent than in some product market reforms that we cover in Chapter 11.

However, this confrontational strategy does not always have to be successful. In fact, while the pension reforms put forward in the UK by the Thatcher government were a political success, other attempts at imposing a parliamentary majority failed, for example, Berlusconi's 1994 pension reform plan in Italy, Juppé's 1995 targeted pension reform in France, and Rasmussen's 2003 labour market reform in Denmark.

Furthermore, there is another important dimension to assessing the success or failure of a reform which one must not overlook: *politically* successful reforms need not be an *economic* success. To highlight the danger of giving excessive leeway to a president or a parliamentary majority in pushing ahead with reforms, we examine the corporate governance reforms in Russia. The dismantling of the Soviet system left the democratic opposition virtually unable to block reforms—even misguided ones. Indeed, the lack of an organized opposition made it impossible to block *ex ante* reforms that had to be undone *ex post* anyway. Beyond such "pathological" cases, the insights of this case study apply also to the UK, as some of the reforms implemented in the 1980s had to be (partially) reversed.

The case studies presented in this chapter highlight some interesting regularities in the steps that a reform-minded government has to take. Strong governments—backed by large majorities in Parliament and, possibly, specific interest groups—may be willing to enter the initial phase of *commitment building* to reform for different reasons. Pro-reform electoral platforms, ideological push, or external constraints may represent powerful determinants. Yet, when the reform plan aims at reducing the cost of the welfare state, this becomes a critical political move, since there are typically few electoral incentives, if any, in democracies to retrench welfare systems[1] (Ney, 2003; Pierson, 1996).

The *coalition building* stage instead relates to the process of identifying which actors may be instrumental to the success of the reform. The latter is then tailored in such a way that these actors support the government's proposals. As we shall see with the case of Russia, however, this component of the strategy may prove very costly in terms of eventual efficiency.

Comparison between these different reforms shows the strengths and weaknesses of this confrontational strategy of exploiting a parliamentary majority. Understanding these aspects will help us appreciate the comparative value of the reform strategies which are covered in other chapters.

9.1. The 1986 Social Security Act in the UK

The retrenchment of the public pension system achieved by the Conservative government of Mrs Thatcher in 1986 constitutes a clear example of exploitation of a parliamentary majority. Moreover, it represented a distinct break with previous pension policies aimed at increasing the role of the state in providing retirement income. The 1986 reform followed a large swing in the political mood over the pension problem, as well as—more generally—over the role of the state, which took place in the early 1980s, and which was clearly present in the pension debate. Already in 1980, the Conservative government had shifted pension indexation from

---

[1] Regarding the UK 1986 pension reform described in the following section, the Conservative government managed this *commitment building stage* by providing the public with a large amount of evidence on the impact of aging (see Nesbitt, 1995). Through this evidence, the government supplied an official justification and built momentum for the reform. Yet, according to some scholars—see Pierson (1994) and Jessop *et al.* (1988)—the government was essentially willing to move along with this reform for ideological reasons, which they refer to as "Thatcherite".

wage growth to inflation, thereby reducing pension spending over the long run, as the value of pension benefits to retirees ceased to grow at the rate of the economy.

In the early 1980s, the Conservative government initiated the commitment building phase of the eventual 1986 pension reform by expressing its deep concern about the future level of pension spending. Two explanations were offered: the expected aging of the population was predicted to undermine the financial sustainability of the public pay-as-you-go (PAYG) pension scheme, and the future completion of the phasing-in of the SERPS scheme, which—having reached its maturity—would have paid pension benefits to a larger fraction of retirees. As argued by Nesbitt (1995), during this phase the government was very active, producing a wide range of evidence on these issues. Already in 1982, a Report by the Government Actuary provided projections on pension spending. This government behaviour was largely different from the experience of other European countries in which little information on pension spending and on the impact of the demographic trend on spending was released (see below and Boeri et al., 2001).

A major boost to this commitment building phase of the pension reform process was given by the large victory by the Conservative Party in the 1983 British election. The Conservatives received 42.4 per cent of the votes—down from 43.3 per cent in the 1979 general election—but obtained 396 seats—57 seats more than in the previous Parliament (see Table 9.1). The big loser from the 1983 election was the Labour Party, which experienced a sharp decrease in its share of votes and seats. Former Labour voters channelled their support towards the Liberal Democrats, which almost doubled its share of votes, and obtained 23 seats.

The majoritarian features of British elections played a crucial role in this circumstance. This majoritarian system penalizes small or medium-sized parties that do not have a geographical characterization. A party that turned out to be second in each district, hence receiving a significant share of votes, would not obtain any seat. On the other hand, a party reaching a relative majority in half of the districts would obtain 50 per cent of the seats in Parliament with little more than 25 per cent of the votes. In 1983, the British majoritarian system favoured the Conservatives in this way, since the flow of votes from the Labour Party to the relatively small Liberal Democrats allowed the Conservatives to prevail in several electoral districts and hence win additional seats. Despite the decrease in vote share from 43.3 per cent in 1979 to 42.2 per cent, the Conservative

Table 9.1 Vote shares and parliamentary seats in British elections, 1979–1992

Year	Conservative Party		Labour Party		Liberal Democrats	
	Votes (%)	Seats	Votes (%)	Seats	Votes (%)	Seats
1979	43.3	339	36.9	268	13.8	11
1983	42.4	396	27.6	209	25.4	23
1987	42.4	375	30.8	229	12.8	17
1992	41.9	336	34.4	271	17.8	20
1997	31.5	165	44.4	418	17.6	46

Source: Bonoli (2000).

Party enjoyed a more comfortable majority in Parliament—around 63 per cent of the seats—than in 1979—around 55 per cent of the seats.

Backed by a strong majority in Parliament, in November 1983, the government launched an "Inquiry into Provision for Retirement", chaired by the Secretary of State, Norman Fowler. The goal of this committee was to analyse the two hot problems of the pension debate: the portability of occupational pension plans and the forecast cost of public pension schemes. Contrary to the British tradition, this Inquiry did not constitute an independent committee; it was instead composed of politicians— namely some ministers in the Conservative government—and by actuarial and insurance industry representatives. Notably, employees, retirees, and union representatives found no place on the committee.

The work developed by this committee was contained in two publications. A background paper (DHSS, 1984) reviewed the issues in the pension debate, which had already been discussed by other political and social players, and provided additional evidence on the importance of the two problems at stake: the limited portability of the occupational pension plans and the expected increase in public pension spending, blamed on population aging. Next, the Green Paper, "Reform of Social Security" (DHSS, 1985b), contained the Inquiry's main message. The committee strongly supported the view that each individual had the right to a personal pension, not linked to employers' contribution. Regarding the public pension system, their bold proposal was to abolish the public earnings related pillar (SERPS). This Green Paper entirely expressed the philosophy of the committee: the role of the state in the pension industry had to be reduced, by dropping the SERPS; whereas there was scope for more private intervention through the introduction of personal rights to a pension. This publication also brought the commitment building phase to an end.

The coalition building phase of the 1986 pension reform lasted only six months and featured a reduced interaction, in which few political and social actors played a relevant role. The government had already made clear its intention to exclude the representatives of the employees, of the retirees, and of the unions from the decision process. During the coalition building phase, the government continued with this strategy by accepting critical remarks from a few players only.

The most controversial reform measure had been proposed by the Secretary of State Norman Fowler: the abolition of the public earnings related pillar (SERPS). Clearly, the Labour Party, the Unions, and several charity organizations, such as Age Concern, fiercely opposed this measure, which largely reduced state responsibility for providing retirement income, especially to low-income workers. Their studies, submitted to the Inquiry, underlined the risk of a large increase in poverty among the elderly, and called for an increase of the state coverage in pensions. Perhaps surprisingly, the main organizations in the private pension industry also opposed the dismantling of SERPS. According to Atkinson (1991), the private pension industry organizations were not so pleased to open up their industry to low-income workers; they would have preferred to keep targeting middle- and high-income individuals. Companies running occupational pension plans, on the other hand, were afraid of possible demographic inbalance in occupational plans, due to large flows of young workers opting out of occupational plans in favour of private personal plans.

However, according to Bonoli (2000), the most influential criticisms came from within the government, that is, from the Treasury. Unlike other players, the Treasury was concerned about the cost of abolishing SERPS. The Treasury argued that, since past obligations to SERPS were to be met, and hence current pensions had to be paid, the abolition of SERPS would have led to a double burden of taxation during the phasing-out period, as current workers were to contribute towards current retirees' pensions as well as to their own future (private) pensions.

A later publication by the government's "Inquiry into Provision for Retirement" Committee, the White Paper "Programme for Action" (DHSS, 1985a) concluded this brief coalition building phase. To meet the opposition by the Treasury—and by private pension industry organizations—the Committee proposed a watered-down reform with a reduction in SERPS coverage, rather than its abolition.

The reform measures proposed by the White Paper were then implemented in the 1986 Social Security Act. This reform profoundly reshaped the mix of private and public provision in the British pension system. As shown in Figure 9.1, social spending in the UK had been constantly increasing since the Second World War. The 1986 reform measures reduced public responsibility for retirement income, while private pension plans were introduced and contracting-out of occupational plans was made easier.

The reduction in the role of SERPS was achieved by decreasing the replacement rate from 25 per cent to 20 per cent of earnings, by increasing the number of years used for calculating the average wage used in the pension benefit formula, from the best 20 years to the entire working history, and by reducing the survival pension benefit to 50 per cent of the retiree's pension.

Why did the Conservative government commit to retrenching the public pension system? Unlike other countries, such as for instance Italy (see the discussion in the next chapter), the British system did not face immediate financial solvency or sustainability problems; yet the Conservative government decided to face the pension issue, by setting up a massive information campaign to increase awareness about the forecast future cost of the public system, *vis-à-vis* population aging. Although some scholars (see Bonoli, 2000) have suggested that this political move was due to Mrs Thatcher government's underlying ideology of limiting public intervention in the economy, other scholars (see Jessop *et al.*, 1988)

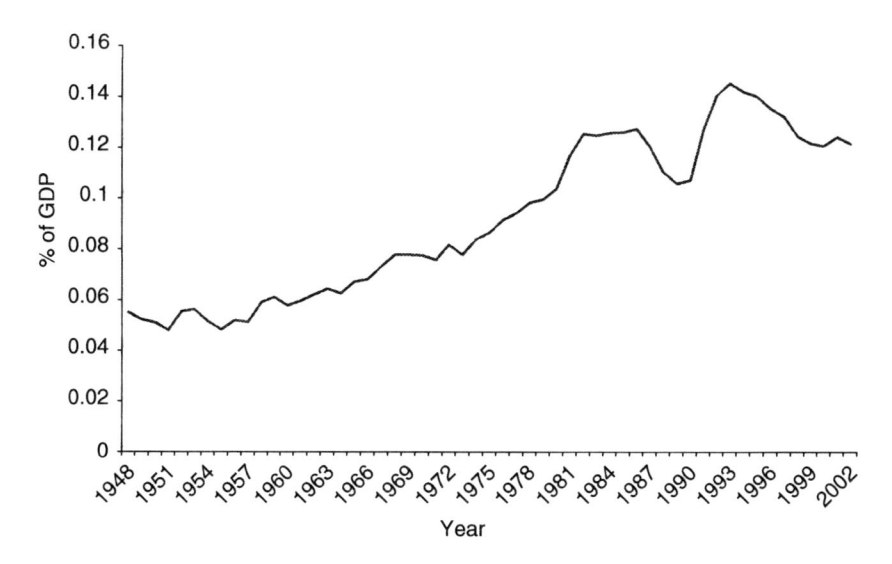

Fig. 9.1 Social spending over GDP in the UK, 1948–2002
Source: National Statistic Office.

have instead argued in favour of the existence of a close link between this government economic policy and its electoral success.

Thatcherism—the set of economic policies aimed at decreasing state intervention—might have represented a political strategy. According to this view, the Conservative government proposed a set of policies— among them the 1986 pension reform—which was clearly targeted at upper-middle and high-income citizens. Poor individuals were not represented in the Conservative Party's platform, perhaps because they were considered as ideologically opposed to the Party, and hence difficult to swing (see Persson and Tabellini, 2000, for a discussion of the relevance of swing voters).

The key political player in this Conservative strategy was the middle-class. The 1986 pension reform, and all other measures aimed at creating an economy with an "extended capitalism", had to be beneficial to middle-income voters. To the extent that the introduction of new instruments for retirement income increased the economic well-being of the upper-middle class, it had the power to maintain the Tories' vote share.

This view is broadly in line with the data reported in Table 9.2 on the use of personal plans by individuals in different classes of income in 1996. Ten years after the reform, private pensions were still not very relevant for the 20 per cent poorest retirees. However, they already constituted a sizeable share of retirement income for individuals in the fourth quintile and, as expected, for the 20 per cent richest retirees, for whom they constitute more than a third of their retirement income. Moreover, as shown in Table 9.1, the Conservative Party did not pay any electoral price for retrenching the welfare state, since in the elections that took place in 1987—the year after the pension reform—they obtained the same share of the vote, 42.4 per cent, as in 1983, although their seats in Parliament went down from 396 to 375.

Table 9.2 Retirees' income by income group and composition

Source	Quintiles				
	1	2	3	4	5
State pension	71.31	59.89	50.05	38.80	23.37
Means-tested benefits	9.40	13.48	19.90	11.26	5.49
Other benefits	6.44	8.27	8.94	12.30	9.56
Private pensions	7.97	13.41	15.05	26.61	38.11
Investment	3.84	3.57	3.74	6.72	13.24
Earnings	0.97	1.39	2.31	4.31	10.24

Source: Emmerson and Johnson (2001).

Another peculiar element of the 1986 British pension reform, as compared to the reform process in other European countries, is the almost complete absence of a coalition building phase. As argued above, the Conservative government was unwilling to compromise with other political or social players. The only criticism that was incorporated in the implemented reform had come from the Treasury, that is, from within the government.

The Conservative Party's decision not to make any concessions to the demands of social actors, such as employees' representative or unions, or to the political opposition, the Labour Party, in the pension reform measures was possible because of the relatively unchecked dominance of the ruling party in the British political system. As shown in Table 9.1, the Conservative Party enjoyed a large majority in Parliament, thanks to the majoritarian features of the electoral system. Hence, because of the institutional design of the British political system, no veto player existed in the political arena, with the notable exception of the members of the government, such as the Treasury (see also Spolaore, 2004).

The only relevant political check for the government was political accountability at future elections. As argued above, this element was taken into account by the Conservative government, whose 1986 pension reform did in fact target middle-class (swing) voters. Moreover, the structural weakness of the Labour Party reduced political competition in the UK over the period 1979–92, thereby providing more leeway for the policies of the Conservative Party.

9.2. "Pushing reforms": the role of momentum

The example provided by the reform of the pension system in Great Britain shows two interesting elements. First, a strong majoritarian government can push reforms ahead even though they may a priori hurt a majority of the population. Yet, even a government as strong as Thatcher's had to tailor its reforms in such a way as to retain support from relevant groups in the population (Section 9.3, however, shows that even majoritarian governments may fail in this strategy). Second, forging ahead with reforms has the potential to create momentum for other reforms. Designing reforms appropriately, the Conservative government managed to maintain its vote share, and even increase its parliamentary majority, thanks to an increasingly divided opposition.

How to Gain Political Support for Reforms

With a view to the countless reforms to be pushed ahead, Russia in 1991 adopted a semi-presidential system with strong powers to the president, effectively making the electoral system close to the US majoritarian system. In light of the successful reforms carried out in the UK, and of the American President's ability to forge ahead with reforms, this choice indeed seemed advisable. Yet, the experience of Russian reforms eventually proved quite different from what was expected at the time. As this case study shows, what appeared to be a strength of the majoritarian system, namely its ability to facilitate the passage of harmful reforms despite opposition from the street, proved to be a curse in the case of Russia.

A critical difference between Russia and the UK was that, at least at the beginning of transition, the power of the government (or rather, as we shall see, its *apparent* power) did not primarily depend on its potential electoral success, but rather on the support of narrow, though powerful, groups. Therefore, reforms were actually tailored to *bribe* these groups. Because of this different source of power, the government had to rely even more on momentum to pass its reforms, before the opposition could recover. On its side, the population let the government pass its reforms, but simply refused to comply with the new rules. As a result, reforms were pushed too far and too fast on paper but led to only minimal structural adjustment in reality. Clearly, this dual evolution undermined the stability of the country. Eventually, it fed a major macroeconomic imbalance that materialized into the rouble crisis that arose on 17 August 1998.

How could this happen? In short, both Russian reformers and international institutions feared that, if reforms were not implemented sufficiently rapidly and drastically, any electoral backlash might induce a reversal to communist interventionism. There was thus a strong desire to exploit the (potentially) narrow window of opportunity provided by the election of President Yeltsin to advance reforms as swiftly as possible. This was meant to create momentum, that is, to coordinate expectations towards the pursuit of reforms. Instead, it essentially generated a widespread belief (which turned out to be correct) that these reforms were totally disconnected from reality.

Needed reforms were broad ranging, and included "establishing property rights, hardening budget constraints, building a healthy banking system, and ensuring true domestic competition" (Wyplosz, 1999). Even among those macroeconomists who were involved in advising Russia, a general consensus had emerged that failing to pass adequate microeconomic reforms would have undermined stabilization policies and restructuring (Fischer and Sahay, 2000). For these reasons, all reforms going in that direction were most welcome and, indeed, there was no lack of formal legislative change under Yeltsin, prodded by the IMF's conditionality lending, which often came in unprecedented degree of detail.

Hence, *on paper*, Russia adopted most of the suggested regulatory framework, but reliable enforcement failed to materialize: in practice, the powerful interests that the government wanted to protect were allowed to ignore most rules. All these reforms failed because of *state capture* by narrow but powerful interest groups. For this reason, Russians did not actually believe in these reforms and hence did not comply. They could have tried to press the government to change its course of action, and implement better reforms. However, it is not even clear that the population could understand which reforms were most needed, as the notion that the public had to be informed came only much later.

Reform implementation: 1991–1998[2]

After a period of partial and inconsistent reforms under Gorbachev, the demise of the Soviet Union in the autumn of 1991 opened the way for an ambitious "shock-therapy" programme, launched along lines comparable to the 1990 Polish plan (Lipton and Sachs, 1992). Following price liberalization, the Gaidar government tightened credit in January 1992 to encourage microeconomic restructuring. The critical phase of this policy required resisting pressures for reflation and compensatory bail-outs, and ultimately forcing real adjustment. In Russia, the actual adjustment response was very limited, and most trade bills went unpaid. The policy collapsed by the summer, when trade arrears rose to three times total bank credit, with a massive bail-out funded by money printing by the CBR (Central Bank of Russia). The bail-out validated collective inertia and led to new cycles of accumulation and bailing out of arrears (see Fig. 9.2). High inflation in 1992–4 essentially wiped out domestic savings.

At the same time, under an extremely *laissez-faire* policy of minimal bank capital requirements, the number of banks increased rapidly, from fewer than 10 to over 2,500. Many such "banks" performed cash management, capital flight, and whitewashing services for enterprises or shadowy organizations. Well-connected banks thrived on managing the balances of federal or local authorities. Banks also held on to transfer payments, indirectly collecting a large inflation tax. Bank supervision

---

[2] This section draws on the chronology of events in Perotti and Sgard (2000).

How to Gain Political Support for Reforms

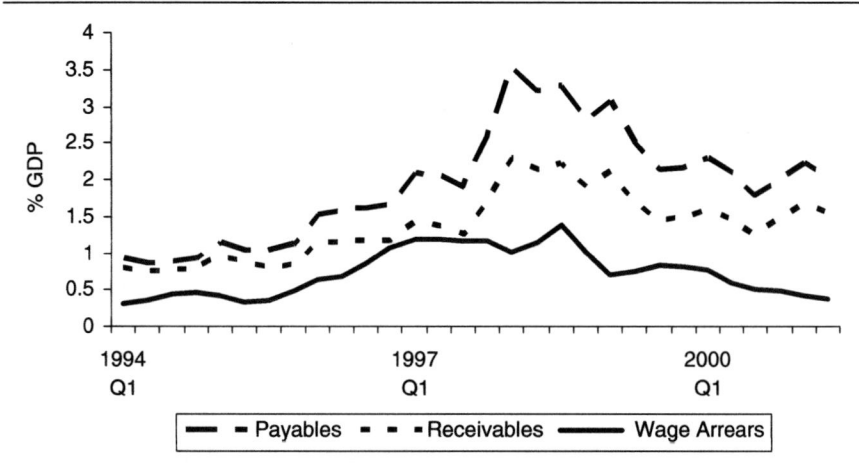

Fig. 9.2 Dynamics of payables, receivables, and wage arrears
Source: Perotti (2002).

performed perfunctorily, monitoring compliance with the formalities of regulations rather than with their content. Pure Ponzi schemes became common—one can, for instance, remember the large MMM collapse in 1994.[3]

When stabilization policy from 1995 onward froze the printing presses, there was a last chance to tighten financial discipline. Yet, the government had lost further support, and was by then at the mercy of special interests. It thus shifted to a different form of *ex post* laxity, substituting loose enforcement for loose money, condoning non-payment and asset-stripping while stoking trouble for later. The CBR kept administering merely cosmetic supervisory controls. Thanks to falling interest rates and strong inflows, the growth rate became marginally positive in 1997 (see Fig. 9.3).

A stronger political leadership could have controlled capital flight, but it would have had to challenge powerful interests as well as disapproval from the West. In practice, the government was unable to enforce even tax collection. Banks took advantage of stabilization and the progressive overvaluation of the rouble, by borrowing massively abroad. While some

---

[3] The MMM Bank in Russia has proved to be nothing more than a spectacular scam in recent times. Founded by Sergei Mavrodi in 1991, MMM offered fantastic returns to investors and was considered an exemplary business success at the time. By the summer of 1994, however, this apparent success proved to be a Ponzi-type pyramid scheme. The bank collapsed and left millions of Russians ruined.

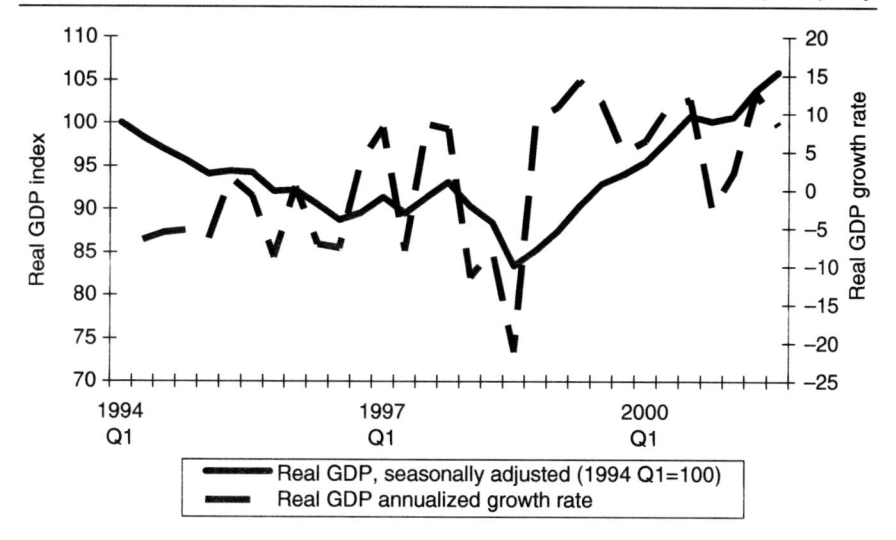

Fig. 9.3 Real GDP growth
Source: Perotti (2002).

of these inflows were invested in the GKO market (Russian government bonds), most simply returned to the West as capital flight.[4]

A new government was brought in in March 1998, on a mandate to restore fiscal responsibility. Politically weak, its few reforms went unimplemented, tax collection did not improve, and capital kept flowing abroad.[5] Several large private banks became visibly insolvent. Only the arrival of the first tranche of an IMF loan delayed the final meltdown.[6] However, this IMF loan fled the country at extraordinary speed, leaving no choice to the government but to devalue and announce a moratorium on the debt, a *de facto* default.

Regulatory and governance capture under Yeltsin

It is important to realize that the failure of economic reforms in Russia was due to a *deliberately* poor design, compounded by a diffuse cynical

---

[4] In addition to their ability to lobby and bribe, Russian banks also enjoyed *de facto* immunity thanks to their link to criminal elements. In the language of the FBI Director Louis French: "Organized crime shaped the post-communist Russian banking industry and now manages it".

[5] A rare glimpse into asset-stripping emerged when officers at the Bank of New York were found guilty of aiding the stealing and exporting of several billion dollars from InkomBank.

[6] Yet, even the average Russian investor could not anticipate the default. Only a few influential Russian bankers managed to capture the last rounds of dollar reserves from the Central Banks just before the collapse.

response by the population, which rationally chose a collective inertial (non-)response to the new rules. State capture reduces the credibility of the authorities, as they are expected to bend rules themselves to accommodate special interests. Coupled with the high average adjustment costs faced by the militarized and monopolized Soviet economy, this created an expectation of a critical mass of non-compliance which overwhelmed even proper intentions, thus reinforcing resistance to adjustment (see also Roland and Verdier, 2003).

ENTERPRISES

Under poor legal enforcement, control rights are very valuable (Modigliani and Perotti, 2000; Bebchuk, 1999). Control generates access to cash-appropriating activities. Privatization thus granted insiders great discretion to capture resources, without exposing them to binding "rules of conduct"[7] (Filatotchev *et al.*, 1999). The overwhelming empirical evidence suggests that privatization failed to improve performance (Earle and Estrin, 1998). The incentive for managers to restructure, retain cash flow, and reinvest it internally did not exist in Russia. On the contrary, manager-owners protected their own interests by stripping assets and transforming them into cash (cash-stripping). Stripping assets destroyed long-term value, but cash was more appropriable than what managers could gain as value-optimizing shareholders (see Black *et al.*, 2000; Johnson *et al.*, 2002). Converting enterprise assets into cash also allows managers to appropriate value. As a result, firms avoided cash payment and often failed to pay altogether.[8] Since non-payment was so widespread, it also minimized the risk of prosecution. Settlement of payment obligations just became a matter of bargaining.

BANKS AND BANKING SUPERVISION

Financial deregulation generated such a surge in the number of banks operating in the country that the supervisory capacity of the CBR was rapidly overwhelmed. As a result, banks could easily avoid performing their presumed function (lending) and instead acted as money launderers.

---

[7] This outcome compares unfavourably with the Chinese experience of central control over major resources while allowing liberalization on new ventures (Roland, 2001*a*, 2001*b*).

[8] A related view is that barter was consequently used as collateralized trade credit. Marin and Schnitzer (1999, 2002, 2003) argue that barter supported trade between firms with tightly integrated production. Thanks to mutual bargaining power, trading via barter provides a form of collateral. Barter offers the sole transacting solution when managers have incentives to strip cash.

Connected lending (loans to friends) simply became outright transfers; cash could vanish, leaving no trail. The ability of bankers to "transfer" cash in such a way gave them an amazing power to capture policies. One example of their political power is reflected in the incredible story of Russian bankruptcy laws. The first general bankruptcy law in 1990 was extremely pro-debtor and thus toothless. Furthermore, as a result of intense lobbying, the new legislation explicitly stated that it would not be applicable to banks: no law on bank bankruptcy was passed until the crisis. *De jure*, Russian banks could not go bankrupt.[9]

Policy changes since the crisis

Three important elements have changed in Russia since the crisis. The main change is certainly political: a major recentralization of power, supported by a population exhausted by pervasive abuse and appalled by the implosion of the state. As a result of political consolidation under Putin, state capture was drastically reduced and fiscal authority restored. In addition, the devaluation has revived domestic production. Thus the trade-off faced by managers between cash-stripping and productive activity has since shifted. As a result, firms again started using cash payments in place of barter; stripping was reduced, and capital flight has slowed (see Fig. 9.4). The high oil price was certainly also a blessing. Coupled with tighter spending discipline, it helped generate a fiscal surplus, granting Russia a modest financial buffer. Even the government has taken to paying its bills.

Currently, Russia perhaps needs simple regulatory solutions, ones that can be easily implemented and monitored: its simplified fiscal code has been quite successful. More importantly, these reforms must be robust to opportunistic behaviour such as that described above.[10] On the other hand, such abuse has now become less easy. Yet, although Putin ensured political stability and established restraints on plunder and pillage, the cost has been high in terms of independent institutions outside the political centre. Russia is thus regressing towards a society based on fear, just as it needs to develop a more open and democratic process.

---

[9] Even the rights of the CBR to withdraw a bank licence were unclear. Tighter legislation was passed in 1999 under IMF pressure, but few significant banks have been closed since.

[10] Glaeser and Shleifer (2001) show that when regulatory enforcement is difficult, quantity restrictions, while less efficient, may be preferred to other restrictions, which are easier to circumvent.

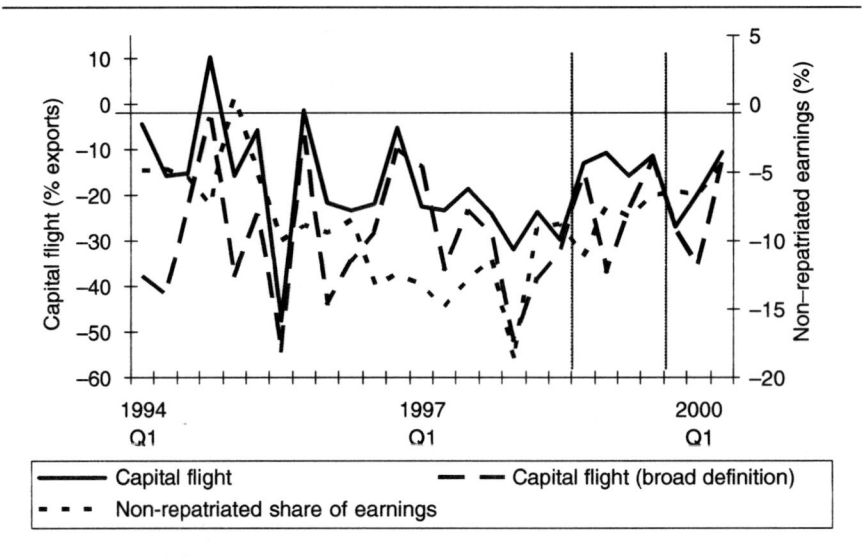

Fig. 9.4 Capital flight
Source: OECD, Employment Outlook.

9.3. Strengths and caveats: a tale of three failures

These two reform experiences show that exploiting a parliamentary majority can provide astounding reforming power to the government. This is, however, not always true. The countries studied above are majoritarian. A proportional representation system may bring up hurdles that prevent this confrontational approach to reforms from being successful.

Next, as the contrasting experiences of the UK and Russia showed, the *identity* of the relevant "veto players" is of primary importance in determining the unfolding of events. Major structural reforms can be both a political success and an economic failure when their design leads to regulatory capture or (in the pathological case of Russia) to *state* capture.[11]

This latter problem characterized the aftermath of the 1986 pension reform pushed forward by the Thatcher government. The liberalization induced by this reform largely increased the scope for private provision of retirement income; yet, the functioning of the private pension industry in the following years featured large and frequent mismanagements.

---

[11] Other examples are large privatization programmes in Chile in the late 1970s and in Mexico in the 1980s. In some early Latin American privatization programmes, large private investors were grossly favoured in the privatization of large state banks. This enabled these investors to acquire control over a number of privatized firms. In all these cases, the abuse of bank resources for private purposes led to brutal financial crises, which forced renationalization of most of these groups.

Low-earners who opted out of the public scheme into a private plan were at times palmed off with inadequate personal pension plans which worsened their economic position. As a result, partial reversals of this reform followed from 1995 to 1999 in an attempt to improve the economic well-being of these individuals *vis-à-vis* their retirement income provisions.

Thus, in some cases, exploiting a strong parliamentary majority to impose reforms *excessively* facilitates the task of the reform-minded government. In other cases, however, it may simply *not be feasible* in the face of *de jure* or *de facto* veto players. As the following examples show, the problem of political feasibility is pervasive.

Possible losers from the reform may represent a substantial share of the population, or benefit from strong political representation—as with the elderly. They may also be concentrated in the political constituency of the ruling government. In such instances, the government's electoral incentives will likely block any reform attempt, at least in the absence of external constraints. Also, a government with a large parliamentary majority need not be strong: it may lack internal cohesion—this is particularly evident in coalition governments—or it may face powerful social or economic actors who are able to effectively counteract the government's reforming efforts. The failure of the 1994 Berlusconi reform project in Italy and of Juppé's 1995 targeted pension reform in France are examples of the latter case. Besides, the unsuccessful attempt by the Rasmussen government to continue reforming the Danish labour market suggests that social dialogue is necessary in some consensus democracies.

The failure of the 1994 Berlusconi's pension reform project

Since the beginning of the 1990s the Italian political system had undergone major changes, largely induced by the so-called "Mani Pulite" (Clean Hands) operation, mainly led by a few Milan-based judges. These judges were prosecuting high-profile businessmen and national politicians, after discovering numerous bribes paid by companies to receive preferential treatment in public auctions. The extent of the phenomenon was so massive that a majority of members of the 1992 Parliament were being investigated. Meanwhile, and partially as a response to this situation, two referendums profoundly reshaped the Italian electoral system. In the 1994 election, three-quarters of the Parliament (Lower House) were elected with a majoritarian (single district) system, and the remaining part with the previous proportional system.

How to Gain Political Support for Reforms

In May 1994, the centre-right coalition, led by a media tycoon, Silvio Berlusconi—who had just launched his own political party, Forza Italia—won the general elections. As shown in Table 9.3, his government enjoyed a large majority in the Lower House. Berlusconi was hence leading a potentially strong, coalition government.

What triggered the Berlusconi government's commitment to a new pension reform was external constraints. Despite the Amato reform in 1992 (see discussion in Chapter 10), pension spending had not decreased. Meanwhile, pressure on Italy was mounting: international bodies, such as the IMF, the World Bank, and the European Commission, wanted it to adopt deeper structural reforms in an attempt to satisfy the Maastricht requirements. Given that the government was led by a businessman, and with Lamberto Dini (a former Italian central banker) as Treasury Minister, expectations of further reforms were particularly high.

The reform plan presented by the Berlusconi government—the plan was mainly elaborated by Lamberto Dini—aimed at a further sizeable decline in pension spending, although not as large as in the case of the previous (Amato) reform. The reduction of the net pension wealth of the workers was estimated to be around 27.5 per cent, as opposed to 52.9 per cent in the Amato reform. The spirit of the reform was to restrict eligibility, to reduce generosity, and to provide incentives for private pension plans.

This attempt to retrench the public pension system failed during the coalition building phase, due to the fierce opposition of two crucial veto players: the unions and Lega Nord, a pivotal party in the Berlusconi

Table 9.3 Votes and shares at the 1994 elections (lower house)

	Proportional		Majoritarian	Total
	Votes (%)	Seats	Seats*	Seats*
Alleanza Nationale	13.5	23	86	109
Forza Italia	21.0	30	67	97
Lega Nord	8.4	11	111	122
CCD	—	—	32	32
PSD	20.4	38	77	115
PPI	11.1	29	4	33
Rifondazione Comunista	6.0	11	29	40
Green Party	—	—	11	11
Other (left)	—	—	37	37
Patto Segni	4.7	13	9	22
Berlusconi Government				360

Note: * Candidates that in the majoritarian districts were elected under the banners of Patto per l'Italia, Polo del Buon Governo, Polo della Libertà, and Progressisti are imputed to the different parties.
Source: Cattaneo Institute.

coalition government. Unlike the Amato government in the preceding reform (see Chapter 10), the Berlusconi government decided not to negotiate the reform with the unions nor with the opposition. The effects of this move—highly criticized by the Italian President, Scalfaro—can be detected in the relatively even split of the cost of the reform among the generations chosen by the government: middle-aged and elderly voters. These are the unions' main constituency, but were among those set to experience the largest reduction in net pension wealth. Massive strikes broke out in October 1994, with millions of citizens taking to the streets; as the unions fought to protect the interests of their median members.

However, and this is crucial to an explanation of the failure of the Berlusconi government's pension reform, one of the main parties in the government—Lega Nord—decided to oppose the reform, despite having participated in its commitment building phase. The reasons of Lega Nord—a right-wing party—were no different from those of the unions, historically tied to the centre-left parties. Since one of the most relevant measures was to restrict eligibility, particularly for seniority pensions, the reform was effectively reducing the pension claims of individuals located in the northern regions, where these early retirement pensions are concentrated, and where the political constituency of Lega Nord is located. This is shown in Figure 9.5, which displays expected share of seniority pension over the 1995–2005 period and the number of votes for Lega Nord

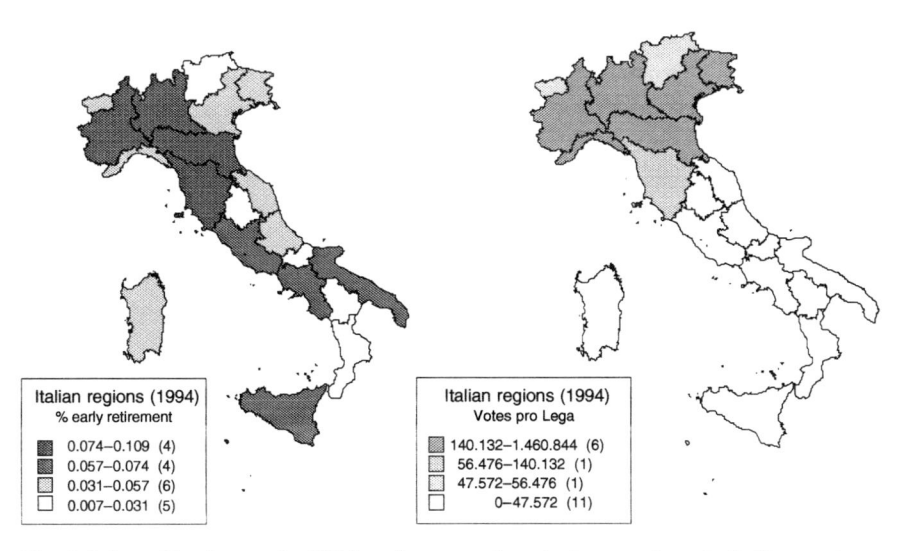

Fig. 9.5 Lega Nord votes in 1994 and expected seniority pensions in Italian regions
Source: Authors' calculations.

by region. Rather than being politically accountable for the loss of the reform to its voters, Lega Nord preferred to abandon the government—a confidence vote was requested together with the Partito Democratico della Sinistra (PDS)—thereby blocking the pension reform.

Juppé's 1995 blocked pension reform project

The story of Juppé's failed reform is somehow similar: like Berlusconi, he tried to take advantage of the momentum created by reforms that had been passed previously. In contrast with Italy, however, he opted for a very targeted reform package. For this reason, perhaps, he was expecting little resistance from the population.

In 1993, after the UDF and RPR right-wing parties had won a 54 per cent parliamentary majority, a plan to reform the French pension system was launched. As in the cases studied above, the main goal of the reform was to curb the generosity of the public pension system. Yet, these reforms had left untouched the position of the workers in the public sector—amounting to 5.5 million highly unionized employees. In 1995, Jacques Chirac was elected President and, following his victory, he nominated Alain Juppé as the new Prime Minister. His mandate was to pursue these unfinished reforms.

Given the fresh popularity of his party, the strategy adopted by Mr Juppé was to reform rapidly. With the power of his majority, Mr Juppé did not look for a wide consensus with social partners (who had opposed the previous reform). Moreover, he targeted his pension reform on the sectors that had been left untouched by reforms in 1993, such as railways, mining, electricity, and culture.

The targeted pension schemes were offering bonuses that were generally absent in the private sector: the reference wages were the last six months instead of 25 years' wages; the basic pension rate was higher (75%);[12] and fewer years of work were needed to obtain a full pension.

The opposition that met Mr Juppé's reform attempt was much stronger than expected. Even before negotiations with social partners could be started, the reform plan was violently rejected by unions. Demonstrations were organized, rallying more than 1 million people in the streets. As a consequence, the project was immediately called off.[13]

---

[12] Workers in the private sector can of course benefit from complementary schemes. But still, these would not fill the gap with the conditions of the public scheme.

[13] The project was introduced 15 November 1995. Strikes and demonstrations took place all over the country from 24 November up until 16 December when the project was withdrawn.

The main cause of failure was the inability of Mr Juppé to build a sufficient political coalition for his reform either in the working population, or among the representatives of his political coalition. Expecting less fierce opposition and, probably, stronger support from his party, the Prime Minister had bluntly introduced his project to social partners and to the media. No debate had been organized prior to this introduction. Nor did the reform try to compensate potential losers—in contrast to previous reforms. As a consequence, the population had been left uninformed, and Juppé never won the support of the electorate.

Blaming only the government for the violence of the opposition would not, however, be fair. The role of the unions was also paramount in this failure. One of the main unions, the CFDT, had split in the late 1980s, because some in the CDFT thought that their leaders were excessively lenient towards the reforms of successive governments. A spin-off had thus been created (namely SUD), which radicalized the debate. For this reason, the communist-based CGT, which is particularly prevalent in public administrations and in large public companies, feared that opening negotiations with the government would generate the same type of outcome in its ranks. Probably, Mr Juppé had thought that the unions had been weakened by the split of the CFDT. Instead of this, competition between the SUD and the CGT crystallized opposition, and resulted in the massive demonstrations described above. This combination of a (deliberate) absence of preparation of the population with (unwitting) radicalization of the opposition is at the heart of the 1995 reform failure in France.

The failure of Rasmussen's 2003 labour market reform project

Between 1994 and 1999, five years of pervasive labour market reforms had taken place in Denmark (see Chapter 10). The Danish labour market had been thoroughly reshuffled and most workers experienced substantial changes in the protection of their job or in the (still generous) unemployment benefits. In 2003, the Conservative government—formed in late 2001 by the Conservative Party and the Liberal Party—tried to forge ahead with further reforms. Like Juppé, the hope was that the momentum of the previous reforms would facilitate the process. Moreover, the proposed reform of the unemployment insurance system was also fairly targeted and aimed at reducing its cost.

Originally, the Minister of Employment outlined four proposals: (1) a reduction of the eligibility threshold so that only people working less than 21 hours a week (instead of 28) would be entitled to benefits; (2) temporary agency workers, casual workers, and freelance workers would no longer receive extra benefits on a permanent basis and a maximum of 52 weeks' benefit would apply to all employees; (3) employees with a monthly wage over) £3,360 would have their first benefit postponed; and (4) the rate of benefit would be based on average salary over the past six months instead of the original three months (in order to stimulate long-term employment relationships).

The employers' organization criticized the first two measures on the ground that they would significantly reduce the flexibility of employment (part-time work), and would be critical in building and industrial industries. The Danish People's Party (supporting the coalition) was also sceptical about this set of reforms. As a result, the government had to withdraw these two proposals. It also proposed to use average salary over the last 12 months instead of three in measure (4). Yet, this revised proposal met strong opposition from the employers' organization, and from two out of three workers' unions. The employers' organization suggested that it would not promote flexibility, while the unions argued that the change would be detrimental to the philosophy of an insurance system. The fact that unemployment was rising at that time might have reinforced the strong opposition of social partners. Eventually, the whole project was withdrawn in late 2003.

In 2004, the coalition tried once again to propose cuts in the benefit system, in order to remove inefficiencies.[14] The targets were supplementary benefits in case of temporary lay-offs and the level of insurance for high-paid workers. Again the centre-right minority government had to withdraw the proposals in the face of a threat to disrupt the upcoming collective bargaining round.

---

[14] Employers and employees could collude to take advantage of a system based on revenue rather than on income taxes. In this set-up, potential inefficiency stems from the fact that employers do not contribute proportionally to their firing behaviour, and that none of the labour market actors pay directly for the insurance benefits.

10
Widen Your Political Base

The reform experiences presented in the previous chapter may suggest that whether or not reform measures are adopted essentially depends on the ability of the political leaders to impose them on the population and/or on the various special interest groups. According to this view, a country's ability to reform largely hinges upon its institutions, that is, upon the rules that determine the relative power of the government. If the institutional design creates "strong" governments, the country will have an improved capacity to pass reforms, but if institutions deliver "weak" governments, special interests will systematically prevail, and even valuable reforms will fail. Furthermore, this approach implies that countries in need of structural reforms should change their institutions to reinforce the government's ability to *commit* to reforms, to weaken the power of special interest groups, and to limit the number of possible veto players.

Yet, these conclusions would be unwarranted, as other reform experiences and governments strategies have proved that governments actually have a wider palette of recipes for reform at hand, according to the specific economic and political scenario, and that sometimes oppositions have to be circumvented rather than overpowered.

This chapter analyses a scenario in which the institutional design does not offer—*de jure* or *de facto*—sufficient political strength to the government; and focuses on economic reforms where the distribution of costs may easily be identified, although benefits may be uncertain. In this political and economic environment, the government may need to turn opponents into supporters: if *commitment* ability is relatively low, the government has to improve its *coalition building* strategy. This strategy of *widening the political base* for the reform is, indeed, more common in countries where the government has less political power due to institutional design or to strong opposition by powerful interest groups. Interestingly, such reforms need not be less efficient—although some measures often had to be watered down, and thus became less effective. In the most successful cases (such as the Danish labour market reforms), the government managed to turn oppositions round by modifying the distribution of benefits. In other cases, the enactment of the reform had to be substantially delayed, to secure the support of the present veto players.

Evidently, buying off oppositions may well come at a substantial cost. For this reason, the presence of strong veto players may indeed prevent some reforms from being enacted, and valuable opportunities are thus missed. In other cases, though, tilting the incentives of the policymakers—thereby *forcing* the government to widen support for a reform— helps build consensus in the population and facilitates the reform process, instead of crystallizing confrontations.

This tailoring strategy can go into remarkable detail in an attempt to protect the economic surplus of some groups. We found it quite striking, for instance, that the success or the failure of pension reforms in Italy essentially hinged on how surpluses and costs were divided. As we saw in Chapter 9, trying to force a reform on the aging Italian population stood little chance of success. By contrast, overtly breaching the social contract ended up creating much less turmoil once the government accepted the need to shield older sections of the population from the burden of adjustment, shifting this burden to younger (and politically less active) parts of the population. In this specific example, Italy gave up some of the benefits of faster and more efficient reform for the sake of political realism. These tailored reforms ended up protecting those who had contributed to the Italian pension system during their working life. The "forceful" option might have been to partly deprive them of their pensions, while leaving bigger benefits to younger generations. The various pension reforms passed in Italy, together with Berlusconi's failed attempt covered in the previous chapter, provide a complete overview of the benefits of *widening political support*. In a similar way, early in their transition to a market economy, Central and Eastern European countries (CEECs) tailored their privatizations explicitly to widen political support for their reforms. The forceful option might have been less palatable to the masses, but would presumably have been more efficient.

The main message conveyed by the case studies analysed in this chapter is thus that reforms can succeed even with "weak" governments. The view that a stark, confrontational style is a necessary condition to reform successfully would thus be mistaken in this economic and political scenario. In the cases studied in this chapter, the governments had to look for ways that made their re-tailored reforms closer to a Pareto improvement. Yet, not all reforms could be made entirely efficient: in a second-best world, the fate of a well-thought-out reform depends more on the government's ability to distribute the benefits than on its ability to maximize them.

10.1. *Flexicurity* in Denmark

OECD studies (1999) rank Denmark as one of the most flexible countries in terms of employment protection, close to the UK or the USA, since economic reasons can easily be invoked for laying off workers regardless of their age, social condition, or tenure. As in the USA, there is no general legal provision giving protection from unfair dismissal, while legal lay-off compensations are minimal: none before 12 years of tenure, and peaking at three months after 18 years of tenure. This framework results in a very small number of cases being brought for unfair dismissal (0.004% of employees, compared to 0.5% in France for instance). These dispositions were left unchanged after the 1994–9 reform.

This flexibility on the employment side has typically been balanced by very strong protection on the unemployment side. Before 1994, unemployment benefits could run for up to nine years. Training periods and subsidized job offers were usually not proposed before the end of a first period of 2.5 years, and if they were accepted by unemployed workers, these programmes used to renew the right to benefits. Moreover, these benefits represented (and still represent) up to 90 per cent of the previous wage— with a ceiling at approximately 1,500 euros per month. The Danish system hence represented one of the most generous unemployment insurance schemes among OECD countries, especially for low-paid workers.

This institutional framework created a strong *constituency effect*, as defined by Saint-Paul (2002*b*). On the one hand, employees accept the flexibility of employment (and hence a high probability of losing their jobs) in exchange for a generous unemployment insurance system and because they do not lose any social rights. Moreover, trade unions encompass both employed and unemployed members. Consequently, they do not only defend the position of employees, nor do they fear losing members when jobs are destroyed (see Calmfors and Driffill, 1988; Jørgensen, 2003). On the other hand, employers do not finance the social cost of job turnover by themselves. The unemployment system allows them to recruit workers easily (even for short periods) and to adjust their workforce in line with the evolution of demand. Additionally, the system is not always financially balanced and, regularly, the state finances the deficit of unemployment insurance.

Yet, at the beginning of the 1990s, Denmark experienced a trough and the economy did not recover before 1994. In 1993, real GDP increased by only 0.8 per cent. Consequently, the unemployment rate peaked at 12 per cent and did not decrease significantly until 1995 (see Fig. 10.1), which jeopardized an insurance scheme designed in times of low unemployment.

The Danish political background is easily described as a long sequence of coalition governments between minority parties, since no single party has had a majority in parliament since 1909. Seats in the Danish parliament are allocated to the parties on a proportional representation basis, so that the constitution of the "Folketing" closely reflects the diversity of political preferences of the population. In most legislatures, centrist parties have determined which side was able to form a majority in the Folketing and therefore which party was in power. Yet, governments have been able to collaborate with both sides of the parliament thanks to the Danish tradition of compromise and consensus.

This tradition is also present among social partners, and the relative instability of coalitions is compensated by their high representativeness. The foundation of social dialogue institutions in Denmark dates back to

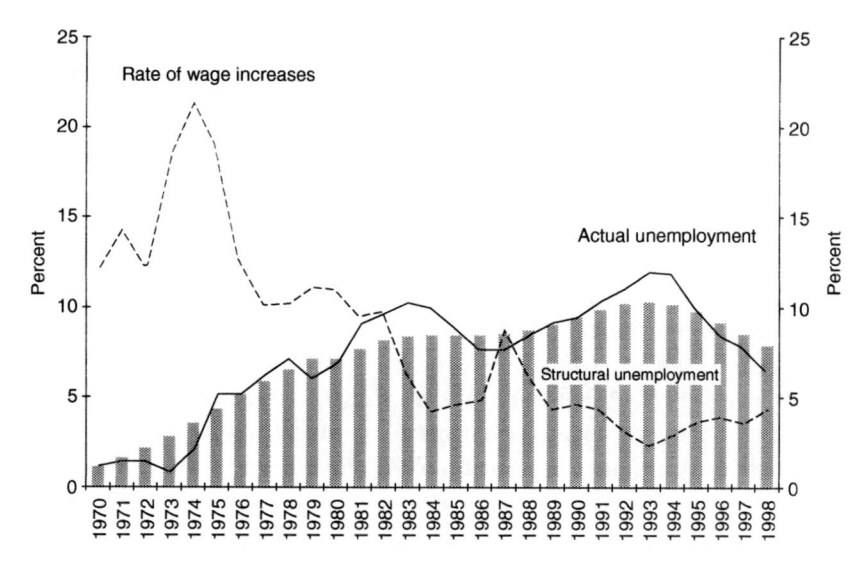

Fig. 10.1 Developments in unemployment, structural unemployment, and rates of wage increases in Denmark, 1970–1998

Source: OECD, Employment Outlook.

the late nineteenth century.[1] Labour market organizations have early been in charge of such diverse matters as work organization, working hours, and minimum wage levels (Jørgensen, 2003). Moreover, workers who become unemployed retain membership of their original trade union, which broadens the scope of interest of these organizations (that is why trade union membership peaked at 84% of workers after the recession, in 1995).

The tradition has always been one of stable collective agreements, with the possibility for collective actors to locally adapt rules to circumstances or to the specificities of a branch. Collective agreements are submitted to the vote of members, which gives them democratic support, and governments rarely interfere with this social dialogue—although contacts between labour market organizations and political parties are frequent. One consequence is that some workers are covered by collective agreements (some 25% of the active population in the late 1990s). Another consequence is that open conflicts between the government and labour market organizations can happen, such as in 2001 (see Chapter 9). But overall, compared to other (south) European countries the system of trade unions in Denmark is both highly representative and unitary, with a strong ability to coordinate at all levels.

Some consensus for a reform of the unemployment insurance scheme was hence needed exactly as unemployment was peaking—the population exposed to the reform was largest—and some of the workers still employed were unsure about the future of their jobs, since the recovery had not started yet. The Danish labour market reform was hence designed and discussed at a difficult time; yet, the crisis seemed to stimulate rather than hinder the reform momentum. The strong pressure exerted by financial constraints helped the relevant actors reach an agreement on the need to reform the scheme and thus to introduce more financial discipline. Simultaneously, a plan to kick-start the economy was introduced. This was instrumental in maintaining the support of the former reform. But the consensus was also built on the need to achieve more social integration, since the unemployment policy (unemployment insurance but also active labour market policies) had turned out to be ineffective at preventing the rise of long-term unemployment and inactivity (see

---

[1] The industrial Danish Federation of Trade Unions (LO) was founded in 1896, and the Danish Federation of Employers (DA) was established in 1898. The organization of white-collar workers is more recent with the Central Confederation of Salaried Employees (FTF) founded in 1952 and the Central Confederation of Professional Associations (AC) founded in 1972.

Fig. 10.2). Indeed, the reform was a mix of social discipline and social integration efforts, since it also tackled the integration of the long-term unemployed through both financial incentives and active labour market policies. The latter aspect of the reform was actually a response to the increased uncertainty facing the unemployed.

Within this political and social scenario, in 1993 the Social-Democratic Party took office and soon started a coalition building effort to reform the unemployment benefit system, based on the 1992 report of the "Zeuthen Commission". The main concern was the relative inefficiency of the system, which relied too heavily on pure benefits and lacked active labour market policies. As a result, the system was not able to prevent the creation of long-term unemployment, while many job vacancies were left unfilled. Indeed, before 1993, activation policies (placement on training programmes, short-term employment offers, and so on) were offered at pre-determined times during the unemployment period, and just before the end of the initial period of eligibility. Since enrolment in these programmes opened a new period of benefits, these activation policies were used as a way to extend the initial benefit period to nine years.

The first phase of the reform took effect on 1 January 1994, while the unemployment rate was peaking at 12.5 per cent, but also the first signs of recovery from the severe recession of the early 1990s were emerging. This phase relied on three principles: (1) emphasis on individual and regional labour market needs, (2) regional implementation of labour market policies according to objectives designed at national level, and (3) participation of labour market organizations in the implementation of policies

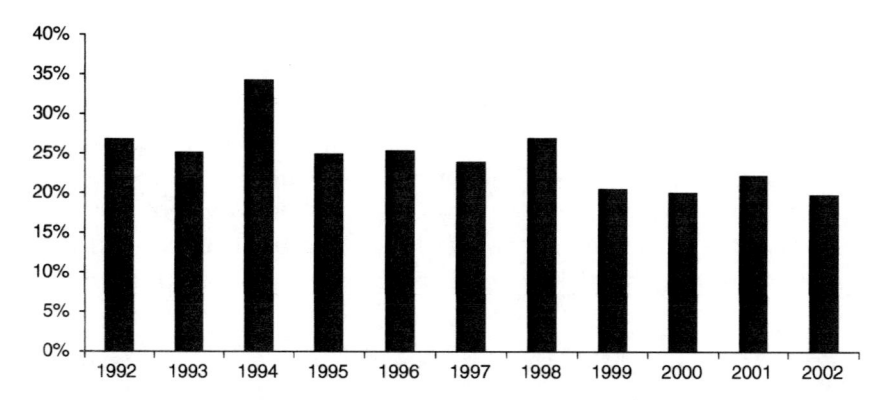

Fig. 10.2 Share of unemployed workers with seniority over 12 months, Denmark
Source: OECD, Employment Outlook.

at the regional level. Moreover, participation in activation policies would not open a new period of benefits.

Within the same reform framework, in 1995 the duration of insurance was reduced to a maximum of seven years and participation in activation programmes became compulsory (with the threat of cutting benefits in case of refusal). In 1996, the second phase started. The compulsory activation phase was set to occur two years after the beginning of the unemployment period (six months for people under the age of 25 and with no diplomas), the maximum duration of benefits was reduced to a maximum of five years including activation programmes. Finally, in 1999, a third round of measures set the activation phase one year after the beginning of the unemployment registration, while reducing the maximum duration of benefits to four years (3.5 years for anybody under 25), including activation.

To summarize, over the 1994–9 period, the maximum duration of benefits was reduced from nine to four years, and a "duty" of activation was introduced after one year (or six months if under 25), while the level of benefits remained unchanged. The minimum period of contribution was increased from 26 to 52 weeks (six months for workers less than 25). Moreover, training, sabbatical, and parental leaves were introduced to promote job rotation between employed and unemployed people.

Overall, the Danish experience is an example of social disciplining and social integration efforts (Larsen, 2004) jointly decided and implemented by the social partners (from initial commitment through to final agreement). It was a challenging reform that transformed a generous but passive unemployment insurance scheme into an active device targeted at the least employable workers.

10.2. Mass privatizations in Central and Eastern European transition countries

The soviet style of economic planning had generated a situation of general shortage (see e.g. Kornai, 1980 and Roland, 2000). Unemployment was non-existent; each individual firm preferred to hoard labour to maintain an internal supply of labour. Employers thus constantly tried to maintain workers "in-house", even though some of them might be redundant. To that end, enterprises developed a wide-ranging series of non-monetary perks (see e.g. Milanovic, 1995, and Brada, 1996). Workers had thus acquired significant rents: they could work little, be paid a comparatively high real wage (in kind, in many cases), and they were protected from grim unemployment spells despite the blatant inadequacy and poor competitiveness of their production.

Accordingly, one of the primary *economic* goals of transition was to restore productive efficiency and force supply to adapt to demand (quite the opposite to central planning times). This required a massive reallocation of factors of production (Aghion and Blanchard, 1994; Castanheira and Roland, 2000). However, reorganizing production proved extremely difficult, and contributed to the dramatic output fall that was observed early in transition (Roland and Verdier, 1999). Advancing further with structural reforms was thus likely to face increasingly strong opposition from the population, who were primarily confronted with their *negative* effects.[2]

Political objectives of privatization

To maintain momentum and eventually improve productive efficiency (which was the only way to generate windfalls from reforms), management decisions needed to be "depoliticized", in the words of Boycko *et al.* (1993). Privatizing *en masse* was seen to be a necessary step in that direction.[3] However, one must realize that one of the "desired" effects of privatization was to generate further adjustments, including a reduction in employment where necessary (see Brickley *et al.*, 2000; Claessens and Djankov, 1999; Gonenc *et al.*, 2000; Megginson and Netter, 2001; Megginson *et al.*, 2001; Sheshinski and López-Calva, 2003, among others, for more detail about the observed effects of privatizations). Therefore, privatization had the potential to reinforce opposition to pro-reform parties, which could have sparked a reversal of the reforms achieved until then. Reformers thus needed a "tool" that could, at the same time, accelerate the reform process *and* "buy" wider support in the population.

Most reforming governments in transition countries designed their privatization programmes with that objective in mind. The idea was essentially to *give* ownership to the population (essentially for free), for the sole purpose of getting support for other reforms in exchange (see Biais and Perotti, 2002 for a formalization of this argument). To quote Boycko *et al.* (1993: 147–8):

The goal of governments that launch privatisation always is to gain support.... Mass privatisation fits this mandate particularly well because it is perceived by the

---

[2] See also Chapter 9, Section 9.2, where we showed how some reforms in Russia could even be targeted at the population, granting *de facto* exemptions to the highest classes in the population.

[3] By contrast, China adopted a dual-track approach to improve managerial decisions in firms. See Roland (2000, ch. 6).

general populace as the only part of the economic reform that can unambiguously benefit them. Unlike price liberalisation, monetary tightening, and reduction of government spending,... privatisation allocates shares to the people for free... — typically a popular measure.... The need to gain support for reform is the political argument for privatising rapidly.

Along the same lines, Brada (1996: 67) summarizes the reformers' political objective as follows: "the state's monopoly... must be broken so that countervailing sources of political influence may emerge (Berger, 1992). Otherwise, the *nomenklatura*, managers of state-owned firms and former bureaucrats, may sabotage or block economic reforms".

The risks of excessively underpricing state-owned enterprises (SOEs) during privatization were already known at the time. Bolton and Roland (1992), for instance, had clearly warned governments against such a strategy. Their analysis demonstrates that underpriced privatization can endanger macroeconomic stability because it foregoes excessive amounts of government revenue. The subsequent rouble crisis episode is but one concrete example of such mismanagement (see also Chapter 9, Section 9.2).

Despite this risk, most transition economies opted for rapid privatization schemes, at the expense of government revenue. To reinforce support for their programme (or for themselves), many reformers refrained from selling state firms during privatization—even in exchange for future repayments (i.e. from providing some type of a loan to the buyers, as Bolton and Roland (1992) were advising). Instead, most mass privatization schemes relied on "vouchers" that were distributed to the population— essentially for free. Although inefficient, such schemes were popular because they effectively transferred ownership to the population at large, and vouchers could easily be sold for cash.

As we know, privatization programmes can potentially serve two goals: generating finance for the government and improving microeconomic efficiency. Most governments in transition deliberately abstained from aiming at the former objective. What about the second?

Economic objective: restore efficiency

Microeconomic efficiency relates to two different dimensions. To achieve efficiency, the output of a firm should be sold at a price close to its marginal cost of production. Moreover, the firm should be induced to adopt an "efficient" cost structure. That is, the management of the firm must have appropriate incentives to reduce operating costs. These incentives are typically provided by market competition, appropriate governance structure, and hard budget constraints. However, SOEs tend to be largely shielded from these constraints (see also Schmidt, 1997; Shleifer, 1998; Sheshinski and López-Calva, 2003). In addition, under state ownership, the management may be induced also to pursue *political objectives* that are orthogonal to efficiency. This is why Boycko *et al.* (1993) stressed the need to "de-politicize" the production process. However, in the presence of monopoly power, there may be a trade-off between these two dimensions: state control may help reduce monopoly rents, at the expense of potentially more distorting incentives to reduce costs.

Megginson and Netter (2001) summarize this trade-off in the following way: "if there are no externalities in production and consumption, the product is not a public good, the market is not monopolistic in its structure, information costs are low etc...", then there is no reason for any form of state intervention. In particular, any SOE in that market should be privatized. Indeed, as noted by Brickley *et al.* (2000), "the price system motivates better use of knowledge and information in economic decisions ... it provides stronger incentives for individuals to make productive decisions". Last, state ownership or state control over capital supply typically reinforces the problem of soft-budget constraints (Kornai, 1980, 1986; Dewatripont and Maskin, 1995; Roland 2000, ch. 12). For all these reasons, state control was clearly introducing more inefficiencies than it could correct.

Privatization thus *had to* improve microeconomic efficiency—without generating too much opposition. To this end, it *had to* improve the match between management and productive equipment. This clearly required the replacement of most existing managers, who were generally not appointed because of their management ability (see Winiecki, 1996).

How did governments actually design their privatization programmes? First, one must realize that *all* countries resorted to more than one scheme. Countries that relied on mass privatization schemes for the bulk of the industry did *sell* specific firms as well. One perfect example is that of the Czech Republic, which pursued a mass privatization programme (see below) as well as targeted privatization of its main car producer, Škoda (Chapter 12).

A brief account of some mass privatization programmes

Here, we briefly describe some of the main privatization schemes that were used in transition countries. For a much more careful account, see

Roland (2000, ch. 10), who also provides a deep survey of the different theories of privatization that are applicable to transition countries. Brada (1996) provides more detail about the amounts involved and the resulting distribution of ownership.[4]

In a nutshell, their evidence shows that only two countries primarily tried to *sell* SOEs, namely Eastern Germany and Hungary. Eastern Germany is of course a special case. First of all, one must realize that, if mass privatization schemes had to be used to buy out support in many countries, Western Germany had already made a substantial "gift" to Eastern Germany by accepting a 1:1 conversion rate between the two German marks. Second, the reunification implied that enormous resources could be poured into the privatization process by other means than give-aways. As evidenced by Brada (1996), despite the attempt at *selling firms for cash*, the eventual flow of resources largely went from the government to the new owners. Even though the *Treuhandanstalt* (the German privatization agency) managed to raise $50 billion from the sale of these firms, it had to spend $243 billion in the process, to a large extent to sustain restructuring. Of course, most of the other countries could not afford such expenses, which in any case did not seem to yield impressive results.

Hungary is another particular case. Famous for having had the deepest privatization programme in all Central and Eastern Europe (Canning and Hare, 1996), in contrast to many other countries, Hungary bet on economic efficiency gains (instead of pure underpricing) to generate popular support. The bulk of privatization thus occurred through *sales*—often to foreign investors, who accounted for about half of the total sales of assets.[5] Moreover, to maintain a high sale value for these firms, the government opted for a *gradual* privatization scheme (the process, however, accelerated in a second phase). What made this choice potentially worthwhile on a political economy basis is that Hungary's reform programme was considered trustworthy by Westerners, since pre-transition reforms (with the Velvet Revolution) had created sufficiently sound grounds for reforms. Policy reversals were thus less to be feared.

The programme established in Poland was quite different. It was a mixture of direct sales and of mass privatization. In the early years of

---

[4] See also Welch and Frémond (1998) and Bortolotti and Siniscalco (2004) for a review of different methods of privatization.

[5] That aspect deserves attention. Privatization to foreigners often triggers substantial opposition from nationals, and is therefore avoided, despite its obvious benefits in terms of potential FDI. The particular position of Hungary did allow the government to rely on substantial inflows of FDI to ensure that opposition and discontent would not grow excessively. The resulting productivity improvements, which were substantial, proved that strategy right.

transition, the goal of policy-makers was to create a functioning capital market. Hence, some firms were privatized through direct sales to (often foreign) strategic investors and stock-market flotation. Firms were selected for privatization by the government, and restructured to make them attractive to potential buyers. However, opposition to this privatization process rapidly organized itself, partly thanks to pre-transition reforms that had reinforced unionization inside firms. This opposition, together with the limited capacity of the government to identify which firms to privatize and how to restructure them, led to a protracted privatization process which turned out to be less successful than expected. Following the insights proposed above, the reaction of the government was to spread the benefits of privatizations more widely. To this end, a National Investment Fund programme was introduced. This led to the voucher privatization of about 10 per cent of state firms, with a complex management and ownership structure.

The Czech Republic instead started immediately with a mass privatization programme, where most firms would be handed over to the population. From the start, firms were distributed for a fraction of their real value, which generated popular support for the reforms initiated by the government of Vaclav Klaus. Moreover, "thanks" to the lack of pre-transition restructuring, unions could not manipulate, or oppose the process, which ensured its success (Roland, 2000). Thanks to the appropriate timing of this privatization programme with respect to the elections, Vaclav Klaus secured his popularity, and could obtain his re-election as Prime Minister in 1996. He was also elected as President in 2003.

To end this brief overview, we should also consider the case of Russia, whose hectic corporate governance reforms were described in Chapter 9, Section 9.2. As we showed there, reforms were characterized by very weak enforcement of private property, exceptions for some oligarchs, and strong collective inertia in the population. Lack of trust in reforms and in the government, together with rising inequalities, meant that, to ensure the success of its privatizations, the government had largely to "bribe" potential shareholders. The method chosen in Russia was thus to give the bulk of firms for free, and to *insiders*. Considering the two potential economic objectives of privatization (raising revenue and improving microeconomic efficiency), this probably represented the worst possible option. Give-aways imply that no revenue is raised. Next, privatizing to insiders implies that the governance of the firms is unlikely to be dramatically improved. For instance, Russian firms were riddled with labour hoarding. Restructuring thus required lay-offs in most firms. Yet, this decision was left to incumbent managers and workers themselves. Clearly, the rationale behind such a choice must be found in its political effects. In a country where profitability was very low and property rights improperly established, citizens preferred to maintain the rents they reaped through control of their firm rather than diversify their portfolio and obtain a fraction of the firms' small official profits.

In all cases, however, state and privatized firms had to adjust to survive. Competition from abroad and from newly created private businesses remained inescapable for most firms. Government budget constraints also tightened sharply (most of the time when a crisis occurred), which implied that state firms' budget constraints eventually hardened as well. One therefore observes that significant defensive restructuring also occurred in SOEs (see e.g. Bevan *et al.*, 1999).

10.3. The season of reforms in Italy

Throughout the mid-1980s, Italian public pension expenditure rose consistently, from less than 1 per cent of GDP in 1951 to above 10 per cent in the mid-1980s (see Fig. 10.3); while the proportion of elderly individuals (of more than 60 years) in the population increased from 12 per cent in 1951 to 21 per cent in the mid-1980s. This hike in pension spending was mainly due to an extension of pension coverage, to relaxation of the eligibility criteria, and to an increase in the generosity of pension benefits. Three types of pension benefits drove this expansion: early retirement (or seniority), non-contributive (social) and disability benefits. The early retirement provision, initially introduced in 1956, allowed generous pension benefits to be awarded after a small contributory period, regardless of the worker's age, and become a popular early pathway from the labour market in the late 1960s, as labour market conditions worsened and several elderly workers were forced to retire early in order to avoid unemployment. Non-contributive (or social) pensions and even disability benefits, which were not contingent on physical disability but on inability to earn income (see Franco, 2002), represented instead instruments of income support to elderly people in the poorer regions.

This rapid increase in spending was not unique to the pension system; indeed, the entire Italian welfare state, government consumption, and public employment experienced sustained growth after the Second World War. Several scholars have associated this characteristic policy-making by

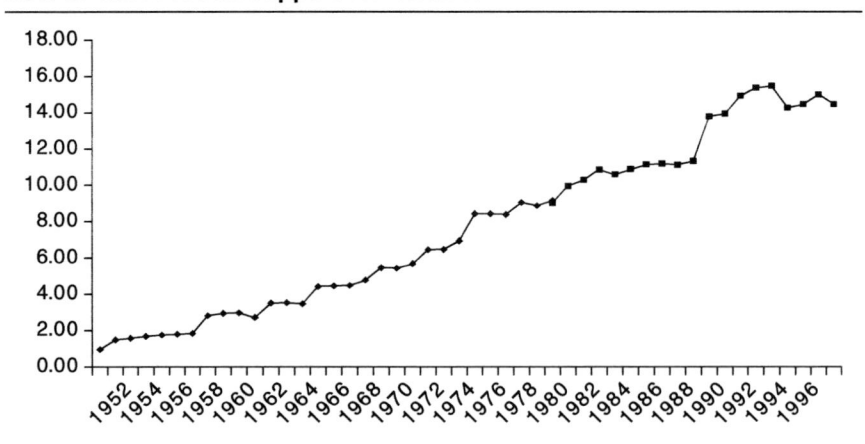

Fig. 10.3 Social security expenditure as a proportion of GDP in Italy
Source: OECD, National Account Statistics, Ferrara (1984).

the Italian government with some institutional features of its political system. In particular, its high degree of party fragmentation (see Sartori, 1982) has often been blamed for producing weak coalition governments unable to keep control of the spending.

In the 1990s, however, Italy experienced a crucial break with its past, since three major reforms were approved in 1992 (Amato), 1995 (Dini), and 1997 (Prodi) in an attempt to provide a progressive stabilization of pension expenditure as a proportion of the GDP, and hence to ensure the long-run sustainability of the system, as well as its financial solvency in the short run.

In 1992, on the eve of the reform period, the Italian pension system was a generous, unfunded, defined benefit system. Despite a 26.4 per cent payroll tax on labour earnings, the private employees' scheme (FPLD, "Fondo Pensioni Lavoratori Dipendenti") featured a large deficit financed through general taxation. Old-age pension spending was equal to almost 15 per cent of GDP, while the share of the elderly in the population was up to 25 per cent. The mandatory retirement age, under the FPLD scheme, was 60 years for a male worker and 55 for females; yet, regardless of their age, workers were eligible for a seniority pension, provided that they had at least 35 years' worth of contributions.

The first successful reform of the Italian pension system was carried out in 1992 by a coalition government formed after the May 1992 elections—the last political elections held with a purely proportional system. The coalition was composed of four parties—PSI, DC, PSDI, and PLI—and was led by a Socialist Prime Minister, Giuliano Amato.

The main event that eventually triggered the 1992 reform occurred in February 1992—even before the election that led to the Amato coalition government—when Italy, under the government led by the Christian Democrat Giulio Andreotti, decided to sign the Maastricht Treaty, thereby committing itself to meet its requirements on inflation and public finances, namely on government deficit and public debt. Faced with these *external constraints*, upon forming his government, Amato asked the parliament to be given large powers in order to reshape the public sector, and in particular the pensions system. In September 1992, Italy was hit by a major financial crisis, as the lira came under strong speculative attack and eventually had to devaluate and exit the European Monetary System. After September 1992, the need for pension reform became evident to a broad swathe of public opinion. The aim of the Amato reform was mainly to guarantee the financial solvency of the pension system in the short run and to stabilize pension expenditure as a share of GDP, by introducing less generous criteria for computing pension benefits, and by restricting eligibility, in particular with respect to retirement age.

The coalition building phase that followed was favoured by wide recognition of these external constraints and by the compromising style of the Amato government (Ferrera and Gualmini, 2004, refer to this situation as an emergency political exchange). Indeed, unions initially opposed any pension reform, although this behaviour partly changed after the September 1992 financial crisis. Interestingly, union leaders were barracked by the crowd on public occasions in September and October 1992 for their willingness to negotiate with the government. Amato's key move to obtain the unions' consensus was to design a long transition period for the reform. Existing pension claims by workers with more than 15 years of contributions in 1992 were not touched. The new rules applied only to the newly hired, and in a pro-rata fashion to those workers with less than 15 years of contributions.

When implemented, the Amato reform was to produce a gradual tightening of eligibility requirements, over a transition period estimated to last two or three decades. For instance, the retirement age was to increase to 60 years for women and 65 for men. The generosity of pensions was reduced by modifying the pension benefits' calculation.[6] Finally, pension benefits were automatically indexed to inflation rather than to nominal

---

[6] The reference wage to be considered for this calculation was changed from the average wage over the five years prior to retirement to the average wage during the entire working career, with past earnings being capitalized at the cost of living index plus 1% per year. Although the replacement rate was not modified—remaining equal to the number of years of contribution multiplied by a 2% rate of return—the average pension decreased, due to a small average reference wage for a typical worker using the new calculation.

wages, although the government was allowed to adopt ad hoc intervention through the Budgetary Law. This last element probably represented the single most effective measure of the Amato reform in containing pension spending and was a rather unique case of reduction in the pension benefits of *current* retirees. After this reform, pension benefits differed in real terms according to the year of retirement, and elderly individuals saw the purchasing power of their pensions decrease over time, thereby raising equity concerns and pressure for redistribution (see Gronchi, 1998; Gronchi and Aprile, 1998; and Rostagno, 1996).

To explain the political support in favour of—and the opposition to—this reform, it is useful to identify the effects of the reform measures on economic well-being, as measured by the net pension wealth of the agents—workers and retirees—covered by the social security system. Net pension wealth is defined as the discounted value of future pension benefits which an individual is entitled to receive under the current legislation, minus the discounted value of her future contributions to the system. A reduction in the net pension wealth of an agent measures the costs of such a reform to this individual. Beltrametti (1995 and 1996) estimated the variations in individual net pension wealth by age induced by the Amato reform, as well as by the Dini reform and by the Berlusconi government's attempt.

According to these estimates, the Amato reform was sizeable, as it reduced the workers' net pension wealth by 52.9 per cent. Both workers and retirees had to foot the bill of the adjustment towards a more financially balanced system, although in rather unequal shares, since, as shown in Table 10.1, most of the reduction in the net pension wealth was sustained by the young cohorts—more than 100 per cent for the individuals aged 30 years or less, and only less than 5 per cent for workers and retirees aged 60 years or more. The long transition period designed by Amato was hence crucial in limiting the effect of the reform on elderly workers and retirees, who constituted the unions' main constituency,[7] thereby reducing their opposition.

Yet, three years later a new reform was implemented. After the Berlusconi government was brought down because of its reform attempt, a technical[8] caretaker government, led by the former Treasury Minister in the Berlusconi

---

[7] Brugiavini *et al.* (2001) provide supporting evidence in favour of the existence of a "seniority bias" in the union representatives' behaviour in welfare state policy decisions, according to which union representatives tend to give more weight to the interests of middle-aged and elderly workers.

[8] According to Ferrera and Gualmini (2004), a government is "technical", as opposed to political, if almost all members are non-elected. They are typically chosen among professionals, in particular institutions, such as the Bank of Italy, and in academia, because of their specific skills or knowledge, but have no marked political affiliation.

Table 10.1 The effects of the reforms on net pension wealth by age

	Amato Reform[a]			Berlusconi Proposal[a]			Dini Reform[a]	
	Before	After	Δ	Before	After	Δ	After	Δ
15–19	28	−31	−59	−48	−52	−4	−56	−8
20–24	152	−50	−202	−101	−116	−15	−128	−27
25–29	276	−43	−319	−112	−131	−19	−145	−33
30–34	347	46	−301	−20	−56	−36	−63	−43
35–39	415	198	−217	139	71	−68	99	−40
40–44	504	282	−222	227	174	−53	227	0
45–49	497	349	−148	306	251	−55	306	0
50–54	533	441	−92	402	338	−64	402	0
55–59	394	360	−34	339	238	−101	339	0
60–64	183	177	−6	168	160	−8	168	0
65+	79	76	−3	74	74	0	74	0
Workers	3.407	1.802	−1.605	1.375	997	−378	1.225	−151
Retirees	2.660	2.527	−133	2.710	2.710	0	2.710	0

Note: [a] In billion of Italian lire in 1992.
Source: D'Amato and Galasso (2002).

government, Lamberto Dini, was formed in January 1995. This government enjoyed the support in Parliament of some of Progressisti (PDS, PPI, and other parties, apart from Rifondazione Comunista) and by Lega Nord, which had been elected in the centre-to-right coalition.

Unsurprisingly, the Dini government continued with the previous government commitment to reform the pension system—Dini was the Treasury Minister responsible for the reform plan in Berlusconi's government—in an economic situation characterized by continuous devaluations of the lira. Dini did not renege on the urgency of a further pension reform, which actually represented one of the four institutional goals of his caretaker government; however, his approach to obtaining the necessary support for reform was different from the Berlusconi government's.

Its compromising style resembled the successful approach of Amato in 1992, and in fact, the unions agreed on negotiating with the new government. According to Ferrera and Gualmini (2004), unions were indeed keener on a government supported by a centre-to-left majority in Parliament. Additionally, the economic constraints had become more binding, as the economic situation was worsening, as shown by the benchmark interest rate differential with Germany, which started to increase.

However, the most relevant factor in obtaining the unions' support as well as in persuading Lega Nord, which had previously opposed a pension reform, was again the long transition period envisaged by the reform. Although the Dini measures were substantially different from the previous reforms, as they introduced a structural change in the Italian pension system, the same transition path as in the Amato reform was chosen. In 1992, workers with 15 years of contributions were shielded by the reform measures, which were then applied pro rata to the other workers. In 1995, a similar exemption was awarded to workers with 18 years of contributions. As displayed in Table 10.1, however, despite using the same cut-off as in 1992, in 1995 the split of the costs among the different generations was more uneven.

The Dini reform redesigned the architecture of the Italian pension system, which shifted from a defined benefit (DB) scheme to a notional defined contribution (NDC) system. The role of the state in the pension industry remained a dominant one. However, workers were not promised a given pension, almost independently of their previous contributions; on the contrary, with this NDC scheme, individual pension benefits were entirely linked to the worker's lifetime contributions.[9] Within this NDC framework, seniority pensions—whose eligibility was exclusively based on having reached a minimum contribution period, regardless of the worker's age—were eliminated, and more flexibility was provided over the retirement decision, with individuals allowed to retire between 57 and 65 years old, but with pension benefits being reduced accordingly.

Interestingly, the most highly criticized feature of this reform has been the long length of the transition to a new regime entirely shaped by the Dini reform. Several scholars—see Franco (2002) and references therein—have argued that the transition from the pre-1992 to the new regime has been and will continue to be too slow and gradual, thereby inducing only a slow improvement in the financial sustainability of the system, while violating a simple notion of intergenerational equity, since the burden of the transition has been shifted onto the younger generations of workers.

Yet, this highly controversial measure—on grounds of both equity and efficiency—represented the key modification in the reform package, with respect to the Berlusconi plan, discussed in Chapter 9, which failed in 1994, allowing the necessary political support for reforming the system to be built. Indeed, the Dini reform was also milder, with a reduction in the net pension wealth of the workers of only 11 per cent. However, as suggested by the estimates in Table 10.1, the political success of this reform,

---

[9] In particular, these contributions were capitalized at an interest rate equal to average nominal GDP growth, and—once at retirement—the capitalized contributions were transformed into an annuity through a conversion coefficient which depends negatively on the expected life at retirement and positively on the actual retirement age. A full description of the Dini reform measures and an evaluation of its effects is given in Brugiavini and Galasso (2004).

as opposed to Berlusconi's attempt, is mainly due to its placing the costs of the reforms on the young generations of workers. With a majority of the voting population in 1995 being over 44 years,[10] the Dini reform did not touch the vested interests of a majority of voters—workers and retirees. To these middle-aged and elderly individuals, the reform was costless, while ensuring the short-run financial solvency of the system, and hence the payment of their accrued pension benefits. Similarly, this reform package did not limit current middle-aged and elderly workers' rights to a seniority pension, thereby avoiding opposition by Lega Nord, as well as by the unions.

---

[10] See D'Amato and Galasso (2002) for a quantitative appraisal of the effects of population aging on political representation and hence on the long-term political sustainability of the pension system in Italy.

11
Divide and Conquer

Despite its political correctness, the strategy of widening the political base for reform by emphasizing social dialogue—as described in the previous chapter—is not always viable. On several instances, reforms are bound to have a negative effect on the vested interests of powerful economic, social, or political actors, so that *buying out* their opposition may become too costly in economic or political terms. In this chapter, we concentrate on the economic scenarios in which a reform—typically the liberalization of a market or the retrenchment of a programme of the welfare state—tends to create diffused, but uncertain gains, for instance to current or future taxpayers, while causing clearly identifiable costs to a relatively concentrated group of individuals. The liberalization of the taxi or of several legal services in many European countries represent good examples of these reforms.

In an alternative economic scenario examined in this chapter, the vested interests damaged by a reform are so tightly entrenched that the strategy of widening the political base for reform through social dialogue would need the support of virtually all social or political actors. Also in these cases, buying out the opposition through targeted concessions is not feasible without a massive watering down of the reforming effort.

Interestingly, both features are typically present in non-manufacturing industry. One peculiarity of non-manufacturing is that it is the area of economic activity in which regulation and public intervention have traditionally been most pervasive, but also where the scope for change is often considered to be largest, as reforms in this area remain—at least nominally—at the top of the political agenda of many governments. Yet, non-manufacturing industries are often sheltered from international trade, swamped with government regulations, and characterized by entrenched interests common to consumers and producers. To see this, consider a possible telecommunication reform: the elimination of rents both to the producers and to the workers and the possible increase in the cost to the consumers—if the industry is initially subsidized—will likely create stiff resistance to reform by several potential voters of all parties across the political spectrum. Since the possible gain from such reform is spread out among all taxpayers, the political cost of reforming will likely outweigh the political benefits. In fact, the history of reforms in this area has both bright and dark spots, as there are probably as many successful reforms as failed attempts. Several of the cases analyzed in this chapter will thus draw from this industry, which constitutes a privileged viewpoint for analysing the interplay of the different forces acting on reform, such as public and private interests and the political and institutional setting.

When *buying out* opponents to a reform becomes too costly in economic or political terms, policy-makers have to follow a different route and try to separate the entrenched interests of the different actors—rather than compensate them. Unlike in the previous chapter, the aim of this *divide and conquer* strategy is not to spread benefits, but rather to concentrate costs. On some occasions, this will require targeting some particular groups of individuals, who will have to foot the bill; whereas, at other times, a gradual approach to reform will be required in an attempt to initially reduce the rents appropriated in the market and only later to liberalize it. The former strategy, named *divide et impera*, is described in the next section; while the gradualist approach, named the *trickle-down effect*, is summarized in Section 11.2.

11.1. Divide et Impera

The Latin motto, *divide et impera*, may provide a good representation of a successful strategy often applied to reforming the non-manufacturing industry. The core message is to try to separate the interests of the actors, such as producers, consumers, workers, and even politicians who initially oppose the reform plan. Since this division typically cannot be achieved along political lines, policy-makers often have to devise a plan that separates this *ex-ante* coalition of interests into winners and losers. The case studies analysed below demonstrate how this strategy has been applied in the telecommunications industry to separate the interests of producers and workers and in the several subsidized sectors to break the coalition between producers and consumers.

This strategy proved to be particularly effective in reforming the non-manufacturing market, in which a strong regulatory status quo typically arises. In fact, most non-manufacturing regulations have at least some grounding in public interest. Market failures (e.g. due to economies of scale or information asymmetries) abound in many non-manufacturing industries and some form of government intervention is often necessary to ensure productive efficiency and protect consumers.[1] Nonetheless, public interest explanations of existing regulations also have several limitations, as they often fail to balance the expected benefits of regulation with the potential costs of government failure[2] and to explain regulatory inertia, that is, the persistence of regulatory restrictions even when the original reasons for regulation have disappeared, and—more importantly—resistance to regulatory reform.

Additional explanations of the existence of non-manufacturing regulation concentrate instead on private interest. According to these theories (see Olson, 1965; Stigler, 1971; Peltzman, 1976 and 1989; Becker, 1983), regulations are shaped, twisted, and preserved by the attempt of some economic agents (entrepreneurs, workers, consumers, and/or bureaucrats) to maintain or generate political power or economic rents for their own benefit. Agents can do so either by directly controlling the regulatory process or by lobbying politicians and government officials that influence or take regulatory decisions.

The influence of special interests on non-manufacturing regulation has distinctive features, since it is *convergence* of special interests—rather than the conflicts among different groups of rent-seekers—that represents the overriding factor explaining regulatory outcomes in non-manufacturing industries over the past decades. For instance, in industries with natural monopoly elements (such as energy, telecommunications, or railways) political clout has been strengthened by widespread public ownership, the large size and the dominant market shares of incumbent firms, and by high unionization rates within them. In more competitive non-manufacturing industries (such as road freight, retail distribution, or professional services), where the average size of firms is small, trade associations have often been able to develop effective lobbying bodies, which have sometimes taken advantage of institutional channels to

---

[1] Many authors have extensively reviewed the conditions under which government regulation (and, in the limit, public ownership) of business activities are justified on economic grounds. See, for instance, Laffont and Tirole (1993), Hart *et al.* (1997) and, for applications to specific industries in OECD countries, the papers in OECD (2001).

[2] Government failure occurs when well-intentioned policies (targeting aggregate welfare) have effects that are costlier than the market failures they aim to correct. The interplay between *politicians* and *special interest groups*; electoral pressures that distort the application of policies; regulatory capture; and unforeseen side-effects of policies (such as disincentives or externalities); and so on help explain such government failures (see Chapter 8).

promote the industry's interests in local or national regulations. This has created influential industry-specific domestic lobbies characterized by a convergence of interests between employers and employees.

Several factors have also ensured convergence of the interests of large portions of intermediate and final consumers. In many non-manufacturing industries, industry lobbies were able to gather support from consumers by arguing that regulation was essential to guaranteeing service quality, safety, and/or security of supply.[3] In natural monopoly industries, the widespread subsidization of some of the industries' products (such as local communications, passenger transport, or electricity consumption above or below certain thresholds) naturally rallied consumers towards existing regulatory arrangements. In sum, regulatory arrangements in non-manufacturing industries have been sustained by compact interest blocks cutting across different categories of economic agents.

Furthermore, the non-manufacturing sector has traditionally been sheltered from international competition either because it produced intrinsically non-tradable products (e.g. household and personal services) or because its markets had remained mainly domestic until recently (e.g. due to natural monopoly characteristics). Also, some non-manufacturing industries have been sheltered for a long time from foreign equity participation for "strategic" reasons (e.g. air transport, energy, telecommunications).

The following two case studies suggest viable paths to reform which involve the separation of the coalition of vested interests that opposes any change of the status quo. In particular, the parallel experiences of France and Italy in the liberalization process of the telecommunications—triggered both by technological reasons and by EC regulation requirements—highlight the negative role of direct ownership and control by the state of legal monopolies in generating an entrenched coalition of interests between employers and employees. These coalitions are cemented by the sharing of pecuniary and non-pecuniary rents, related to workers' privileges and status, enhancing resistance to change. Prior privatization of the industry or the existence of private contracts for the industry's employees—as in the case of the Italian telecoms—may greatly enhance the probability of liberalizing the market and increase the speed of the process. Reforms in other non-manufacturing sectors may need to overcome the opposition of incumbents with market power and

---

[3] These arguments in favour of existing regulations were voiced particularly loudly in air and rail transport, energy and professional services, but also played a role in rallying support for regulations in road freight and retail distribution.

consumers with status quo bias. In these instances, the policy advice is to liberalize first those services or products that account for large share of firms' intermediate inputs, but a relatively small share of consumer expenditure. This has indeed been the case with several non-manufacturing sectors which were more oriented to business than to final consumers, such as international financial services and road freight in the transport sector.

11.1.1. *Privatize or corporatize: Telecom Italia versus France Telecom*

Some reforms—typically in the product market—involve taking away rents (often reducing or modifying perceived "acquired" rights) across social groups. For example, competition policies affect the rents of both entrepreneurs and their workers, who share the same rents. In such instances, resistance from the beneficiaries of such rents or acquired rights is the major stumbling block on the road to reform.[4] Clearly, the strength of resistance in an industry is affected by the size of rents and by the ability of workers and firms to organize and coordinate. This relates both to the intrinsic characteristics of the industries and to the degree of market and bargaining power allowed by product and labour market institutions. Ceteris paribus, the higher actual and prospective rents, the larger are the incentives to preserve and/or increase market or bargaining power.

A measure of the prospective rents to the workers is provided by wage premia (see the recent estimates by Jean and Nicoletti, 2002, for non-manufacturing industries in the 1990s), although workers in sheltered markets may also accrue non-pecuniary rents, such as lower work effort and job security. Indeed, Jean and Nicoletti (2004) show that, especially in industries in which public ownership is significant, non-pecuniary rents can be more important than wage premia, leading to a non-monotonic relationship between premia and product market regulation (including public ownership). Interestingly, the correlation across countries and industries between the extent of reform and job tenure, which represents a possible measure of non-pecuniary rents, is negative, as shown at Figure 11.1. Thus, it would seem that, where these rents are higher, it has proved more difficult to implement reforms.

---

[4] This resistance is further enhanced by the fact that some of the rents are "capitalized" out of the economic system (the "taxi-cab medallion problem"), so that they are embodied in the price of assets or factor incomes of some agents, even though they did not originally benefit from the redistributive policies (e.g. subsidies, discretional licensing systems, etc.) that generated the rents. In these cases, natural resistance against reforms that eliminate rents is compounded by a feeling of unfairness *vis-à-vis* policy outcomes that makes the political viability of reforms even more difficult. (We owe this point to Koromzay, 2004.)

Divide and Conquer

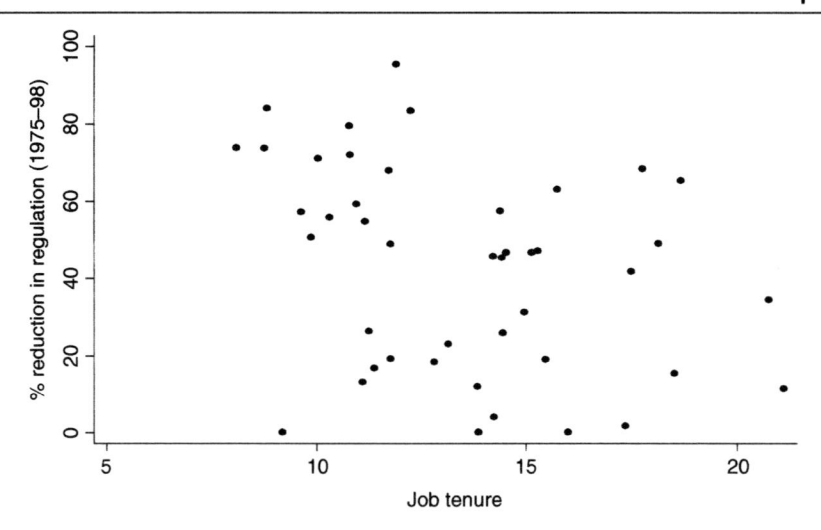

Fig. 11.1 Workers' non-pecuniary rents and regulatory reform
Source: Nicoletti (2006).

Naturally, workers' rents can take a host of other forms, which are embodied neither in tenure nor in estimated premia. Important examples are reduced workers' effort, special contractual arrangements concerning working conditions, or privileged pension schemes. In state-owned non-manufacturing enterprises, these are sometimes compounded by public-law work contracts which ensure a degree of job protection much higher than in the private sector. These favourable conditions provide insiders with a powerful incentive to lobby against attempts to change the legal status and/or the ownership structure of the firm or to open up the market to new entrants when the incumbent enterprise has a monopolistic or dominant position.

The parallel privatization experiences of the French and Italian telecoms in the 1990s provide some hints regarding the impact of these factors on the success and speed of the reform process in the telecommunication market. In fact, while at the beginning of the 1990s, telecommunications workers in the fully state-owned and public-law French telecommunications company (France Telecom) were hired on public-law contracts and had privileged retirement schemes, workers in the state-controlled (but corporatized, partially private and listed) Italian telecommunications companies (STET-SIP-Italcable) had private contracts and were part of general social security arrangements.[5]

---
[5] Analogously, workers in the fully state-owned and public-law French gas company (Gaz de France) had public-law contracts and special retirement schemes, while workers in the

In France, telecommunications were run as a fully public legal monopoly from 1889 to 1997, when the incumbent operator was partially privatized. The incumbent remained an integral part of the telecommunications ministry until 1991, when two public-law companies (*"établissements publics"*), France Telecom (FT) and La Poste, were created. The board of FT included government' representatives, staff members, and independent "experts" named by the government. Employees in FT also retained civil servant status and a special pension scheme and fund. As in the rest of the public sector, FT was a stronghold of the unions,[6] which had successfully opposed early attempts to reform the sector involving the separation of responsibilities for market regulation from the public telecommunications operator (PTO).[7]

At the beginning of the 1990s, the need to implement the EC telecommunications liberalization agenda and the globalization of business strategies in the telecommunications sector accelerated attempts to reform this industry. Although it became evident that the governance structure of FT severely constrained the ability to raise sufficient funds, internationalize the business, and conclude the business alliances needed to face competition, due to political and trade union opposition, the initial attempts to corporatize FT by modifying the inherited governance structure failed.

In 1993, the *"projet Longuet"* proposed under Balladur's centre-right government was blocked by strikes involving 75 per cent of FT's workforce, which opposed the change in their public employee status, while the CEO (Suard) did not provide much support to the project either. In 1995, under the Balladur and Juppé centre-right governments a new project was blocked by strikes involving 65 per cent of FT's workforce, even though the proposed plan would guarantee civil servant status and pension privileges to current (but not future) employees in the new corporation. Interestingly, despite strong support by the management[8] and by some politicians seeking to use fresh cash coming from the possible sale of FT shares to finance other public enterprises, the two main candidates

publicly controlled (but corporatized, partially private, and listed) Italian gas companies (Italgas-Saipem) had ordinary contracts and social security schemes.

[6] According to data by Visser and Ebbinghaus (2000), union density in French PTT was double the average union density in the economy as a whole.

[7] In 1986, an attempt to create a separate regulator (Commission Nationale de la Communication et des Libertés) failed due to trade union opposition. In 1991, however, the separation was made through the creation of the Direction Générale de la Réglementation within the telecommunications ministry.

[8] Paradoxically, open support for the project was one factor leading to the replacement of the CEO Roulet by the government.

in the presidential elections, Chirac and Jospin, showed an ideological aversion to markets, reflected in the attachment to the idea of *"service public à la française"*, which (contrary to EC directives) cannot envisage that universal service can be ensured other than by a public monopoly.

A corporatization project finally went through at the end of 1996—under the Juppé government—partially forced by the external constraint of imminent EC liberalization, and despite union unrest, strong political opposition (leading even to a confidence vote), and a legal challenge in the Supreme Court. It involved new concessions such as the maintenance of special pension rights and civil servant status for current employees *as well as* new ones (but only those hired before 2002).

Since corporatization, partial privatization plans were implemented after further concessions were made—such as early retirement, new hiring, and an extended notion of universal service obligations—and over one-third of FT's equity was handed to the private sector by means of an initial public offering (IPO) (coupled with an employee share ownership plan) in October 1997, with the approval of the majority of trade unions.

Yet, as a result of hesitations and delays in reform—due both to the resistance of vested interests and to ideological reasons—90 per cent of FT's employees still retained civil servant status in 1999,[9] and the government still currently owns 55 per cent of FT. Delays in bringing about strategic alliances, in restructuring to face competition, and in opening up capital led FT perilously close to bankruptcy in 2002, with equity prices dropping dramatically. A drastic restructuring plan, involving 14,500 job cuts in 2004 and heavy financial support from the state, had to be negotiated with the EC.

The Italian experience of liberalization of the telecommunications industry was somewhat different. Since 1881, telecommunications services in Italy were delivered by a mixed public-private system and in 1997 the incumbent operator was completely privatized. Initially—the first comprehensive telecommunications law dates back to 1925—the service was provided by five regional private legal monopolies in a regime of state concession, while another private company, Italcable, managed international telecom cable linkages. By 1965, several changes had occurred and the market was dominated by a newly formed company, SIP; yet, with the exception of the public company ASST, all the companies in the industry were listed on the stock exchange. The Italian

---

[9] The resulting paradox is that after the partial privatization 75 per cent of the employees owned company stock even though most of them had risk-free jobs!

telecommunications industry kept this structure until 1994, when Telecom Italia (TI), a subsidiary of STET—a subholding of the state holding IRI—was created by a merger of SIP, Italcable, Iritel (formerly ASST), and two other companies.

In contrast with France, most Italian telecommunications companies have hence remained semi-public joint-stock corporations (with either a majority or a strong minority of shares in private hands) listed on the stock exchange and subject to private company law.[10] Perhaps more importantly, employees in these companies were hired under private job contracts with old-age pensions covered by the general social security scheme. Unlike in France, union density in telecommunications was not higher than in the private sector, though there was a special collective agreement covering this sector, consistent with the industry-level bargaining that prevailed in Italy until 1993. The exception in the Italian telecommunications industry that followed the "French" model was ASST, which until 1994 depended directly upon the telecommunications ministry, with employees having civil servant status. It is thus not surprising that resistance to changes in the structure of the telecoms industry came almost exclusively from ASST, and from the Catholic trade union (CISL), which, however, had a small percentage of workers in the telecommunications industry.

Despite some political interference and populist management of tariff regulation, SIP was generally run as a private company, aiming at maximizing value for shareholders, and was in fact one of the most profitable companies of the public (IRI) conglomerate. Yet, the lack of a clear regulatory framework and the need to meet the EC agenda on liberalization led to plans to restructure the sector, notably by bringing ASST within STET control.[11]

These plans were delayed due to political resistance (mainly by the Christian Democrats) and to some union opposition (CISL), until in the aftermath of the corruption scandals and during a major economic crisis the restructuring was finally carried forward as part of the 1993 privatization plan, which included STET among the companies to be sold. In 1994, Telecom Italia was created as a subsidiary of STET, incorporating among others SIP, Iritel (former ASST), and Italcable. Given the mixed

---

[10] In 1993, 42 per cent of SIP's equity was held by 63,000 estimated private shareholders, while 52.2 per cent of STET's equity was held by 28,000 private shareholders. 49.8 per cent of Italcable's equity was held by 7,200 private shareholders. Both SIP and STET were also listed on foreign stock exchanges.

[11] In 1988, IRI's chairman (Prodi) suggested the unification of STET, SIP, ASST, Italcable, and Telespazio in one subholding of IRI (super-STET).

public–private shareholdings in these companies, after the merger, around 45 per cent of Telecom Italia's equity was already owned by private shareholders. The implementation of the plan met virtually no trade union opposition, even though few guarantees were offered to former ASST employees, such as a one-time option to move to another public administration. In subsequent years, further restructuring and complete privatization went through relatively swiftly. In 1995, TIM was separated from Telecom Italia. In 1997, STET and Telecom Italia were merged in view of privatization, which was completed at the end of the year, just before the EC deadline for the complete liberalization of telecommunications services.

From a comparison of the parallel liberalization experiences of the French and the Italian telecommunications industry under the common external constraints of the EC liberalization agenda, an interesting lesson for reform may be drawn. Cross-country differences in companies' ownership structure, legal status, stock-market listing, and industrial relations systems can go a long way towards explaining differences in regulatory reform outcomes. The degree of resistance to change by workers in these companies crucially depends on these institutional arrangements, and inheriting one or the other can seriously impair or significantly facilitate privatization and liberalization efforts.

The pre-existing corporate structure of the telecommunications industry played a crucial role. Unlike in France, in Italy telecom joint-stock companies were subject to private company law and controlled by the government only at a distance. Being partly private and listed on the stock-market, their strategies were business oriented. Moreover, EC state aid constraints were tighter for Italy than for France precisely because of IRI's governance structure. But most importantly, the majority of employees had no special status relative to their fully private counterparts and did not enjoy specific pecuniary or non-pecuniary rents. In comparison with the difficulties that the opening up of France Telecom's capital had to endure, no significant trade union or political opposition to restructuring or privatization was recorded in the case of Telecom Italia.

Also, other framework conditions play a role. While in France there existed a pervasive ideological attachment to the idea that public service should be ensured by fully-public legal monopolies, in Italy the feeling was rather a lack of trust in the effectiveness of the public enterprise system, due to corruption scandals and widespread inefficiency.

From the point of view of policy, the interplay between institutional arrangements and workers' resistance to change suggests that, in countries where non-manufacturing markets are dominated by public monopolies sharing pecuniary and non-pecuniary rents with their employees, viable reform trajectories require early corporatization, followed by partial privatization as well as partial liberalization of market segments in which new entrants can bring competitive pressures to bear on the dominant company's entrenched industrial relations habits, eventually leading to a harmonization of labour practices with private sector standards. In cases in which incumbents enjoy legally enforceable privileges related to the type of contract or pension arrangements, there would seem to be little alternative but to design compensatory mechanisms of the kind described above.

11.1.2. Break vertical chain: intermediate goods

Some reforms of the product market must overcome the resistance of a coalition of producers and consumers, who—on some occasions—share the rents or acquired rights generated, for example, by some competition policies. In particular, in some non-manufacturing industry, reforms may meet the opposition of incumbents with market power and consumers with status quo bias.

The attitude of final and intermediate consumers of the products that are being liberalized is crucial for the success of reforms, as consensus for reform often depends on the perceived repercussions on the purchasing power of consumers, as well as on the expected fall in input costs (or enhancements in quality and variety of the goods or services). In fact, the probability of success of a liberalization reform will depend on the *share* of the consumers' and final producers' expenditures that are affected by reforms. It is hence not surprising that, of all reforms, liberalization of trade in manufactured goods was the front runner and the least controversial (at least until recently), since it was a relatively secure way of increasing purchasing power and the range and quality of goods for a majority of consumers as well as of reducing the cost and increasing the range and quality of inputs for a majority of firms.

In the non-manufacturing sector, however, matters are more complex, though the same logic should broadly continue to apply. On the final consumer side, part of the increased complexity stems from the fact that, in many of these industries, the uncertainty of reform outcomes may become much larger. This is especially true in areas where the existence of natural monopoly elements or other market imperfections makes outcomes heavily dependent on the ability of policy-makers to design regulation that accounts for information asymmetries, and mimics competitive outcomes.

Furthermore, while trade protection generally distorts relative prices in favour of a very limited section of the population, restrictive non-manufacturing regulation often translates into substantial subsidies given to a relatively large group of consumers (e.g. prices well below cost in local transport, low electricity use or local fixed telecommunications). Thus, there can be powerful forces pushing final consumers towards a status quo bias. From the point of view of intermediate consumers, things are complicated by the fact that entrepreneurs in non-manufacturing industries often operated in a "closed loop". They formed, therefore, a solid (and in some industries large) social block against change, opposing widespread support for reform among manufacturing entrepreneurs. Due to these complications, in utilities and service industries, the influence of the share of final and intermediate consumption affected by the reform is likely to be more ambiguous than in manufacturing.

Figure 11.2 (panels A and B) plots a measure of country-specific reform in three broad non-manufacturing aggregates (the percentage change in the corresponding indicators over the 1975–98 period) against the shares represented by these aggregates in intermediate and final consumption[12] (respectively) in the early 1990s. These simple bivariate relationships can only give a suggestive feeling for the underlying phenomena, not least because they fail to properly account for potential endogeneity problems.[13] However, judging from them, it appears that larger shares in *intermediate* consumption are indeed associated with wider *changes* in regulation, while larger shares in *final* consumption are associated with greater regulatory *persistence*. Put differently, industries that undergo deeper reforms are those accounting for a larger share of firms' inputs and a smaller share of consumers' budgets. This suggests that economy-wide pressures for reform are stronger when these are likely to affect significantly economy-wide production costs, but opposite pressures come from the consumers' side (more on this below).[14]

Hence, the policy implication is that to maximize the chances of success the first step should be to liberalize services or products that account for a relatively small share of consumer expenditure but a large share of firms'

---

[12] Here, summary indicators of reform for industry aggregates were obtained by weighting the indicators for the individual industries by the average OECD share of each industry in total business sector employment.

[13] Of course, there is also an obvious endogeneity problem when one tries to relate consumption or input shares to reform, since these shares may change over time precisely as a consequence of reform.

[14] By and large, the same kind of bivariate relationship continues to hold at the level of the single industry aggregate. However, the negative link between consumer shares and regulatory reform appears to be most evident in the energy sector.

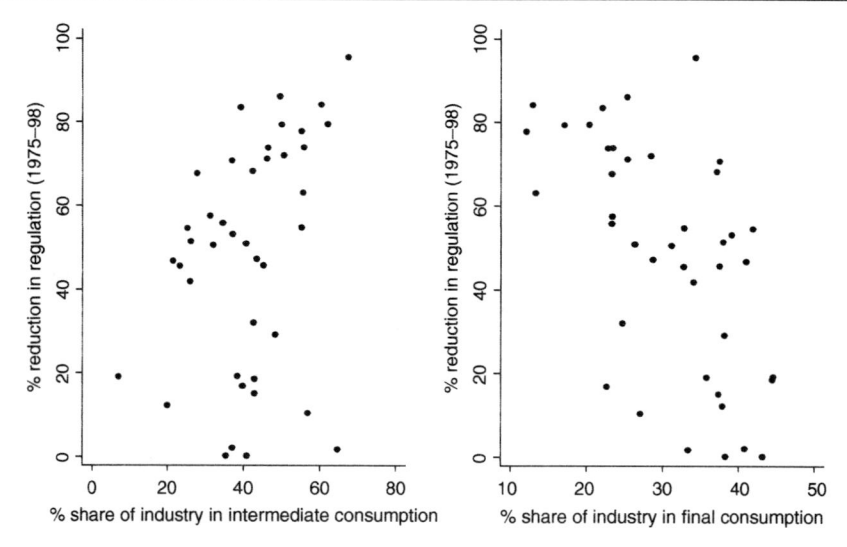

Fig. 11.2 Regulatory reform versus intermediate and final consumption (by country and industry)
Source: Nicoletti (2006).

intermediate inputs. This is so for three reasons: first, because the number of firms using non-manufacturing inputs is often larger than the number of their producers that enjoy market power; second, because the fall in prices and the output expansion expected after liberalization helps to widen and strengthen the coalition between firms using these inputs and those producing them competitively; and third, because potential consumer opposition to liberalization is minimized. The recent history of the liberalization process provides some examples of this successful strategy.

The first non-manufacturing activity to be liberalized in most countries (removing price controls and barriers to international trade) was international financial services. These services are mostly used as an intermediate input by firms. Liberalization was not perceived as threatening by consumers or workers and, indeed, met very little opposition. Incumbents did not oppose it because it created more profit opportunities, and featured no downside for incumbents because (unfortunately) in most countries they still remain sheltered from takeover due to FDI restrictions in the banking sector. Some positive spillover effects of this reform were the additional constraints liberalization placed on the conduct of macro and budgetary policies.

Analogously, early attempts to liberalize the transport sector concentrated on road freight (and later on rail freight), where freight transport is clearly almost exclusively an intermediate input for manufacturing firms. As pointed out by the OECD indicators, this was the case in almost all OECD countries, with the clearest cases being the USA, where reforms began in 1978, and a few other countries (Canada, New Zealand, Australia, and the UK) where liberalization was implemented even earlier. More generally, in a majority of OECD countries, road freight was liberalized well before other industries. In this case, though, incumbent opposition was stronger and the outcome of the reform process depended on how far institutions "voiced" them. For instance, reforms failed in countries where the institutional setting associates incumbents with decisions concerning new entry and prices (e.g. Italy).

Similarly, when the EC agenda for reforming telecommunications gradually opened up markets to competition, it started precisely from industry segments producing mainly services for businesses. EC directives first, liberalized in 1990, data transmission and so-called "value-added" services.[15] Moreover, several EU countries anticipated the EC agenda by opening up to competition long-distance services well before 1998 (Sweden, Denmark, Finland). These services had also been opened up at the beginning of the decade by early reformers such as the USA, the UK, Japan, and New Zealand. Businesses are also the largest consumers of long-distance services. These liberalizations often met stiff opposition from incumbents, but the political influence of the supporting coalition was much stronger. Predictably, there was no consumer opposition to such liberalizations.

Finally, when considering the liberalization of those regulated product markets mainly targeted at final consumers, reform policies should contemplate compensation mechanisms for consumers who are likely to be harmed. For instance, as telecommunications services were being liberalized, several OECD countries created mechanisms through which the costs related to universal service obligations imposed on incumbent operators (or new entrants alike) could continue to be financed even after the necessary realignment of tariffs on costs and the elimination of state aid to telecommunications companies (for examples, see Gönenç et al., 2001).

11.2. Trickle-down effects

When vested interests in a market or welfare programme are so tightly entrenched that social dialogue is not a feasible option for reform, rather

---

[15] Previously, the market for handsets and other terminals had been liberalized and several provisions had harmonized telecommunications standards across EU countries.

than trying to move ahead with a massive watering down of the reforming plan, policy-makers may adopt a strategy of gradual reforms. The underlying idea is to create a *trickle-down* effect both with*in* market and *across* markets: the initial reform generates a *chain reaction* that creates favourable conditions for reforms either with*in* the same market—for instance, a gradual move from privatizing to liberalizing—or *across* markets—for example, from the product to the labour market.

In order to overcome the resistance of incumbents or insiders, initial reforms require either putting pressure on their vested interests, their rents, their market shares, and/or their governance systems or—alternatively—changing the relative importance of the social or political actors. The Spanish labour market reform of the 1980s, which largely liberalized the use of temporary contracts, represents a good example of the latter strategy. In fact, ten years after this reform, permanent workers had lost their prominent role in the labour market and some reform to the degree of protection of regular jobs was hence possible. This case study will be analysed in Section 11.2.2 below.

In non-manufacturing industries, on the other hand, policy-makers trying to overcome the resistance of incumbents to regulatory change need to put pressure on their rents, their market shares, and/or their governance systems. For instance, the competitive pressures generated by the opening up of one market may reshuffle the coalition of interests in ways that favour the liberalization of other markets, by increasing the rewards from reforming. Instances of these *trickle-down* effects in the non-manufacturing sector are provided in the next section.

11.2.1. *Market power and gradual reforms*

Potential resistance to non-manufacturing reform by entrepreneurs may be measured by their market rents. Although only very sparse hard evidence is available on product market rents in utilities and services industries, using the few internationally comparable estimates of non-manufacturing mark-ups in the 1990s, Figure 11.3 suggests that (on average across countries) there is an inverse relationship between market power and reform outcomes. Market power is lowest in transport, where reforms have been deepest, and it is highest in energy, where reforms were fewer, while the communications industry holds an intermediate position. However, country-specific data show that extensive telecommunications reforms have been associated with moderate mark-ups, low concentration ratios, and high entry rates, suggesting that market power has significantly decreased over time in reforming countries.

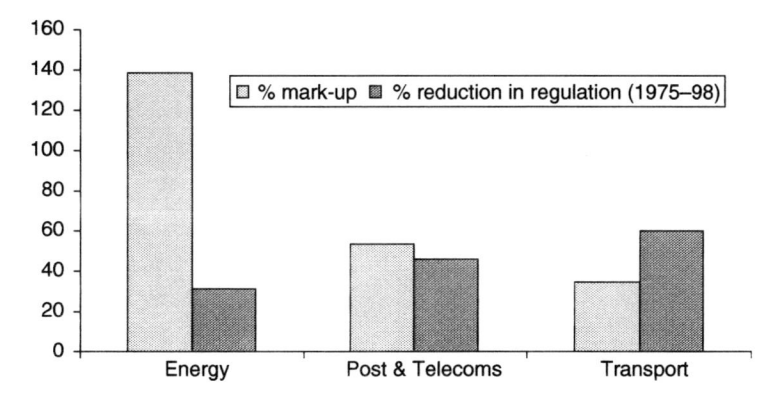

Fig. 11.3 Product market rents and regulatory reform (industry averages across countries)

Source: Nicoletti (2006).

To implement regulatory changes in these markets, policy-makers hence need to introduce gradual reforms that erode incumbents' market power and rents, in order to weaken their resistance. Indeed, this process is constantly under way partly as a by-product of increased globalization of trade and investment flows. Increasing trade in goods and tradable services (such as financial, communication, and transport services) puts pressure on regulatory arrangements that damage efficiency and raise costs for intermediate and final consumers. As noted above, liberalization of services in other countries also provides ways around restrictive domestic regulations by creating cream-skimming opportunities for international competitors. This tends to compress rents and erode the market shares of regulated firms in markets that tend to become contestable. Moreover, liberalization of international investment flows, and the associated wave of mergers and acquisitions, puts stress on rigid governance systems (such as public ownership) that circumscribe corporate strategies for domestic markets, leading to losses in competitiveness and market leadership. Thus, in some cases, globalization has pushed incumbents themselves to join the ranks of those in favour of privatization and reform, at least to the extent that this would not jeopardize their dominant position in the market (Levy and Spiller, 1999; Noll, 1999).

Indeed, in concomitance with the major drive for product market reforms, the intensity of trade in both goods and services rose sharply in the OECD area over the 1990s, and FDI (another form of services trade

How to Gain Political Support for Reforms

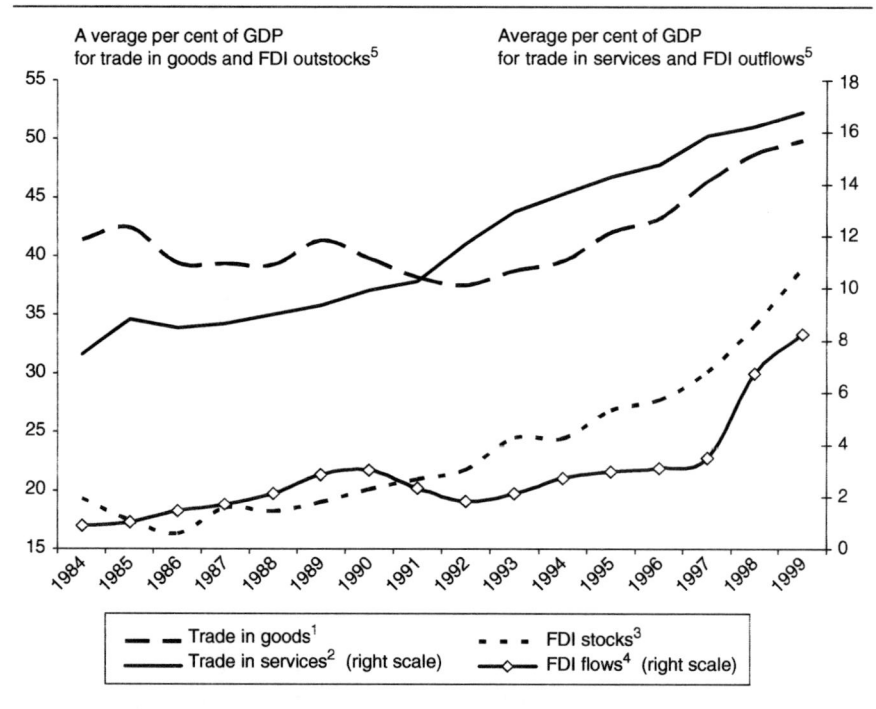

Fig. 11.4 Trade and FDI patterns in the OECD

Notes:

[1] Trade in goods is defined as the sum of the exports and imports of goods realized between a reporting country and the OECD area.

[2] Trade in services is defined as the sum of exports and imports of services realized between a reporting country and the world (due to the lack of OECD-specific data, services trade cannot be defined relative to the OECD area).

[3] FDI stock is the sum of inward and outward positions of the average country in the OECD area.

[4] FDI flow is the sum of yearly investment inflows and outflows of the average country to the OECD area.

[5] Simple average of the rations of OECD countries

Source: Nicoletti *et al.* (2003).

through commercial presence) almost doubled (Fig. 11.4).[16] Interestingly, available cross-country evidence suggests that both services trade and FDI intensities are inversely related to the stringency of domestic regulations (Fig. 11.5). Clearly, the direction of causality could go both ways: relatively stringent domestic regulations could deter services trade

---

[16] It should be noted, however, that only part of reported FDI flows translates into an increase in activity of foreign affiliates in non-manufacturing industries. Many of them are related to manufacturing activities, merger and acquisition (M&A) activities, minority equity participations, or reinvested earnings. The available data on foreign affiliates, however, tend to confirm the picture provided by FDI data.

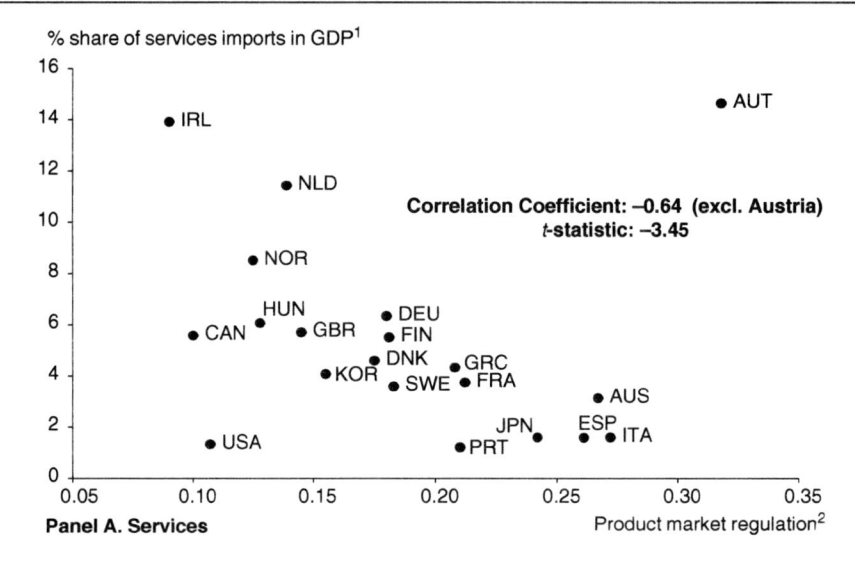

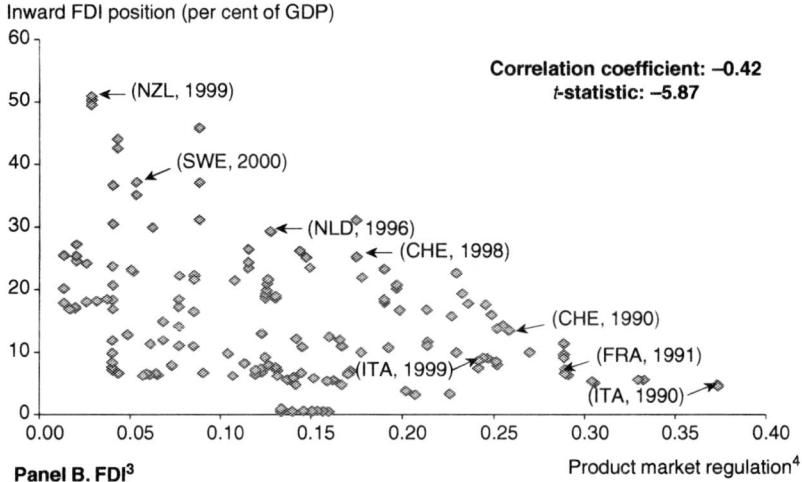

Fig. 11.5 Non-manufacturing regulation, services imports, and inward FDI, 1998

Notes:

[1] The position of Austria reflects the exceptionally high share of service trade accounted for by tuorism.

[2] Weighted average of regulatory indicators in 12 non-manufacturing industries. 0–1 scale from least to most restrictive of competition.

[3] Each point shows the combination of regulation and FDI in a given country and period. Some of these country/period contributions are shown for illustrative purposes.

[4] Product of the indcator of economy-wide regulation in 1998 and the indicator of barriers to entry in seven non-manufacuting industries over the 1980–98 period. 0–1 scale from least to most restrictive of competition.

Source: Nicoletti *et al*. (2003).

and FDI,[17] but weak services trade and FDI intensities might also be discouraging efforts at (or undermining support for) reforming regulations in a competitive sense.

This observation carries an important policy implication: opening up trade in services industries where opposition to reform is lowest can have positive repercussions for the viability of reform in other services industries where vested interests are stronger. In particular, several authors (see Li *et al.*, 2001) have stressed the influence of the liberalization of international financial flows on the drive to liberalize telecommunications. This is mainly due to technological reasons. Managing larger financial flows and providing more diverse financial services required massive data transmission capacity and timely exchange of information. In other words, financial development became increasingly complementary to communications. Hence, especially in urban areas of the most developed countries, financial liberalization created a strong constituency for a more flexible, demand-driven and innovative communications industry. It also disadvantaged on global financial markets financial businesses whose domestic communications services were inefficient and costly. For instance, OECD (1994) reports that in 1991 the difference between the cost of communications from Italy to the UK and the cost of communications from the UK to Italy ranged from 50 to 80 per cent (depending on which of the two competing British operators was providing the service). Awareness of this kind of competitive disadvantage, which also penalized EU countries *vis-à-vis* the USA and Japan, was one of the primary factors underlying the EC 1987 "Green Book on the Development of Telecommunications equipment and Services". It is not a coincidence, therefore, that telecommunications liberalization took off in the USA and the UK, where the largest financial industries are located.

Another element that can contribute to a switch in attitudes among domestic producers towards reforms improving production flexibility and efficiency is the presence of foreign affiliates, enjoying forward technology and knowledge spillovers from their home companies. Of course, foreign affiliates also constitute interest groups of their own, whose attitudes towards reform are not necessarily univocal. To the extent that they enjoy market power, they may join the ranks of those that oppose reform. But, if they are "challengers" of incumbent firms they will also directly lobby the

---

[17] See Nicoletti *et al.* (2003) and Mirza and Nicoletti (2004) for multivariate empirical analyses of the linkages between product market regulations and bilateral FDI and services trade.

government to remove restrictions that impinge on their ability to compete effectively.[18]

Hence, another way for the policy-maker to increase consensus for domestic product market reforms is by removing protections against foreign ownership of domestic firms or creating wedges in domestic markets where foreign services providers can force their way in. Indeed, removal of FDI restrictions has been an important element of product market reform in the OECD area (Fig. 11.6, Panel A), and regulatory reform appears to have been deeper in industries and countries where the share of foreign affiliates in output has grown larger (Fig. 11.6, Panel B).[19] Moreover, there are several examples of wedges used by foreign providers, which during the 1990s were instrumental in stimulating wider non-manufacturing liberalization. In air transport, opening up routes to cabotage by low-cost airlines had similar effects. In electricity, certain regulatory authorities (e.g. in Italy) widened access by foreign producers using "direct lines"—independent of the national transmission grid—as a means to increase competitive pressures on the domestic market.

Finally, another strategy of gradual reforming is to open up a market segment to competition while keeping regulation unchanged for incumbents. This occurred, for instance, with international long-distance communications in the UK and several other countries. The regulated price structure inherited by the incumbent from the period in which he held a legal monopoly was typically characterized by prices well above cost in long-distance communications and below cost in local communications. New entrants in the long-distance market could therefore easily compete on prices, eroding the incumbent's market share precisely in those services that ensured its overall profitability. Faced with this threat, incumbents moved from a position of passive resistance to reform to a position of more active support for regulatory changes, involving, for instance, the rebalancing of tariffs in favour of a more cost-oriented profile.

---

[18] As noted above, the attitude of foreign affiliates towards trade openness is less ambiguous, since (save for special cases) they will tend to lobby for trade liberalization (Gawande et al., 2004).

[19] A related issue is what determines the attitude of domestic and foreign lobbies towards FDI policy. While research in this area has not been extensive, Facchini and Willmann (2001) stress the role played by factor complementarities. They note that a factor will have an incentive to lobby for the removal of any distortion in the flows of its complements, since its marginal productivity is increasing in it.

How to Gain Political Support for Reforms

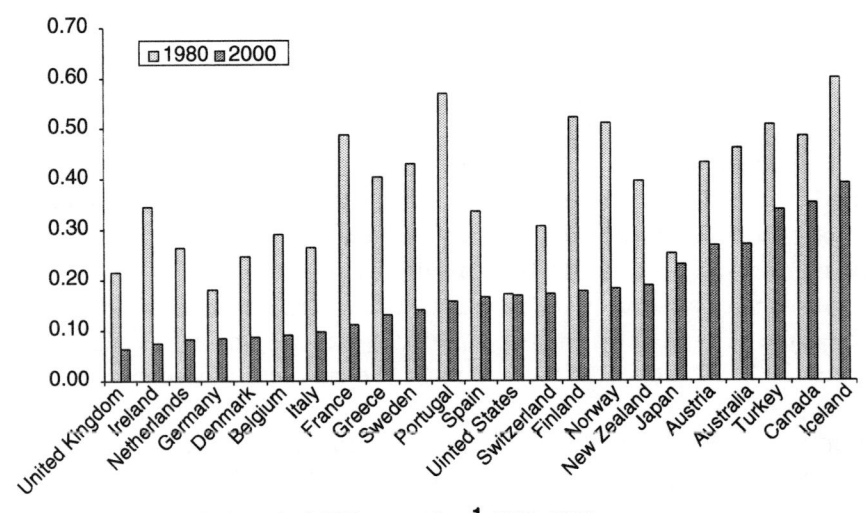

Panel A. FDI restrictions in OECD countries,[1] **1980–2000**

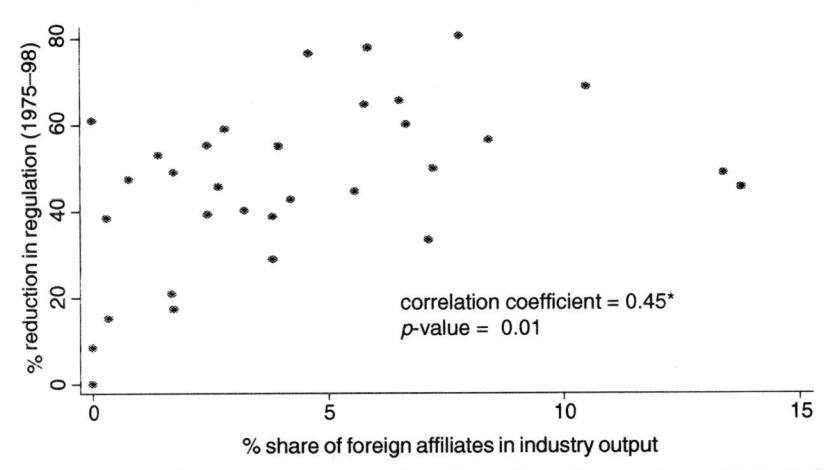

Panel B. Foreign affiliates and non-manufacturing reform (by country and industry)

Fig. 11.6 Regulatory reform and FDI openness

Note:

[1] The indicator ranges from 0 (least restrictive) to 1 (most restrictive). The most recent year for which data are available varies across countries between 1998 and 2000. For details, see Golub (2003).

Source: Nicoletti (2006).

11.2.2. *The 1994–1997 reforms of EPL in Spain*

Before the reform season started in 1994, Spanish permanent jobs used to be among the best-protected jobs in Europe. Severance payments amounted to 45 days of pay for every year of tenure, with a ceiling at

42 months, and 3.5 years of pay in unfair individual dismissal cases. Indeed, even after the 1994–7 reforms, the OECD (1999) kept ranking the Spanish labour market among the least flexible in terms of employment protection laws. This rigidity of the labour market is counterbalanced by the low coverage of unemployment insurance. Although initial benefits represent 70 per cent of the last wage—reduced to 60 per cent after six months—and maximum duration is equal to 24 months, eligibility is determined by the worker's previous contributions. To obtain 12 months of benefits, a worker must have contributed between 3 and 3.5 years. Hence, the system mainly targets long-term employees, while several workers, especially those with short-term employment, are not protected.

The combination of strict employment protection regulations (EPL) and low unemployment insurance coverage is consistent with the main goal of protecting permanent workers (see Boeri *et al.*, 2004), who represent two-thirds of employees, and almost all union members. The unemployed and workers on short-term contracts are instead virtually unprotected by both instruments—EPL and unemployment insurance—according to a dualism generated mainly by the employment protection laws. The protection of permanent workers has historically been the main goal of the Spanish unions—UGT (Workers' General Union) and CC.OO. (Workers' Commissions)—since the end of Franco's dictatorship. This element constituted a crucial feature in the development of the Spanish labour market, given the role of these unions since the political transition to democracy in the last 1970s, when conditions emerged for social dialogue and centralized action strategy involving numerous contacts between government and employers' organizations. Yet, due to some reforms unilaterally passed by the Socialist government in the mid-1980s, relations between the government and unions become more problematic until the beginning of the 1990s, when the Economic and Social Council was created to organize social dialogue at the national level between workers' unions and employers' organizations. On the one hand, the government needed to resort again to social bargaining in order to moderate wages and to lower inflation (in line with the EMU convergence criteria). On the other hand, the unions—which were losing ground at the firm level—sought to restart the dialogue at the national level partly to avoid being excluded from major reforms. Since the mid-1990s, unions have hence followed a more pragmatic approach with employers and governments, although they retain a strong veto power through the ability to organize national strikes (as occurred in 2002 against the unemployment insurance reform).

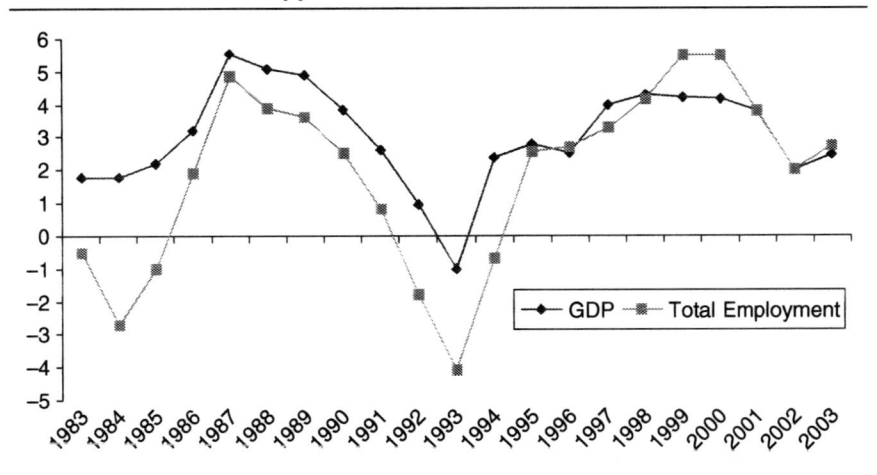

Fig. 11.7 GDP and total employment changes (%) in Spain
Source: INEM.

The seeds of the 1994–7 reforms of the permanent labour market contracts are to be found in the 1984 reform that liberalized the use of temporary contracts. According to these new regulations, temporary contracts could be created up to a maximum duration of three years, well above the limits imposed on such contracts by most European countries. Little or no termination compensation was offered to workers and massive opportunities to use these temporary contracts were provided. As a result, the stock of temporary contracts mushroomed from 11 per cent to 33 per cent a—while permanent contracts declined—and in 1997 they represented 96 per cent of the annual job creation flows.

Between 1992 and 1994 Spain, like many other European countries, experienced a serious recession: for instance, in 1993 GDP decreased by 1 per cent and total employment by 4 per cent (see Fig. 11.7). In this difficult scenario, the Socialist government launched an extensive and far-reaching reform of labour legislation in an attempt to increase the flexibility of a labour market characterized by an unemployment rate above 20 per cent and by a share of workers under fixed-term contracts of 33 per cent. Besides revising several regulations on special working hours and laying the foundations for the revised regulation of the collective bargaining system, the reform restricted the conditions of use of temporary contracts to temporary causes, re-targeted the "employment promotion" fixed-term contracts to hard-to-place workers and—more importantly—reduced the costs of individual dismissal, thereby affecting the vested interests of permanent workers.

Divide and Conquer

Clearly, the reform that reduced the cost of laying off permanent workers was opposed by the unions, since the core of union members felt threatened by massive dismissals, due also to the reduction in permanent jobs during the 1993 recession (see Fig. 11.8) and to increasing economic uncertainty. Yet, this opposition was not massive and the reform measures were eventually implemented.

The explanation proposed by Dolado and Jimeno (2004), who investigate the evolution of the ratio of regular permanent employees relative to the active population, highlights the role played by the previous 1984 reform, which liberalized temporary contracts. By 1994, as displayed in Figure 11.9, the share of regular or permanent workers in the total active population had dropped below 50 per cent, due to the growing number of temporary workers. To the extent that the government—or the unions— care about the median voter in the labour market, where the electoral base is composed of all actual and potential workers, by 1993 the median voter was no longer an insider (or permanent worker), but rather an outsider (a temporary worker or unemployed). This may account for the behaviour of the unions *vis-à-vis* a reform that enhanced the probability of temporary workers or unemployed individuals obtaining permanent jobs, at the cost of lowering job security for the incumbents. As such, the role of the 1984 reform hence proved to be crucial in creating the conditions—ten years later—for the reform of permanent contracts.

The 1994 reform, however, had little impact on the mix of temporary and permanent contracts, as the stock of short-term contracts in the

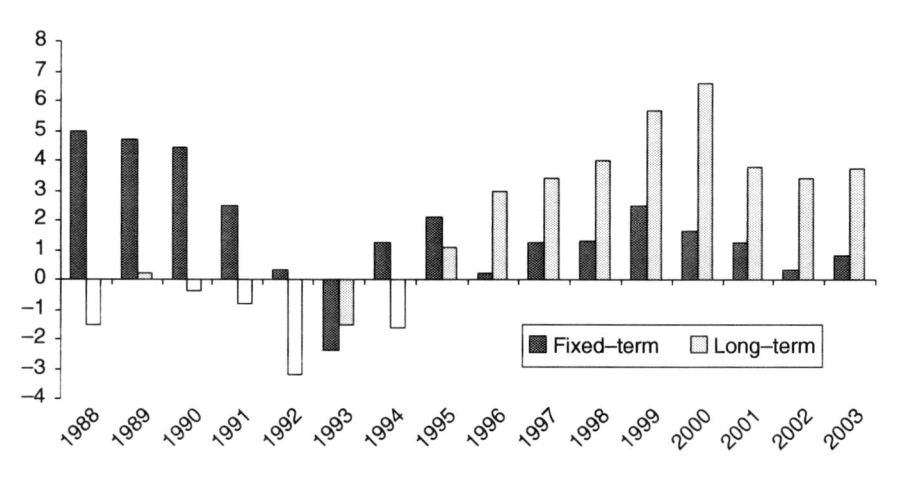

Fig. 11.8 Net employment variation by type of contract (thousands)
Source: Consejo Economic y Social, 2004.

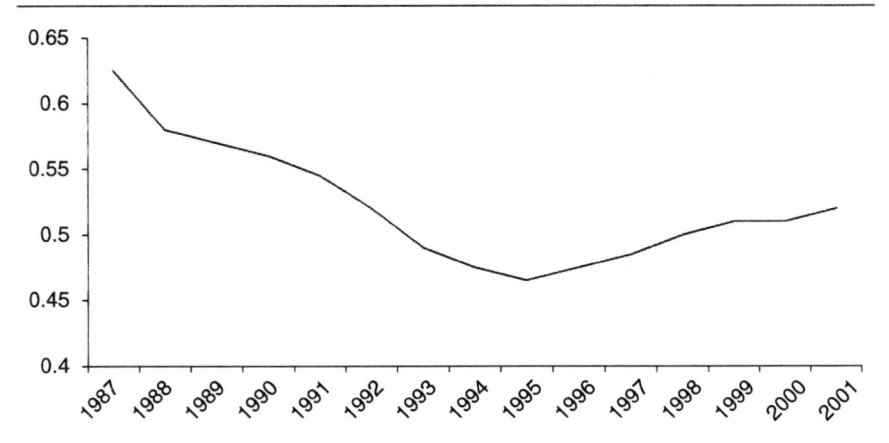

Fig. 11.9 Regular long-term employees as a proportion of the active population
Source: Dolado and Jimeno (2004).

economy peaked at 35 per cent in 1995. This was probably due to the limited increase in the relative cost of short-term contracts *vis-à-vis* permanent jobs, despite the restrictions imposed on their use. By 1997, when a new reform of the labour market took place to tackle this problem, economic conditions had greatly improved. With a GDP growth rate of around 3 per cent, but partly as a result of the 1994 reform, permanent employment had bounced back, although temporary jobs still constituted 33 per cent of all jobs in 1997. Several conditions favourable to reform emerged, since there was a general consensus over the necessity to reduce the share of temporary jobs in the economy and hence to continue the path of the 1994 reform. Moreover, there was less uncertainty about the future—and hence about the winners and losers from the reform (Saint-Paul (2002 *b*)'s "identifiable effect")—and fewer employees were exposed to an immediate impact from such a reform.

The 1997 reform's coalition building phase included a long round of negotiation initiated by the Conservative government, which led the social partners to sign cross-sectoral agreements on employment protection legislation and collective bargaining. The main goal of the reform was to promote permanent employment and to reduce employment insecurity. A *permanent employment promotion contract* was introduced over a four-year period, targeted at young and elderly unemployed individuals (aged below 30 or above 45 years) and at those temporary workers whose contract was transformed into a permanent one. It differs from the common permanent contract in that compensation for unfair individual lay-off and social charges were reduced, since the compensation payable by the employer went from 45 to 33 days per year of service up to a maximum of 24 months' pay (instead of 42). Combined with the 1994 reform that abolished the necessity for administrative authorization and introduced the "objective" reason for lay-offs, this measure significantly reduced the cost of separation in these new contracts. Furthermore, social contributions on these contracts were substantially cut. The reform also introduces some measures sponsored by the unions, such as better regulation of training, part-time and discontinuous contracts and additional rights for temporary workers. Moreover, it attempted to correct some of problems posed by the chaotic collective bargaining structure in the country. The reform brought new issues to the negotiation table, such as the possibility of nationwide sectoral collective agreements on occupational structures, career structures, pay structure, and disciplinary systems.

12
Exploit External Constraints

The reform strategies presented in previous chapters emphasized the crucial role of *coalition building* and *commitment building* in different economic and political scenarios. A large parliamentary majority may be sufficient to build commitment to "push ahead" with reforms; if this tilts expectations towards the perception that reforms are inescapable, the government may generate a "snowball" effect for reforms (see Chapter 9). Yet, this straightforward confrontational strategy may also bring reforms to standstill, as governments may be held up by a handful of opponents who block the reform. Alternative strategies that take account of differences in the economic and political environment aim at improving the coalition building effort, as shown in Chapters 10 and 11.

In this chapter, we consider a scenario, in which policy-makers may resort to external constraints to strengthen their *commitment* ability to reform. Interestingly, this circumstance is unrelated to the political and economic scenarios analysed in previous chapters, since external constraints may occur regardless of the political strength of the government and may become binding in several economic areas.

Yet, relying on imposed constraints on reform may only be rational in a second-best world. In principle, constraints decrease the number of available options, and should therefore reduce potential benefits. However, in the absence of such constraints, governments may fail to confront the opposition of special interest groups (SIGs) (Grossman and Helpman, 2001) or they may abstain from implementing unpopular reforms due to electoral concerns. The idea of relying on external constraints is thus of value in strengthening the position of reform-minded governments *vis-à-vis* these SIGs and in providing a blame-avoidance strategy to governments timorous of electoral backlashes. Raising hurdles typically increases the bargaining power of these governments, and facilitates efficiency-enhancing reforms. Obviously, opponents of reform will also oppose the imposition of such external hurdles, which will be deemed 'anti-democratic'. Oppositions to WTO rules, to the Stability Pact, to IMF conditionality rules, or to the EU *Acquis Communautaire* are only a few examples. Such external constraints produce a strait-jacket that limits the government's freedom of movement. But they provide even more of a strait-jacket for opposing lobby groups. In that case, they can actually be welcomed by a government that wants to bypass oppositions, without having to take the blame for the reform (see also Chapter 10).

Examples of exploitation of external constraints to pass reforms abound: many governments benefit from being blamed by the OECD or the IMF for undertaking too few structural reforms or for running excessive deficits. This helps them confront opposition when they propose reforms that can then be marketed as unavoidable. In a somehow similar manner, delegating monetary policy to an independent central bank can be seen as the self-imposition of an external constraint (Kydland and Prescott, 1977; Rogoff, 1985; Persson and Tabellini, 2000).

To illustrate the benefit of these external constraints, we cover two emblematic cases in this chapter. These case studies are provided by the privatization of significant car producers in two transition countries: the Czech Republic and Ukraine. Transition countries, more than others, were facing substantial aggregate uncertainty at the outset of transition. Which was "the best" way to reform was highly uncertain; and so was the potential outcome of each reform strategy. There were thus strong tensions between different groups in the population. The Czech Republic was, however, provided with clear-cut incentives, thanks to the opportunity of developing its exports to Western Europe and, later, of joining the European Union. This effect was so strong that the literature now considers this "EU accession effect" as having been of primary importance for the success of transition in many countries (see Roland, 2000, ch. 8). Ukraine provides a valuable contrasting case. It could pursue its reforms in a more independent manner for several years. In spite of (or because of) this freedom of action, the privatization of its main car maker, AvtoZAZ, proved much less successful.

12.1. Škoda (Czech Republic) and AvtoZAZ (Ukraine)

As we stressed in Chapter 10, the governments in transition countries had to privatize many of their enterprises. Not all of them were privatized through mass privatization. For obvious reasons, car producers were generally one of the exceptions. Indeed, car production requires intensive know-how and relies on modern technologies. Moreover, know-how requirements impose substantial fixed costs. Hence, only a limited number of competitors can survive in world markets. That is why the recovery of national car producers called for external support and expertise. Conversely, foreign potential acquirers were interested in the considerable growth potential of Central and Eastern European markets.[1]

Background information

In the Soviet system, the automobile industry enjoyed the status of a 'strategic industry'. Moreover, the automobile industry was important for collective identity reasons. One of the main conditions imposed by both the Czech and the Ukrainian governments was precisely the safeguard of national models and, above all, the survival of the national brand after privatization.

Both the Czech *Škoda Avtomobilová A.S.* and the Ukrainian *AvtoZAZ* car producers were among the oldest and most important producers in the region: in 1989, Škoda employed 21,000 workers and its production attained some 180,000 cars per year. AvtoZAZ had comparable production capacities, producing 150,000 cars per year and employing 18,000 workers.

On the face of it, both companies also experienced a similar process of privatization. Both companies were (partially) sold to a foreign partner.[2] These privatization processes were also outstanding regarding the amounts of foreign direct investment involved. In Škoda's case, the offer of Volkswagen represented the highest single FDI in the Czech economy. The privatization of AvtoZAZ took place later. Had it been better managed, it probably would have generated the greatest inflow of FDI ever experienced in Ukraine.

Despite these apparent similarities, the privatization processes of the two companies led to drastically different outcomes. The reasons for these differences lie in the economic and political conditions in each country; in the attitude of their governments; and in the objectives pursued by foreign investors. The cases of Škoda and AvtoZAZ illustrate how inappropriate political decisions by a government can lead to enormous

---

[1] At the start of transition, there were only 80 cars per thousand inhabitants in Central and Eastern Europe, compared to 500 in the European Union (Dörr and Kessel, 2002: 5).

[2] It should be remembered that privatization through sale to a foreign investor was rather atypical for both the Czech and the Ukrainian government.

losses in terms of economic potential, despite relatively similar economic conditions.[3]

Economic conditions

Czechoslovakia, unlike many other transition economies in Central Europe, started its journey to a market economy from virtually full state ownership: in 1989, only 2 per cent of all registered assets belonged to the private sector (Dyba and Svejnar, 1995: 29). The price system was highly distorted, and the labour force concentrated in the industry—it accounted for about 47 per cent of GDP, compared to 36 per cent in other Visegrad countries (Roland, 2000: 6). The average size of national enterprises was also significantly larger: 96 per cent of total employment was concentrated in firms with more than 500 employees (Roland, 2000: 7). In many respects, the Czech economy was thus quite close to that of the Ukraine and other former USSR countries.

Both the Czech and Ukrainian Republics were particularly hard-hit by price liberalization and the break-up of the CMEA.[4] Their difficulties were worsened by political break-ups—that of Czechoslovakia and that of the Soviet Union. Central and Eastern European Countries (CEECs) also experienced a dramatic output fall in the first years of transition, and the automobile industry was hit particularly strongly. The reason lies precisely in the failure of these car producers to be in line with the technological developments of the global automotive industry. Because of their lack of competitiveness, sales plummeted; underutilization of production capacities worsened, and their financial position became critical.

The survival of Central and Eastern European automotive enterprises required significant restructuring and modernization. However, the tight financial situation of these companies made it impossible to generate the necessary cash-flows either within the company or through the sole support of national financial markets. Therefore, external funds were indispensable.

12.2. The Privatization of Škoda

Like all automobile producers in transition economies, Škoda faced a deep decline in demand. Depressed internal demand, combined with the

---

[3] This explains our choice of the two firms: in the car industry, government policies towards foreign investors were similar across Central European countries (cf. Werner, 2004: 2–3, 11–15). Comparing a Central European and an Eastern European country extends the scope of our comparative study.   [4] CMEA—Council for Mutual Economic Assistance.

company's technological lag, led to productivity decay. In 1991, Škoda's losses amounted to nearly CZK 800 million ($27 million). Still, several foreign car makers were interested in cooperating with Škoda. Two candidates were still active at the end of the bidding race: the French company Renault and the German Volkswagen Group. A noteworthy detail is that the Czech political leadership (including President Havel) was, mainly for political reasons, strongly in favour of the French producer (Dörr and Kessel, 2002: 10), whereas the German Volkswagen Group had the support of Škoda's workforce and management.[5] The ambivalent preferences of the Czechs, together with the uncertainties surrounding which strategy to adopt in Škoda's best interests, protracted the negotiations. In the end, the offer of Volkswagen, which proposed an investment programme of over DM 9 billion tipped the balance in its favour.[6]

The interest of Volkswagen (VW) in the joint venture was twofold. One goal was to gain market shares in transition economies. A second objective was to meet international competition. In the case of Škoda, VW's strategy of "integrated peripheral markets" aimed at gaining access to a cheap and skilled labour force.[7] At the same time, production facilities close to Germany allowed exports to the West.

The final agreement between the Czech side and the German car maker was concluded in the form of a joint venture in April 1991. VW was to gradually assume the ownership of Škoda and to increase the Czech company's annual production capacity from 200,000 to 450,000 vehicles by 2000. To achieve this goal, VW offered DM 500 million for a 31 per cent stake in Škoda at the creation of the joint venture.

Control rights

The crucial aspect of the initial agreement concerned the *management* of the joint venture: although the Czech government retained a control stake in Škoda, it was committed to refraining from interfering in the management of the company, effectively accomplished by VW. In exchange, VW committed to managing the joint venture separately,

---

[5] According to Dörr and Kessel, 2002 (11–12), "Skoda workers threatened strike and resistance if Renault were to be chosen. The overwhelming vote of Skoda employees was influenced not only by the economically more advantageous offer of VW but also by the better social benefits and pay VW generally provided".

[6] Renault's proposal involved an investment plan of "only" DM 5 billion (see Dörr and Kessel, 2002).

[7] Indeed, the labour costs are currently about 25 per cent of those in Germany and were significantly lower throughout the 1990s.

as one member of its car maker Konzern (which, besides VW, includes Audi and Seat) and not as an integral part of VW.

Temporary (!) protection

Strong competition among the Visegrad countries for foreign investment provided robust arguments and strong negotiating power to the German investor. As a result, the government offered special conditions to VW: "Despite the government's proclaimed principle of equal treatment for all foreigners investing in Czechoslovakia, the government did negotiate special entry conditions for foreign investors into some ventures with state-owned firms. The VW-Škoda arrangement, which waived anti-monopoly provisions, provided a number of trade barriers against imports of competing cars, and involved the government in business negotiations, is the most visible example of such an arrangement" (Bohatá, 2000: 172).[8] One such trade barrier provision, which followed the creation of the joint venture, was the establishment of a 14 per cent import tariff on vehicles. In other words, at the same time as it invested in Škoda, VW acquired quasi-monopoly powers in the Czech market for a period of four years. The *temporary* nature of this protection deserves special attention. While such protections can generate soft-budget constraints, Castanheira and Roland (2000) and Castanheira (2003) highlight that *temporary* protections have the power to foster investment and accelerate restructuring. However, the government must be able to commit to this course of action. The desire to create a break with the communist past of the country and to redirect itself towards Western Europe fortunately provided such a commitment incentive (Roland, 2000, ch. 8).

From the creation of the joint venture, a number of important changes were carried out by the German investor to consolidate and improve the competitive position of the Czech company. In particular, the administrative structure of the company was made to resemble VW's. The efficient restructuring of production and distribution procedures, together with relatively low labour costs and well-trained workers, resulted in substantial productivity growth (about 7–10% annually over that period), and allowed the company to become competitive in European markets. The government, on its side, fulfilled its commitment by adopting a "hands-off" policy.

---

[8] These favourable trade provisions were completed by the Association Agreements with the EU, signed in 1991, and provided direct and indirect trade incentives to invest in the Visegrad countries.

Commitment

During this process, the attitude of the Czech government was rather unusual. It continued to resist the strong public pressures that demanded government intervention. In 1993 and 1994, the break-up of Czechoslovakia, together with stagnating international markets, prevented VW from attaining its promised objectives: the joint venture was loss-making, and production and investment plans were revised downwards. The government could have tried to force VW into maintaining the initial investment and production plans. Instead, the government acknowledged it would be difficult to change business partner at this stage, and allowed VW to raise its stake in Škoda up to 60.3 per cent in December 1994 and then to 70 per cent in 1995. At that time, the government's residual share of 30 per cent was intended to be sold as shares without voting rights. However, VW was eventually allowed to assume total ownership of the company in May 2000.

The success of Škoda is so striking that it now became an extensively studied case (see Fig. 12.1). Its results are indeed remarkable: Škoda's annual production attained 460,000 vehicles in 2001; almost three times more than in 1991. Its most recent model is produced on one of the most advanced assembly lines in the world, and Škoda became one of the most efficient units in the VW group. It exports more than 80 per cent of its production and accounted for one-seventh of all Czech exports in 2002.

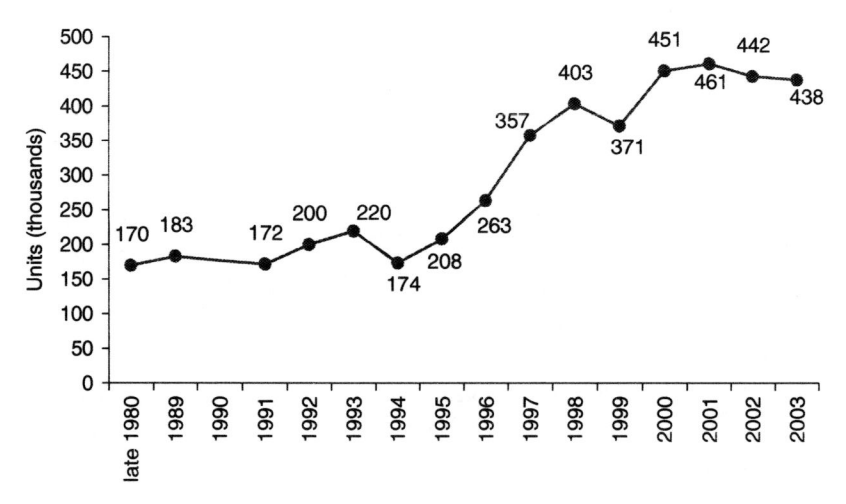

Fig. 12.1 Production of Škoda

Source: Auto Katalog, various issues; Lastauto Omnibus Katalog, various issues, Škoda Annual reports.

The success of Škoda's privatization was due, first of all, to the governmental position, clearly defined at the beginning of the joint venture with VW. Using the "external anchor" offered by Western Europe, it could commit to an efficient course of action, thereby creating appropriate incentives for both VW and Škoda. The commitment of the government not to interfere in the management of the company, even though it retained its control stake, allowed VW to achieve all the (defensive and strategic) restructuring the company required. Another important aspect reinforcing these incentives is the short-term nature of protectionist measures. Lastly, Škoda benefited from VW's need to thrive in the "integrated peripheral markets" of the European Union. That is, the strengthening of Škoda's competitiveness was the main objective of both the Czech government and the German VW Group. The congruence of their objectives was one of the reasons for the survival of the project, in spite of the major crises and conflicts the joint venture faced in 1993–4.

12.3. The privatization of AvtoZAZ

Ukraine is famous for its sluggish economic and political adjustments, and for being the country in transition that experienced the sharpest and longest fall in output (see Fig. 12.2, and Roland, 2000: 20). Reforms proceeded slowly, and there were few privatizations. However, in this country

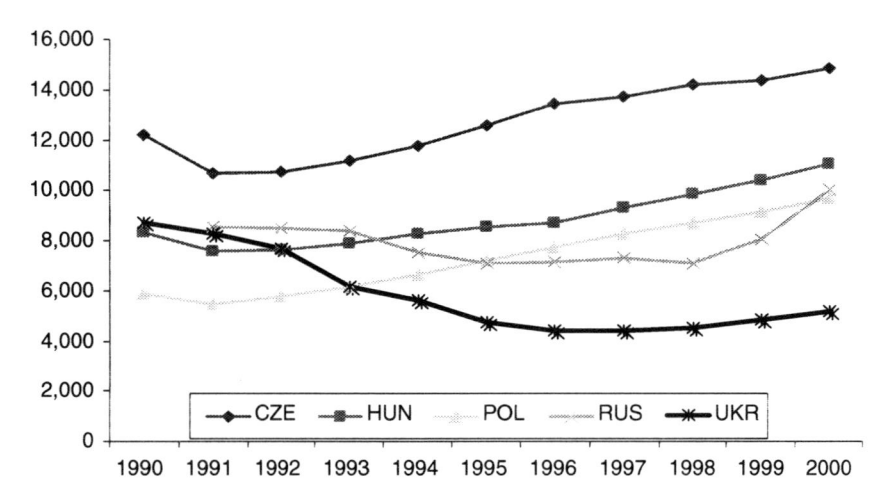

Fig. 12.2 Output in PPP ($ in current prices)
Source: PWT Mark 6.1.

too, AvtoZAZ was one of the exceptions. Still, in a country where reforms were limited, and where ambition to promote the development of a "real" market economy was doubtful, this privatization process was bound to be quite different from that of Škoda.

Any explanation of the differences observed in the two privatization processes would be incomplete if it did not take into account both the initial conditions of these two countries and the differences in their more recent economic and political reforms.

One aspect that proves significant in the progress of reforms in CEECs is the proximity of the country to the European Union (see Roland and Verdier, 1999, and Roland, 2000, ch. 8). This effect is two-pronged. First, being "close to Brussels" increases the attractiveness of a country for international investors. Second, the subsequent prospect of joining the European Union provided proper incentives to establish high standards of democracy within extremely limited periods. Accession prospects also reduced uncertainty for investors, and led to significant transfers from the EU. Potential accession to the EU served as a valuable "external constraint" on the reform process in these countries.

By contrast, a country such as Ukraine could not reap the benefits of this outside anchor. Its privatization process was as slow as in Russia (see Table 12.1), and it had stirred up substantial resistance. The privatization of AvtoZAZ was nevertheless initiated in 1997, within this political context. The attractiveness of AvtoZAZ to international investors was limited. They had had ample time to realize that the economic and political evolution of Ukraine was hectic and uncertain, and most investors were scared away by insiders (industrial lobbies) who were politically strong and opposed to the privatization of AvtoZAZ.

Finally, unlike the Czech Republic, the government of Ukraine was not representative of the majority of the people in Ukraine. Representation was weak, because voters' power was also. As a corollary, the motivations behind the privatization of AvtoZAZ were far removed from efficiency

Table 12.1 Private sector share in GDP

	1990	1991	1992	1993	1994	1995	1996	1997	1998
Czech Republic	10	15	30	45	65	70	75	75	75
Poland	30	40	45	50	55	60	60	65	65
Hungary	25	30	40	50	55	60	70	75	85
Ukraine	10	10	10	15	40	45	50	55	55
Russia	5	5	25	40	50	55	60	70	70

Source: EBRD Transition Reports (1999–2002).

improvement. The government essentially wanted to attract capital from abroad to prevent the outright bankruptcy of the company. The poor management of the company, together with the continued fall in GDP, had indeed led to a sharp decline in production: from about 156,500 cars in 1992, to only 94,000 cars in 1994 and 58,984 cars in 1995.[9]

Control rights

The main companies that revealed their interest were General Motors, Fiat, and Daewoo. Few details are known about the negotiation process between these companies and the Ukrainian government since it took place in a completely non-transparent manner. Still, it was quite clear from the start that the Ukrainian government wanted to retain direct control over the "strategic" decisions that AvtoZAZ would have to make. One such "strategic" decision was that the production of the only national model, the Tavria had to be perpetuated.[10] Another was that employment would have to be maintained, at all costs. Clearly, such constraints limited the freedom of the management to enhance productivity.

The most attractive proposition—in the eyes of the Ukrainian government—emanated from the South Korean car producer Daewoo. Officially, the selection of Daewoo was justified by its investment plan, which was by and large superior to the other bids. Daewoo proposed $1.3 billion of direct investment (the highest foreign direct investment the country would ever have received), promising to maintain employment unchanged (at 18,000 workers), and to increase the annual production up to 255,000 cars within four years. In comparison, General Motors initially proposed to invest $23 million to produce 25,000 Opel Vectra per year. Later, it increased its bid to $60 million, and production of 60,000 cars per year. As for the employees, only 1,000 workers were considered necessary for such production volumes. The "non-negligible" question of whether the "generous" offer of Daewoo was at all realistic was, of course, of secondary importance for the ex-Soviet Republic leaders. Actually, some specialists and people in Ukraine still believe that the attraction of this offer was not unrelated to personal favours offered to some of the leaders.

---

[9] Some attempts were made to find national financing. However, national investors (such as "Prominvestbank") were sceptical about the value of such investment without any restructuring (Piskovyi, 2001). Moreover, the managers of the company preferred a foreign investor (bringing more funds) rather than a national one.

[10] The Tavria model was put into production in 1987 in order to replace the old model, the Zaporozhets. By 1997, this model was suffering from a poor image: it was clearly outdated, of poor comfort, and had mediocre performance.

Why cast doubt on this investment plan?

The reasons to doubt the realism of the plan are first, because the production of AvtoZAZ accounted for only 6,881 cars in 1996. Second, the volume of *total* car sales in the Ukrainian market only amounted to 200,000 units, and the constraints imposed on the management of AvtoZAZ would not have enabled it to develop a strong export capability. Besides, the total sales of Daewoo in the whole European Union only attained 200,000 cars in 2000. Consequently, a sales target of 255,000 cars per year, that is, 127 per cent of the national market, appears clearly unrealistic. Third, Daewoo was already facing obvious financial troubles before it assumed joint ownership of AvtoZAZ, and had substantial excess capacity worldwide.[11] Hence, there was little doubt that Daewoo was interested above all in obtaining substantial protection to achieve a monopoly position in the Ukrainian market. As we will see, the organizational form chosen for the new Company AvtoZAZ–Daewoo was particularly appropriate for these purposes. Among other things, the central role assumed by government was perfect to guarantee that soft-budget constraints could be sustained for a long period.

Despite the questionable financial position of Daewoo Corporation, the negotiation process resulted in an agreement, signed in September 1997, creating a joint-stock company AvtoZAZ–Daewoo.[12] The statutory fund of the joint venture was contributed by both parties in equal shares, where Daewoo's contribution amounted to $150 million in cash. To repeat, the fact that 50 per cent of the newly created joint venture would belong to the state is explained by the desire of the government to retain control of the new firm. It was also an additional "insurance" for insiders and for Daewoo that soft-budget constraints and preferential conditions could be maintained.

Temporary (?) protection

As with the privatization of Škoda, generous protections and preferential treatment were offered to Daewoo. Among these conditions, the most important ones were (1) the adoption of a law promoting automobile

---

[11] These problems were common to many Korean firms and were one of the reasons why the "Asian Crisis" occurred a few months later.

[12] The corporate structure then became the following: the government would remain the unique owner of AvtoZAZ (probably to avoid using the politically sensitive word, of "privatization"). However, AvtoZAZ was stripped of its labour force and productive equipment, which were entirely transferred to the joint venture. That transfer represented the 50% contribution of the Ukrainian side to the joint venture.

production in Ukraine and (2) the introduction of import restrictions on used cars.[13] The former, adopted in September 1997, consisted of substantial tax privileges for investors in the automobile industry and the granting of exemptions from import duties and other foreign trade regulations under the (rather "precise") conditions, that only AvtoZAZ–Daewoo could meet. These measures were to be applied until 2008 (i.e for more than ten years). Another "welcoming present" consisted in debt write-offs for AvtoZAZ, and the restriction that public organizations could only purchase cars produced in Ukraine (i.e. by AvtoZAZ–Daewoo). All the objections raised by other investors in the Ukrainian car industry were completely ignored.

Even though some may argue that such measures may be necessary to protect an infant industry, there is no doubt in the present case that they had strongly negative implications in terms of potential catching up. Some authors even contend that these protectionist measures were responsible for the almost complete destruction of the Ukrainian car industry (see e.g. Szyrmer, 2000: 16).

The players

What led to these choices? Lobbies played a crucial role in the negotiation process. First, some non-official voices argue that Daewoo managed to attract strong support among the political elites of the country. Second, there was significant lobbying in favour of Daewoo by the main actors involved in this process, in particular by the incumbent managers of the company. The employees of AvtoZAZ also backed the proposal of Daewoo unanimously, against the offer of General Motors, which proposed to lay off 95 per cent of the staff. It should also be noted that time constraints were getting very tight: with 18,000 employees, AvtoZAZ only produced 6,881 cars in 1996, and 1,000 cars in 1997. Although Daewoo's offer was clearly unrealistic and socially costly in the long run, the interests of the employers and employees of the firm were given outright preference over that of the population: through tax privileges and duties exemptions, the government sacrificed potential gains in efficiency.

Admittedly, Daewoo did not obtain such favourable conditions without having itself to offer an (unrealistically?) ambitious development plan for the company. In return for all the protectionist measures it obtained, the

---

[13] The new law stipulated that import of cars more than five-years old and/or worth less than $5000 would be forbidden.

How to Gain Political Support for Reforms

South Korean car maker agreed to issue a $1.1 billion loan to AvtoZAZ, with no guarantees from the government's side. That loan would be used to restructure production plants in accordance with Daewoo's production technologies, and to improve the production of the famous Ukrainian Tavria model. Furthermore, the AvtoZAZ–Daewoo company promised to reinvest its profits in the development of the Ukrainian car industry.

The outcome

From the first year of operations, the company's production was far below its minimum targeted level of 100,000 vehicles: only 24,000 cars were produced. Out of these, only 11,700 could actually be sold. The managers of AvtoZAZ–Daewoo put the blame on falling national demand and delays in the introduction of a new car model (see Fig. 12.3).

External experts instead think that a more important reason lies in the poor performance of the joint venture. The new Korean models were quite unpopular in Ukraine, and AvtoZAZ–Daewoo failed to improve the quality of the pre-existing Tavria model. The effort of the management indeed focused on improving the appearance of that model. This led to a change in the image of the Tavria model: instead of being perceived as a "low quality and low price" car, it became a "low quality but quite expensive" one. Finally, some of the protectionist measures put in place expressly to protect the car maker did not significantly affect imports.

Lack of commitment

The main explanation may, however, be found in the lack of commitment on both sides to the deal. The financial situation of Daewoo rapidly became alarming. Since the government had not devised anyway to make Daewoo stick to its promises, none of the latter was fulfilled. There is no evidence that the loan ever materialized. Concomitantly, the plants were not restructured. Going from bad to worse, instead of trying to produce cars in Ukraine, Daewoo used its international excess capacity (estimated at some 2 million units in 1998) to ship already built cars to a factory in Odessa and, after a minimal addition of value by Ukrainian labour, sold them as domestic cars: " 'They' ll [the Daewoo Nexias] have their wheels taken off in Varna, Bulgaria,' said Vladimir Ushakov, an Odessa shipping professional. 'Then the Koreans will bring the wheels in separately and put them on. Voila!' says Ushakov, 'A Korean car made in Ukraine!' " (Korshak, 1998).

On 1 January 1999, 13,000 unsold cars (i.e. more than the equivalent of the previous year's sales) were stocked in the AvtoZAZ plant. Only two

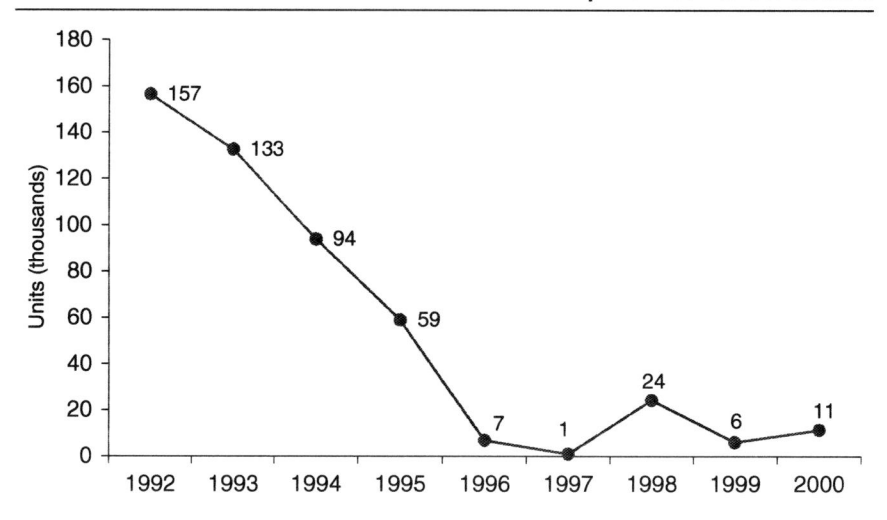

Fig. 12.3 Production of AvtoZAZ
Sources: Auto katalog, various issues; Lastauto omnibus katalog, various issues, Transporama.

years after the creation of the joint venture, the privatization of AvtoZAZ to the South Korean car maker had resulted in blatant failure: despite the the government's protectionist measures, the company had not managed to conquer the Ukrainian market.

Despite (or perhaps because of) these developments, the government set up a programme to selling the shares still in its possession and to delegate the entire management of the joint venture. However, the pressure from insiders went in the opposite direction: "As long as the joint venture [AvtoZAZ–Daewoo] is at stage of *gaining strength*, it would be better for the government to remain the chief property holder, to manage us and to help us" (AvtoZAZ Deputy Director, M. Lastovetsky, quoted in Korshak, 1998—emphasis added). To spare the interests of the insiders and to create support for this additional privatization step, the programme maintained some of the initial conditions that had already undermined the first phase of privatization. Namely, potential buyers would have to run the firm "efficiently". The meaning of the word "efficient", however, still meant that all workers would remain employed.

Unsurprisingly, in September 2000, this attempt to sell state shares failed for lack of bids. The Daewoo Corporation was already bankrupt, and rare were any other firms interested in AvtoZAZ, which was producing at less than 10 per cent of capacity and unable to sell its own production.

How to Gain Political Support for Reforms

External constraints, external players, and light at the end of the tunnel

As observed before, critical conditions are sometimes necessary to force governments into undertaking necessary reforms. The huge losses of AvtoZAZ, together with the ever-increasing deficit of the Ukrainian government and with external pressures, probably explain how AvtoZAZ may eventually escape the vicious circle we described.

By 1998, the overall economic situation in Ukraine had followed the same course as AvtoZAZ. The financial needs of the Ukrainian government had been increasing as well: in 1997, the public deficit was reaching 7 per cent of GDP (the limiting measure imposed by the IMF for the continuation of financial cooperation was 2.5%). The government kept relying on foreign borrowing, but the difficulties in its relations with the IMF and other international financial institutions, made further loans increasingly difficult to obtain.

External constraints were thus tightening. In line with our argument, these helped shift the balance of power away from industrial lobbies. The government was now forced to design a privatization plan that aimed to raise $1 billion in revenues through the privatization of key state-owned enterprises (SOEs), such as Zaporozhstal (the biggest steel producer), Tsentrenergo (power generator), Ukrainian International Airlines (already partly owned by Swissair), and, of course, AvtoZAZ.

As a result, the Ukrainian government had to sell many more shares in AvtoZAZ than initially desired. Eventually, a majority stake of 82 per cent was put on offer, at the beginning of 2001. After several unsuccessful attempts, AvtoZAZ was privatized to a national car distributor, Ukravto, at a discount price. As to Daewoo's shares in AvtoZAZ–Daewoo, the bankruptcy of the latter partner forced it to sell its 50 per cent share to 'Hirsch&Co,' which acted on behalf of an undisclosed actor. The latter announced officially that it would not interfere with the management. Ukravto therefore became the *de facto* manager of the company. However, Ukravto being a national car *distributor*, and not a car producer, its main efforts focused on defensive restructuring and on improving the distribution of cars in Ukraine. Together with this defensive strategy, it signed several agreements with foreign car makers (such as Daimler-Chrysler and Opel, which is part of the initially rebuffed GM group) for the knock-down production of their models by AvtoZAZ. This conservative strategy led to positive results. Production and sales significantly increased and, in 2002 and 2003, demand was so high that it exceeded the production capacities of the AvtoZAZ plants. Hence, the prospects of the company have now improved.

Other external constraints materialized as well, which forced the Ukrainian government to start lifting its protective measures. The protectionist measures had induced the European Union to intervene and oppose them. They were declared to violate existing agreements between the EU and Ukraine. Therefore, the Ukrainian side was invited to change its legislation and to make it consistent with its international commitments. The Ukrainian government eventually accepted the invitation and, after several years of reflection, partially waived quantitative restrictions on the imports of used cars.[14]

12.4. Broader Evidence

While these two case studies provide strong evidence about the value of external constraints, one may still question whether or not there is any *systematic* relationship between the tightness of external constraints and the intensity of privatizations. Such evidence can be found in Bortolotti and Siniscalco (2004, ch. 3), who analyse the determinants of privatization on a panel data set that represents about 60 per cent of all privatizations realized over the 1977–99 period. Their regression analysis shows, among other things, that high government debt (typically an external constraint) is a strong determinant of the intensity of privatization. The privatization policies initiated in Italy in 1993 and in many other countries thus appears to result directly from the need to find extra finance.

Also, the decision to comply with the Maastricht Treaty criteria—and hence to enter the eurozone—helped many European countries accelerate their privatization process. Beyond privatizations, the evidence provided in Chapter 8 suggests that external constraints imposed by the Maastricht Treaty and, subsequently, by the Stability Pact helped these European countries increase the pace of their reforms, as was shown in Figures 8.4 and 8.5.

---

[14] In reaction to these amendments, the General Director of AvtoZAZ–Daewoo, Wang Yang Nam, declared that they represented a direct and unambiguous violation of the guarantees set forth by Section 2 of the law of Ukraine "On the Regime of Foreign Investment" and that the Korean side would take some measures and make Ukraine pay moral damages according to Article 10 of the abovementioned law. Hence, "Cabinet members are now racking their brains over the issue of how to kill two birds with one stone, satisfy the EU and to comfort the investor" (Mr Papashev, Chairman of the AvtoZAZ–Daewoo joint venture, in Brovkin, 2000).

Yet, the recent breach of the Stability Pact by France and Germany may call into question the validity of these external constraints, which are—or at least have been—directly agreed upon by the countries' governments. Initially, the creation of the Pact was suggested by Germany in an attempt to create a straitjacket that would prevent "deficit-prone" countries (such as Belgium and Italy) from abusing the common euro currency and free-riding on the credibility generated by fiscally virtuous countries, such as, of course, Germany. Indeed, the Pact has mainly benefited these "deficit-prone" countries. As showed by Bris *et al.* (2004), the real effects of the euro (namely, an increase in corporate investment) materialized in these countries more than in initially virtuous ones. Furthermore, the existence of these *external constraints* helped them commit to pursuing reforms that reduced their structural deficit, implement pension reforms (see Chapters 9 and 10), and initiate other structural reforms (see Chapters 8 and 9).

Still, there is an important difference between a "self-imposed" external constraint, and one genuinely imposed from the outside. In fact, recent popular opposition to EU rules of conduct eventually weakened the will of the French and German governments, which were believed by their own electorates to be in a position to water down the Pact. Having to choose whether to maintain or to lift the Pact, these governments gave in to electoral pressure and decided to display "national strength" in controlling EU rules, although it is not self-evident that this move will be beneficial to Europe, nor even to them. By contrast, such a choice was not available to the Czech nor (recently) to the Ukrainian governments but the fact that their constraints were binding actually helped them.

13
How to Reform: Pulling the Strings

Confronted with increasing globalization, intensifying international competition, or the rise of newly industrializing countries such as China, European countries are called to the difficult task of adjusting their economies to move ahead. Europe must develop its growth potential, create jobs, and adapt its various welfare systems to the new economic and demographic realities. Appropriate responses to these challenges may bring substantial economic gains; yet several obstacles stand in the way.

A first task is clearly to identify which reforms to implement. It is conventionally recognized that, in Europe, increasing reliance on markets (e.g. through deregulation, privatization, and a better provision of incentives in the labour market) should generate large gains.[1] The analysis in the first part of this volume suggests that product market reforms generally do bring such benefits. Yet, their outcome is not always certain, as there can be mishaps (especially in slowly innovating industries), transitional costs (as evidenced by the case of the UK—see Part I), and redistributive aspects. Beyond the difficult exercise of accurately identifying the benefits attached to each possible reform, political obstacles systematically arise to oppose reforming efforts.

This report has examined how political opposition materializes, and suggested strategies for reform-minded governments to prevail. Our cases studies show that opposition to reform may come from a handful of individuals or from numerous groups in society; that it may be due to different motivations, and that it may lead even valuable reforms to be blocked. Typically, uncertainty about the winners and losers from a reform creates substantial *ex ante* opposition, even if the reform *ex post* benefits a majority of the individuals. This *status quo bias* has long been

---

[1] This view, of course, extends well beyond Europe, and has been termed "Washington concensus". However, many aspects of the consensus have received sharp criticism, partly due to the failures of some unaccompanied liberalization reforms in transition and in developing countries. See also the discussion by Vito Tanzi in this volume for a longer-term perspective.

acknowledged in the literature (see Fernandez and Rodrik, 1991; Dewatripont and Roland, 1992), and shows that political support for a proposed reform may not be an accurate measure of the reform's true economic value. A benevolent policy-maker may hence wish to push through even unpopular reforms, but opportunistic, office-seeking policy-makers will be more anxious to avoid electoral backlashes. Sometimes, however, losers—and thus opponents—are clearly identifiable, whereas potential winners—and hence likely supporters—may be uncertain. The nature of the opposition depends also on whether the electorate at large is concerned, or only specific groups in the population. In the former case, the success or failure of the reform essentially hinges on its electoral support, while in the latter case, it is the balance of power between politicians and special interest groups that matters. Frequently, however, the two aspects are intertwined.

How can policy-makers successfully cope with such multi-faceted opposition? To identify successful strategies for reform, we examined a broad set of reform experiences through the lens of existing theories of reform. Unlike previous works, our case-study approach emphasized—in a rather systematic manner—the crucial role of the political institutional and economic "framework" conditions. Unsurprisingly, no "one-size-fits-all" strategy emerges; yet, some general lessons may be drawn by potential reformers depending on the economic and political "framework conditions".

Through our case studies, we examined different political economic scenarios. A scenario combines an economic characterization of the market or welfare system to be reformed and a description of the political institutions and of the *de facto* veto players which determine the political strength of the government. Among the possible configurations that may emerge from the interplay between the political power of the policy-makers and the nature of the opposition to reform—driven by economic incentives—our case studies identify four relevant scenarios—which need not be mutually exclusive. For each scenario, we identify a successful recipe for reform, which emerges as the winning strategy from our large set of case studies.

The first scenario features a strong government, backed by a large parliamentary majority, and wide-reaching economic reforms which could potentially affect every citizen. The benefits of the reform materialize with a substantial lag, and there is uncertainty about the identity of the winners and losers. In this environment, the core "recipe" for a strong government is to push the reform through—using its political strength—while relying on subsequent support as the effects of the reform settle in. This clearly resembles the strategy adopted by Mrs Thatcher in the 1980s, when she bluntly exploited her parliamentary majority to impose reforms, in a rather non-consensual way. In this case, oppositions were brushed aside, and reforms made a *political* success. Yet, since oppositions are muted, they cannot elicit information about the costs of reform that the reformers may have failed to discern. Also, some other governments which attempted to adopt the same strategy did not succeed. What are the conditions that make such a strategy potentially successful?

The framework conditions that played in favour of Mrs Thatcher's reforms are, in part, institutional: in a country with majoritarian elections, featuring a divided opposition, where votes were increasingly dispersed across Labour and the Liberal Democrats, the Tories enjoyed a parliamentary edge which allowed them to pursue further reforms. Furthermore, the main opponents did not manage to veto the reform by means other than electoral either, due to weakened unions. This combination of a specific institutional framework and a weak opposition allowed the government to force reforms.

Three other countries (Italy, France, and Denmark) tried to adopt this confrontational strategy under rather different framework conditions, and failed. Their institutional design provided less strength to the government, while wage bargaining was more institutionalized—implying that coalitions of citizens would have more power to veto reforms. In the case of Italy, Mr Berlusconi's government attempted to impose a pension reform à la Thatcher, but stern opposition forced early elections. In the case of France, Mr Juppé's government tried to retrench specific pension schemes, and was forced to step down. In Denmark, the attempt by the Rasmussen government to bypass the conventional consensual approach in modifying labour market regulations aborted his reform efforts. In all these cases, we find that the conjunction of elements that allowed Mrs Thatcher to bypass the coalition building stage was absent. Failing to acknowledge this difference prevented these governments from pursuing their reform efforts, independently of their parliamentary strength.

The second scenario considers instead "weak" governments—either *de jure*, by institutional design, or *de facto*, because of strong interest groups. Yet, our case studies highlight that the relative weakness of a government needs not be a handicap. Relying on an appropriate strategy, several wide-reaching economic reforms—in pension or labour market— were successfully implemented even by weak governments. In this environment, the "recipe" is to tailor the reform so as to *widen the political base* in favour of the reform. Since the government has less political weight to bluntly commit to reforming, the reform measures are designed in order to "buy" support from a broad section of the population. This strategy is crucial in electoral politics, as opposed to special interest politics. When most of the population may be affected by a reform proposal, the primary incentive of the government is to get closer to the most active social players—such as unions and employers' associations in pension reforms—and popular support at least within its electoral constituency. The success of the reform hence depends on the government's ability to produce benefits to all these groups. Clearly, the need to ensure such support may lead governments to sacrifice some economic efficiency to ensure the reforms' political feasibility.

Labour market reforms in Denmark are an emblematic case of the successful use of social dialogue. Due to a tradition of consensual negotiations between representatives of the workers and of the employers, based on an understanding of the need to maintain economic efficiency to secure sustainable welfare levels, Denmark managed to reinforce both the flexibility of employment and to strengthen the incentives to work, in the midst of an economic slowdown. Simply, to ensure wide enough support in the population, compensating measures had to be found, essentially by means of a sufficiently tight safety net. In Italy, where labour unions are sufficiently strong to bring a government down, but social dialogue is less of a tradition than in Denmark, major pension reforms were implemented by achieving support in the population and from the unions. To this end, long transitory periods of adjustment had to be introduced, thereby foregoing the benefits of more radical reforms. Yet, the strategy of widening popular support allowed Italy to go much further than the had uncompromising style been adopted. The case of mass privatizations in Central and Eastern European countries also suggests that the design of privatization schemes was not meant to maximize efficiency, but rather to buy out support for other reforms, such as price liberalization. Here as well, gaining political support for reforms was crucial to making the democratic and economic transitions successful.

The third scenario identifies a situation in which a government—possibly, but not necessarily, weak—faces reforms in an economic environment characterized by a tight web of entrenched interests who will strongly oppose any reforming effort. In this situation, the "recipe" is to *divide and conquer*. When the option of widening the political base is not feasible, because spreading benefits over a wide section of the population is overly costly or because the groups that may stand to lose from the reform are better organized politically, governments may use divide-and-conquer tactics to concentrate the costs of a reform onto specific groups of individuals. This strategy helps untie the web of entrenched interests

How to Reform: Pulling the Strings

which would have opposed the reform, and divide them into (a larger group of) supporters, who will mute (a small group of) opponents. This strategy proved successful in implementing labour market reforms in Spain, and in beginning the reforming process of non-manufacturing industries in most European countries, yet it failed in countries with strong social dialogue, where imposing reforms may disrupt social links and become extremely costly for society, as the case of Denmark in Chapters 9 and 10 reveals.

The last scenario analyzed in this part of the book is almost unrelated to the economic and political characterization of the previous scenarios of reform: it identifies the existence of external constraints that require policy-makers to adopt—often unpopular—reform measures. While weak governments may need these constraints to build commitment to reform, even strong governments may benefit from the availability of a blame-avoidance strategy to limit electoral backlashes after unpopular reforms.

Our case studies consistently suggest that acknowledging or *exploiting* these *external constraints* can thus be a highly efficient way of building commitment to pursue reforms. For instance, the case of Russia, with the Yeltsin governments clearly falling prey to special interest groups, and the privatization of the major Ukrainian car producer, AvtoZAZ, were confused and highly inefficient until external constraints forced these two governments to redirect their efforts. Relying on *external constraints* has also been a deliberate strategy in Europe, where governments unwilling to take the blame for unpleasant, though necessary, reforms were supporting reforms at the European Union level, in order to then market these reforms as inescapable at the national level; however, this blame-avoidance strategy may have recently backfired, as suggested by the French and Dutch referendums on the European Constitution.

In a first-best world, imposing additional constraints can only reduce the value of the attainable goal. In a second-best world, however, with the economic and political constraints we have described above, adding hurdles can be a valuable (though somewhat undemocratic) way to build commitment, tame oppositions, or to restore the incentives for government to aim at aggregate efficiency rather than giving preference to special interest groups. In practice, European economic history has shown that governments may, at times, gain from having some options removed from their set of feasible alternatives.

In other cases, as in the transition countries, constraints are truly external; they come from a situation of economic crisis, or from international organizations that refuse to rubber-stamp the actions of the government. In that case, those promoting efficiency-enhancing reforms may gain bargaining power *vis-à-vis* the opponents of reforms, and the country at large may gain. Particularly in the presence of a web of overly strong special interest groups, which can neither be bought off via a spreading of benefits, nor broken up via concentration of costs on a sufficiently narrow subgroup, external constraints can be instrumental in making reforms inescapable. Yet, this option may also turn out to be extremely risky and costly on some occasions, as external constraints may prevent the government from implementing valuable policies supported by a large majority of the population.

No "one-size-fits-all" strategy thus exists. We hence warn policy-makers not to automatically adopt best practices that have worked in different political and economic environments, while instead encouraging them to pay close attention to the framework conditions underlined in this report. What this strategy is and how gradual it should be is likely to depend on the sector or market to be reformed and on the political and social institutions of the country under analysis. Yet, one general result seems to come out on the role of information. Particularly when the effects of reforms are hard to grasp and when they are expected to materialize over a long time horizon, government may gain further support by providing information about the short-and long-term benefits to be expected from the reform, as well as about the costs of maintaining the status quo. Boeri *et al.* (2002), for instance, showed that agents who were more informed about the future of pensions were significantly more supportive of pension reforms; they were knowledgeable about the true costs and future prospects of the existing system.

References

Acemoglu, D., Robinson, J., and Verdier, T. (2003), "Kleptocracy and Divide-and-Rule: A Model of Personal Rule". MIT mimeo.

Aghion, P. and Blanchard, O. (1994), "On the Speed of Transition in Central Europe", in Stanley Fischer and Julio J. Rotemberg (eds.), *NBER Macro economics Annual 1994*, Cambridge, Mass.: MIT Press.

Atkinson, A. B. (1991), "The Development of State Pensions in the UK", Discussion Paper no. WSP/58, London School of Economics.

Baron, D. (1994), "Electoral Competition with Informed and Uninformed Voters", *American Political Science Review*, 88, 33–47.

Bebchuk, Lucian (1999), "A Rent-Protection Theory of Corporate Ownership and Control", NBER Working Paper no. 7203, Cambridge, Mass.

Becker, G. (1983), "A Theory of Competition among Pressure Groups for Political Influence", *Quarterly Journal of Economics*, 98, 371–400.

Beltrametti, L. (1995), "Le Pensioni tra Solidarietà e Sostenibilità", *Il Ponte*.

—— (1996), *Il Debito Pensionistico in Italia*, Bologna: Il Mulino.

Berger, P. (1992), "The Uncertain Triumph of Democratic Capitalism", *Journal of Democracy*, 3, 7–16.

Bernheim, B. Douglas and Whinston, Michael D. (1986), "Menu Auctions, Resource Allocation, and Economic Influence", *Quarterly Journal of Economics*, 101, 1–31.

Bertola, G. and Boeri, T. (2004), "Product Market Integration, Institutions and the Labour Market", mimeo, IGIER, Bocconi.

Bevan, A., Estrin, S., and Schaffer, M. (1999), "Determinants of Enterprise Performance during Transition", CERT Discussion Paper no. 99/03.

Biais, B. and Perotti, E. (2002), "Machiavellian Privatization", *American Economic Review*, 92(1), 240–58.

Black, B., Kraakman, R., and Tarassova, A. (2000), "Russian Privatization and Corporate Governance: What Went Wrong?" *Stanford Law Review*, 52, 1731–808.

Black, D. (1958), *The Theory of Committees and Elections*, Cambridge: Cambridge University Press.

Blanchard, O. and Giavazzi, F. (2003), "The Macroeconomic Effects of Regulation and Deregulation in Goods and Labor Markets", *Quarterly Journal of Economics*, 118, 879–909.

Boeri, T., Börsch-Supan, A., and Tabellini, G. (2002), "Pension Reforms and the Opinions of European Citizens". *American Economic Review*, 92, 396–401.

—— Brugiavini, A., and Disney, R. (eds.) (2001), *"Pensions: More Information, Less Ideology"*, Berlin: Kluwer Academic Publisher.

—— Conde-Ruiz, J. I., and Galasso, V. (2004), "Cross-Skill Redistribution and the Tradeoff between Unemployment Benefits and Employment Protection", IGIER mimeo.

Bohatá, Marie (2000), "Škoda Automobilová a.s.", in Saul Estrin, Xavier Richet, and Josef C. Brada (eds.), *Foreign Direct Investment in Central Eastern Europe: Case Studies of Firms in Transition*, New York: M. E. Sharpe.

Bolton, P. and Roland, G. (1992), "Privatisation in Central and Eastern Europe", *Economic Policy*, 15, 276–309.

Bonoli, G. (2000), *The Politics of Pension Reform*, Cambridge: Cambridge University Press.

Bortolotti, B. and Siniscalco, D. (2004), *The Challenges of Privatization: An International Analysis*, Oxford: Oxford University Press.

Boycko, M., Shleifer, A., Vishny, R. W., Fischer, S., and Sachs, J. (1993), "Privatizing Russia", Brookings Papers on Economic Activity no. 1993(2), 139–92.

Brada, J. C. (1996), "Privatization is Transition—Or is it?", *Journal of Economic Perspective*, 10, 67–86.

Brickley, J. A., Smith, C. W., and Zimmerman, J. L. (2000), "Incentives in Nonprofit Organizations: Evidence from Hospitals", Working Paper, University of Rochester.

Bris, A., Koskinen, Y., and Nilsson, M. (2004), "The Real Effects of the Euro: Evidence from Corporate Investments", CEPR Discussion Paper no. 4521.

Brovkin, Dmytro (2000), "Daewoo Issues Ultimatum", *The Day*, no. 14.

Brugiavini, A., Ebbinghaus, B., Freeman, R., Garibaldi, P., Holmund, B., Schludi, M. and Verdier, T. (2001), "What do Unions do to the Welfare State?" in T. Boeri, A., Brugiavini, and L. Calmfors (eds.), *"The Role of the Unions in the Twenty-First Century"*, Oxford: Oxford University Press.

—— and Galasso, V. (2004), "The Social Security Reform Process in Italy: Where do we Stand?" *Journal of Pension Economics and Finance*, June, 1–31.

Calmfors, L. and Driffill, J. (1988), "Bargaining Structure, Corporatism and Macroeconomic Performance", *Economic Policy*, 6, 14–61.

Canning, A., and Hare, P. G. (1996), "Political Economy of Privatization in Hungary: A Progress Report", Centre for Economic Reform and Transformation mimeo.

Castanheira, M. (2003), "Public Finance and the Optimal Speed of Transition", *The Economics of Transition*, 11(3), 435–62.

—— and Esfahani, H. (2003), "The Political Economy of Growth: Lessons Learned and Challenges Ahead", in Gary McMahon and hyn Squire (eds.), *Explaining Growth. A Global Research Project*, New York: Palgrave MacMillan.

—— and Roland, G. (2000), "The Optimal Speed of Transition: A General Equilibrium Approach", *International Economic Review*, 41(1), 219–39.

CC.OO. (2004), "El empleo en España", *Confederacion Sindical de Comisiones Obreras*, no. 52.

Claessens, S. and Djankov, S. (1999), "Politicians and Firms in Seven Central and Eastern European Countries", Policy Research Working Paper Series 1954, The World Bank.

Consejo economico y social (2004), *España 2003, Mémorià sobre la situaciòn socio-economica y laboral*, Madrid: Cousejo economico e social.

References

Crepaz, M. L. (1998), "Inclusion versus Exclusion: Political Institutions and Welfare Expenditure", *Comparative Politics*, 31, 61–80.

Cukierman, A. and Tommasi, M. (1998). "When Does it Take a Nixon to Go to China?" *American Economic Review*, 88, 180–97.

D'Amato, M. and Galasso, V. (2002), "Assessing the Political Sustainability of Parametric Social Security Reforms: The Case of Italy", *Giornale degli Economisti e Annali di Economia*, 61(2), 171–213.

Dewatripont, M. and Maskin, E. (1995), "Credit and Efficiency in Centralized and Decentralized Economies". *Review of Economic Studies*, 62, 541–55.

—— and Roland, G. (1992), "Economic Reform under Political Constraints", *Review of Economic Studies*, 59, 595–620.

—— —— (1995), "The Design of Reform Packages under Uncertainty", *American Economic Review*, 85, 1207–23.

DHSS (United Kingdom, Department of Health and Social Security) (1984), "Population, Pension Costs and Pensioners' Income: A Background Paper for the Inquiry into the Provision for Retirement", London.

—— (1985a), "A Programme for Action, White Paper", London.

—— (1985b), "Reform of Social Security, Green Paper", London.

Diermeier, D. and Feddersen, T. (1998), "Cohesion in Legislatures: The Vote of Confidence Procedure", *American Political Science Review*, 92, 611–21.

Dolado, J. and Jimeno, J. (2004), "Contratacion Temporal y costes de despido en España: Lecciones para el futuro desde la perpectiva del pasado", Documento de Trabajo 48, Fundacion Alternativas.

Dörr, Gerlinde, and Kessel, Tanja (2002), "Cooperation and Asymmetry: The Development Profile of an East-West Corporate Project", WZB working paper FS II 02–201.

Downs, A. (1957), *An Economic Theory of Democracy*, New York: Harper and Row.

Dyba, K. and Svejnar, J. (1995), "A Comparative View of Economic Developments in the Czech Republic", in J. Svejnar (ed.), *The Czech Republic and Economic Transition in Eastern Europe*, San Diego: Academic Press.

Earle, J. and Estrin, S. (1998) "Privatization, Competition, and Budget Constraints: Disciplining Enterprises in Russia", London Business School mimeo, London.

—— and Sabirianova, K. (2002), "How Late to Pay? Understanding Wage Arrears in Russia", *Journal of Labor Economics*, 20(3), 661–707.

Emmerson, C. and Johnson, P. (2001), "Pension in the United Kingdom", in R. Disney and P. Johnson (eds.), *Pension Systems and Retirement Income across OECD Countries*, Cheltenham: Edward Elgar.

European Bank for Reconstruction and Development (various years), *Transition Report*, London: EBRD.

Facchini, G. and Willmann, G. (2001), "The Political Economy of International Factor Mobility", SIEPR Working Paper 00–20, Stanford University.

Fernandez, R. and Rodrik, D. (1991), "Resistance to Reform: Status Quo Bias in the Presence of Individual Specific Uncertainty", *American Economic Review*, 81, 1146–55.

Ferrera, M. (1984), Ie Welfare in Italia. Sui luppo e crisi in prospettira comparata, Il Mulino, Bologna.

Ferrera, M., and Gualmini, E. (2004), *Rescued by Europe?* Amsterdam: Amsterdam University Press.

Filatotchev, I., Wright, M., and Bleaney, M. (1999), "Privatization, Insider Control and Managerial Entrenchment in Russia", *Economics of Transition*, 7(2), 481–504.

Fischer, Stanley, and Sahay, Ratna (2000), "The Transition Economies after 10 Years", IMF Working Paper no. 00/30, Washington, DC.

Franco, D. (2002), "Italy: A Never-Ending Pension Reform", in M. Feldstein and H. Siebert (eds.), *Social Security Pension Reform in Europe*, Chicago: University of Chicago Press.

Gawande, K., Krishna, P., and Robbins, M. (2004), "Foreign Lobbies and US Trade Policy", NBER Working Paper no. 10,205.

Glaeser, E. and Shleifer, A. (2001), "A Case for Quantity Regulation", Harvard Institute of Economic Research Paper no. 1909, Jan.

Golub, S. (2003), "Measures of Restrictions on Inward Foreign Direct Investment for OECD Countries", *OECD Economic Studies*, no. 36.

Gonenc, R., Maher, M., and Nicoletti, G. (2000), "The Implementation and the Effects of Regulatory Reform: Past Experience and Current Issues", OECD Economics Department Working Paper no. 251.

—————— (2001), "The Implementation and the Effects of Regulatory Reform: Past Experience and Current Issues", *OECD Economic Studies*, no. 32.

Gronchi, S. (1998), "La sostenibilità delle nuove forme previdenziali ovvero il sistema pensionistico tra riforme fatte e da fare", *Economia Politica*, 15, 295–315.

—— and Aprile, R. (1998), "The 1995 Pension Reform: Sustainability and Indexation", *Labour*, 12, 67–100.

Grossman, G. and Helpman, E. (2001), *Special Interest Politics*. Cambridge, Mass.: MIT Press.

Hart, O., Shleifer, A., and Vishny, R. W. (1997), "The Proper Scope of Government: Theory and an Application to Prisons", *Quarterly Journal of Economics*, 112(4), 1127–61.

Havas, A. (2000), "Changing Patterns of Inter- and Intra-Regional Division of Labour: Central Europe's Long and Winding Road", in Humphrey, J., Lecler, T., and Salerno, M. (eds.), *Global Strategies and Local Realities: The Auto Industry in Emerging Markets*, Basingstoke: Macmillan, 234–62.

Hinich, M. J. (1977), "Equilibrium in Spatial Voting: The Median Voter Result is an Artifact", *Journal of Economic Theory*, 16, 208–19.

—— Ledyard, J. O., and Ordeshook, P. C. (1972), "Nonvoting and the Existence of Equilibrium under Majority Vote", *Journal of Economic Theory*, 44, 144–53.

Holzmann, R. and Hinz, R. (2005), *Old-Age Income Support in the 21st Century: An International Perspective on Pension Systems and Reform*, Washington, DC: World Bank.

Hotelling, H. (1929), "Stability in Competition", *Economic Journal*, 39, 41–57.

INEM: Instituto de Empleo Servicio Pùblico de Empleo Estatal, Ministerio de Trabajo y Asuntos Sociales, online at www.inem.es.

References

Jean, S. and Nicoletti, G. (2002), "Product Market Regulation and Wage Premia in Europe and North America: An Empirical Investigation", OECD Economics Department Working Paper no. 318.
—— (2004), "Regulation and Wage Premia", GEP Research Paper 04/26, Leverhulme Centre for Research on Globalisation and Economic Policy, University of Nottingham.
Jessop, B., Bonnet, K., Bromley, S., and Ling, T. (1988), *Thatcherism: A Tale of Two Nations*, Cambridge: Polity Press.
Jimeno, J. (2002), "A Gradualist Approach at Labour Market Reforms: Employment Policies in Spain (1976–2001)", Working Paper for the conference, Beyond Transition—Development, Perspectives and Dilemmas, Case Foundation, Center for Social and Economics Research, 12–23, Apr.
Johnson, S., Macmillan, J., and Woodruff, C. (2002), "Courts and Relational Contracts", *Journal of Law, Economics, and Organization*, 18, 221–77.
Jørgensen, H. (2003), "The Role of the Trade Unions in Social Restructuring in Scandinavia in the 1990s", *Revue française des affaires sociales*, 4.
Kniazhanski, Vitalyi (2000), " О легкомысленном лоббизме и его последствиях", *The Day*, no. 206.
Kornai, J. (1980), *Economics of Shortage*, Amsterdam: North-Holland.
—— (1986), *Contradictions and Dilemmas*, Cambridge, Mass.: MIT Press.
—— (1998), "The Concept of the Soft Budget Constraint Syndrome in Economic Theory", *Journal of Comparative Economics*, 26: 11–17.
Koromzay, V. (2004), "Some Reflections on the Political Economy of Reform", Comment presented at the international conference on Economic Reforms for Europe: Growth Opportunities in an Enlarged European Union, Bratislava, Slovakia, 18 Mar.
Korshak, Stefan (1998), "Ukraine: Daewoo/AvtoZAZ joint venture stalls", RFE, May.
Koval', Rostyslav (1998), "АвтоЗАЗ-Daewoo: GM, третім будеш?" *Галицькі Контракти*, no. 12.
Krueger, Anne O. (1974), "The Political Economy of the Rent-Seeking Society", *American Economic Review*, 64, 291–303.
Kydland, F. and Prescott, E. (1977), "Rules rather than Discretion: The Inconsistency of Optimal Plans", *Journal of Political Economy*, 85, 473–91.
Laffont, J. J. and Tirole, J. (1993), *A Theory of Incentives in Procurement and Regulation*, Cambridge, Mass.: MIT Press.
Larsen, F. (2004), "The Importance of Institutional Regimes for Active Labour Market Policies—The Case of Denmark", Working Paper, Danish National Centre for Labour Market Research (CARMA).
Levy, B. and Spiller, P. T. (1994), *The Institutional Foundations of Regulatory Commitment: A Comparative Analysis of Telecommunications Regulation*, Oxford: Oxford University Press.
Li, W., Xu, C. L., and Qiang, Z-W. (2001), "The Political Economy of Privatization and Competition: Cross-Country Evidence from the Telecommunications Sector", CEPR Discussion Paper no. 2825, London: Centre for Economic Policy Research.

Lijphart, A. (1999), "Patterns of Democracy", Yale University.
Lindbeck, A. and Weibull, J. (1987), "Balanced-Budget Redistribution as the Outcome of Politicial Competition", *Public Choice*, 52, 273–97.
Lindbeck, A. and Weibull, J. (1993), "A Model of Political Equilibrium in a Representative Democracy", *Journal of Public Economics*, 51, 195–209.
Lipton, David, and Sachs, Jeffrey (1992), "Prospects for Russia's Economic Reforms", Brookings Papers 2, 213–83.
Marin, D. and Schnitzer, M. (1999), "Disorganization and Financial Collapse", CEPR Discussion Paper no. 2245, London.
—— —— (2002), *Contracts in Trade and Transition: The Resurgence of Barter*, Cambridge, Mass.: MIT Press.
—— —— (2003), "Creating Creditworthiness through Reciprocal Exchange", *Review of International Economics*, 11(1), 159–74.
Megginson, W. L., Nash, R. C., Netter, J. M., and Poulsen, A. B. (2001), "The Choice of Private versus Public Capital Markets: Evidence from Privatizations", University of Georgia mimeo.
—— and Netter, J. M. (2001), "From State to Market: A Survey of Empirical Studies on Privatization", *Journal of Economic Literature*, 39, 321–89.
Meyer, Klaus E. (1998), "Multinational Enterprises and the Emergence of Markets and Networks in Transition Economies", Centre for East European Studies Working Paper no. 12.
Milanovic, B. (1995), "The Distributional Impact of Cash and In-Kind Transfers in Eastern Europe and Russia", in D. van de Walle and K. Nead (eds.), *Public Spending and the poor: Theory and Evidence*, Baltimore and London: Johns Hopkins University Press for the World Bank, 489–520.
Mirza, D. and Nicoletti, G. (2004), "Is There Something Special about Trade in Services?" Paper presented at the EIIE (Empirical Investigations in International Economics) conference in Ljubljana, Slovenia, 9–11 June.
Modigliani, Franco, and Perotti, Enrico (2000), "Security Markets versus Bank Finance: Legal Enforcement and Investor Protection", *International Review of Finance*, 1(2), 81–96.
Mueller, D. C. (2003), *Public Choice III*, Cambridge: Cambridge University Press.
National Statistic Office, online at www.statistics.gov.uk.
Nesbitt, S. (1995), "British Pension Policy Making in the 1980s: The Rise and Fall of a Policy Community", Aldershot: Avebury.
Ney, S. (2003), "The Rediscovery of Politics: Democracy and Structural Pension Reforms in Continental Europe", in R. Holzmann, M. Orenstein, and M. Rutkowski, *"Pension Reform in Europe: Process and Progress"*, Washington, DC: The World Bank.
Nicoletti, G. (2006), "The Political Economy of Product Market Reform", fRDB occasional paper.
—— G., Golub, S. S., Hajkova, D., Mirza, D., and Yoo, K. Y. (2003), "The Influence of Policies on Trade and Foreign Direct Investment", *OECD Economic Studies*, no. 36.
Noll, R. G. (1999), "The Economics and Politics of the Slowdown in Regulatory Reform", *Brookings Institution Domestic Economics Working Papers*, no. 1.

References

OECD (1994, 1999, 2001), *Employment Outlooks*.

OECD, National Account Statistics, various issues.

Olson, M. (1965). *The Logic of Collective Action: Public Goods and the Theory of Groups*. Cambridge, Mass.: Harvard University Press.

—— (1982), *The Rise and Decline of Nations*. New Haven: Yale University Press.

Peltzman, S. (1976), "Toward a More General Theory of Regulation", *Journal of Law and Economics*, 19, 211–40.

—— (1988), "The Growth of Government", in G. Stigler (ed.), *Chicago Studies in Political Economy*, Chicago and London: University of Chicago Press, 3–84.

Perotti, E. (2002), "Lessons from the Russian Meltdown", CEPR Policy Paper no. 9.

—— and Gelfer, S. (2001), "Red Barons or Robber Barons? Governance and Investment in Russian Financial-Industrial Groups", *European Economic Review*, 45, 1601–17.

—— and Sgard, J. (2000), "The Russian Meltdown", mimeo, University of Amsterdam.

Persson, T., Roland, G., and Tabellini, G. (1997), "Separation of Powers and Political Accountability", *Quarterly Journal of Economics*, 112, 1163–202.

—— —— —— (1998), "Towards Micropolitical Foundations of Public Finance", *European Economic Review* 42, 685–94.

—— —— —— (2000), "Comparative Politics and Public Finance", *Journal of Political Economy* 108(6), 1121–61.

—— —— —— (2003), "How Do Electoral Rules Shape Party Structures, Government Coalitions and Economic Policies?", Berkeley mimeo.

—— and Tabellini, G. (2000), *Political Economics: Explaining Economic Policy*, Cambridge, Mass.: MIT Press.

Pierson, P. (1994), *"Dismantling the Welfare State?"* Cambridge: Cambridge University Press.

—— (1996), "The New Politics of the Welfare State", *World Politics*, 48, 143–79.

—— and Weaver, K. (1993), "Imposing Losses in Pension Policy", in K. Weaver and B. Rockman (eds.), *"Do Institutions Matter? Government Capabilities in the United States and Abroad"*, Washington, DC: Brookings Institute.

Piskovyi, Volodymir (2001), "Капкани для «АвтоЗАЗу» на додачу до наявних, заводу намагаються запропонувати нові", *Zerkalo Nedeli* (electronic version), no. 20(344) 26 May.

Robinson, J., Torvik, R., and Verdier, T. (2002), "Political Foundations of the Resource Curse", CEPR DP 3422.

Rogoff, K. (1985), "The Optimal Degree of Commitment to an Intermediate Monetary Target", *Quarterly Journal of Economics*, 100, 1169–89.

Roland, G. (2000), *Transition and Economics: Politics, Markets and Firms*, Cambridge, Mass.: MIT Press.

—— (2001*a*), "The Political Economy of Transition", *Journal of Economic Perspectives*, 16(1), 29–50.

—— (2001*b*), "Ten Years After... Transition and Economics", *IMF Staff Papers*, Special Issue 48(0), 29–52.

—— and Verdier, T. (1999), "Transition and the Output Fall", *The Economics of Transition*, 7(1), 1–28.

Roland, G. and Verdier, T. (2003), "Law Enforcement and Transition", *European Economic Review*, 47(4), 669–85.

Rostagno M. (1996), "Il percorso della riforma: 1992–1995. Nuovi indicatori di consistenza e sostenibilità per il FPLD", in F. Kostoris Padoa Schioppa (ed.), *Pensioni e risanamento della finanza pubblica*, Bologna: Il Mulino.

Saint-Paul, G. (2000), *The Political Economy of Labour Market Institutions*, Oxford: Oxford University Press.

—— (2002a), "Macroeconomic Fluctuations and the Timing of Labour Market Reforms", CEPR Working Paper no. 3646.

—— (2002b), "The Political Economy of Employment Protection", *Journal of Political Economy*, 110, 672–704.

Sartori, G. (1982), *Teoria dei Partiti e caso Italiano*, Milan: Sugar Co Edizioni.

Schmidt, K. (1997), "Managerial Incentives and Product Market Competition", *Review of Economic Studies*, 64, 191–213.

Sheshinski, E. and López-Calva, L. F. (2003), "Privatization and its Benefits: Theory and Evidence", *CESifo Economic Studies*; 49(3), 429–59.

Shleifer, A. (1998), "State versus Private Ownership", *Journal of Economic Perspectives*, 12(4), 133–50.

Škoda (2004), "Annual Report 2003", Internet version (www.skoda-auto.cz).

Spolaore, E. (2004), "Adjustments in Different Government Systems", *Economics and Politics*, 16(2), 117–46.

Stigler, G. (1971). "The Theory of Economic Regulation", *Public Choice*, 13, 91–106.

Szyrmer, Janusz (2000), "Post-Soviet Transition: Problems, Lessons, and Solutions", in J. Szyrmer and D. Snelbecker (eds.), *Reforms in Ukraine: Ideas and Actions*, Kiev: Harvard/CASE "Alterpres".

UGT (2004), "Balance de la Legislatura y Propuestas de UGT ante las Electiones Generales", *Union*, Feb.

Visser, J. and Ebbinghaus, B. (2000), *Trade Unions in Western Europe since 1945*, London: Macmillan.

Welch, D. and Frémond, O. (1998), "The Case-by-Case Approach to Privatization: Techniques and Examples", World Bank Technical paper no. 403.

Werner, Robert (2004), "Location, Cheap Labour and Government Incentives: A Case Study of Automotive Investment in Central Europe since 1989", Columbia Business School Working Paper.

Winiecki, J. (1996), "Impediments to Institutional Change in the Former Soviet System: A Property-Rights-Based Approach", in L. J. Alston, T. Eggertsson, and D. North (eds.), *Empirical Studies in Institutional Change*, Cambridge: Cambridge University Press.

World Bank (1994), *Averting the Old Age Crisis*, Washington, DC: Oxford University Press and World Bank.

Wyplosz, Charles (1999), "Ten Years of Transformation: Macroeconomic Lessons", Paper presented at the World Bank ABCDE conference, Washington, DC.

Comments

Gérard Roland

This is a welcome report on the political economy of reforms, blending in a nice way facts, theory, and case studies. The political economy of reforms has been a very important topic of research in the transition from socialism to capitalism (Roland, 2000). It has attracted the interest of all those also interested in the political economy of reforms in other regions of the world and has been integrated into the new field of political economics (see e.g. Drazen, 2000). It seems particularly relevant today in the context of the European Union, where there is a growing perception that institutional reforms are needed. Individual member states face the dual challenge of reform of the pension system and of the welfare state on one hand and reforms in the labour market on the other hand. Reforms in capital markets, product markets, and higher education are also high on the agenda. There is indeed a growing concern that Europe has stopped bridging the gap with the USA and that it is starting to lag behind. More and more economists are convinced that structural reforms are the key to higher growth in Europe. Further relaxation of monetary policy without structural reforms would be misguided.

The report uses the new tools of the political economy of reforms to analyse particular reforms. In order to give a succinct account of the content of the report, I will use Table C2.1, where each row stands for a particular reform and each column stands for a particular variable that plays a role from the point of view of the political economy of reforms. These variables can be justified by the extensive literature dealing with the subject. I will not do any survey of that literature here but will just mention briefly the role of the different variables in the columns of Table C2.1.

How to Gain Political Support for Reforms

Table C2.1 The political economy of reforms

	Electoral system	External constraint	Emergency	Spillover from other reforms	Commitment Building	Divide and rule	Experimentation
Pensions	x	x	x		x	x	
Labour market		x	x	x	x		
Product market		x		x		x	x
Privatization	x	x			x	x	
Corporate governance					x		

The *electoral system* contrasts the difference between majoritarian systems and proportional systems. The former usually have a smaller number of parties competing for seats and coalition governments are therefore much less frequent (for recent theory and empirical analysis of the effect of electoral systems on party and coalition formation, see Persson et al., 2003). As a consequence, governing parties do not have to work out compromises with their coalition partners or face hold-up threats from the latter. The *external constraint* refers to obligations stemming from participation in the EU (mainly entry to EMU for eurozone countries and entry to the EU for accession countries), conditionality imposed by IMF or World Bank loans. The role of *emergency* refers to large negative external shocks such as speculative attacks or large terms of trade shocks that force countries to react. The *spillover from other reforms* relates to complementarities between reforms in the sense that, for example, reforms in the product markets can affect the distribution of costs and benefits of reform in the labour market. The notion of *commitment building* refers to the fact that governments signal their commitment to the implementation of particular reforms because credibility matters for the success of reforms. Building commitment can, however, take many forms: large information campaigns to explain the government's views and intentions with respect to particular reforms, the launching of a wide social dialogue to try to convince social groups of the correctness of the reform packages projected, explicit coalition-building for specific reform packages in order to demonstrate that a wide majority can be won to approve a given reform package, and so on. *Divide-and-rule tactics* are a more cynical way of getting reforms through and the literature on this dates back at least to Machiavelli and even to Sun Tzu. *Experimentation* refers to the use of partial or localized reform as a method of "trial and error" to learn more about the effect of reforms with uncertain outcomes. These variables play a different role depending on the kind of reform that is being implemented, with some playing a more prominent role in some cases and other variables in other cases.

The section of the report on pension reform emphasizes mostly the role of the electoral system but also most of the other variables with the exception of experimentation and spillovers. The main comparison is between the experience of the UK and that of Italy. The difference between both reforms sheds light on the difference between electoral systems. In the UK, the Conservative government of Margaret Thatcher was able to exploit its parliamentary majority emanating from the majoritarian electoral system in order to push through a rather radical pension reform. The majoritarian system allowed the government to push through its preferred policy without having to make any compromise. This stands in contrast to Italy where pension reform occurred under a mostly proportional electoral system. There the reform was much more gradual and attempted to build a broad enough coalition, which meant that the effects of the reform have been pushed into the future, hurting mainly today's young while protecting the older generations. The reform itself was mainly motivated by Italy's fiscal imbalances and the requirements of entry into the EU. It was pushed through after dialogue with different parts of civil society such as the trade unions and other representatives of social groups.

The section of the report on labour market reform contrasts the experience of Spain and Denmark. Both countries stand at the opposite ends of the spectrum of labour market flexibility, with Denmark at the high end of flexibility and Spain at the high end of rigidity. On the other hand, Denmark has a high level of social insurance whereas Spain has a low level. The report documents, however, that in both cases, labour market reforms (a reduction in the length of benefit entitlements in Denmark and a reduction of firing costs in Spain) were passed only through social dialogue. They were motivated by the macroeconomic situation and the effect of increased economic integration and further liberalization of factor markets within the EU.

The section on product markets takes a more comprehensive approach and returns to cross-country analysis to understand the variation in the extent and timing of reforms in the different member states. One of the main lessons of that chapter is that reforms could usually pass via the use of "divide-and-rule" tactics (Dewatripont and Roland, 1992) that isolate and even disenfranchise specific interest groups opposed to deregulation and competition reform. Experimentation was, however, also used in some cases.

The section on privatization seems close to the case of pension reform. The electoral system also played an important role, with the UK again being the forerunner of privatization programmes. Macroeconomic factors such as fiscal imbalances and the external constraint of entry into the EU played a more important role in other countries. Divide-and-rule tactics were also important in the sense that privatization in different sectors was usually approached on a sequential basis.

The section on corporate governance presents an interesting contrast between the privatization of Škoda in the Czech Republic and of AvtoVAZ in the Ukraine. The success in building commitment in the Czech Republic seems to be the main difference between the experiences.

Are there some general lessons we can learn by confronting these experiences about the main path to success in structural reform? An important question that emerges is whether electoral reform is a key to reforms or whether, on the contrary, one cannot avoid major efforts in consensus-building. The argument that a majoritarian electoral system should be adopted because it helps to pass reforms more easily may be valid in some cases but is a poor argument in general. Indeed, constitutional choices should be defended not on the basis of short-term or even medium-term considerations, even less on the basis of a particular agenda. It is long-term considerations that are relevant here, taking the maximum possible number of contingencies into account. From a normative point of view, constitutional choices should be defended using "behind the veil of ignorance" arguments. A pure majoritarian logic has advantages from the point of view of reform agendas but also has many less palatable features. In particular, it makes it possible to hurt minority groups and leave them without protection. Independently of the question of the optimal electoral choice in a given country, it seems that forms of consensus-building are not only inevitable in a democracy, they are desirable.

I found it striking when reading the report to see the contrast between the emphasis on "divide and rule" in some cases and consensus-building in others. A possible hypothesis is that consensus-building is more important when reforms relate to general interest politics whereas divide and rule is very useful when reforms relate to special interest politics. A possible reason is that reforms in the realm of general interest politics touch large groups of the population whereas reforms in the realm of special interest politics touch more targeted narrow groups. But that is not enough. The arithmetics of voting will in my view not get us far enough in understanding this difference. Even when the arithmetics of voting would allow some reforms to pass, consensus-building is still often sought in reality. A deeper reason for consensus-building is probably the fact that all social orders are based on explicit or implicit social pacts whereby different groups recognize the legitimate interests of other groups and thus promise not to hurt these interests. Many of these social pacts have involved forms of "give and take" at a particular moment in time as well as mutual promises not to affect the legitimate interests of the social groups constitutive of the social order. Reforms that can be seen as "breaching the social pact" lead to immediate distrust between social groups and can very quickly spoil the social climate in a country. Therefore, new forms of consensus must be sought to modify existing social pacts or to adopt new ones that are more adapted to the evolution of the times. In contrast, special interest politics often involve illegitimate interests and the struggle of well-organized minorities to maintain economic rents derived from economically inefficient outcomes. In practice, it is not always easy to distinguish between reforms that relate to general interest politics and those that relate to special interest politics. However, I think one must be especially careful about reforms that are perceived to call into question social pacts that have been constitutive of the existing social order. Let me give a few examples. One of today's prime targets for pension reform is the generous pension system for employees in the public sector. However, in many countries, when public sector pensions were adopted, they were seen, together with employment security, as a *quid pro quo* for accepting lower wages than private sector employees. Plans to cut down public pensions, especially in the context of "divide-and-rule tactics" can thus be perceived as a breach of an existing social pact. A similar argument can be made with respect to unemployment benefits and to large parts of the European welfare system. In the post-Second World War era, their establishment was seen as the price of social peace. A similar argument, though a weaker one in my view, could be made with respect to some European pacts. The dreaded Common Agricultural Policy (CAP) was established as a price for France to accept trade liberalization within Europe, which was thought mostly to benefit Germany. Similarly, the Structural Funds were established to bring Spain and Portugal within the EU because they expected to bear initial economic suffering from the Single Market. Perceptions of breach of an important social pact lead to withdrawal of trust that can be very detrimental when it comes to future deals and pacts. There is the implicit notion that many actions are not allowed under a social pact and that the breach of a pact and of mutual trust allows destructive and aggressive actions between social groups.

How to Gain Political Support for Reforms

The importance of consensus-building implies that governments that are keen on implementing reforms must signal their true intentions and define goals of reform that are believable by and acceptable to the largest number of people. Fear of deceit is a powerful factor in generating opposition to reforms. Obviously, the attitude towards reform also depends not only on the government's efforts in generating consensus but also on the structure of civil society institutions. Here, I think the classical Calmfors–Driffill (1988) idea that corporatist regimes with full centralization of wage bargaining do better than those that are less centralized but not completely decentralized is relevant. Indeed, social partners who negotiate in a centralized setting tend to internalize more the effect of different decisions as well as the impact of non-reform and will thus take a more responsible attitude towards reform. Improving some of the institutions of social dialogue within European countries to make the social partners more responsible seems a worthwhile objective.

An idea that does not seem to be mentioned in the report and that plays an important role is the dual-track principle in implementing reforms (Lau *et al.*, 2000). The idea of the dual track is to design a reform that is Pareto improving in the sense that the efficiency gains from the reform can be reaped while nobody is made worse off. In China, this happened by allowing all enterprises to undertake market transactions at free prices while maintaining their contractual obligations resulting from the plan. The market track thus created efficiency gains while the plan track maintained the existing rents of producers and consumers. Applications of the dual-track principle are reform-specific but usually rely on some form of grandfathering. This principle seems to have been applied to the case of pension reform in Italy since the reformed system applies mostly to younger people entering the job market while others, who started with the old system, will keep it until it is phased out. The dual-track principle seems also to be applied in the Spanish labour market where some workers have rigid indeterminate contracts while others have very flexible contracts. The dual-track principle would call for new "reformed contracts" for newcomers while keeping the status quo for existing workers. Another example is that it seems that when wage cuts are implemented in enterprises, this happens usually via lower wages for new hires, explaining why variation in the entering wage seems to be one of the biggest sources of wage variation, abstracting from seniority (Baker *et al.*, 1994). Applications of the dual-track system, while attractive for economists who like the principle of Pareto improvement and see it as an interesting tool of consensus-building, can, however, appear to be socially divisive and perceived as unfair. Our current economics tools do not fully allows us to understand this but it seems that analysis of fairness by behavioural economists is going in that direction (Rabin, 1993).

In concluding and in relation to my last remarks, I would like to throw out a few unorthodox ideas that deserve our attention when thinking about reforms. It seems to me that there has been an exaggerated emphasis on the analysis of pure economic interests. While interests are extremely important in a political economy set-up, I believe they are not the only source of behaviour of political and economic agents and that this leads to quite different stances on reality. To take an example, recent demographic shifts (a higher share of the elderly) should predict an absence of pension reform or even a worsening of the situation in most advanced industrialized countries because the old carry more political weight. However, this is not exactly what we observe. Pension reforms, even timid ones, are being put forward by different European governments. Why is this the case? Here it seems to me that beliefs about the world and changes in these beliefs play an important role in shaping policies and reforms. I think it is difficult to rationalize all political actions as corresponding to well-understood interests of particular groups. There are also many actions and policies based on beliefs (that turn out to be wrong most of the time). Beliefs about the economy after the Second World War were much more interventionist and statist than now. Who knows what the beliefs of the times will be in 20 years? Many actions to fight unemployment have been based on wrong views about unemployment. Economists have often also espoused wrong ideas and convinced policy-makers of them, not necessarily because they were "playing to the interests" of special groups but because of wrong beliefs and misguided analysis. To the extent that we are making progress in our scientific understanding of the economy, we as economists can therefore play a helpful role in helping to influence beliefs in the right direction, promote more efficient social pacts, and help the general public understand the smokescreen of special interest. Our understanding of many aspects of economic systems is, however, often too rudimentary to claim confidently that we can predict with accuracy the outcome of specific reforms. The experience of the transition process from socialism to capitalism should be a useful reminder of the gaps in our knowledge. This leaves room for experimentation with policy reform, a topic that is neither sufficiently emphasized nor sufficiently appreciated by economists in my view (see e.g. Dewatripont and Roland, 1995). So, there is room both for debate and to influence each other's beliefs as well as for policy experimentation in building coalitions to promote reforms away from inefficient status quos.

References

Calmfors, L. and Driffill, J. (1988), "Centralization of Wage Bargaining", *Economic Policy*, 6, 12–61.

Baker, G. Gibbs, M., and Holmstrom, B., (1994), "The Wage Policy of a Firm", *The Quarterly Journal of Economics*, 109(4), 921–55.

Dewatripont, M., and Roland, G. (1992), "Economic Reform and Dynamic Political Constraints", *Review of Economic Studies*, 59, 703–30.

—— —— (1995), "The Design of Reform Packages under Uncertainty", *American Economic Review*, 85, 1207–23.

Drazen, A. (2000), *Political Economy in Macroeconomics*, Princeton: Princeton University Press.

Lau, L., Qian, Y., and Roland, G. (2000), "Reform without Losers: An Interpretation of China's Dual-Track Approach to Reforms", Journal of Political Economy, 108(1), 121–43.

Persson, T., Roland, G., and Tabellini, G. (2003), "How do Electoral Rules Shape Party Structure, Forms of Government and Economic Policy?" Mimeo.

Rabin, M. (1993), "Incorporating Fairness into Game Theory and Economics", *American Economic Review*, 83(5), 1281–302.

Roland, G. (2000), *Transition and Economics: Politics, Firms, Markets*, Cambridge, Mass.: MIT Press.

Stefano Scarpetta

This is an interesting study dealing with a difficult, but essential, topic: the political economy of structural reforms. It provides a wealth of information on country experiences and, as such, it is an important contribution to those who would like to know more about the complex chemistry of "getting it done".

The study highlights a number of important points. The *first* is about the role of different electoral systems in shaping the reform process. Galasso *et al.* argue that majoritarian systems may promote more rapid reforms, but run greater risks of reversal if the majority changes in parliament. By contrast consensus democracies may lead to a more gradual approach to reforms, but possibly more consistent reform strategies over time. Electoral systems also interact with framework conditions, which is the *second point* discussed in this study. Framework conditions include the nature and strength of the different opposition groups; the relationships between different opposition groups and whether it is possible to disentangle them to reduce opposition to reforms; and the nature of the reforms themselves, which shapes the dynamic process of coalition building and implementation. The *third point* is about commitment building—those factors that push governments to engage their political "capital" in pursuing difficult reforms. The list here is rather long, but the authors highlight three broad factors: (1) economic opportunities related to technological progress and globalization; (2) the real (and perceived) "cost" of the status quo, in terms of low growth, high unemployment, or even widening social disparities; (3) external forces related to multilateral or regional agreements or to changes occurring in neighbouring countries; and (4) ideology, which drives governments with strong majorities along a given reform path even if the economic rationale or public support are not strong. The *fourth point* is about the optimal sequencing of reforms. Reforming certain markets (the "easy" ones) before others may enable positive synergies (the "trickle down effects") to be exploited. And sequencing reforms may also help to disentangle interest groups and thus avoid strong opposition (the "divide-and-conquer" strategy).

In my comments, I will discuss these points while reviewing some of the reform episodes discussed in this study: (1) pension reforms in the UK and Italy; (2) labour market reforms in Denmark and Spain; and (3) product market reforms in Europe.

How to Gain Political Support for Reforms

What we know that (possibly) ain't so

Before moving to these reform episodes, however, a word of caution is needed. The authors stress in several places that there is not a *one model fits all*, and that market and country specificities play a major role in shaping successful reforms. One cannot agree more with the authors on this point. But then the authors indulge in identifying *"recipes"* or *"lessons"* for the future as if they felt obliged to provide normative guidelines. While I agree with the authors that there is a lot to learn from the reform episodes discussed in their study, I also believe that these episodes do not really allow us to write recipes that could be easily followed in other countries/markets. It is precisely the complexity of framework conditions, political systems, and interactions within (and across) markets that make the political economy behind these observed reforms rather unique. Should we then abandon the case-study approach used in this study? No, not at all. But policy-makers and economists would still have to do their homework and figure out whether, and how, a successful reform in another country could be replicated in their own country.

This issue is of relevance also in light of the remarks made in the first study in this book, namely that it is often difficult to identify the *where to go*, or the institutional or policy settings that a given country should move towards. This point is not new, and it is well documented in the extensive literature on the success and (often) failures of reforms in many countries (see e.g. Rodrik, 2003; Easterly, 2001). This literature indicates that many growth successes of the past two decades concern countries that have followed very "heterodox" policies (East Asia, China), while many growth failures are in countries that have followed more traditional market-oriented strategies (notably in Latin America).[1] Even in the OECD countries, key institutional and policy settings differ substantially and these differences cannot be easily mapped into better or worse economic outcomes. Japan is a straightforward example of a country that managed a protracted period of sustained growth in the post-war period, despite its fairly restrictive product market regulations, active industrial policy, and

---

[1] As Summers (2003) recalls, the growth record of some developing countries over the past decades is consistent with some of the *higher-order* economic principles: a semblance of property rights, sound monetary policy, fiscal solvency, and some market-oriented incentives. But these higher-order principles of sound economic management do not map onto unique institutional arrangements. The examples of heterodox approaches abound: China with its dual-track approach to agricultural liberalization at the margin; South Korea and Taiwan with heavy reliance on public enterprises and aggressive industrial policy until the mid-1980s. And failures in countries which have adopted more conventional market-oriented approaches also abound, as the experience of many countries in Latin America shows.

lifetime employment in core firms, all recipes which are at odds with the standard principles of a sound market economy. The Nordic countries have developed a very generous and costly system of social protection, but have still managed to promote high participation in the labour market and strong growth. The list is long and points to the fact that even in countries at a similar stage of economic development, fundamental aspects of the institutional settings differ, and these differences are not mapped one to one onto different economic performances. And if it is difficult to clearly identify the *where to go* of structural reforms, it is even more difficult to identify the *how to get there*, which is the subject of this study.

HOW TO RATIONALIZE THE WELFARE STATE: PENSION REFORMS IN ITALY AND THE UK

"Back against the wall" hypothesis

Both Italy (in the 1990s) and the UK (in the 1980s) passed major reforms of their pension system. Galasso *et al.* argue that the main commitment building in Italy was the widespread perception that the status quo—not only in the pension system—was no longer sustainable and Italy needed a major overhaul of its economic system. This perception was reinforced in 1992, when Italy was hit by a major financial crisis leading to devaluation of the Italian lira and exit from the European Monetary System. And only a few months before, Italy had signed the Maastricht Treaty, imposing on itself the commitment of converging towards strict (at least for Italy) requirements on inflation, government deficit, and public debt. In the UK, a strong majority of the Thatcher government, coupled with a strong ideology, were behind the pension reform. Ideology, however, can hardly suffice to boost unpopular reforms. As in Italy, in the UK at the time of the first Thatcher government there was a mounting feeling that the status quo was no longer viable. Indeed, the Conservative government of Mrs Thatcher was elected in 1979 after the so-called "Winter of Discontent", characterized by many strikes and instability (see e.g. Bean and Symons, 1989). At the time, the UK had a large fiscal deficit, high inflation, and one of the highest unemployment rates in Europe. All in all, there seems to be a common factor behind both pension reforms: in both Italy and the UK, there was a growing feeling that the status quo was no longer viable, the so-called *there is no alternative* (TINA) hypothesis. It should be stressed, however, that many other countries have experienced very difficult economic conditions and yet have not embarked on major reforms. In other words, it is not clear how bad economic conditions should be—and how long it takes for the population at large to perceive them as such—before enough consensus is built behind reformers.

Strong politicians, or not!

The Italian pension reform has other interesting "political economy" features. The year of the pension reform, 1992, is also the beginning of *mani pulite*, a major inquiry about political corruption and bribery. Most of the parties in the government were hit by mounting scandals and this probably weakened their ties with the electorate. So the "external forces" (restore the financial solvency of the pension system and meet the Maastricht obligations) were coupled with a vacuum of power in which a determined prime minister was able to push for an unpopular reform. Therefore, while in general a strong political leadership is needed to boost the reform agenda—as in the case of Mrs Thatcher—in some cases, a weakened of fragmented political power may create a window of opportunity for technocrats to pass needed reforms.

The devil is in the detail

The Amato pension reform also suggests that sometimes focusing on less visible, but important, components of the status quo may reap great benefits without arousing fierce opposition. Indeed, while the Amato reform foresaw a very long implementation period to protect insiders, it also shifted indexation of pension benefits from nominal wages to prices. This component of the reform had a significant impact on current retirees: the change in indexation implied that benefits would differ in real terms according to the year of retirement, and retirees should expect their living standards to decline over time. Yet, this potentially controversial element of the reform did not attract a lot of attention or resistance, which was concentrated on the symbols of the pension system, such as the age of retirement in the case of the pension reform.

Majoritarian versus consensus

Drawing on the Italian and British pension reform episodes, Galasso *et al.* also argue that consensus democracies—such as Italy, in their view—are more likely to implement gradual reforms to reduce opposition forces. Slower progress, as was certainly the case with the Amato reform, is compensated by a lower risk of reversal, often a characteristic of majoritarian systems. But gradual reforms may also imply insufficient effects, requiring further changes. This was indeed the case with the Amato reform, since the very long transition phase (more than two decades) was not enough to restore the financial solvency of the pension system, and Italy had quickly to embark on further reforms. Since the 1992 Amato reform, Italy had four other "reforms"—including the most recent by the actual government—and one failed attempt (by the Berlusconi government in 1994). This arguably created a great deal of uncertainty, and probably led to some irrational responses by would-be pensioners who withdrew from the labour market in anticipation of other more restrictive changes in the future. Hence, if gradualism means ineffective changes, it may not be associated with greater stability in the reform path, but rather uncertainty, which may partly jeopardize the expected outcomes of reforms.

LABOUR MARKET REFORMS: THE CASE OF DENMARK AND SPAIN

Involving key stakeholders

Galasso *et al.* have chosen two successful labour reforms in countries with very different institutional settings. Both Denmark and Spain were characterized by worsening labour market conditions at the time of the reform—a fact which supports the TINA hypothesis. Given their proportional representation systems, both countries pursued a consensus building approach, involving social partners and especially unions in the design of their labour reform. This approach has also been used in several other European countries, most notably by the Dutch government in 1982 with the famous Wassenaar Agreement. An open question is what to do in other countries where social partners are not highly representative and/or fragmented but still very vocal, as in France and many other countries around the world.

The Danish and Spanish examples also have important differences that are not sufficiently emphasized in the study. Denmark is the champion of the so-called "flexicurity", a combination of generous support to the unemployed and labour market flexibility through low dismissal costs.[2] This policy mix has guaranteed sufficient dynamism in the labour market, while ensuring adequate income security for the workers. The 1994 Danish reform discussed in the study implied a slight reduction in the generosity of unemployment benefits and, more importantly, a tightening of eligibility conditions. This reform was also accompanied by greater effort to help the unemployed to (re-)gain employment, through public and private job training, job search, and targeted education with support from employment services. Tightening eligibility criteria was largely

---

[2] See OECD (2004).

perceived as improving the fairness of the system rather than reducing its generosity, and reinforcing the "activation" of the unemployed contributed to reducing the length of joblessness. Two aspects of the Danish "flexicurity" system are difficult to export to many other countries. First, the activation system is very costly—total expenditure on labour market policy accounts for almost 5 per cent of GDP. Second, unions are directly involved in running unemployment benefit funds, which gives them the appropriate incentives for promoting efficiency in the utilization of these funds.

Trial and errors

The Spanish reform in 1997 focused on reducing compensation for unfair dismissal for workers under a regular contract. This reform cannot be assessed in isolation, but rather represents the last step of a "trial and error" process that started a decade before. The story of employment protection reform in Spain starts in the mid-1980s. The government at the time attempted to promote flexibility in the rather sclerotic Spanish labour market by liberalizing temporary contracts. This type of contract remained fairly restrictive from an international perspective, but became more attractive to employers if compared to the even more restrictive regular contract. Since then, Spain experienced one of the most dramatic shifts from permanent to temporary employment and, at the beginning of the 1990s, had more than one-third of its workforce under temporary contracts, while the unemployment rate approached 20 per cent.[3] In 1994, Spain attempted to counteract these trends—which were widely perceived as inefficient by both employers and workers—by tightening temporary contracts again, but the effects were very small. The 1997 reform should be considered in this context: by then it was obvious that this asymmetric liberalization of labour contracts was not working and the government finally decided to liberalize regular contracts. The Spanish lesson is important also for other European countries that have pursued this asymmetric approach to labour reforms.

REFORMS IN THE NON-MANUFACTURING SECTOR

External forces to commitment building

This is the only section of the study that provides a cross-country analysis instead of country case studies. It draws from the extensive work done at the OECD over the past few years in assessing progress in product market

[3] See e.g. Dolado *et al.* (2002).

Comments

reforms. The authors argue that commitment building in product market reforms is partly exogenous. Technological advances and globalization have created enormous competitive pressures on manufacturing. In turn, the manufacturing sector is creating stronger pressure for more efficient services and this trickle-down effect has motivated major changes in a number of utility industries.

Unbundle interests

The key to success in reforming the service sector, the authors argue, is to unbundle entrenched private interests and to exploit possible synergies: that is, by progressing gradually from the easy to more difficult areas, the reformer may enjoy some *bandwagon* effects as new competitive forces in one area will raise pressure for reforms in other areas. Galasso *et al.* propose to start by eliminating price distortions and "phasing out" institutions that give voice to special interest groups, for example, by creating independent regulatory authorities.

Interactions between product and labour markets

One issue that the authors could have explored in more detail is the interaction between reforms in product and labour markets. Product

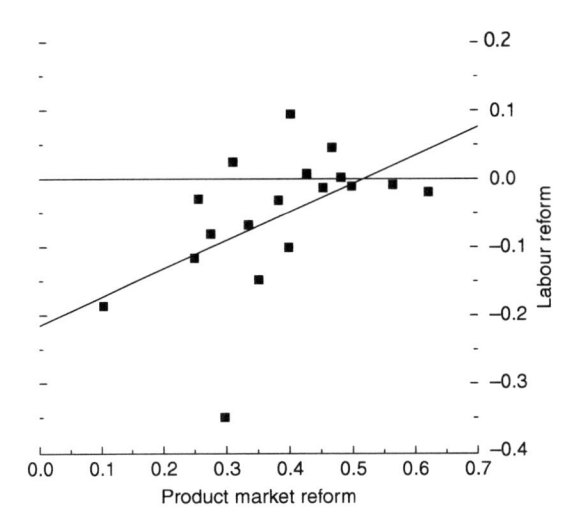

Fig. C2.1 Product and labour market reforms, 1982–1998

Notes: The labour reform index includes: the index of employment protection legislation (see Nicoletti *et al.*, 1999); the duration of unemployment benefits; and the indicator of the unemployment benefit replacement rate.

Source: IMF (2004).

How to Gain Political Support for Reforms

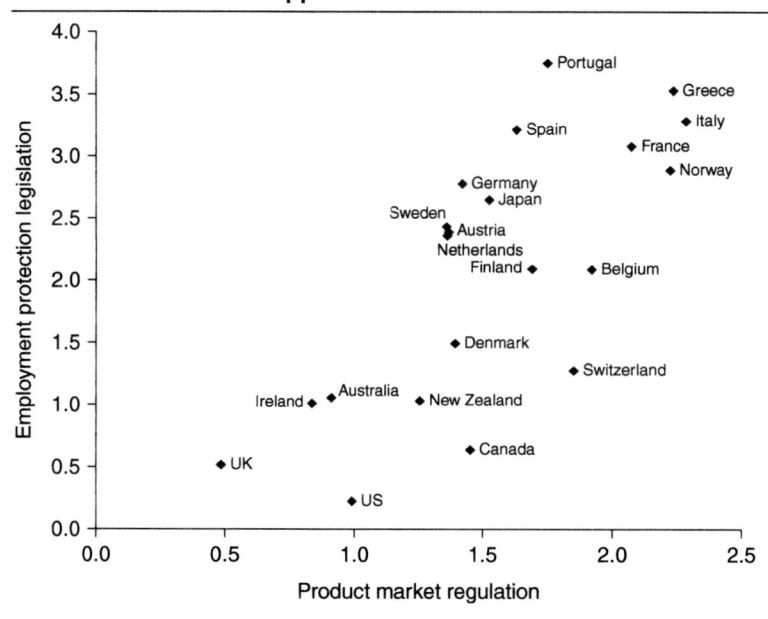

Fig. C2.2 Product market regulations and employment protection regulations, 1998

Notes: Correlation 0.73; *t*-statistic 4.72.
Source: Nicoletti *et al.* (1999).

market reforms are likely to benefit consumers at large, but may also create pressure to reform other, more difficult, areas like the labour market. Indeed, by reducing market rents and stimulating greater dynamism in the economy, product market reforms are likely to boost changes in the labour market, including the attitude of unions (e.g. Calmfors, 1993). At the same time, labour market reforms may enhance the effects of product market reforms on labour (e.g. Blanchard and Giavazzi, 2003). And there could be important synergies in joint reforms (e.g. Coe and Snower, 1997). Does the empirical evidence support these hypotheses? A recent chapter of the IMF, *World Economic Outlook* (2004), provides some support. It suggests that countries that have liberalized the goods market more aggressively have also made significant reforms in the labour market (see Fig. C2.1). This adds to the OECD evidence of a very close cross-country correlation between the regulatory stance in the goods and labour markets; that is, countries with stringent regulations in one market also tend to have stringent regulations in the other market (see Fig. C2.2). And looking at the evolution of product and labour reforms, Nicoletti and Scarpetta (2004) found that it is indeed the combination of rigid regulations in labour and product markets that has the worst impact on the economy, and that combined reforms may reap the largest benefits.

References

Bean, C. R. and Symons, J. (1989), "Ten Years of Mrs. T.", CEPR Discussion Paper no. 316.

Blanchard, O. and Giavazzi, F. (2003), "Macroeconomic Effects of Regulations and Deregulation in Goods and Labor Markets", *Quarterly Journal of Economics*, 118(3), 879–907.

Calmfors, L. (1993), "Centralisation of Wage Bargaining and Macroeconomic Performance: A Survey", *OECD Economic Studies*, no. 21, Paris.

Coe, D. and Snower, D. (1997), "Policy Complementarities: The Case for Fundamental Labour Market Reform", IMF Staff Papers, no. 44, 1–35.

Dolado, J. J., Garcia, C., and Jimeno, J. F. (2002), "Drawing Lessons from the Boom of Temporary Jobs in Spain", *Economic Journal*, 112(480), F270–295.

Easterly, W. (2001), "The Elusive Quest for Growth: Economists' Adventures and Misadventures in the Tropics", Cambridge, Mass.: MIT Press.

International Monetary Fund (2004), *World Economic Oulook–2004*, Apr.

Nicoletti, G. and Scarpetta, S. (2004), "Do Regulatory Reforms in Product and Labor Markets Promote Employment: Evidence from OECD Countries", Paper presented at the ECB–CEPR Conference on What Helps or Hinders Labour Market Adjustments in Europe?, 28–9 June, Frankfurt am Main.

———— and Boylaud, O. (1999), "Summary Indicators of Product Market Regulation with an Extension to Employment Protection Legislation", OECD Economics Department Working Paper no. 226, Paris.

OECD (2004), *Employment Outlook—2004*, Paris.

Rodrik, D. (2003), "Growth Strategies", CEPR Discussion Paper no. 4100.

Summers, Lawrence H. (2003), "Godkin Lectures", John F. Kennedy School of Government, Harvard University (Apr.).

Final Remarks

Christopher Pissarides

1. Services are an important input into industry and other services. The demand for services by business has risen faster than the demand by consumers and a major contribution of the first report is to quantify the demand for services by business. But services remain a highly regulated sector in Europe and because of the regulation, services are probably a more expensive input than they need be. If they are deregulated their unit price should fall, business costs should fall, and efficiency should increase. It is surprising that the report finds ambiguous empirical results—have we measured the input of services and regulation correctly?

2. What will be the effect of deregulation on employment? It is likely to be negative in the sectors affected, at least in the short run. It is a fact that the share of employment increases in industries that have low TFP growth. Services have been attracting a lot of employment in rich economies because they are labour intensive and there is demand for their output. If deregulation raises their productivity, as expected, this will necessarily mean lower employment in their sectors, unless demand for their output is price elastic. But in either case, overall welfare will increase because the wealth created by the higher productivity will create demand elsewhere and labour will move to those sectors. So deregulation of services is likely to create some structural change, with some interim unemployment, which is probably the reason for the resistance to reforms by workers.

3. Service deregulation is likely to increase the level of productivity because of the reduction in costs, but it is not likely to increase the rate of growth of productivity. Sometimes reform can bring unexpected one-off benefits that cannot be quantified in a formal econometric model and I was disappointed not to see some examples in the reports. For example,

one of the benefits of the privatization and deregulation of the railways in the UK has been the release of a lot of land for use by other sectors. Big plots of land near the city centre that belonged to the railways were underutilized because of public ownership. Once privatization arrived, many of these plots were sold to the private sector for development. Careful planning can benefit other sectors, such as retailing, culture, and the arts (as for example in the case of the new British Library, built on former railway land).

4. A neglected point in the report is that sometimes restrictions in service industries are caused by labour market and other types of regulation. For example, the retail sector may not have enough employment because of high minimum wages; the retail and other sectors that require land may be affected by regulation of land use; and many service industries are dominated by small firms and regulation of firm entry could restrict the sector's expansion. But in some service industries, for example, the professions, barriers to entry are imposed by the incumbents—with support from policy.

5. Globalization is not a force pushing for reform of services because services are traded much less than manufacturing. Reform pressures have to come from within the country, and they will not benefit the incumbents. In the professions, the people who vote for reforms (e.g. the politicians) are often beneficiaries of the regulation, for example, many politicians are practising lawyers, so they do not have an incentive to push for the reform of legal services. The actors involved in services are different from those in manufacturing. They are more educated and there are more women. Also, the vested interests are less sharply divided between capitalists and workers. This has two implications. The first is that expansion of service provision and improvements in quality require good education and training. And the second is that the reform process will be more difficult because the incumbents may form coalitions against reforms, avoiding internal conflict and not associating with sharply divided political parties.

6. One of the biggest gaps between the USA and Europe in the provision of high-level services concerns management services. Europeans are not as good as Americans at getting trained to run one's own business and updating the skills of the workforce to make it more adaptable to new conditions. This educational gap is likely to affect services more severely than other sectors of the economy. If the expansion of management education and lifelong learning in Europe succeeds, deregulation reforms will be more easily implemented because there will be new managers

Final Remarks

pushing for conditions to create new businesses quickly and efficiently. Workers will also not be worried about job insecurity because their lifelong learning experience will help them get jobs quickly elsewhere, or adapt to new conditions within their own firm. Support for reform could come from a new class of outsiders—new managers, highly trained workers, women with good education, and so on.

7. Have we learned about the turnaround of US productivity in the 1990s and why it was not matched in Europe? The reports emphasize product market regulation; however, I think more important here is labour-market regulation and the attitudes of the main actors. Europe's preoccupation in the 1980s was to create more jobs to bring unemployment down. The US success in the 1990s was due largely to industrial restructuring and the introduction of more employer-friendly management techniques. The result of these changes in the USA was more uncertainty for the workers, both in connection to what they did within their firm and in connection to job security. But it made it easier for US firms to reorganize and adopt new office techniques when, for example, IT became available. In Europe, the "social partners" were less willing to accept bigger insecurity for the workers, necessitated by change, because having just come out of the jobless growth of the 1980s, there was aversion to adopting new techniques of industrial organization that would have involved large-scale restructuring and displacement of workers.

André Sapir

Since the mid-1970s, average growth in the European Union (EU) has been declining decade after decade. During this period, Europe's potential growth has fallen by one full percentage point. According to most estimates, the EU's potential growth is now only 2 per cent a year, compared with almost 3.5 per cent in the USA. This appears to be the result of two trends: declining productivity growth and inefficient use of labour.

Recognition of the need to improve Europe's economic performance has driven EU policy for the past two decades. In the mid-1980s, the Single Market Programme (SMP) was conceived as an antidote to "eurosclerosis". Yet it has failed to generate higher growth. Apart from the costs of German reunification, there are three main reasons for this (Sapir, 2004).

First, the SMP was never fully implemented. Since 1993, the single market has been a reality for goods. On the other hand, service markets remain highly fragmented. Yet, as the excellent report by Riccardo Faini and his co-authors argues, efficient provision of services is crucial for the competitiveness of modern economies.

The importance of a single market for services for the competitiveness of the European economy was already identified 20 years ago by the European Commission in its famous White Paper on the completion of the internal market. It stated that: "In the Commission's view, it is no exaggeration to see the establishment of a common market in services as one of the main preconditions for a return to economic prosperity. Trade in services is as important as trade in goods... [Hence], the Commission considers that swift action should be taken to open up the whole market for services" (Commission of the European Communities, 1985: 26–7).

The key role of services was again highlighted by the European Commission a few years later in a study on the potential impact of the SMP, which stated that: "The importance of market services goes far beyond their share in economic activity. Most services... play an essential role in market economies as basic infrastructure for all other economic activities. The efficient provision of services is, therefore, a prerequisite for overall competitiveness... The White Paper on the completion of the internal market was a major attempt by the Commission to create a truly integrated European market. *Whereas the internal market programme can be regarded as the final step towards the free movement of goods inside the Community, it must be recognised that for services it amounts to the beginning of the last step to freedom*" (Buigues and Sapir, 1993, p. xi; emphasis added). Unfortunately, this statement still holds today.

Second, the conception and implementation of the SMP were rooted in yesterday's thinking—based on the assumption that Europe's fundamental problem was the absence of a large internal market that would allow European companies to achieve big economies of scale. It has now become clear that the problem lay elsewhere. In the modern world, characterized by rapid technological change and strong global competition, what European industry needs is more opportunity for companies to enter new markets, more retraining of labour, greater reliance on market financing, and higher investment in both research and development and higher education.

Third, the SMP excluded the liberalization of labour markets, which largely remains the prerogative of member states. Yet without such reform and greater labour mobility within and across companies, the liberalization of product markets is unlikely to trigger the reallocation of resources necessary to produce higher growth.

The Lisbon Agenda, which aims to make Europe "the most competitive and dynamic knowledge-based economy in the world" by 2010, can be viewed as an attempt to achieve higher growth by tackling precisely these three flaws. Lisbon seeks to speed productivity growth by removing barriers to product market entry, by fostering innovation, and by improving education systems. At the same time, it aims to ensure that labour is used more efficiently by reforming labour markets and social policies. The Lisbon Agenda rightly sets ambitious goals. Sadly, the EU is not on track to achieve them. The problem lies in both the multitude of targets and the weakness of the instruments.

Effective implementation of the Lisbon strategy requires focusing on growth and establishing a new relationship between EU and national policies. The role of EU institutions—particularly the Commission—in coordinating and enforcing commonly agreed disciplines is crucial, and probably needs to be strengthened. At the same time, EU institutions must increasingly act as facilitators. Sticks are important, but so are carrots. The EU should move towards a more incentive-based approach that treats member states as partners (Sapir *et al.*, 2004).

Consider the way the EU spends its budget. Public spending at the Union level accounts for barely 2.5 per cent of total public spending in the EU. Hence value added by the EU budget is bound to be insignificant unless it is focused on a limited number of areas or serves as a catalyst for coordinating efforts by member states. Giving the highest priority to growth implies that a larger share of the EU budget should be channelled towards growth-enhancing projects that offer EU-wide benefits—such as R&D and higher education—and towards low-income members with the greatest need and potential for catching up. By contrast, spending on agriculture, the largest item in the EU budget, should gradually shift to national budgets in line with the principles of fiscal federalism and subsidiarity.

There is little doubt that Europe's growth problem is first and foremost a problem of raising potential growth through appropriate structural reforms. At the same time, however, it must be recognized that the current slow recovery in the euro area also points in the direction of a lack of sufficient domestic demand.

The question arises, therefore, concerning the relationship between structural reforms and macroeconomic policy. In particular, the question arises as to whether Europe today needs a "two-handed approach", combining supply-side and demand-side measures, as argued 20 years ago by Blanchard *et al.* (1985).

Although the Lisbon Agenda has not delivered, it would be wrong to say that EU member states have not attempted to implement structural reforms. However, the success rate has been far from satisfactory, especially in France, Germany, and Italy, which together account for three-quarters of the euro area GDP.

There is a distinct possibility that the current lack of domestic demand in the euro area is precisely caused by the uncertainty concerning the implementation of structural reforms in its largest economies. As some economists have argued, part of the problem may be caused by the introduction of the euro, which removes an important incentive for structural reforms due to the different levels of responsibility between structural reforms (national level) and monetary policy (euro area level). To overcome this coordination problem, these economists have argued that structural reforms should be coordinated across EU countries. "This [would] allow the [European Central Bank] to engineer a monetary expansion in the Union at the same time as all member countries engage in structural reforms, thus implementing the two-handed approach at a union-wide level" (Bentolila and Saint-Paul, 2001).

The Lisbon Agenda can also be viewed as an attempt to solve this coordination problem.

Final Remarks

In conclusion, Europe's current growth difficulty is reminiscent of the problem already diagnosed 20 years ago. Although the context has changed somewhat, the current remedy—the Lisbon Agenda—is also reminiscent of the remedy proposed then.

References

Bentolila, S., and Saint-Paul, G. (2001), "Will EMU Increase Eurosclerosis", in Charles Wyplosz (ed.), *EMU: Impact on Europe and the World*, Oxford: Oxford University Press.

Blanchard, O., Dornbusch, R., Drèze, J., Giersch, H., Layard, R., and Monti, M. (1985), "Employment and Growth in Europe: A Two-Handed Approach", Center for European Policy Studies, 21 (June). Reprinted as "Occupazione e crescita in Europa: un intervento su due fronti", *Giovnale degli Economisti e annali di economica*, Nov.–Dec. 3–36.

Buigues, P., and Sapir, A. (1993), "Market Services and European Integration: Issues and Challenges", in Pierre Buigues, Fabienne Ilzkovitz, Jean-François Lebrun, and André Sapir (eds.), *Market Services and European Integration: The Challenges for the 1990s, European Economy*, Luxembourg: European Commission.

Commission of the European Communities (1985), "Completing the Internal Market", White Paper from the Commission to the European Council, Milan, 28–9 June.

Sapir, A. (2004), "Higher Growth should be Barroso's Priority", *Financial Times*, 22 July.

—— Aghion, P., Bertola, G., Hellwig, M., Pisani-Ferry, J., Rosati, D., Viñals, J., and Wallace, H., with Marco Buti, Mario Nava, and Peter M. Smith (2004), *An Agenda for a Growing Europe: The Sapir Report*, Oxford: Oxford University Press.

Vito Tanzi[1]

INTRODUCTION

Fashion plays a bigger role in economics than is generally realized. Until the early 1980s there was little or no talk about "structural reform" and one would have been at a loss to define what the expression meant. I recall the negative reaction to probably the first paper on structural policy written at the IMF in the mid-1980s (see Tanzi, 1987). Until that time the economic discussion had dealt mostly with a few macroeconomic variables such as the exchange rate, the interest rate, the fiscal deficit, the current account, and credit expansion. The one department in the Fund that dealt routinely with the "reform" of a sector was the Fiscal Affairs Department. Its main preoccupation was tax reform. Both the Fund and the World Bank had introduced so-called structural adjustment loans (SAL) on extended fund facilities (EFF). These, however, were programmes that extended from one to three years the time during which countries had to adjust their macroeconomic variables. The expression "structural reform", meaning the redesign of several institutions or sectors in an economy came with the supply-side "revolution" of the early 1980s. This "revolution" shifted the attention of economists and policy-makers from the demand to the supply side of the economy and thus to structural reform.

In that first Fund paper, after arguing about the importance of structural policies and making the argument that, over the long run, macroeconomic developments are largely the result of the structural characteristics of various sectors, I predicted that structural reforms would meet far more opposition than the demand-management policies then in fashion. The experience of many countries over the past two decades has convinced me that my prediction was correct.

In my remarks today, I shall discuss why there is so much opposition to structural reform. I will also briefly address the question of the conditions that may help promote these reforms. I will draw mainly from my seven years of experience as a Division Chief and 20 years as a Director in one of the largest and busiest departments in the Fund. I will also draw from my two-year stint as an Undersecretary in the Italian government. The Fund's experience gave me access to ministers and high-level officials in a large

---

[1] Comments delivered at the Conference on "Structural Reforms without Prejudices", organized by the Debenedetti Foundation in Lecce (Italy), 19 June, 2004.

number of countries. The Italian experience gave me access to the relevant committees in Parliament—the Budget and the Finance Committees.

I will organize my remarks under three headings. They characterize some of the obstacles encountered by structural reform. The three headings are: (*a*) philosophical; (*b*) political; and (*c*) technical. This characterization, while helpful, is somewhat artificial because the three categories tend to overlap a great deal. After discussing these obstacles, I will conclude with a few general remarks.

PHILOSOPHICAL OBSTACLES

If we consider economic developments over a long time, say a century, rather than over a shorter period, say a decade, we can observe major changes in attitude towards the role of the state in the economy and towards economic policies. These changes have inevitably resulted in pressures for policy changes. For example, over the past century there have been swings from "*laissez-faire*" (until the 1920s) to the "mixed economy" (from around 1930 to 1960); from the mixed economy to fully fledged "welfare states" in many European countries during the period 1960–80; after 1980, from the welfare state to the "third way", which was a kind of welfare state "lite". From the third way in the 1980s to the Washington Consensus in the early 1990s, there was a kind of return to *laissez-faire*. In the late 1990s, we start observing some "reform fatigue" that may take us some way back from the Washington Consensus.

What it is important to realize is that each of these changes calls for particular "structural reforms". For example, the transition from *laissez-faire* to a mixed economy called for a larger role for the state. This call had the endorsement of Keynes, who, in a book written in 1926, argued for the change. Roosevelt, with his New Deal, implemented some of the changes. This change began also the process towards the establishment of public enterprises and the nationalization of some private enterprises. In Italy, for example, in the 1930s, IRI, a government institution, acquired many enterprises. IRI was liquidated only recently after the wave of privatization in the 1990s. On the other hand, the Washington Consensus called for the privatization of public enterprises, a policy that had started with the advent of Thatcher in the UK a decade earlier. Over the years, there were calls for high tax rates and for low tax rates; for high import duties and for low import duties; for occasional price controls and for no price controls; for indexation of wages and for no indexation. It is obvious that the prevailing economic thinking at any one time has called for different and often for "structural reforms" that may contrast with those promoted in earlier periods.

Final Remarks

Fifty years ago, the "desired" structural reforms were those that *increased* the role of the state and many mainstream economists, including those at Harvard and MIT, argued for these reforms. In the 1990s, the "desired" reforms were those that *reduced* the role of the state. Given the inevitable lags in implementation, this means that the current structural arrangements are largely those desired a few decades ago. Just think of the policies with respect to pensions.

Mainstream economists, and I place myself among them, now argue for changes in these arrangements in the same way as mainstream economists (including Keynes at the time) argued for changes in the arrangements of the past. The question is whether the mainstream economists of today are ahead of the curve. Obviously not everyone agrees that the structural arrangements that today's economists would like to have in place are more desirable than the ones that they would like to replace. The latter were set up in the past and were the arrangements preferred decades ago.

In some parts of the world (e.g. Latin America and, perhaps, Eastern Europe), some political leaders have been arguing that the Washington Consensus was tried and the results were not the ones promised or hoped. Whether it was truly tried remains an open question.

The views of some leading economists (Joe Stiglitz, Dani Rodrik, and others) have given a strong "voice" to these positions. For those who do not share his views, and they include most economists, it must be discomforting to realize that Stiglitz's (2003) book on globalization, published in the year after he got the Nobel Prize, is the only book in economics to have made the bestseller's list, and in more than one country. This means that many people were interested in, or shared, his views. The increasing unevenness of the income distributions of many countries in recent years has raised additional concerns about the impact of the structural reforms that economists have been advocating. In any society, there are some individuals much better prepared or much better connected who can take advantage more quickly than the rest of the population of the opportunities offered by structural reforms. Thus, at least at the beginning, these reforms may affect the income distribution in ways that are not welcome and, thus, give rise to opposition to them. In conclusion, It is a mistake for us economists to assume that we speak universal and permanent truths or that we speak for the masses. We need to recognize that the population at large, including individuals who end up in parliaments or in the government, may not see the world through the same lenses as we see it.

Final Remarks

We economists have a particular way of looking at the world and convince ourselves that it is the only, or the only right, way. The trouble is that we often fail to convince others that this is so. We forget that most of those who make economic decisions are not economists. They are often intelligent people with different professional backgrounds who see the world through different prisms or paradigms. Issues that are very important to economists (e.g. "welfare costs") are often almost meaningless to these people. I have often been reminded of the famous question asked by someone, probably not an economist, about 40 years ago: how many Harberger triangles does it take to fill an Okun's gap? Non-economists do not understand Harberger triangles that deal with welfare costs but they do understand Okun's gaps that deal with unemployment.

As a group, we economists have not done a good job in teaching the general public the *basic* principles of economics. We spend too much time refining abstract theories and building abstract models and not enough teaching the general public important concepts. We are almost embarrassed to spend our time in this prosaic activity and tend to look down on those who do. At the same time, we are often puzzled that the conclusions of our abstract models do not drive the world.

Having spent much of my professional life on the policy side of economics, and having talked to more economic or finance ministers than most economists do, I am acutely aware of the limited influence that economic theory has on policy decisions. Take, as an example, the so-called "optimal taxation theory". This is the theory that has dominated the teaching of taxation in graduate schools for the past 30 years. Hundreds of articles, refining that theory, have been published in academic journals and at least two economists connected with it have been given Nobel Prizes. Students in top graduate schools learn little else on taxation today. Yet its impact on tax reforms so far has been close to zero. Tax reforms continue to be made mainly by lawyers who know nothing about optimal taxation but know a lot about the tax systems of various countries. As Keynes could have said, tax reforms continue to be guided by the thinking of dead (or almost dead) economists!

Why do we allocate so many resources to such activity rather than to the teaching of broad and useful tax principles to students and to the general population?

If the support for structural reforms comes from largely theoretical arguments presented in articles published in economic journals that few read, and not from more accessible, intuitive arguments, the popular and political backing necessary for structural reform will remain weak.

Final Remarks

The international organizations (IMF, World Bank, OECD, EBRD, EC, etc.) have become the most forceful proponents for structural reforms. In my biased view, they do a better job than academic economists in presenting the arguments for reform, mainly because the incentives under which the economists that work for these organizations operate are different from those of their academic colleagues. Thus, the leverage that these organizations have on the policies of countries has become an important determinant of the speed with which reforms can be introduced. So-called think-tanks, such as the Debenedetti Foundation, can play an important educational role but it is more difficult for them to be seen to be as objective and as non-committed as international organizations.

There remains a fundamental problem related to the present enthusiasm shown by mainstream economists for the kind of structural reforms that have been analysed in the reports presented at this conference and for similar reforms. To convince the general public (and the politicians) of the benefits that would derive from these reforms, it would be necessary or useful to have facts because, as I have argued, theoretical arguments are not sufficient. But as the reports presented today themselves indicate, and as Nietzsche once famously said, "there are no facts, only interpretations". Is our (i.e. economists') recent attitude *vis-à-vis* the structural reforms justified by the availability of "facts"? Or does it depend on value judgements that determine what we consider "good" structural reforms? In the absence of non-contested facts, who decides whether a reform is successful or not? Is it the economists, even though there may be disagreement even among them, as there was at this conference? Is it the politicians? Or is it the public?

It would be useful to have facts that do not lend themselves to varying interpretations, but this may be difficult or impossible. Until that time comes, our policies will be driven mainly by value judgements even though we may not recognize them as such. But, as argued earlier, value judgements tend to change over time even though we economists do not seem to be aware of this. We must also be careful that our a priori value judgements about many of these reforms (free trade is good; free capital movement is good; unregulated labour market is good; an unregulated goods market is good, etc.), do not influence the analyses that generate the empirical results (the "facts") that we use to justify the reforms.

I have often observed that people with different value judgements tend to get different *empirical* results, that is different "facts". I have also observed that the different value judgements that predominate in different periods tend to generate results that are consistence with these judgements. For example, as long as high marginal tax rates were considered desirable, in the 1950s and 1960s, most studies did not find negative effects associated with their use. When the value judgement charged in favour of lower tax rates (with the Laffer curve and supply-side economics), studies started finding results that were consistent with the new thinking. Was this change in empirical results due to better estimation techniques, as often argued, or to different value judgements that affected the design of the experiments?

In conclusion, let us be aware that, like all social sciences, economics is influenced by the prevailing value judgement of each period. The illusion of an economic science free of value judgement is just that, an illusion.

POLITICAL OBSTACLES

Obstacles of a more political nature often interfere with, or prevent, the introduction of structural reforms. Let me mention some of them.

The people elected to parliament are often *elected with the support of groups or lobbies* who benefit from particular policies. We vote for those who will protect *our* personal interests not the general interest, whatever that is. Thus, indirectly, many members of the legislature reflect the current structural arrangements. When the proposed structural reforms conflict with these interests, those that we have elected will oppose the reforms.

Experience with structural reforms indicates that they often generate *costs in the short run and benefits some time later*. Chile and New Zealand, or even Ireland, indicate that, for several years after the reforms were made, the countries had little to show for them. The benefits came later and, in some cases, several years later.

Given the time horizon of politicians, it is not surprising that for them this is often not a good bargain. They may have to bear the costs while others reap the benefits. This is especially the case with pension reform. It is for these reasons that reforms should always be proposed at the beginning of a legislature in the hope that the government will reap the benefits before the next election.

To be enacted, major structural reforms need strong and persuasive mentors to explain them in terms that the citizens can understand and to push for their enactment. But mentors need to be fully attuned to the reforms. They must be convinced of their merit and must have the capacity to communicate with the public why the reforms are necessary and why now. Leaders who do not fully share the rationale for the reforms, or who are not good communicators, will not be able to convince the public that the reforms are needed. Thatcher and Reagan were examples of leaders who had strong convictions and the ability to communicate their views in a way that the citizens of their countries could understand.

The problems come with "reluctant reformists" or with leaders who want to make reforms without political costs or short-term citizens' sacrifices. If a minister starts his mandate with the promise that he will not take one dime out of the pockets of the citizens, or that a major tax reform will be done without *any* taxpayer experiencing an increase in taxes, it is likely that reforms will not take place. Or, if they do, that they will be modest ones.

Cohesion within the government is important, especially when the government is a coalition government. A reform programme must be a "programme" and not a collage of independent pieces. The members of the government (the various ministers) *must act as a team*. They must decide the basic strategy and must support one another. If a government spends its time and effort coordinating divergent views of ministers or parties, it will not be able to convince the public about the needed reforms because it will not, itself, be able to develop or establish a clear sense of direction. When they take place, discussions or disagreements must be carried out away from the media. They must not spill out in the open. A strong prime minister, or a powerful finance minister, must be able to consolidate the views and present them as "the" government's position. If this cannot be done, there is no effective government.

In the literature, too much attention is given to the conflicts between the executive and the legislative branches or within the legislative branch and not enough to the *conflicts within the executive*. This literature has concluded that a majoritarian or presidential form of government has an advantage over a proportional system. But even a majoritarian government can develop problems of coordination between ministries or within the executive. Just read *The Price of Loyalty*, the book on O'Neill's experience as the US Treasury Secretary or observe developments within the Berlusconi government of 2001.

TECHNICAL OBSTACLES

One of my professors at Harvard who got the Nobel Prize in Economics—Simon Kuznets—used to repeat the mantra: *Data before Analysis. Analysis before Policy or Prescription.*

Final Remarks

I have been impressed over the years by how little this advice is followed and how little *serious* effort is made within governments to determine what can be expected from a reform. Often a kind of theology drives decisions. Theology, or ideology to choose a different term, tends to make data collection or analysis apparently unnecessary. The truth does not need analysis. Thus arguments in favour of some policy changes tend to be based on faith or, even worse, on dishonest statements based on hope. When this is the case, the proposed changes, or the reforms, will be questioned and will not be supported by the public.

The lack of good data and good analysis contributes to the creation of more uncertainty about the benefits and the costs of a reform. It also increases for economic operators the value of waiting so that the reforms made do not have a quick effect on economic activity. At times, the estimates available provide a range of costs and benefits so large as to make them useless. Thus, we often find situations in which the potential losers, and there are always some, feel very strongly about the losses from the reform while the benefits are not only widely distributed, as often recognized, but also less firmly determined.

Under the best of circumstances, there will be asymmetry between the knowledge about the benefits from a reform that is available within the government and that available to the population at large, especially when few think-tanks are available to increase the information to the population. If the reputation, for candour and honesty, of the government is not high, because in the past it has not been right or honest, its estimates of benefits will be challenged. In this context, think-tank institutions and international organizations can play an important role if they are seen as competent and objective.

The full impact, or even the benefits, of a reform often depends on whether other reforms accompany it. This is the classic second-best argument. A reform enacted in isolation in one sector may not generate the hoped-for benefits. This, for example, has been shown by various studies on the impact of free trade or free capital movement on particular countries. Thus the question of sequencing is highly relevant. A "big bang" approach might have many advantages but the capacity of a government and a public administration to deal with several reforms at the same time may be limited.

An economic minister does not himself need to be a Nobel Laureate in economics to be a good minister. In fact, it may even be argued that it is better if he is not an economist. What is important is that (*a*) he surrounds himself with capable economists and other advisers; (*b*) he encourages them to give him their objective opinions; and (c) he has the honesty and the humility to listen seriously to those opinions. The most dangerous combination is one in which the minister feels that he knows all the answers and surrounds himself with individuals who tell him what he wants to hear or simply write briefs supporting his ideas. Under these circumstances, the reforms enacted will have little probability of being good ones.

SAND VERSUS OIL IN THE ECONOMIC MACHINE

The reports that have been presented at this conference are valuable descriptions of reforms in the area of pensions, labour, product markets, privatization of public enterprises, and corporate governance. All these are areas that could benefit from structural reforms that increase the efficiency of the economy and reduce the role of the state in economic decisions. Thus, I am glad to see these analyses. However, it is my opinion that at least in some countries and especially in Italy, the final results from these structural reforms will largely depend on what happens in two other areas that have not been addressed in the Reports.

I would have liked to see chapters dealing with reforms in (a) the public administration and (b) the justice system. These are the areas that can provide oil for the economic machine of a country or that can put sand in the mechanism of that machine. It is in these areas that the American economy retains a substantial advantage over several European economies. American operators spend little time worrying about the effectiveness of justice or public administration. On the other hand, these are aspects that continually worry Italian or, say, Russian economic operators or enterprises. Shortcomings in these two areas can neutralize or reduce the benefits from structural reform in other areas.

To this audience, it may not be necessary to mention that much recent economic literature has concluded that the protection of property rights, broadly defined to include intellectual property, and the enforcement of contracts are two fundamental elements that make an economy grow. Poorly functioning public administrations and justice systems create a kind of bad cholesterol that damages the economic system. Some international comparisons that have provided "soft" data on the quality of the institutions that deal with these aspects have indicated large differences across countries. See, for example, the *Global Competitiveness Reports*. Perhaps a report that dealt with these issues could be very useful. I hope that at some future time the Rodolfo Debenedetti Foundation will prepare reports on these issues. They could study the experiences of countries that have achieved successes in reforming these areas.

Finally, while we should continue to study the important reforms in the labour market, the product market, the privatization of public enterprises, and other similar ones, let us not forget that, using an analogy, buildings are not only destroyed by hurricanes, earthquakes, tidal waves, tornados, and other catastrophic events, but also by termites in their foundations. In many countries, there are often mini impediments to the efficient allocation of resources and to growth. These impediments, like termites, do not attract much attention. They are rarely studied. At times, these impediments are the product of culture; at times, they reflect the political power of particular groups; at other times, they reflect regulations imposed by *local* governments and by non-governmental associations. Individually, these impediments may not appear important. Taken together, they may be major impediments to growth and full employment.

References

Keynes, J. M. (1926), *The End of Laissez-Faire*, London: Hogarth Press.
Stiglitz, J. (2003), *Globalization and its Discontents*, New York: W.W. Norton & Company Inc.
Suskind, R. (2004), *The Price of Loyalty: George Bush, the White House, and the Education of Paul O'Neill*, New York: Simon & Schuster.
Tanzi, V. (1987), "Fiscal Policy, Growth and the Design of Stabilization Programmes", in Vito Tanzi, *Public Finance in Developing Countries*, Cheltenham: Edward Elgar; 1st pub. in *External Debt, Savings and Growth in Latin America*, IMF, 1987.

General Index

Note: Index includes all cited authors.

Acemoglu, Daron 7, 160, 161 n2
Acquis Communautaire (EU) 233
advertising, and professional services 57
Agcom (Italy) 43
Aghion, P 18, 194
Aldi 68
Alesina, A 18
Allegra, E 19, 101
Allianz 85
Amato, Giuliano, and Italian pension reform 200–2, 274
Andreotti, Giulio 201
Aprile, R 202
Asda 64
ASST 213, 214
Atkinson, A B 170
AvtoZAZ, and privatization of:
  background to 234–5, 240–1
  creation of AvtoZAZ-Daewoo joint venture 242
  Daewoo's investment plan 241, 243–4
  doubts over Daewoo's plans 242
  failure of 245
  government conditions 241
  impact of external constraints 246–7
  improved prospects for 246–7
  lack of commitment 244–5
  outcome of 244
  role of lobbying 243
  temporary protection 242–3

Baily, M N 121, 129
Baker, G 268
Balladur, Edouard 212
Balto, D A 67 n10
Baron, D 159
Bartelsman, E J 116, 121
Barton, D 120
Basu, Susanto 131, 137

Bean, C R 273
Bebchuk, L 178
Becker, G 159, 208
Beeching Reports 47
beliefs, and impact on reforms 269
Beltrametti, L 202
Benfratello, L 101
Bentolila, S 8, 285
Berger, P 195
Berliner Wasserbetriebe 85
Berlusconi, Silvio 148, 251
  and pension reform 181–4
Bernheim, B D 160
Bertola, G 5, 18, 155
Bevan, A 199
BG Transco 37
Biais, B 194
Bishop, M 121
Black, B 159
Black, D 178
Blair, Tony 147
Blanchard, O 5, 8, 18, 127, 161 n3, 194, 278, 285
'Blue Laws' 62
Boeri, T 5, 7, 18, 155, 168, 227
Bohatá, M 237
Bolton, P 195
Bonoli, G 170, 171
Bortolotti, B 197 n4, 247
Boycko, M 194–5, 196
Boylaud, O 63 n7
Brada, J C 193, 195, 197
Brickley, J A 194, 196
Bris, A 248
British Gas 34, 36–7, 38, 39
British Telecom 41–2, 43, 44, 45
Brovkin, D 247 n14
Brugiavini, A 202 n7, 204 n9
Buigues, P 284

297

General Index

Bundesbahn 49
Button, K J 120

Calmfors, L 189, 268, 278
Campbell, James I 73
Canning, A 197
Cartel Office (Germany) 65
Carter, C 120
Castanheira, M 108, 158, 161 n2, 194, 237
Caves, R 120, 121
Central and Eastern European Countries (CEECs):
  and impact of proximity to European Union 240
  and privatization 193–4
    Czech Republic 197–8, 233–9
    Eastern Germany 197
    economic objectives 194, 195–6
    Hungary 197
    Poland 197–8
    political objectives 194–5
    Russia 198–9
    Ukraine 239–47
    widening political support for 188
Central Bank of Russia 175, 176, 178
Central Electricity Generating Board (CEGB) 27, 28–9
Centrica 37
Charles II 72
Chile 292
China, and dual-track principle 268
Chirac, Jacques 184, 213
civil society, and structural reform 268
Claessens, S 194
Clarke, R 120
Coe, D 278
collective action processes:
  and actors in 158–9
    political elites 158
    special interest groups 158–9
    voters 158
  and economic rents 161
  and gradual versus one-off reforms 163
  and rules:
    constitutional arrangements 160
    lobbying 159–60
    system of political representation 160
    voting 159
  and status quo bias 162, 249–50
    non-manufacturing reform 216–17
  and uncertainty 163
commitment building, and structural reform 145, 167, 168, 232, 264, 266, 271

Common Agricultural Policy 161, 267
compensating measures, and structural reform strategy 154–5, 219
competition:
  and benefits of 18
  and economic performance 21–3
  and electricity industry 26
    liberalization of 32–4
  and energy sector liberalization 26
  and gas industry 26
    liberalization of 38–40
  and innovation 21–2, 121
  and liberalization 24–5
  and productivity 21–2, 116
    agency models 118
    bargaining models 118–19
    frontier studies 120
    intra-firm contracts 116–17
    non-frontier studies 120–1
    privatization 122
    welfare implications 119
  and professional services 54, 56–7, 58, 60
  and telecommunications liberalization 46
Competition Commission (UK) 43, 64
competitiveness, and service sector 89, 107
concentration, and productivity 120–1
consensus-building, and structural reform 266–8
constitutional arrangements:
  and collective action processes 160
  and structural reform 266
  see also electoral systems
contracts, and enforcement of 295
Conyon, M 101
Crepaz, M L 160
Criscuolo, C 101, 121
Czech Republic:
  and economic conditions 235
  and privatization programme 196, 197–8
  and Škoda privatization:
    background to 234–5
    control rights 236–7
    government commitment to 238–9
    success of 238–9
    temporary protection 237
    Volkswagen joint-venture 236

Daewoo, and AvtoZAZ privatization:
  creation of joint venture 242
  doubts over plans for 242
  failure of 245
  investment plan 241, 243–4
  lack of commitment 244–5
  outcome of 244

role of lobbying 243
temporary protection 242–3
Davies, S 121
de Boer, Willem 130
Debenedetti Foundation 291, 295
Denmark:
    and coalition government 190
    and collective agreements 191
    and labour market:
        flexibility of 188–9
        reform of 185–6, 275–6
        unemployment insurance reform 191–3
    and social dialogue institutions 190–1
deregulation, see liberalization
Deutsche Bahn AG 49
Deutsche Post AG 78, 81
Deutsche Reichsbahn 49
Deutsche Telekom AG 41, 44
Dewatripont, M 163, 196, 249, 265, 269
Dhrymes, P J 121
Diermeier, D 160
Dini, Lamberto 182
    and Italian pension reform 202–5
divide and conquer, and structural reform
    strategy 149, 164, 264, 265, 266
    framework conditions for 252–3
    French telecommunications
        reforms 212–13
    Italian telecommunication
        reforms 213–15
    regulation in non-manufacturing 207–9
    rents of involved groups 210–11
    special interest groups 208–9
Djankov, S 194
Dobson Consulting 67, 68
Dolado, J 8, 229, 276 n3
Doms, M E 101, 116, 121
Dörr, G 234 n1, 236
Downs, A 159
Drazen, A 263
Driffill, J 189, 268
dual-track principle 268–9
Dyba, K 235

Earle, J 178
Easterly, W 272
Eastern Germany, and privatization
    programme 197
Ebbinghaus, B 212 n6
economists, and role of 288–92
education, and service sector reform 281–2
efficiency, in microeconomic theory 195–6
electoral systems:
    and collective action processes 160

and Denmark 190
and Italy 181
and Russia 174
and structural reform 264, 265, 266, 271
and United Kingdom 168–9, 173
electricity industry, liberalization of:
    and competition 26
    and economic outcomes:
        prices 33
        productivity 31–2, 34
    and European Union reform agenda 28
    and evaluation of 34
    and Germany 30–1
    and Italy 30
    and pre-privatization structure 27–8
    and regulation 31
    and United Kingdom 28–30
emergency, and structural reform 264
Emmerson, C 172
employment:
    and energy sector liberalization 26
    and impact of deregulation 280
    and liberalization 25, 53–4, 105, 108, 132–3
    and retail industry liberalization 69
    and structural reform 5
    and telecommunications
        liberalization 44, 46
employment protection legislation (EPL):
    and comparison with unemployment
        benefits 6–7
    and Denmark 188–9
    and Spanish reforms (1994–97) 226–31, 276
EnBW 31
Enel 27, 28, 30
energy sector, liberalization of 25–7
    and competition 26
    and effects of restructuring 26
    and electricity industry:
        economic outcomes 31–3
        European Union reform agenda 28
        evaluation of 34
        Germany 30–1
        Italy 30
        pre-privatization structure 27–8
        regulation 31
        United Kingdom 28–30
    and employment 26
    and gas industry:
        economic outcomes 38–40
        European Union reform agenda 35–6
        evaluation of 40
        Germany 37–8

299

General Index

energy sector, liberalization of (*cont.*)
    Italy 37
    pre-privatization structure 34–5
    regulation 38
    United Kingdom 36–7
  and prices 26
  and productivity 26
Eni group 34, 37
entrepreneurship 137
E.On 31
Esfahani, H 158, 161 n2
Estrin, S 178
Etro, F 18, 22
European Commission 182
  and professional services
    liberalization 55–6
  and single market for services 283–4
European Commission Directives:
  and energy sector liberalization 25
    electricity industry 28
    gas industry 35–6
  and liberalization 24
  and postal service liberalization 74
    authorization policy 76–7
    National Regulatory Authority 74–5
    reserved areas 75–6
    universal service policy 75
  and railway liberalization 47
  and telecommunications
    liberalization 41, 219
European Monetary Union (EMU) 11
European Union:
  and *Acquis Communautaire* 233
  and budget of 284–6
  and economic leadership 138
  and economic potential of 138–9
  and environmental change in 4–5
  and identifying appropriate reforms 249
  and impact on transition countries 240
  and labour market reform, limited
    impact of 4
  and liberalization of product markets 11
  and Lisbon Agenda 17, 56, 74, 284
  and need for reform 249, 263
  and poor economic performance 17,
    135, 283
    factors affecting 137
  and productivity, comparison of Europe
    and USA 126–8, 282
  and service sector 2
  and Single Market Programme 4, 283
    based on old thinking 284
    exclusion of labour market
      liberalization 284
    failure to implement for services 283–4
  and Stability Pact 149, 247
    breaches of 248
    opposition to 233
  and Structural Funds 267
experimentation, and structural
  reform 264, 265
external constraints, and structural reform
  strategy 149–50, 164, 232–3, 247–8, 264
  AvtoZAZ privatization 233–5, 239–47
  framework conditions for 253–4
  Italian pension reform 182, 201
  Škoda privatization 233–9

Facchini, G 225 n19
Feddersen, T 160
Fernandez, R 162, 249
Ferrera, M 201, 202 n8, 203
Ferrovie dello Stato 47, 49, 50
Fiat 241
Filatotchev, I 178
financial services, and liberalization of 218
  impact of 224
firms, and competition and productivity:
  agency models 118
  bargaining models 118–19
  frontier studies 120
  intra-firm contracts 116–17
  non-frontier studies 120–1
Fischer, S 174
Fondazione Rodolfo Debenedetti (fRDB) 7–8
foreign direct investment (FDI) 221–4
  and impact of regulation in
    services 101–4, 106–7
  and productivity 101
  and removal of restrictions on 225
Forza Italia 182
Foster, L 121
Fowler, Norman 169, 170
France:
  and energy sector liberalization 26
  and pension reform 184–5
  and productivity:
    comparison of Europe and USA 126–8
    electricity industry 132
    mobile telephony 131
    retail sector 129–31
    road freight 132
  and Stability Pact 248
  and telecommunications
    liberalization 209, 211
    corporatization 212–13
    impact of institutional structure 215
    partial privatization 213

France Telecom 149, 211
  and corporatization 212–13
  and partial privatization 213
Franco, D 204
Frémond, O 197 n4
French, Louis 177 n4

Galasso, V 204 n9
gas industry, liberalization of:
  and competition 26–7
  economic outcomes:
    competition 38–40
    productivity 38
  European Union reform agenda 35–6
  evaluation of 40
  Germany 37–8
  Italy 37
  pre-privatization structure 34–5
  regulation 38
  United Kingdom 36–7
Gawande, K 225 n18
General Agreement on Trade in Services
  (GATS) 91
General Motors 241
Germany:
  and electricity industry liberalization 30–1
    pre-privatization structure 27–8
    prices 33
    self-regulation 31
  and energy sector liberalization 26
  and gas industry liberalization 37–8
    competition 39–40
    pre-privatization structure 34
    regulatory framework 38
  and postal service liberalization:
    authorization policy 80
    comparison with Italy and UK 80–2
    National Regulatory Authority 77–8
    reserved areas 79
    universal service policy 78–9
  and productivity, retail sector 129–31
  and professional services 59
    self-regulation 56
  and railway liberalization 49
    pre-privatization structure 47
    productivity 52
    regulatory framework 51
  and regulation in services:
    impact on foreign direct
      investment 101–4
    impact on manufacturing 97–101
  and retail industry liberalization:
    comparison with Italy and UK 66–71
    competition and fair trade policy 63
    opening hours restrictions 62
    planning/construction restrictions 62
  and service sector:
    openness to trade 90
    as supplier of inputs 91–5
  and Stability Pact 248
  and telecommunications
    liberalization 42–3
    pre-privatization structure 41
    prices 44–5
    productivity 44
    regulatory framework 43–4
  and water industry liberalization 85
    regulatory framework 85–6
    service quality 88
Geroski, P 121
Gestore Rete Trasmissione Nazionale
  (Grtn) 30
Giavazzi, F 5, 18, 133, 161 n3, 278
Girma, S 101
Glaeser, E 179 n10
globalization 221
Gönenç, R 194, 219
Gorbachev, Mikhail 175
Görg, H 101, 102
government, and structural reform:
  coalition building 145, 167, 187
    Danish unemployment insurance
      reform 192
    French pension reform 185
    Italian pension reform 182–3, 201
    Spanish labour market reform 230
    UK pension reform 170, 173
  commitment building 145, 167, 168, 232,
    264, 266, 271
  failure to inform citizens 3
  institutional structure 187
  and motives behind 145–6
  reluctance to implement 2–3
  see also structural reform strategy
Gramel, S 83 n21, 85 n24
Green, A 120, 121
Greenaway, D 102
Griffith, R 101, 102
Griliches, Z 121
Gronchi, S 202
Grossman, G 158 n1, 159, 160, 232
Grünhagen, M 62, 64
Gualmini, E 201, 202 n8, 203

Häfner, P 47 n2
Hare, P G 197
Harris, R 101
Hart, O D 118, 208 n6

General Index

Hart, P 120
Haskel, J 44, 102, 118, 121
Havel, Vaclav 236
Health and Safety Executive (UK) 50
Hellwig, M 76, 78, 81, 82
Helpman, E 158 n1, 159, 160, 232
Henry VIII 72
Hermalin, B E 118
Hill, Rowland 72
Hinich, M J 159
Hinz, R 143 n1
Holzmann, R 143 n1
Hotelling, H 159
Howenstine, N 101
human capital 138
Hungary, and privatization programme 197

Inderst, R 63 n6
Information Technology sector, and productivity growth 128–9
innovation 137–8
  and competition 21–2, 121
institutional structure:
  and ability to reform 187
  and structural reform 268
intermediate sectors, and structural reform strategy 217–19
International Express Carriers Conference 73
International Monetary Fund (IMF) 149, 246, 287
  and Italian pension reform 182
  and opposition to 233
  and Russian reforms 175, 177
investment, and liberalization 54
Ireland 292
Istat (Italian statistical office) 45
Italcable 213
Italy:
  and electricity industry liberalization 30
    pre-privatization structure 27–8
    prices 33
    productivity 31–2
    regulatory framework 31
  and employment protection/ unemployment benefits trade-off 8
  and energy sector liberalization 26
  and gas industry liberalization 37
    competition 39
    pre-privatization structure 34–5
    regulatory framework 38
  and Maastricht Treaty 201
  and pension reform 9
    Amato reforms (1992) 200–2, 274–5
    assessment of 273–5
    Berlusconi's failure (1994) 181–4
    Dini reforms (1995) 202–5
    external constraints 201
    rise in pension spending 199–200
    tailoring division of cost/benefits 188
  and postal service liberalization:
    authorization policy 80
    comparison with Germany and UK 80–2
    National Regulatory Authority 77–8
    reserved areas 79
    universal service policy 78–9
  and productivity, comparison of Europe and USA 126–8
  and professional services 59
    self-regulation 56
  and railway liberalization 49
    pre-privatization structure 47
    prices 52
    productivity 51–2
    regulatory framework 50–1
    service quality 53
  and regulation in services:
    impact on foreign direct investment 101–4
    impact on manufacturing 97–101
  and retail industry liberalization 65
    comparison with Germany and UK 66–71
    competition and fair trade policy 63
    opening hours restrictions 62
    planning/construction restrictions 62
  and service sector:
    openness to trade 90
    as supplier of inputs 91–5
  and telecommunications
    liberalization 42, 209, 211, 214–15
    impact of institutional structure 215
    pre-privatization structure 41, 213–14
    prices 45
    regulatory framework 43
  and water industry liberalization 83–5
    prices 86
    regulatory framework 85
    service quality 87

Jean, S 18, 210
Jensen, J B 101
Jessop, B 167 n1, 171
Jimeno, J 229
Johnson, G 118
Johnson, P 172
Johnson, S 178

Jørgensen, H 189, 191
Jospin, Lionel 213
Juppé, Alain 148, 184–5, 212, 251
justice system 295

Kay, J 121
Kessell, T 234 n1, 236
Keynes, John Maynard 288, 289
Klaus, Vaclav 198
Kornai, J 193, 196
Koromzay, V 210 n4
Korshak, S 244, 245
Krueger, A O 160
Kuznets, Simon 293
Kydland, F 233

labour markets:
  and employment protection/
    unemployment benefits trade-off 6–7
  and interactions with product
    market 4–6, 277–9
  and reform of 265
    compensating measures 154
    Denmark 185–6, 191–3, 275–6
    gradual introduction of 8–10
    impact on employment 5
    liberalization 133
    limited impact of 4
    Spain 149, 226–31, 275–6
Laffont, J J 208 n6
Landier, Augustin 127
Lastovetsky, M 245
Lau, L 268
Lega Nord 182–4, 203
Levy, B 221
Li, W 224
liberalization:
  and competition 24–5
  and employment 25, 53–4, 105, 108, 132–3
  and impact of 105
  and investment 54
  and labour market reform 133
  and need for improved policy design 108–9
  and potential benefits of 109
  and prices 25, 105
  and productivity 24, 25, 105, 107, 131–2, 280
  and service sector 18
    impact of 135
    impact on manufacturing 97–101
    resistance to 107–8

see also energy sector; postal service;
  professional services; railway industry;
  retail industry; telecommunications;
  water industry
Lidl 68
Lijphart, A 160
Lindbeck, A 159–60
Lipton, D 175
Lisbon Agenda 17, 56, 74, 284–6
Ljundqvist, L 7
lobbying:
  and AvtoZAZ privatization 243
  and collective action processes 159–60
López-Calva, L F 194, 196

Maastricht Treaty 201, 247
McKinsey Global Institute 64, 129, 130, 131
Mankiw, N G 119
manufacturing:
  and decline in protection 90–1
  and impact of regulation in
    services 97–101, 136–7
    foreign direct investment 101–4
  and service sector 19–20
  as supplier of inputs 89, 91–6, 106
Marin, D 178 n8
market power, and gradual introduction of
  reforms 220–5
Martin, R 101
Martin, S 121
Maskin, E 196
Mavrodi, Sergei 176 n3
Mayes, D 120
Megginson, W L 194, 196
Mercury 41
Milanovic, B 193
Mirza, D 224 n17
Mittelstaedt, R A 62, 64
MMM Bank 176
mobile telephony, and productivity 131
Modigliani, F 178
Monopolies and Mergers Commission
  (UK) 43
monopoly, and service sector 2
Monti, Mario 56
Mueller, D C 159
multinational enterprises (MNEs):
  and impact in host country 102
  and productivity 101–2
  and reform 224–5

National Grid Company 29
National Power 29

303

General Index

Nesbitt, S 167 n1, 168
Netter, J M 194, 196
New Electricity Trading Agreement 29, 33
New Zealand 292
Ney, S 167
Nickell, S 116, 118, 121
Nicoletti, G 18, 19, 22, 63 n7, 91, 101, 210, 223, 224 n17, 278
Nietzsche, Friedrich 291
Noll, R G 221
North, Douglass 158
Nuclear Power 29

Oates, W 12
Office of Fair Trading (UK) 64
Office of Passenger Rail Franchising (UK) 50
Office of Rail Regulator (UK) 49–50
OFTEL 45
OFWAT (UK) 83, 85, 86
Olley, S 121
Olson, M 159, 160, 161, 208
O'Mahony, M 69, 121, 130
Organization for Economic Cooperation and Development (OECD) 4, 91
overmanning, and liberalization 25

Pakes, A 121
Panzar, J 75
Parker, D 121
Partito Democratico della Sinistra (PDS) 184
Paulus, M 76, 78, 81, 82
Peltzman, S 208
pension reform 166
  and compensating measures 154–5
  and France 184–5
  and impact of electoral system 265
  and Italy:
    Amato reforms (1992) 200–2, 274–5
    assessment of 273–5
    Berlusconi's failure (1994) 181–4
    Dini reforms (1995) 202–5
    external constraints 201
    tailoring division of cost/benefits 188
  and public sector 267
  and United Kingdom:
    aftermath of 180–1
    assessment of 273–5
    Social Security Act (1986) 167–73
Perotti, E 175 n2, 178, 194
Persson, T 159, 160, 172, 233, 264
Phillippon, T 8
Pierson, P 167
Piskovyi, V 241 n9

Pissarides, C 6
Poland, and privatization programme 197–8
political economy, and structural reform 145, 158
  and actors 158–9
  see also reform process, political economy of
political elites 158
Pollitt, M 121
Portugal 8
Post Office (UK) 41
postal service, liberalization of:
  comparison of performance (UK-Italy-Germany) 80–2
  European Union reform agenda 74
    authorization policy 76–7
    maximum reservable area 75–6
    National Regulatory Authority 74–5
    universal service policy 75
  implementation in Germany, Italy and UK 77
    authorization policy 80
    National Regulatory Authority 77–8
    reserved areas 79
    universal service policy 78–9
  pre-liberalization structure 72–4
  and remail 73
Postcomm (UK) 77, 78–9
PowerGen 29
Prescott, E 233
prices:
  and electricity industry liberalization 32–3
  pre-privatization practice 28
  and energy sector liberalization 26
  and gas industry liberalization 38
  and liberalization 25, 105
  and railway liberalization 52, 53
  and telecommunications liberalization 44–5, 46
  and water industry liberalization 86, 88
private interest, and regulation 208
privatization:
  and productivity 122
  and productivity growth 22
  and transition economies 193–4, 196–9
    Czech Republic 197–8
    Eastern Germany 197
    economic objectives 194, 195–6
    Hungary 197
    Poland 197–8
    political objectives 194–5
    Russia 198–9
  see also liberalization

product markets:
  and interactions with labour market 4–6, 277–9
  and reform of:
    delegation to supranational authorities 11
    political difficulties with 10–11
    unsustainability of marginal 10
productivity:
  and comparison of Europe and USA 126–8, 282
    role of Information Technology sector 128–9
    role of retail sector 129–31
  and competition 21–2, 116
    agency models 118
    bargaining models 118–19
    frontier studies 120
    intra-firm contracts 116–17
    non-frontier studies 120–1
    welfare implications 119
  and concentration 120–1
  and electricity industry liberalization 31–2, 34
  and energy sector liberalization 26
  and foreign direct investment 101
  and gas industry liberalization 38
  and liberalization 24, 25, 105, 107, 131–2, 280
  and privatization 22, 122
  and railway liberalization 51–2, 53
  and reallocation 121
  and retail industry liberalization 69–71
  and service sector, impact of regulation 97–101, 106, 136–7
  and stagnation of growth in 17
  and telecommunications liberalization 44, 46
  and water industry liberalization 86, 88
professional services, liberalization of:
  and advertising 57
  and competition 54, 56–7, 58, 60
  and Germany 59
  and Italy 59
  and need for 59
  and reform proposals 56–7, 60
  and regulatory framework 54–5, 56
  and resistance to 57, 59–60
  and role of European Commission 55–6
  and slow pace of 58
  and structural issues:
    absence of competition 54
    restrictions 55
    self-regulation 54–5, 59

  and United Kingdom 58
property rights 295
protection:
  and AvtoZAZ-Daewoo joint-venture 242–3
  and manufacturing 90–1
  and service sector 2, 90, 91
  and Škoda-Volkswagen joint-venture 237
public administration 295
public interest, and regulation 208
public sector, and pension reform 267
Putin, Vladimir 179

quality of service:
  and railway liberalization 53
  and telecommunications liberalization 45–6
  and water industry liberalization 86–8

Rabin, M 269
Railtrack 48, 49
railway industry, liberalization of:
  economic outcomes:
    prices 52, 53
    productivity 51–2, 53
    service quality 53
  European Union reform agenda 47
  evaluation of 53–4
  Germany 49
  Italy 49
  pre-privatization structure 47
  regulatory framework 49–51
  United Kingdom 48–9
  unanticipated benefits 280–1
Rasmussen, Anders Fogh 148, 251
  and labour market reform 185–6
Reagan, Ronald 293
reallocation, and productivity 121
reform process, political economy of:
  and actors:
    political elites 158
    special interest groups 158–9
    voters 158
  and benefits of reform:
    economic 157
    ideological 158
    political 158
  and economic rents 161
  and gradual versus one-off reforms 163
  and obstacles to reform:
    philosophical 288–92
    political 292–3
    technical 293–5

305

General Index

reform process, political economy of: (cont.)
  and rules:
    constitutional arrangements 160
    lobbying 159–60
    system of political representation 160
    voting 159
  and status quo bias 162, 249–50
    non-manufacturing reform 216–17
  and uncertainty 163
Regev, H 121
regulatory framework:
  and correlation across domains 4
  and electricity industry liberalization 31
  and gas industry liberalization 38
  and impact on manufacturing:
    foreign direct investment 101–4, 106–7
    productivity 97–101, 136–7
  and need for stability in 109
  and non-manufacturing sectors 207–9
  and postal service liberalization:
    authorization policy 76–7, 80
    National Regulatory Authority 74–5, 77–8
    reserved areas 75–6, 79
    universal service policy 75, 78–9
  and private interest 208
  and productivity 131–2
  and professional services 54–5, 56, 59
  and public interest 208
  and railway liberalization 49–51
  and regulatory inertia 208
  and retail industry liberalization:
    competition and fair trade policy 62–3
    deregulation in Germany 64–5
    deregulation in United Kingdom 63–4
    opening hours restrictions 61–2
    planning/construction restrictions 62
  and service sector 2, 280
    as cause of restrictions 281
    impact on foreign direct investment 101–4, 106–7
    impact on manufacturing 97–101
  and telecommunications liberalization 43–4
  and water industry liberalization 85–6
Regulierungsbehörde für Telekommunikation (RegTP) 77, 79, 81
remail 73
research and development 137–8
retail industry, liberalization of:
  and comparison of performance (UK-Italy-Germany) 68–9, 71, 129–31
  concentration 67–8
  discounters 68
  employment 69
  large retail formats 68
  productivity 69–71
  and Germany:
    competition policy 65
    opening hours 64–5
    planning/construction policy 65
  and industry characteristics 60–1
  and Italy 65
  and regulatory framework:
    competition and fair trade policy 62–3
    opening hours restrictions 61–2
    planning/construction restrictions 62
  and United Kingdom:
    competition policy 64
    opening hours 63–4
    planning/construction policy 64
Rete Ferroviaria Italiana 49, 50
Rewe 68
rigidities:
  and European economic growth 126
  and ignorance of time-series properties 4
  and service sector 2
road freight:
  and liberalization of 218–19
  and productivity 132
Robinson, C 101
Robinson, J 161 n2
Rodrik, D 162, 249, 272, 289
Rogerson, C 75
Rogoff, K 233
Roland, G 163, 178, 193, 194, 195, 196–7, 198, 233, 235, 237, 239, 240, 249, 263, 265, 269
Roosevelt, Franklin D 288
Rosen, A 118
Rostagno, M 202
Royal Mail 81
Ruhrgas 34
Russia, and reform process:
  failure of 174
    enforcement 175
    majoritarian political system 174
  policy changes since the crisis 179
  political consequences of 179
  privatization programme 198–9
  reform implementation (1991–1998) 175–7
  reforms required 174–5
  regulatory and governance capture 177–8
    banks and banking supervision 178–9
    enterprises 178
  state capture by interest groups 175
RWE 31, 85

Sachs, J 175
Safeway 64
Sahay, R 174
Sainsbury 64
Saint-Paul, G 9, 189, 285
Sapir, A 283, 284
Sargent, T J 7
Sartori, G 200
Scarpetta, S 18, 19, 22, 91, 101, 278
Scharfstein, D 118
Schmidt, K 196
Schnitzer, M 178 n8
Scottish Hydro 29
Scottish Power 29
self-regulation, and professional services 54–5, 59
Sembenelli, A 101
service sector 17–18
  and absence of European single market for 2
  and benefits of competition 18
  and competitiveness 89, 107
  and definition of 89–90
  and education 281–2
  and impact of reform 20, 280
    incumbents 281
  and increasing economic role of 89, 106
  and intensification of trade 221–4
  and liberalization 18
    impact of 135
    intermediate sectors 217–19
    resistance to 107–8
  and manufacturing 19–20
  as supplier of inputs 89, 91–6, 106
  and openness to trade 90
  and pressure for 281
  and protection of 2, 90–1
  and regulation in 280
    as cause of restrictions 281
    impact on foreign direct investment 101–4, 106–7
    impact on manufacturing 97–101, 136–7
  and unbundling interests 277
Sgard, J 175 n2
Sheshinski, E 194, 196
Shimer, Robert 7
Shleifer, A 179 n10, 196
Simpson, H 101
Single Market Programme (EU) 4, 283
  and basis in old thinking 284
  and exclusion of labour market liberalization 284
  and failure to implement for services 283–4

Siniscalco, D 197 n4, 247
SIP 213, 214
Škoda, and privatization of 196
  background to 234–5
  control rights 236–7
  government commitment to 238–9
  success of 238–9
  temporary protection 237
  Volkswagen joint-venture 236
Snower, D 278
social pacts 267
Social Security Act (UK, 1986) 167–73
Southern Electric 29
Spain:
  and labour market reform 149, 275–6
  and productivity 128
  and reform of employment protection legislation (1994–97) 226–31
special interest groups:
  and collective action processes 158–60
  and non-manufacturing regulation 208–9
  and structural reform 266, 267
Spiller, P T 221
spillover effects, and structural reform 264
Stability Pact 149, 247
  and breaches of 248
  and opposition to 233
state capture, and Russian reforms 175
state control, and economic inefficiency 195–6
status quo bias 162, 249–50
  and non-manufacturing reform 216–17
STET 215
Stigler, G 208
Stiglitz, J 289
Strobl, E 101
structural reform:
  and case-study analysis of 1, 144
  and coalition building 145, 167, 187
    Danish unemployment insurance reform 192
    French pension reform 185
    Italian pension reform 182–3, 201
    Spanish labour market reform 230
    UK pension reform 170, 173
  and commitment building 145, 167, 168, 232, 264, 266, 271
  and dual-track principle 268–9
  and failure to communicate benefits of 3
  and gradual introduction of 8–10, 219–20
  and interaction between labour/product markets 4–6
  and international competition 155
  and international trends in 151–4

General Index

structural reform: (cont.)
  and labour markets:
    gradual introduction of 8–10
    impact on employment 5
    limited impact of 4
    unviability of supranational authorities 11–12
  and motives behind 145–6
  and obstacles to:
    philosophical 288–92
    political 292–3
    technical 293–5
  and opposition to 144, 155–6, 165, 206–7, 249–50
    external constraints 232–3
    rents of involved groups 210–11
  and origins of 287
  and political context of 143–4
  and political economy literature of 145
  and political support for:
    exploiting labour/product market interactions 6–8
    obstacles to 2–3
    socio-economic differences 8–9
  and product markets:
    delegation to supranational authorities 11
    political difficulties with 10–11
    reform of 147
    unsustainability of marginal 10
  and sectoral impact of 18–19
  and sequencing of 271
  and unanticipated benefits of 280–1
  and variables affecting 264–5
  and Washington consensus 143
  and winners and losers 165
  see also reform process, political economy of; structural reform strategy
structural reform strategy:
  and absence of common 146, 250, 254, 272–3
  and compensating measures 154–5, 219
  and consensus-building 266–8
  and divide and conquer 149, 164, 265, 266
    framework conditions for 252–3
    French telecommunications reforms 212–13
    Italian telecommunication reforms 213–15
    regulation in non-manufacturing 207–9
    rents of involved groups 210–11
    special interest groups 208–9
  and exploitation of external constraints 149–50, 164, 232–3, 247–8
    AvtoZAZ privatization 233–5, 239–47
    framework conditions for 253–4
    Italian pension reform 182, 201
    Škoda privatization 233–9
  and exploitation of parliamentary majority 148, 164, 165–7, 250–1
    dangers of 166–7
    Danish labour market reform 185–6
    framework conditions for 251
    French pension reform 184–5
    Italian pension reform (1994) 181–4
    need for strong government 165–6
    political feasibility 181
    Russia 174–9
    United Kingdom pension reform (1986 Social Security Act) 167–73
    universal nature of reform 166
  and features of successful 146–7
  and government strength 187
  and gradual introduction 8–10, 219–20
  and market power 220–5
    Spanish EPL reforms (1994–97) 226–31
  and impact on consumers'/final producers' expenditure 216–18
  and intermediate sectors 217–19
  and labour market/welfare state 146–7
  and transition economies 147–8
  and widening of political base 148–9, 164, 187–9
    Danish unemployment insurance reform 191–3
    framework conditions for 251–2
    Italian pension reform (Amato, 1992) 200–2
    Italian pension reform (Dini, 1995) 202–5
    privatization in transition countries 193–9
    tailoring division of cost/benefits 188
Summers, L H 272 n1
supranational authorities:
  and labour market reform 11–12
  and product market reform 11
  see also external constraints
Suskind, Ron 293
Svejnar, Jan 137, 235
Sweden, and pension reform 9
Symons, J 273
Szyrmer, J 243

Tabellini, G 159, 172, 233
Takis, W 75

General Index

Tanzi, V 287
Telecom Italia 41, 42, 214–15
  and privatization of 149
telecommunications, liberalization of:
  and divide and conquer strategy 207
  and economic outcomes:
    competition 46
    employment 44, 46
    prices 44–5, 46
    productivity 44, 46
    service quality 45–6
  and European Union reform agenda 41
  and evaluation of 46
  and France 209, 211
    corporatization 212–13
    partial privatization 213
  and Germany 42–3
  and impact of financial services liberalization 224
  and impact of institutional structure 215–16
  and Italy 42, 209, 211, 214–15
    pre-privatization structure 41, 213–14
    regulatory framework 43
  and United Kingdom 41–2
Tengelmann 68
tertiary sector, *see* service sector
Tesco 64
Thatcher, Margaret 147, 148, 167, 250–1, 265, 273, 274, 293
Thatcherism 172
Thompson, D 121
TIM 215
Tirole, J 208 n6
trade intensity 221–4
trade unions:
  and French pension reform 184–5
  and labour market reform 133
  and Spanish labour market 227, 229
transition economies:
  and impact of proximity to European Union 240
  and privatization 193–4, 196–9
    Czech Republic 197–8, 233–9
    Eastern Germany 197
    economic objectives 194, 195–6
    Hungary 197
    Poland 197–8
    political objectives 194–5
    Russia 198–9
    Ukraine 233–5, 239–47
  and structural reform 147–8
    widening political support for 188
Trenitalia 49, 50, 52

trickle-down effects 220
Tuke, Sir Brian 72

Ukraine:
  and AvtoZAZ privatization:
    background to 234–5, 240–1
    creation of AvtoZAZ-Daewoo joint venture 242
    Daewoo's investment plan 241, 243–4
    doubts over Daewoo's plans 242
    failure of 245
    government conditions 241
    impact of external constraints 246–7
    improved prospects for 246–7
    lack of commitment 244–5
    outcome of 244
    role of lobbying 243
    temporary protection 242–3
  and economic conditions 235, 246
  and privatization, external constraints 246–7
  and slow pace of reform 239–40
Ukravto 246
uncertainty, and reform process 163
unemployment benefits (UBs):
  and comparison with employment protection legislation 6–7
  and Denmark 188–9
    reform of 191–3, 275–6
  and Spain 227
United Kingdom:
  and electricity industry liberalization 28–30
    pre-privatization structure 27–8
    prices 32–3
    productivity 31–2
    regulatory framework 31
  and gas industry liberalization 36–7
    competition 38–9
    pre-privatization structure 34–5
    regulatory framework 38
  and pension reform:
    assessment of 273–5
    Social Security Act (1986) 167–73
  and postal service liberalization:
    authorization policy 80
    comparison with Germany and Italy 80–2
    National Regulatory Authority 77–8
    pre-liberalization structure 72
    reserved areas 79
    universal service policy 78–9
  and productivity, retail sector 129–31
  and professional services liberalization 58

General Index

United Kingdom: (cont.)
  and railway liberalization 48–9
    pre-privatization structure 47
    prices 52
    productivity 51
    regulatory framework 49–50
    service quality 53
    unanticipated benefits 280–1
  and regulation in services:
    impact on foreign direct investment 101–4
    impact on manufacturing 97–101
  and retail industry liberalization 63–4
    comparison with Germany and Italy 66–71
    opening hours restrictions 62
    planning/construction restrictions 62
  and service sector:
    openness to trade 90
    as supplier of inputs 91–5
  and telecommunications liberalization 41–2
    pre-privatization structure 41
    prices 44
    productivity 44
    regulatory framework 43
    service quality 45–6
  and water industry liberalization 83
    prices 86
    productivity 86
    regulatory framework 85
    service quality 86–7
United Nations Conference on Trade and Development (UNCTAD) 103
United States:
  and economic leadership 138
  and productivity:
    comparison of Europe and USA 126–8, 282
    retail sector 129–31
  and service sector 2
United States Postal Service 73
Universal Postal Convention 73
Ushakov, Vladimir 245

van Ark, B 67, 69, 128, 129, 130, 131
Varian, H R 119
Vattenfall Europe 31
venture capital 137

Verdier, T 178, 194, 240
Vickers, J S 116, 119
Visser, J 212 n6
Vivendi 85
Volkswagen, and Škoda privatization 234, 236
  control rights 236–7
  government commitment to 238–9
  success of 238–9
  temporary protection 237
voters, and collective action processes 158, 159

Wal-Mart Stores 61, 65
Wang Yang Nam 247 n14
Washington consensus 288, 289
  and rise of 143
water industry, liberalization of:
  and economic outcomes:
    prices 86, 88
    productivity 86, 88
    service quality 86–8
  and European Union reform agenda 83
  and evaluation of 88
  and Germany 85
  and Italy 83–5
  and pre-privatization structure 82–3
  and regulatory framework 85–6
  and United Kingdom 83
Weibull, J 159–60
Welch, D 197 n4
Werner, R 235 n3
Wey, C 63 n6
Weymarn-Jones, T G 120
Whinston, M D 119, 160
Wik-Consult 76, 77, 79, 80, 81, 82
Williams, B 120
Willmann, G 225 n19
Winiecki, J 196
Wm Morrison Supermarkets 64
World Bank 182, 287
World Trade Organization (WTO) 149
  and opposition to 233
Wragg, R 120
Wyplosz, C 174

Yeltsin, Boris 174, 175

Zeile, W 101